Lecture Notes in Artificial Intelligence   8624

Subseries of Lecture Notes in Computer Science

Nils Bulling   Leendert van der Torre
Serena Villata   Wojtek Jamroga
Wamberto Vasconcelos (Eds.)

Computational Logic in Multi-Agent Systems

15th International Workshop, CLIMA XV
Prague, Czech Republic, August 18-19, 2014
Proceedings

 Springer

Volume Editors

Nils Bulling
Clausthal University of Technology
Adolph-Römer-Strasse 2A, 38678 Clausthal-Zellerfeld, Germany
E-mail: bulling@in.tu-clausthal.de

Leendert van der Torre
Wojtek Jamroga
University of Luxembourg, Campus Kirchberg
6, rue Richard Coudenhove-Kalergi, 1359 Luxembourg, Luxembourg
E-mail: {leon.vandertorre, wojtek.jamroga}@uni.lu

Serena Villata
Inria Sophia Antipolis-Méditerranée
2004, route des Lucioles - BP 93, 06902 Sophia Antipolis Cedex, France
E-mail: serena.villata@inria.fr

Wamberto Vasconcelos
University of Aberdeen, Meston Building
Old Aberdeen, Aberdeen AB24 3UE, UK
E-mail: w.w.vasconcelos@abdn.ac.uk

ISSN 0302-9743   e-ISSN 1611-3349
ISBN 978-3-319-09763-3   e-ISBN 978-3-319-09764-0
DOI 10.1007/978-3-319-09764-0
Springer Cham Heidelberg New York Dordrecht London

Library of Congress Control Number: 2014944725

LNCS Sublibrary: SL 7 – Artificial Intelligence

Typesetting: Camera-ready by author, data conversion by Scientific Publishing Services, Chennai, India

Printed on acid-free paper

Springer is part of Springer Science+Business Media (www.springer.com)

Preface

In this volume, we present the proceedings of the 15th International Workshop on Computational Logic in Multi-Agent Systems (CLIMA XV), held during August 18–19, 2014, in Prague, Czech Republic, and co-located with the 21st European Conference on Artificial Intelligence (ECAI).

Multi-agent systems are systems of interacting autonomous agents or components that can perceive and act upon their environment to achieve their individual goals as well as joint goals. Research on such systems integrates many technologies and concepts in artificial intelligence and other areas of computing as well as other disciplines. Over recent years, the agent paradigm gained popularity, due to its applicability to a full spectrum of domains, from search engines to educational aids to electronic commerce and trade, e-procurement, recommendation systems, simulation and routing, to mention only some.

Computational logic provides a well-defined, general, and rigorous framework for studying syntax, semantics, and procedures for various tasks by individual agents, as well as for interaction amongst agents in multi-agent systems, for implementations, environments, tools, and standards, and for linking together specification and verification of properties of individual agents and multi-agent systems.

The purpose of the CLIMA workshops is to provide a forum for discussing techniques, based on computational logic, for representing, programming and reasoning about agents and multi agent systems in a formal way.

CLIMA XV closely followed the format established by its predecessors, with regular proceedings and two special sessions: Logics for Games, Strategic Reasoning, and Social Choice, organized by Wojtek Jamroga, and Logics for Agreement Technologies organized by Wamberto Vasconcelos.

Strategic reasoning occurs in many multi-agent scenarios. This is evident in theoretical approaches to MAS, as well as in practical solutions used, for example, in computer games, IT infrastructures for e-voting procedures, social network services, etc. The Special Session on Logics for Games, Strategic Reasoning, and Social Choice was intended to be a forum to discuss how formal logic can contribute to our understanding, modeling, and analysis of strategic behavior, and how the metaphors of game and social interaction can help in constructing and using logical formalisms.

A growing number of computer systems are based on software agents, which act on behalf of humans. These agents are becoming increasingly responsible for complex tasks delegated to them, interacting with each other in sophisticated ways so as to forge agreements in the interest of human users. The Special Session on Logics for Agreement Technologies aimed at expanding the state-of-the-art on logic-based approaches and technologies to enable different aspects of many-party agreements and to support the lifecycle of such systems.

Former CLIMA editions have mostly been conducted in conjunction with major computational logic and artificial intelligence events such as CL in 2000, ICLP in 2001 and 2007, FLoC in 2002, LPNMR and AI-Math in 2004, JELIA in 2004 and 2008, AAMAS in 2006, MATES in 2009, ECAI in 2010 and 2012, IJCAI in 2011, and LPNMR in 2013. In 2005, CLIMA VI was organized as a stand-alone event.

This 15th edition of CLIMA received a good number of submissions. The 12 papers presented at CLIMA XV were selected from 20 submissions, on average of very high quality, resulting in a final acceptance rate of circa 60%, in line with the standards of previous editions. Many of those involved in the revision and selection process acknowledged the high quality of the program. In many instances the authors expressed their satisfaction with very informative and constructive reviews, for which CLIMA is renown.

The Program Committee consisted of 66 top-level researchers from 46 institutions located in five continents and 24 countries. Seven additional reviewers helped in the process. The papers in this book have been authored by 50 researchers worldwide.

Further information about CLIMA XV is available from the website http://www-sop.inria.fr/members/Serena.Villata/climaXV.html. General information about the workshop series, with links to past and future events, can be found at http://centria.di.fct.unl.pt/~clima/, the CLIMA workshop series home page.

We thank all the authors of papers submitted to CLIMA XV, the invited speakers, the members of the Program Committee, and the additional reviewers, for ensuring that CLIMA keeps up to its high standards.

August 2014   Nils Bulling
Leendert van der Torre
Serena Villata
Wojtek Jamroga
Wamberto Vasconcelos

Organization

Workshop Chairs

Nils Bulling   Clausthal University of Technology, Germany
Leendert van der Torre   University of Luxembourg, Luxembourg
Serena Villata   Inria Sophia Antipolis, France

Special Session Organizers

Wojtek Jamroga   University of Luxembourg, Luxembourg
Wamberto Vasconcelos   University of Aberdeen, UK

Program Committee

Huib Aldewereld	Delft University of Technology, The Netherlands
Natasha Alechina	University of Nottingham, UK
Jose Julio Alferes	Universidade NOVA de Lisboa, Portugal
Katie Atkinson	University of Liverpool, UK
Matteo Baldoni	University of Turin, Italy
Tina Balke	University of Surrey, UK
Pietro Baroni	University of Brescia, Italy
Stefano Bistarelli	Università di Perugia, Italy
Elise Bonzon	LIPADE - Université Paris Descartes, France
Rafael H. Bordini	FACIN-PUCRS, Brazil
Jan Broersen	Utrecht University, The Netherlands
Nils Bulling	Clausthal University, Germany
Stefania Costantini	University of L'Aquila, Italy
Célia Da Costa Pereira	Université Nice Sophia Anipolis, France
Mehdi Dastani	Utrecht University, The Netherlands
Marina De Vos	University of Bath, UK
Louise Dennis	University of Liverpool, UK
Frank Dignum	Utrecht University, The Netherlands
Catalin Dima	LACL, Université Paris Est - Créteil, France
Juergen Dix	Clausthal University of Technology, Germany
Michael Fisher	University of Liverpool, UK
Sujata Ghosh	Indian Statistical Institute Chennai, India
Massimiliano Giacomin	University of Brescia, Italy
Valentin Goranko	Technical University of Denmark, Denmark
Stella Heras	GTI-IA DSIC UPV, Spain

Additional Reviewers

Wolfgang Dvorak	University of Vienna, Austria
Michał Knapik	ICS PAS, Poland
Bastien Maubert	IRISA, France
Joerg Puehrer	Leipzig University, Germany
Nicolas Schwind	University of Artois, France
Sunil Easaw Simon	CWI Amsterdam, The Netherlands

CLIMA Steering Committee

Thomas Ågotnes	University of Bergen, Norway
Michael Fisher	University of Liverpool, UK
Katsumi Inoue	National Institute of Informatics, Japan
João Leite	New University of Lisbon, Portugal
Leendert van der Torre	University of Luxembourg, Luxembourg

CLIMA Publications

Special Issues

- **Journal of Logic and Computation**, Special issue on Computational Logic and Multi-Agent Systems, guest edited by Nils Bulling, Leendert van der Torre, Serena Villata, Wojtek Jamroga and Wamberto Vasconcelos. Expected, 2016.
- **Argument & Computation**, Special issue on Applications of Logical Approaches to Argumentation, guest edited by João Leite, Tran Cao Son, Paolo Torroni and Stefan Woltran. Expected, 2015.
- **Journal of Logic and Computation**, Special issue on Computational Logic and Multi-Agent Systems, guest edited by João Leite, Tran Cao Son, Paolo Torroni and Stefan Woltran. Expected, 2015.
- **Journal of Logic and Computation**, Special issue on Computational Logic and Multi-Agent Systems, guest edited by Michael Fisher, Leon van der Torre, Mehdi Dastani, and Guido Governatori. Expected, 2014.
- **Journal of Logic and Computation**, Special issue on Computational Logic and Multi-Agent Systems, guest edited by João Leite, Paolo Torroni, Thomas Ågotnes, Guido Boella, and Leon van der Torre. Expected, 2013.
- **Annals of Mathematics and Artificial Intelligence**, 62(1-2), 2011. Special issue on Computational Logic and Multi-Agent Systems, guest-edited by Jürgen Dix and João Leite.
- **Journal of Autonomous Agents and Multi-Agent Systems**, 16(3), 2008. Special Issue on Computational Logic-Based Agents, guest-edited by Francesca Toni and Jamal Bentahar.
- **Annals of Mathematics and Artificial Intelligence**, 42(1-3), 2004. Special issues on Computational Logic and Multi-Agent Systems, guest-edited by Jürgen Dix Dix, João Leite, and Ken Satoh.
- **Annals of Mathematics and Artificial Intelligence**, 37(1-2), 2003. Special issue on Computational Logic and Multi-Agent Systems, guest-edited by Jürgen Dix, Fariba Sadri and Ken Satoh.
- **Electronic Notes in Theoretical Computer Science**, 70(5), 2002. Special Issue on Computational Logic and Multi-Agency, guest-edited by Jürgen Dix Dix, João Leite, and Ken Satoh.

Proceedings

- **Computational Logic in Multi-Agent Systems XV, Proceedings**. Vol. 8624 of Lecture Notes in Artificial Intelligence, edited by Nils Bulling, Leendert van der Torre, Serena Villata, Wojtek Jamroga and Wamberto Vasconcelos. Springer-Verlag Berlin Heidelberg 2014.

- **Computational Logic in Multi-Agent Systems XIV, Proceedings.**
Vol. 8143 of Lecture Notes in Artificial Intelligence, edited by João Leite,
Tran Cao Son, Paolo Torroni, Leon van der Torre, and Stefan Woltran.
Springer-Verlag Berlin Heidelberg 2013.

- **Computational Logic in Multi-Agent Systems XIII, Proceedings.**
Vol. 7486 of Lecture Notes in Artificial Intelligence, edited by Michael Fisher,
Leon van der Torre, Mehdi Dastani, and Guido Governatori. Springer-Verlag
Berlin Heidelberg 2012.

- **Computational Logic in Multi-Agent Systems XII, Proceedings.**
Vol. 6814 of Lecture Notes in Artificial Intelligence, edited by João Leite,
Paolo Torroni, Thomas Ågotnes, Guido Boella, and Leon van der Torre.
Springer-Verlag Berlin Heidelberg 2011.

- **Computational Logic in Multi-Agent Systems XI, Proceedings.**
Vol. 6245 of Lecture Notes in Artificial Intelligence, edited by Jürgen Dix,
João Leite, Guido Governatori and Wojtek Jamroga. Springer-Verlag Berlin
Heidelberg 2010.

- **Computational Logic in Multi-Agent Systems X, Revised Selected
and Invited Papers.** Vol. 6214 of Lecture Notes in Artificial Intelligence,
edited by Jürgen Dix, Michael Fisher, and Peter Novák. Springer-Verlag
Berlin Heidelberg 2010.

- **Computational Logic in Multi-Agent Systems IX, Revised Selected
and Invited Papers.** Vol. 5405 of Lecture Notes in Artificial Intelligence,
edited by Michael Fisher, Fariba Sadri, and Michael Thielscher. Springer-
Verlag Berlin Heidelberg 2009.

- **Computational Logic in Multi-Agent Systems VIII, Revised Selected and Invited Papers.** Vol. 5056 of Lecture Notes in Artificial Intelligence, edited by Fariba Sadri and Ken Satoh. Springer-Verlag Berlin
Heidelberg 2008.

- **Computational Logic in Multi-Agent Systems VII, Revised Se-
lected and Invited Papers.** Vol. 4371 of Lecture Notes in Artificial
Intelligence, edited by Katsumi Inoue, Ken Satoh, and Francesca Toni.
Springer-Verlag Berlin Heidelberg, Germany, 2007.

- **Computational Logic in Multi-Agent Systems VI, Revised Selected
and Invited Papers.** Vol. 3900 of Lecture Notes in Artificial Intelligence
(State-of-the-art Survey), edited by Francesca Toni and Paolo Torroni,
Springer-Verlag Berlin Heidelberg, Germany, 2006.

- **Computational Logic in Multi-Agent Systems V, Revised Selected
and Invited Papers.** Vol. 3487 of Lecture Notes in Artificial Intelligence,
edited by João Leite Leite and Paolo Torroni. Springer-Verlag Berlin Heidelberg, Germany, 2005.

- **Computational Logic in Multi-Agent Systems IV, Revised Selected
and Invited Papers.** Vol. 3259 of Lecture Notes in Artificial Intelligence,
edited by Jürgen Dix and João Leite. Springer-Verlag Berlin Heidelberg,
Germany, 2004.

Early Editions

- Proceedings of the **5th International Workshop on Computational Logic in Multi-Agent Systems** (CLIMA V), edited by João Leite Leite and Paolo Torroni. Lisbon, Portugal, ISBN: 972-9119-37-6, September 2004.
  http://centria.di.fct.unl.pt/~jleite/climaV/climaV-preprocs.pdf
- Proceedings of the **4th International Workshop on Computational Logic in Multi-Agent Systems** (CLIMA IV), edited by Jürgen Dix and João Leite. ITZ Bericht 1(5). Papierflieger Verlag, Clausthal-Zellerfeld, Germany, ISBN 3-89720-688-9, 2003.
  http://centria.di.fct.unl.pt/~jleite/climaIV/climaIV-TR.pdf
- Pre-proceedings of the **3rd International Workshop on Computational Logic in Multi-Agent Systems** (CLIMA III), edited by Jürgen Dix Dix, João Leite, and Ken Satoh. Datalogiske Skrifter 93, Roskilde University, Denmark, ISSN 0109-9779, 2002.
  http://centria.di.fct.unl.pt/~jleite/papers/clima02_procs.pdf
- **ICLP'01 Workshop on Computational Logic in Multi-Agent Systems** (CLIMA II), held in association with ICLP'01, Paphos, Cyprus, December 1, 2001. Organized by Ken Satoh and Jürgen Dix.
  http://research.nii.ac.jp/~ksatoh/clima01.html
- **CL-2000 Workshop on Computational Logic in Multi-Agent Systems** (CLIMA I), held in association with the International Conference on Computational Logic, Imperial College London, UK, July 24-25, 2000. Organized by Ken Satoh and Fariba Sadri.
  http://research.nii.ac.jp/~ksatoh/clima00.html
- **Workshop on Multi-Agent Systems in Logic Programming** (MAS-LP), held in conjunction with the 16th International Conference on Logic Programming, Las Cruces, NM, November 30, 1999. Organized by Stephen Rochefort, Fariba Sadri, and Francesca Toni.
  http://www.cs.sfu.ca/news/conferences/MAS99/

Table of Contents

Main Session

Logics for Agreement Technologies

Logics for Games, Strategic Reasoning, and Social Choice

On the Complexity
of Two-Agent Justification Logic

Antonis Achilleos

The Graduate Center of CUNY, New York, USA
aachilleos@gc.cuny.edu

Abstract. Justification Logic provides a refined version of epistemic modal logic in which the proofs/justifications are taken into account. As a practical tool, Justification Logic has the ability to model argumentation and track evidence in the full logic context, to measure the complexity of the arguments, to keep the logical omniscience at bay, etc. The complexity of single-agent justification logics has been well-studied and shown to be generally lower than the complexity of their modal counterparts. In this paper we investigate the complexity of two-agent Justification Logic. We show that for most cases the upper complexity bounds established for the single-agent cases are maintained: these logics' derivability problem is in the second step of the polynomial hierarchy. For certain logics, though, we discover a complexity jump to PSPACE-completeness, which is a new phenomenon for Justification Logic.

1 Introduction

Justification Logic is a family of logics which models the way justifications interact with statements and can be viewed as an explicit counterpart of epistemic modal logic. It is often the case that we want to express statements of the form "agent A knows/believes ϕ because of *justification t*" and Justification Logic offers the means to formalize situation where either the distinction between different justifications is important, or a given claim is provided together with an appropriate justification for it. This allows for a finer analysis than the one provided by Modal Logic.

The first such system, the Logic of Proofs LP, which is the explicit counterpart of modal logic S4, was introduced in 1995 by Artemov([4]). Since then, several variations have been introduced (ex. [5,9]), which resulted in a wide class of logics to model the interaction between belief, knowledge and justifications. For a comprehensive review of Justification Logic, see [7,6].

Justification formulas are formed using propositional connectives and justification terms: if ϕ is a formula and t a term, $t : \phi$ is a formula. An important aspect of (and to the author an important motivation for) Justification Logic is its complexity properties. Ladner showed in [19] that S4-satisfiability (and thus, provability) is PSPACE-complete. Kuznets proved that LP-provability is in the second level of the polynomial hierarchy and in particular in Π_2^p ([15]). Krupski has shown that LP-provability for formulas of the form $t : \phi$ is in NP ([14]).

N. Bulling et al. (Eds.): CLIMA XV, LNAI 8624, pp. 1–18, 2014.
© Springer International Publishing Switzerland 2014

Under certain reasonable assumptions about the justification terms, there is an easily recognizable class of terms (say, $\mathcal{T}$), such that if a formula ϕ is provable then $t : \phi$ is provable for some $t \in \mathcal{T}$, while when $t \in \mathcal{T}$, the provability of $t : \phi$ is in P([8]). Of course, this does not simplify theoremhood of S4 (which is PSPACE-complete), but it demonstrates the complexity-theoretic difference between determining the provability of a modal statement and determining the provability of a modal statement when given appropriate evidence.

We consider situations with multiple agents and also allow dependencies between agents' justifications and beliefs. In particular, we allow that each agent can be based on a different justification logic. We thus introduce and study two-agent logics which are combinations of two different justification logics as a first step towards a multi-agent justification logic. For some of these logics we discover a complexity jump to PSPACE-completeness. This is a different situation from what is the case for all (pure) justification logics whose complexity has been studied.

Contrary to what is usually the case in Modal Logic, PSPACE-hardness is not achieved through some type of alternation, but by using a formula which forces the satisfiability testing procedure we provide to simulate a polynomial space Turing Machine, using (potentially) an exponential number of steps. In fact, the methods we use have similarities to Fischer's and Ladner's proof in [12] that PDL is EXP-hard, while the methods *and* results are nearly identical for diamond-free (in negation normal form) modal formulas as studied in [2]. For corresponding cases in full Modal Logic, Spaan ([23]) and Demri ([11]) have determined for certain corresponding cases of Modal Logic a jump to EXP-hardness.

The systems we provide can describe settings of multiple (in this case two) agents that receive information from different sources and somehow communicate with each other. Within our formalization we are able to describe situations where each agent can distinguish between different sources (justifications) of information and can take into account how reliable they consider another agent's information.

Other multi-agent justification logics have already been introduced (for example, see [10,22,24]). They present a different approach.

The main result of this paper is Theorem 1, which settles the complexity for all two-agent logics we introduce and informally states that for most of the logics that are presented, the complexity of provability remains in the second level of the polynomial hierarchy. The exceptions for which we observe the complexity jump to PSPACE-completeness are certain combinations of JD and a justification logic which has the Positive Introspection or Factivity axiom, depending on the way these are combined.

A more extensive version of this paper can be found as a technical report [3].

2   Syntax, Axioms, and Semantics

The proofs of some propositions that appear in this section are very similar to the proofs of corresponding results for the single-agent logics and the reader can see

[6,7] or [16] for an overview. The justification terms of the language L^2 include constants $c_1, c_2, c_3, \ldots$ and variables $x_1, x_2, x_3, \ldots$ and if t_1 and t_2 are terms, then the following are also terms: $[t_1 + t_2]$, $[t_1 \cdot t_2]$, $!t_1$. The set of terms will be referred to as Tm. We also use a set $SLet$ of propositional variables, or sentence letters. These will usually be $p_1, p_2, \ldots$. Formulas of the language L^2 include all propositional variables and if ϕ, ψ are formulas, t is a term, and $i \in \{1, 2\}$, then the following are also formulas of L^2: $\bot$, $\phi \rightarrow \psi$, $t :_i \phi$. The remaining propositional connectives, whenever needed, are treated as constructed from $\rightarrow$ and $\bot$ in the usual way: $\neg a := a \rightarrow \bot$, $a \vee b := \neg a \rightarrow b$, and $a \wedge b := \neg(\neg a \vee \neg b)$.

The function of the operators $\cdot, +$ and $!$ becomes clear below as described by the axioms. Intuitively, $\cdot$ applies a justification s for a statement $A \rightarrow B$ to a justification t for A and gives a justification $[s \cdot t]$ for B. Using $+$ we can combine two justifications and have a justification for anything that can be justified by any of the two initial terms – much like the concatenation of two proofs. Finally, $!$ is a unary operator called the proof checker. Given a justification t for ϕ, it gives another one, $!t$, for the fact that t is a justification for ϕ.

The logics use modus ponens as a derivation rule and share all of the following axioms:

Propositional Axioms: Finitely many schemes from classical propositional
   logic;
Application: $s :_i (\phi \rightarrow \psi) \rightarrow (t :_i \phi \rightarrow [s \cdot t] :_i \psi)$;
Concatenation: $s :_i \phi \rightarrow [s + t] :_i \phi$, $s :_i \phi \rightarrow [t + s] :_i \phi$.

where in the above, ϕ and ψ are formulas in L^2, s, t are terms and $i \in \{1, 2\}$.

Depending on the reliability of agent i's justifications, the logic can include Factivity or Consistency for i, or neither:

Factivity: $t :_i \phi \rightarrow \phi$;
Consistency: $t :_i \bot \rightarrow \bot$;
Positive Introspection: $t :_i \phi \rightarrow !t :_i t :_i \phi$,

where in the above, ϕ is a formulas in L^2, t a term and $i \in \{1, 2\}$. If we consider that agent i accepts only justifications that yield truth, then we would include Factivity; if on the other hand i has justified beliefs that are not true, then the agent may at least have justified beliefs that are consistent and in this case the logic would include Consistency for i; when we consider an agent that can even have inconsistent beliefs, then we would include neither of these axioms. If agent i can verify (has a justification for) their own justifications, then the logic would include Positive Introspection for i.

The following axioms give the interactions between the two agents' justifications. As before, depending on the type of interactions we desire to include in our logic, we would include a different set from these axioms.

12-Verification: $t :_1 \phi \rightarrow !t :_2 t :_1 \phi$;
21-Verification: $t :_2 \phi \rightarrow !t :_1 t :_2 \phi$;
12-Conversion: $t :_1 \phi \rightarrow t :_2 \phi$;
21-Conversion: $t :_2 \phi \rightarrow t :_1 \phi$,

where in the above, ϕ is a formula in L^2, t a term.

We would normally expect an agent to have justifications available for certain formulas – at least for the axioms of the logic. These justifications are provided by the constant specification and all agents are aware of these justifications through the Axiom Necessitation axiom. A *constant specification* for a two-agent logic J is any set

$$\mathcal{CS} \subseteq \{c\!:_i A \mid c \text{ is a constant}, A \text{ an axiom of } J \text{ from above and } i \in \{1,2\}\}.$$

We say that axiom A is justified by a constant c for agent i, when $c\!:_i A \in \mathcal{CS}$.

Axiom Necessitation: $t\!:_i \phi$,

where $t :_i \phi \in \mathcal{CS}$, or $\phi = s :_j \psi$ is an instance of Axiom Necessitation and $t =!s$. Therefore, for $i_1, \ldots, i_k \in \{1,2\}$ and $c\!:_{i_1} A \in \mathcal{CS}$, all formulas of the form $!! \cdots !c\!:_{i_k}! \cdots !c\!:_{i_{k-1}} \cdots c\!:_{i_1} A$ are instances of Axiom Necessitation.

We assume that a constant specification $\mathcal{CS}$ has the following properties: each axiom (except for Axiom Necessitation) is justified by at least one constant for every agent, every constant justifies only a certain number (possibly zero) of schemes from the ones above (which implies that if c justifies A for i and B results from A and substitution, then c justifies B for i), and $\mathcal{CS} \in \mathsf{P}$ (i.e. there is a polynomial time algorithm that given some $t :_i \phi \in L^2$, decides whether $t\!:_i \phi \in \mathcal{CS}$).

Combining different logics gives rise to new phenomena, which makes them notable. We may consider situations where two agents are not equally reliable, or we may even consider the two agents to model separate states of belief/knowledge. For example, if agent 2 comes with factivity, $s :_2 \phi$ may indicate knowledge of ϕ, while if 1 comes only with consistency, then $t :_1 \psi$ may indicate belief of ψ. If knowing a fact implies belief of the fact, then 12-Conversion becomes a natural axiom of the logic.

Example 1. An agent has somehow obtained two pieces of evidence, the first being evidence for ϕ and the second for $\neg\phi$. After an additional inquiry the agent discovers that the second piece of evidence has been compromised whereas the first was confirmed. On this basis, the agent attains the knowledge of ϕ. Lets attempt to model this situation in Bi-modal and Two-agent Justification logic. Bi-modal logic is insufficient to model this situation: we need to distinguish between two types of belief: B and K, where K indicates knowledge and B some kind of belief. Then, initially the agent would have the beliefs $B\phi$, $B\neg\phi$, while the fact that the agent determines the first evidence as confirmed can be formalized as $K(B\chi \rightarrow \chi)$. We can already see that Modal logic's language presents difficulties in expressing the desired distinction between the two pieces of evidence. From $B\phi$ we can derive $KB\phi$ (we assume that the agent has at least knowledge of the evidence they have obtained) and from $K(B\phi \rightarrow \phi)$ we can derive $KB\phi \rightarrow K\phi$; from the two we derive $K\phi$ and then ϕ. Similarly we can derive $\neg\phi$ and we reach an inconsistency.

We can formalize the scenario in a natural and intrinsically faithful way using a two-agent justification logic from the above, where $s :_1 X$ stands for 's is an evidence for X' and $t :_2 X$ denotes 't is a conclusive/knowledge producing evidence for X', equipped with 12-Verification. The situation can be formalized by the set $\{u :_1 \phi,\ v :_1 \neg\phi,\ c :_2 (u :_1 X \to X)\}$. This set is consistent, which can easily be satisfied in a model (defined later on). We can derive knowledge of ϕ in the following way: $u :_1 \phi \to !u :_2 u :_1 \phi$ is an instance of the 12-Verification axiom and together with $u :_1 \phi$ yields $!u :_2 u :_1 \phi$ and this in turn together with $c :_2 (u :_1 \phi \to \phi)$ and the application axiom yield $[c \cdot !u] :_2 \phi$. Then, ϕ is known with justification $[c \cdot !u]$.

The above scenario can also be reformulated as a situation of two agents, where the second has more reliable sources than the first (enough to accept only evidence that yield knowledge) and the first one reports to the second one the two pieces of evidence for ϕ and $\neg\phi$; the second agent would then have obtained information about the reliability of the evidence that the first agent provides, i.e. that the second piece of evidence is compromised, while the first one is confirmed. The analysis would then be the same.[1]

Example 2. During a trial, two lawyers, A and B, present evidence to support their case. A presents witness a who claims A's client is right, while B presents witness b who claims B's client is right (and lets assume they both believe their respective witnesses' claims). Furthermore, A also presents document d that strongly support that whoever is right is entitled to receive the sum of $10 from the other. Both lawyers accept the document and their respective witness' claims as valid evidence, while they are aware of (and reject) each other's beliefs on the case. Similarly to the above, this scenario can be formalized by a two-agent logic where both agents are equipped with Consistency and has 12-Verification and 21-Verification. As above, we can see that Bi-modal logic cannot sufficiently formalize the situation.

The axioms for each two-agent logic are provided in Figure 1. Each of the Application, Concatenation, Factivity, Positive Introspection, and Consistency axioms has a version for agent 1 and one for agent 2, depending on what we substitute i for. We say agent 1 is based on logic $\mathcal{J}_1$ and agent 2 on logic $\mathcal{J}_2$ and we choose the axioms' versions for each agent that correspond to the logic the agent is based on. For example, the logic $(\mathsf{JT} \times_C \mathsf{JD4})_{CS}$ is the logic with, the Propositional Axioms axioms, Application, Concatenation, Axiom Necessitation, Factivity for 1, Consistency and Positive Introspection for 2, and 12-Conversion.[2]

If we map each formula to a propositional formula by just removing all terms, it is easy to see that each axiom is mapped to a propositional tautology and that modus ponens preserves the mapping. Thus, we conclude that *each of the logics defined above is consistent.*

The following proposition is a characteristic result in justification logic. It demonstrates that Necessitation in Justification Logic is a derived rule.

---

[1] Of course, we could also handle the situation in Modal Logic by using more modalities. This treatment would not appropriately reflect the nature of the issue, though, and it would be hard to apply the analysis in other similar situations.

[2] The operators we use to combine justification logics are extensions of operators $\oplus$ and $\oplus_\subseteq$ as defined in [23,11] for Modal Logic.

Logic $\mathcal{J}_i$ is	Contributes the Axioms:
For all $\mathcal{J}_i$	*Propositional Axioms:* Finitely many schemes of classical propositional logic; *Application:* $s :_i (\phi \to \psi) \to (t :_i \phi \to [s \cdot t] :_i \psi)$; *Concatenation:* $s :_i \phi \to [s + t] :_i \phi$, $s :_i \phi \to [t + s] :_i \phi$, *Axiom Necessitation*
$\mathcal{J}_i = \mathsf{J}$	No additional axioms
$\mathcal{J}_i = \mathsf{JD}$	Consistency: $t :_i \bot \to \bot$
$\mathcal{J}_i = \mathsf{JT}$	Factivity: $t :_i \phi \to \phi$
$\mathcal{J}_i = \mathsf{J4}$	Positive Introspection: $t :_i \phi \to !t :_i t :_i \phi$
$\mathcal{J}_i = \mathsf{JD4}$	Consistency and Positive Introspection
$\mathcal{J}_i = \mathsf{LP}$	Factivity and Positive Introspection

$\times_\circ$ is	Contributes the Axioms:
$\times$	No additional axioms
$\times_!$	12-Verification: $t :_1 \phi \to !t :_2 t :_1 \phi$
$\times_C$	12-Conversion: $t :_1 \phi \to t :_2 \phi$
$\times_{!!}$	12-Verification and 21-Verification: $t :_2 \phi \to !t :_1 t :_2 \phi$
$\times_{CC}$	12-Conversion and 21-Conversion: $t :_2 \phi \to t :_1 \phi$

Fig. 1. The axioms for logic $J = (\mathcal{J}_1 \times_\circ \mathcal{J}_2)_{\mathcal{CS}}$, where $\mathcal{J}_1, \mathcal{J}_2 \in \{\mathsf{J}, \mathsf{JD}, \mathsf{JT}, \mathsf{J4}, \mathsf{JD4}, \mathsf{LP}\}$, $\times_\circ \in \{\times, \times_!, \times_{!!}, \times_C, \times_{CC}\}$

Proposition 1. *If $\phi_1, \ldots, \phi_k \vdash \phi$, then for any $i \in \{1, 2\}$, there is some term t depending on terms $t_1, \ldots, t_k$, such that $t_1 :_i \phi_1, \ldots, t_k :_i \phi_k \vdash t :_i \phi$.*

Proof. By induction on the proof of ϕ: If ϕ is an axiom, then by the Axiom Necessitation axiom, the proposition holds. Furthermore the proposition obviously holds for any ϕ_j, $j \in \{1, 2, \ldots, k\}$. This covers the base cases. Using the application axiom, if ϕ is the result of $\psi \to \phi, \psi$ and modus ponens, since the proposition holds for $\psi \to \phi$ and ψ, then $t_1 :_i \phi_1, \ldots, t_k :_i \phi_k \vdash r :_i (\psi \to \phi), s :_i \psi$ and thus for $t = [r \cdot s]$, $t_1 :_i \phi_1, \ldots, t_k :_i \phi_k \vdash t :_i \phi$ and this completes the induction. $\square$

We now introduce models for our logic. In the single-agent cases, M-models (introduced in [18,20]) and F-models (introduced in [13,18,21]) are used and they are both useful in the study of complexity issues. We only introduce F-models, which are Kripke models equipped with an additional mechanism to handle justification terms, called an admissible evidence function.

Definition 1. *Let $J = (\mathcal{J}_1 \times_\circ \mathcal{J}_2)_{\mathcal{CS}}$, where $\mathcal{J}_1, \mathcal{J}_2 \in \{\mathsf{J}, \mathsf{JD}, \mathsf{JT}, \mathsf{J4}, \mathsf{JD4}, \mathsf{LP}\}$ and $\times_\circ \in \{\times, \times_!, \times_{!!}, \times_C, \times_{CC}\}$. An F-model $\mathcal{M}$ for J is a tuple $(W, R_1, R_2, \mathcal{E}_1, \mathcal{E}_2, \mathcal{V})$ where W a nonempty set of states (occasionally referred to as worlds), for $i \in \{1, 2\}$, $R_i \subseteq W^2$ is a binary relation on W, $\mathcal{E}_i : (Tm \times L_n) \longrightarrow 2^W$, and $\mathcal{V} : SLet \longrightarrow 2^W$. Furthermore, $\mathcal{E}_1, \mathcal{E}_2$ will often be seen and referred to as $\mathcal{E} : \{1, 2\} \times Tm \times L^2 \longrightarrow 2^W$ and $\mathcal{E}$ is called an admissible evidence function. $\mathcal{E}_1, \mathcal{E}_2$ must satisfy the following natural closure conditions:*

Application closure: *for any formulas* ϕ, ψ *and justification terms* t, s,
$$\mathcal{E}_i(s, \phi \rightarrow \psi) \cap \mathcal{E}_i(t, \phi) \subseteq \mathcal{E}_i(s \cdot t, \psi).$$
Sum closure: *for any formula* ϕ *and justification terms* t, s,
$$\mathcal{E}_i(t, \phi) \cup \mathcal{E}_i(s, \phi) \subseteq \mathcal{E}_i(t + s, \phi).$$
$\mathcal{CS}$-closure: *for any* $t :_i \phi \in cl^2(\mathcal{CS})$, $\mathcal{E}_i(t, \phi) = W$.
Positive Introspection Closure: *When* $\mathcal{J}_i$ *is among* J4, JD4, *and* LP,
$$\mathcal{E}_i(t, \phi) \subseteq \mathcal{E}_i(!t, t :_i \phi).$$
Distribution: *When* $\mathcal{J}_i$ *is among* J4, JD4, *and* LP, *then for any formula* ϕ,
justification term t, *and* $a, b \in W$, *if* $aR_i b$ *and* $a \in \mathcal{E}_i(t, \phi)$, *then* $b \in \mathcal{E}_i(t, \phi)$.
Verification Closure: *When* J *has* ij-*Verification*, $\mathcal{E}_i(t, \phi) \subseteq \mathcal{E}_j(!t, t :_i \phi)$.
Conversion Closure: *When* J *has* ij-*Conversion*, $\mathcal{E}_i(t, \phi) \subseteq \mathcal{E}_j(t, \phi)$.
V-Distribution: *If* J *includes* ij-*Verification, then for any formula* ϕ, *justification term* t, *and* $a, b \in W$, *if* $aR_j b$ *and* $a \in \mathcal{E}_i(t, \phi)$, *then* $b \in \mathcal{E}_i(t, \phi)$.

The accessibility relations, R_1, R_2, *must satisfy the following conditions: for every* $i \in \{1, 2\}$,

- *If* $\mathcal{J}_i \in \{\mathsf{JT}, \mathsf{LP}\}$, *then* R_i *must be reflexive.*
- *If* $\mathcal{J}_i \in \{\mathsf{JD}, \mathsf{JD4}\}$, *then* R_i *must be serial* $(\forall a \in W \,\, \exists b \in W \,\, aR_i b)$.
- *If* $\mathcal{J}_i \in \{\mathsf{J4}, \mathsf{JD4}, \mathsf{LP}\}$, *then* R_i *must be transitive.*
- *If the logic includes* ij-*Verification, then for any* $a, b, c \in W$, *if* $aR_j bR_i c$, *we also have* $aR_i c$.
- *If the logic includes* ij-*Conversion, then* $R_j \subseteq R_i$.

Truth in the model is defined in the following way:

- $\mathcal{M}, u \not\models \bot$ *and if* p *is a propositional variable, then* $\mathcal{M}, u \models p$ *iff* $u \in \mathcal{V}(p)$.
- *If* ϕ, ψ *are formulas, then* $\mathcal{M}, u \models \phi \rightarrow \psi$ *if and only if* $\mathcal{M}, u \models \psi$, *or* $\mathcal{M}, u \not\models \phi$.
- $\mathcal{M}, u \models t :_i \phi$ *if and only if* $u \in \mathcal{E}_i(t, \phi)$ *and for every* $v \in W$ *such that* $uR_i v$, $\mathcal{M}, v \models \phi$.

(W, R_1, R_2) *is called a frame for* J. *We say that* $\mathcal{M}$ *has the Strong Evidence property when for every* $t :_i \phi \in L^2$, $\mathcal{M}, u \models t :_i \phi$ *iff* $u \in \mathcal{E}_i(t, \phi)$.

Proposition 2 (Soundness and Completeness[3]). *Let* $J = (\mathcal{J}_1 \times_\circ \mathcal{J}_2)_{\mathcal{CS}}$, *where* $\mathcal{J}_1, \mathcal{J}_2 \in \{\mathsf{J}, \mathsf{JD}, \mathsf{JT}, \mathsf{J4}, \mathsf{JD4}, \mathsf{LP}\}$ *and* $\times_\circ \in \{\times, \times_!, \times_{!!}, \times_C, \times_{CC}\}$. *Then,* J *is sound and complete with respect to its F-models. Furthermore,* J *is sound and complete with respect to its F-models that have the Strong Evidence property.*

The proof of Proposition 2 is by a canonical model construction (cf. [13]). By a modification of the canonical model construction, we can prove a finite frame property for the logics we presented. Although interesting on its own, the following corollary makes several results easier to prove.

Corollary 1. *Let* J *be a two-agent justification logic as in the assumptions of Proposition 2. If* ϕ *is* J-*satisfiable, then* ϕ *is satisfiable by an F-model for* J *of at most* $2^{|\phi|}$ *states which has the strong evidence property.*

---

[3] If either $\mathcal{J}_1$ or $\mathcal{J}_2$ are JD or JD4, then the requirement that $\mathcal{CS}$ justifies all axioms is necessary.

The ∗-calculus

We introduce the ∗-calculus for logic J on frame $\mathcal{F}$, an invaluable tool when studying the complexity of justification logic.[4] The calculus rules are given in Figure 2. The ∗-calculus is a calculus on ∗-expressions prefixed by states from $\mathcal{F}$. ∗-expressions are expressions of the form $*_i(t, \phi)$, where $t:_i \phi \in L^2$.

∗$\mathcal{CS}(\mathcal{F})$ Axioms: $w *_i (t, \phi)$, where $w \in W$ and $t:_i \phi \in cl_n(\mathcal{CS})$	**∗V($\mathcal{F}$):** If the logic has ij-Verification,
∗App($\mathcal{F}$): $$\frac{w \ *_i (s, \phi \to \psi) \qquad w \ *_i (t, \phi)}{w \ *_i (s \cdot t, \psi)}$$	$$\frac{w \ *_i (t, \phi)}{w \ *_j (!t, t:_i \phi)}$$ **∗C($\mathcal{F}$):** If the logic has ij-Conversion,
∗Sum($\mathcal{F}$): $$\frac{w \ *_i (t, \phi)}{w \ *_i (s + t, \phi)} \qquad \frac{w \ *_i (s, \phi)}{w \ *_i (s + t, \phi)}$$	$$\frac{w \ *_i (t, \phi)}{w \ *_j (t, \phi)}$$
∗Dis($\mathcal{F}$): If $(a, b) \in R_i$ and $\mathcal{J}_i$ has Positive Introspection, $$\frac{a \ *_i (t, \phi)}{b \ *_i (t, \phi)}$$	**∗V-Dis($\mathcal{F}$):** If $(a, b) \in R_j$ and the logic has ij-Verification, $$\frac{a \ *_i (t, \phi)}{b \ *_i (t, \phi)}$$

Fig. 2. The $*^{\mathcal{F}}_{\mathcal{CS}}(\mathcal{J})$-calculus for $(\mathcal{J}_1 \times_\circ \mathcal{J}_2)_{\mathcal{CS}}$ includes the above axioms and rules, for every $i, j \in \{1, 2\}$, $w \in W$, s, t terms, ϕ, ψ formulas, where $\mathcal{F} = (W, R_1, R_2)$

Notice that the calculus rules correspond to the closure conditions of the admissible evidence functions. In fact and because of this, given some frame $\mathcal{F} = (W, R_1, R_2)$ and a set S of ∗-expressions prefixed by states of the frame, the function $\mathcal{E}$ such that

$$\mathcal{E}_i(t, \phi) = \{w \in W \mid S \vdash_{*^{\mathcal{F}}_{\mathcal{CS}}(\mathcal{J})} w \ *_i (t, \phi)\}$$

is an admissible evidence function. Furthermore, if some admissible evidence function $\mathcal{E}'$ is such that such that $w \ *_i (t, \phi) \in S \ \Rightarrow \ w \in \mathcal{E}'_i(t, \phi)$, then for every agent i, term t, and formula ϕ, $\mathcal{E}_i(t, \phi) \subseteq \mathcal{E}'_i(t, \phi)$. When $\mathcal{J}, \mathcal{CS}, \mathcal{F}$ are clear from the context, $*^{\mathcal{F}}_{\mathcal{CS}}(\mathcal{J})$ will be referred to as $*$.

If $\mathcal{CS} \in \mathsf{P}$, then deciding for some finite S and $\mathcal{F}$ if $S \vdash_{*^{\mathcal{F}}_{\mathcal{CS}}(\mathcal{J})} w \ *_i (t, \phi)$ is in NP and here we sketch how to prove this. The nondeterministic algorithm which decides derivability in the ∗-calculus, can first guess the derivation tree, which is bounded in size by $2|t| \cdot |\mathcal{F}|$ and has ∗-expressions for nodes. A notable difference of this procedure from the one in [16] is that rule $*C(\mathcal{F})$ does not

---

[4] The ∗-calculus was first introduced in [14], but its origins can be found in [20]. The form on which the one in this section is based is from [16].

increase the size of the term and can in theory be applied several consecutive times; two or more consecutive applications of this rule contribute nothing to a derivation, though and we can assume they never occur. Cycles in the frame can be treated the same way. At this step the algorithm guesses and for every node $v *_j (s, \psi)$ it fills in v, j, s, but not ψ. Then, the algorithm fills in these formulas for the leaves of the tree by guessing an appropriate formula (or scheme), which could either be an element of S, or in case s is of the form $! \cdots !c$, where c a constant, the formula (scheme in this case – $\mathcal{CS}$ is schematic) can be an axiom. The algorithm then in turn and for each node unifies the formulas of its children trying to result in a valid derivation of $w *_i (t, \phi)$. If it succeeds, then it accepts; otherwise it rejects.

3 Tableaux and Satisfiability - The Method and the Tools

To test the satisfiability of ϕ, we use a tableau procedure, which starts from $0 \, T \, \phi$ and we apply tableau rules to gradually decompose the initial formula and produce more formulas. Formulas used in the tableau are of the form $0.w \, S \, \alpha$, where $w \in \{1, 2\}^*$ is the world prefix, $S \in \{T, F\}$ the truth prefix and α either a formula or a $*$-expression. When all applicable rules have been applied, then we have a complete branch. If either $w \, T \, \bot$ is in the branch, or there are some $w \, T \, a$ and $w \, F \, a$ in the branch then the branch is propositionally closed. If it is not propositionally closed, then W is the set of world-prefixes appearing in the branch. Depending on the logic (and thus on the tableau rules), we can define a frame. On this frame we can run the $*$-calculus to confirm that there is some admissible evidence function $\mathcal{E}$ such that for every $x \, T \, *_i (t, \psi)$, $x \in \mathcal{E}_i(t, \psi)$ and for every $x \, T \, *_i (t, \psi)$, $x \notin \mathcal{E}_i(t, \psi)$.

As an example we give tableau rules for $(\mathsf{JD} \times \mathsf{JD})_{\mathcal{CS}}$:

$$\frac{w \, T \, \phi \rightarrow \psi}{w \, F \, \phi \mid w \, T \, \psi} \qquad \frac{w \, F \, \phi \rightarrow \psi}{\begin{array}{c} w \, T \, \phi \\ w \, F \, \psi \end{array}} \qquad \frac{w \, T \, t :_i \phi}{\begin{array}{c} w.i \, T \, \phi \\ w \, T \, *_i (t, \phi) \end{array}} \qquad \frac{w \, F \, t :_i \phi}{w \, F \, *_i (t, \phi)}$$

For these rules,

$$R_i = \{(w, w.i) \in W^2\} \cup \{(w, w) \in W^2 \mid w.i \notin W\}.$$

Then, $\mathcal{F} = (W, R_1, R_2)$ and $\mathcal{V}(p) = \{w \in W \mid w \, T \, p \text{ appears in the branch}\}$. Let $S = \{w *_i (t, \psi) \mid w \, T \, *_i (t, \psi) \text{ appears in the branch}\}$ and $\mathcal{E}$ be the admissible evidence function such that

$$\mathcal{E}_i(t, \phi) = \{w \in W \mid S \vdash_{*_{\mathcal{CS}}^{\mathcal{F}}(\mathcal{J})} w *_i (t, \phi)\}.$$

$\mathcal{M} = (W, R_1, R_2, \mathcal{E}_1, \mathcal{E}_2, \mathcal{V})$ is a model, as R_1, R_2 are serial and $\mathcal{E}$ is an admissible evidence function. It is not hard to see by induction on the structure of formulas ψ, ψ' that for every $w \, T \, \psi$ and $w \, F \, \psi'$ in the branch, $\mathcal{M}, w \models \psi$ and $\mathcal{M}, w \not\models \psi'$, as long as there is no prefixed $*$-expression $w \, F \, *_i (t, v)$ appearing in the branch that $w \in \mathcal{E}_i(t, v)$. Thus we say the branch is accepting exactly when it is not propositionally closed and there is no prefixed $*$-expression $w\ F\ e$ in the branch such that $S \vdash_* w\ e$.

If there is an accepting branch, then from the above we see that ϕ is satisfiable. On the other hand it is not hard to see how to construct an accepting branch for ϕ given an F-model for ϕ that satisfies the Strong Evidence property: we map each world prefix w to a world $w^{\mathcal{M}}$ of the model such that $0^{\mathcal{M}}$ is a world satisfying ϕ and $w.i$ is mapped to a world accessible through R_i from $w^{\mathcal{M}}$. Then we ensure that we only produce formulas $w\ T\ \psi$ such that the world $\mathcal{M}, w^{\mathcal{M}} \models \psi$ and formulas $w\ F\ \psi$ such that $\mathcal{M}, w^{\mathcal{M}} \not\models \psi$. Thus we ensure the branch is accepting. That the number of formulas in the branch is polynomially bounded results from the observation that the formulas prefixed by distinct world-prefixes are distinct – assuming all subformulas of ϕ are distinct. This means that $(\mathsf{JD} \times \mathsf{JD})_{\mathcal{CS}}$-satisfiability is in Σ_2^p.

For the cases that follow we use a similar tableau procedure and arguments for its correctness and complexity. We will only explain what changes for each case as needed. The propositional rules (the first two) an the rule for $w\ F\ t :_i \phi$ (the last one) remain exactly the same for all logics – we only consider models with the strong evidence property. Notice that to prove the Σ_2^p upper bound for a two-agent logic, it is enough to have a polynomial as a bound on the number of the world-prefixes in a branch of its corresponding tableau. This in turn gives a polynomial as an upper bound for the total size of a branch and thus the time it takes to (nondeterministically) apply all the tableau rules, as each rule increases the size of the branch. Since to decide satisfiability for a formula we need to do just that (nondeterministically run the tableau) and at the end for every prefixed $*$-expression $w\ F\ e$ in the branch we need to determine whether $S \vdash_* w\ e$, we already have a nondeterministic algorithm that runs in polynomial time and uses an oracle from NP.

For several cases it is important to know Lemmata 1 and 2, as well as the finite frame property of these logics, as established by Corollary 1. Lemma 1 describes the situation when the logic is a pair of logics with serial accessibility relations and has both versions of the Verification axiom. On the other hand, Lemma 2 is more general and, perhaps, more surprising. A similar result with a similar proof appears in [1].

Lemma 1. *If ϕ is $(\mathcal{J}_1 \times_{!!} \mathcal{J}_2)_{\mathcal{CS}}$-satisfiable and $\mathcal{J}_1, \mathcal{J}_2 \in \{\mathsf{JD}, \mathsf{JD4}\}$, then there is some $(\mathcal{J}_1 \times_{!!} \mathcal{J}_2)_{\mathcal{CS}}$-model $\mathcal{M} = (W, R_1, R_2, \mathcal{E}_1, \mathcal{E}_2, V)$, where $W = \{u, a_1, a_2\}$, $\mathcal{M}, u \models \phi$, and for $i \in \{1, 2\}\ R_i = \{(x, a_i) \in W^2\}$.*

Proof. Consider an F-model $\mathcal{M} = (W, R_1, R_2, \mathcal{E}_1, \mathcal{E}_2, V)$, having the strong evidence property and such that W is finite (see Corollary 1) and some $u \in W$ such that $\mathcal{M}, u \models \phi$. Let $a_0, b_0 \in W$ such that uR_1a_0 and $a_0R_2b_0$. Then, for $k \in \mathbb{N}$, let $a_{k+1}, b_{k+1} \in W$ be such that $b_kR_1a_{k+1}R_2b_{k+1}$. Then, for every $l, k \in \mathbb{N}$ such that $l < k$, $u, a_l, b_lR_1a_k$ and $u, a_l, b_lR_2b_k$. Since W is finite, there are some $k, k' \in \mathbb{N}$ such that $k < k'$ and $a_k = a_{k'}$ (and thus, $a_k, b_kR_1a_k$ and $a_k, b_kR_2b_k$).

Let $W' = \{u, a_k, b_k\}$, $R_1' = \{(a, a_k) \mid a \in W'\}$, $R_2' = \{(a, b_k) \mid a \in W'\}$, and $V'(p) = V(p) \cap W'$. $\mathcal{E}_i'(t, \psi) = \mathcal{E}_i(t, \psi) \cap W'$ and $\mathcal{E}'$ is then an admissible evidence function. If not, it should violate one of its closure conditions, but it is not hard to see that they are all satisfied.

Then, $\mathcal{M}' = (W', R_1', R_2', \mathcal{E}', \mathcal{V}')$ is a model and we can determine in a straight-forward way that $\mathcal{M}', u \models \phi$. □

Lemma 2. *Let* $\mathcal{J} = (\mathcal{J}_1 \times_\circ \mathcal{J}_2)$ *and for some* $i \in \{1, 2\}$, $\mathcal{J}_i = \mathsf{JD4}$.
If $\mathcal{M} = (W, R_1, R_2, \mathcal{E}_1, \mathcal{E}_2, \mathcal{V})$ *is a* $\mathcal{J}$-*model and* W *is finite, then for every* $a \in W$, *there is some* $b \in W$, *such that* aR_ibR_ib *and for every* $c \in W$, *if there is some* $b' \in W$ *for which* c, bR_ib', *then* cR_ib.

Proof. Consider such an F-model for $\mathcal{J}$, $\mathcal{M} = (W, R_1, R_2, \mathcal{E}_1, \mathcal{E}_2, \mathcal{V})$. For that $a \in W$ let $a_0 \in W$ such that aR_ia_0. Let $S_k = \{x \in W \mid \exists y, a_kR_ix \text{ and not } yR_ia_k\}$ and let $a_{k+1} \in S_k$, if $S_k \neq \emptyset$, and $a_{k+1} = a_k$ otherwise. Then, for every $l, k \in \mathbb{N}$ such that $l < k$, $a, a_lR_ia_k$ and thus $S_k \subset S_l$. But since W is finite, there must be some $k \in \mathbb{N}$ such that $S_k = \emptyset$. □

4   Complexity Results

The results of this section are summed up by Theorem 1:

Theorem 1. *Let* $\mathcal{J}_1, \mathcal{J}_2 \in \{\mathsf{J}, \mathsf{JD}, \mathsf{JT}, \mathsf{J4}, \mathsf{JD4}, \mathsf{LP}\}$, $\times_\circ \in \{\times, \times_!, \times_{!!}, \times_C, \times_{CC}\}$, *and* $\mathcal{J} = (\mathcal{J}_1 \times_\circ \mathcal{J}_2)_{\mathcal{CS}}$. *If* $\mathcal{J}_2 = \mathsf{JD}$, $\mathcal{J}_1 \in \{\mathsf{J4}, \mathsf{JD4}, \mathsf{LP}\}$ *and* $\times_\circ = \times_C$, *or* $\mathcal{J}_2 = \mathsf{JD}$, $\mathcal{J}_1 \in \{\mathsf{JT}, \mathsf{LP}\}$ *and* $\times_\circ = \times_!$, *then* $\mathcal{J}$-*satisfiability is* PSPACE-*complete. In every other case,* $\mathcal{J}$-*satisfiability is in* Σ_2^p.

We do not examine $(\mathcal{J}_1 \times_{CC} \mathcal{J}_2)_{\mathcal{CS}}$, as it is essentially a single-agent logic: it is not hard to see that $t:_1 \phi \leftrightarrow t:_2 \phi$ is a theorem of the logic.

4.1   No Interactions: $\times_\circ = \times$.

Since there are no interactions we simply use the usual rule for $w \, F \, t:_i \psi$ that gives $w \, F \, *_i (t, \psi)$ and one rule for each agent i depending on what $\mathcal{J}_i$ is. These are given in Table 1 together with the corresponding $\mathcal{J}_i$. The reasoning follows the one for the case of $(\mathsf{JD} \times \mathsf{JD})_{\mathcal{CS}}$, except for the case when $\mathcal{J}_i = \mathsf{JD4}$, where when we construct an accepting branch from a model (of finite states and with the strong evidence property), we can use Lemma 2 and thus if we map w to a we map $w.i$ to some b such that aR_ibR_ib.

Of course, when we construct a model from an accepting branch we need to provide a different accessibility relation to account for the different logics. In particular, if $\mathcal{J}_i \in \{\mathsf{J}, \mathsf{J4}\}$, then $R_i = \emptyset$; if $\mathcal{J}_i \in \{\mathsf{JT}, \mathsf{LP}\}$, then $R_i = \{(w, w) \in W^2\}$; if $\mathcal{J}_i = \mathsf{JD}$, as in the case of $(\mathsf{JD} \times \mathsf{JD})_{\mathcal{CS}}$,

$$R_i = \{(w, w.i) \in W^2\} \cup \{(w, w) \in W^2 \mid w.i \notin W\};$$

finally, if $\mathcal{J}_i = \mathsf{JD4}$, then

$$R_i = \{(w, w.i) \in W^2\} \cup \{(w.i, w.i) \in W^2\} \cup \{(w, w) \in W^2 \mid w.i \notin W\}.$$

Table 1. Tableau rules for logics without interactions. We use two of these rules: the ones that correspond to $\mathcal{J}_1$ and $\mathcal{J}_2$.

$$\frac{w\ T\ t:_i\phi}{w\ T\ *_i\,(t,\phi)}\ \mathsf{J}$$

$$\frac{w\ T\ t:_i\phi}{\begin{array}{c}w.i\ T\ \phi\\ w\ T\ *_i\,(t,\phi)\end{array}}\ \mathsf{JD}$$

$$\frac{w\ T\ t:_i\phi}{\begin{array}{c}w\ T\ \phi\\ w\ T\ *_i\,(t,\phi)\end{array}}\ \mathsf{JT}$$

$$\frac{w\ T\ t:_i\phi}{w\ T\ *_i\,(t,\phi)}\ \mathsf{J4}$$

$$\frac{w\ T\ t:_i\phi}{\begin{array}{c}v.i\ T\ \phi\\ w\ T\ *_i\,(t,\phi)\end{array}}\ \mathsf{JD4}$$

where if w of the form $w'.i$, then $v = w'$ and otherwise $v = w$

$$\frac{w\ T\ t:_i\phi}{\begin{array}{c}w\ T\ \phi\\ w\ T\ *_i\,(t,\phi)\end{array}}\ \mathsf{LP}$$

4.2   Verification: $\times_\circ = \times_{!!}$.

When $\times_\circ = \times_{!!}$ and $\mathcal{J}_1, \mathcal{J}_2$ are among JD, JT, JD4, and LP, Lemma 1 applies, so we can base our rules on the three-world models it describes.[5] Then, the remaining argument remains the same as before, except when we define the accessibility relations, depending on the logics, if $\mathcal{J}_i \in \{\mathsf{JT}, \mathsf{LP}\}$, then $R_i = \{(w,w) \in W^2\}$ and otherwise, $R_i = \{(w, 0.i) \in W^2\}$. The rules are in Table 2.

Table 2. Tableau rules for when $\times_\circ = \times_{!!}$

$$\frac{w\ T\ t:_i\phi}{\begin{array}{c}0.i\ T\ \phi\\ w\ T\ *_i\,(t,\phi)\end{array}}\ \mathsf{JD,JD4}$$

$$\frac{w\ T\ t:_i\phi}{\begin{array}{c}w\ T\ \phi\\ w\ T\ *_i\,(t,\phi)\end{array}}\ \mathsf{JT,LP}$$

On the other hand if one of the two agents is based on J or J4, then we can use the same rules and reasoning as for the case when $\times_\circ = \times$.

4.3   Verification: $\times_\circ = \times_!$.

Like before, if one of the two agents is based on J or J4, then we can use the same rules and reasoning as for the case when $\times_\circ = \times$. Thus we only examine the cases when $\mathcal{J}_1, \mathcal{J}_2 \in \{\mathsf{JD}, \mathsf{JT}, \mathsf{JD4}, \mathsf{LP}\}$. For these cases we can use the same rules as in the case where $\times_\circ = \times$ for $\mathcal{J}_2$ as well as one of the following two rules for $\mathcal{J}_1$ (Table 3). The first should be used if $\mathcal{J}_1 = \mathsf{JD}$, the second one if $\mathcal{J}_1 \in \{\mathsf{JT}, \mathsf{LP}\}$ and the third one should be used if $\mathcal{J}_1 = \mathsf{JD4}$.

---

[5] In fact if one of $\mathcal{J}_1, \mathcal{J}_2$ is JT or LP, then only up to two worlds are required in the model, as these logics require reflexivity and not seriality of their accessibility relation.

Table 3. Tableau rules for $\times_\circ = \times_!$

$$\frac{w\ T\ t:_1\phi}{\substack{w.s.1\ T\ \phi \\ w\ T\ *_1(t,\phi)}}\ \text{JD} \qquad \frac{w\ T\ t:_1\phi}{\substack{w.s\ T\ \phi \\ w\ T\ *_1(t,\phi)}}\ \text{JT,LP} \qquad \frac{w\ T\ t:_1\phi}{\substack{v.1\ T\ \phi \\ w\ T\ *_1(t,\phi)}}\ \text{JD4}$$

where for the first two rules, $s \in 2^*$ and $w.s$ has already appeared and for the third one, either w of the form $0.a$, where $a \in 2^*$ and $v = w.s$ where $s \in 2^*$ and $w.s$ has already appeared, or w of the form $0.w_1.1.w_2$ (and $w_1, w_2 \in 2^*$) and $v = 0.w_1$.[6]

The argument for this case is similar to the ones that have already been covered. Notice in all these cases that if in a frame, $aR_2^*bR_1c$, then aR_1c. To justify the third rule, which is different from the ones we have encountered, we gave Lemma 2. Then, when constructing a branch from a model, if w is mapped to u, then we map $w.1$ to such a $b \in W$ as indicated by Lemma 2, such that for every $c \in W$, if there is some $b' \in W$ such that c, bR_1b', then cR_1b. When we construct a model from an accepting branch, we can define W to be the set of all world prefixes that appear in the branch as well as $0.s.1$ for every $s \in 2^*$ such that no world prefix $0.s.i$ where $i \in \{1,2\}$ appears. Then,

$$R_1 = \{(w, w.u.1) \in W^2\} \cup \{(w.1.u, w.1) \in W^2\}.$$

For the first rule we can impose two extra restrictions (without affecting the argument for correctness): we give this rule the lowest priority – it can only be applied when there are other rules to apply – and when it introduces $w.s.1$, then there must be no $w.s.s'$ already in the branch, where s' not empty (i.e. $w.s$ must be maximal). Thus we ensure that for every $w\ T\ t:_i\phi$ that appears in the branch, the rule produces only one formula of the form $w'\ T\ \phi$; this condition gives an upper bound of $|\phi|$ (where ϕ the initial formula) for the number of world-prefixes. When we use the third rule ($\mathcal{J}_1 = \text{JD4}$), then notice that 1 can only appear once in a prefix. Then, the number of prefixes of the form 0.2^* is at most $|\phi|$ and so is for any given $w.1$ the number of prefixes of the form $w.1.2^*$; this gives an upper bound of $O(|\phi|^2)$ on the total number of world-prefixes. The exception is when $\mathcal{J}_1 \in \{\text{JT}, \text{LP}\}$; in that case, if $\mathcal{J}_2 \in \{\text{JT}, \text{LP}, \text{JD4}\}$, we still have at most two prefixes, but $(\mathcal{J}_1 \times_! \text{JD})_{\mathcal{CS}}$-satisfiability is PSPACE-complete (see the case of $(\text{JD4} \times_C \text{JD})_{\mathcal{CS}}$ in subsection 4.4, which is similar).

4.4 Conversion: $\times_\circ = \times_C$.

If $\mathcal{J}_2 \in \{\text{JT}, \text{LP}\}$ then $J \vdash t:_1\phi \rightarrow \phi$. Thus we can use the tableau rules we already used for $((\mathcal{J}_1 + \text{Factivity}) \times \mathcal{J}_2)$ (but using the appropriate version of

---

[6] 2^* is the set of strings that only use 2 as a symbol. If A is a binary relation, then A^* is its reflexive transitive closure. When A is a set (of symbols) and not a binary relation, then A^* is the set of strings that use A as their alphabet. $0.2^* = \{0.a \mid a \in 2^*\}$.

the $*$-calculus) that only produce the world-prefix 0. The cases $\mathcal{J}_1 \in \{\mathsf{J}, \mathsf{JD}, \mathsf{JT}\}$ or $\mathcal{J}_2 \in \{\mathsf{J}, \mathsf{JT}, \mathsf{JD4}, \mathsf{J4}, \mathsf{LP}\}$ are left to the reader and the only cases that will interest us are the ones where $\mathcal{J}_2 = \mathsf{JD}$ and $\mathcal{J}_1 \in \{\mathsf{J4}, \mathsf{JD4}, \mathsf{LP}\}$. In fact, for these cases and in contrast to most cases we have studied, J-satisfiability is PSPACE-complete.

We provide the tableau rules for $(\mathsf{JD4} \times_C \mathsf{JD})_{\mathcal{CS}}$ in Table 4, leaving to the reader to complete the proof and to adjust these to the other cases.

Table 4. Tableau rules for $(\mathsf{JD4} \times_C \mathsf{JD})_{\mathcal{CS}}$

$w\ T\ t{:}_2\,\phi$	$w\ T\ t{:}_1\,\phi$	$w\ T\ \Box\alpha$
$w.2\ T\ \phi$	$w\ T\ *_1\,(t,\phi)$	$w.2\ T\ \alpha$
$w\ T\ *_2\,(t,\phi)$	$w\ T\ \Box\phi$	$w.2\ T\ \Box\alpha$
	$w\ T\ \Box *_1\,(t,\phi)$	where $w.2$ has already appeared

Informally, $w\ T\ \Box\alpha$ stands for v "satisfies" α for every wR_1v and α either a formula or a $*$-expression. When running the tableau we are not guaranteed it will terminate, but we can artificially terminate it after a sufficient length of prefixes is reached (exponential in $|\phi|$, enough to know we have reached the same set of expressions twice), or consider an infinite branch, closed under the rules. When constructing a model from a branch, W is the collection of prefixes (possibly infinite) and

$$R_2 = \{(w, w.2) \in W^2\} \cup \{(w, w) \in W^2 \mid w.2 \notin W\}$$

and R_1 the transitive closure of R_2:

$$R_1 = \{(w, w.u) \in W^2 \mid u \neq \epsilon\} \cup \{(w, w) \in W^2 \mid w.2 \notin W\}.$$

Notice that we can keep exactly one world-prefix in memory each time. The only part of the process which is affected by the frame is the application of rules $*\mathrm{Dis}(\mathcal{F})$ and $*\mathrm{V\text{-}Dis}(\mathcal{F})$ in the $*$-calculus, but these can only be applied to some $a\ *_1\,(t, \psi)$. Then, by induction on the calculus derivation we can push all applications of $*\mathrm{Dis}(\mathcal{F})$ and $*\mathrm{V\text{-}Dis}(\mathcal{F})$ to the leaves of the $*$-calculus derivation, where they are unnecessary, as we can see from the following rules. Furthermore, since we can answer whether $S \vdash_* w\ *_i\,(t, \psi)$ in nondeterministic polynomial time, we can also do that in (deterministic) polynomial space. Since all prefixes are $0.2 \ldots 2$, we don't even need to keep the prefix as is in memory, just its length, which gives us a bound on the space we use.[7]

---

[7] Notice that despite the notational differences (the use of $\Box$ in and the incorporation of $*\mathrm{Dis}(\mathcal{F})$ and $*\mathrm{V\text{-}Dis}(\mathcal{F})$ of the calculus in the tableau), the rules for $(\mathsf{JD4} \times_C \mathsf{JD})_{\mathcal{CS}}$ and the ones for $(\mathsf{LP} \times_! \mathsf{JD})_{\mathcal{CS}}$ and $(\mathsf{JT} \times_C \mathsf{JD})_{\mathcal{CS}}$ are practically identical.

We now prove PSPACE-*hardness for* $(JD4 \times_C JD)_{CS}$-*satisfiability.* The proof is by reduction from a deterministic Turing machine of two tapes (input and working tape) using polynomial space. It closely resembles the one in [12] and has been used in [2] in a more general form to prove similar results. Let the machine be (Q, Σ, δ, s), where Q the set of states, Σ the alphabet, δ the transition function and s the initial state. Let $x = x_1 x_2 \cdots x_{|x|}$ be the input, where for every $i \in \{1, 2, \ldots, |x|\}$, $x_i \in \Sigma$. Since the Turing machine uses polynomial space, there is a polynomial p, such that the working tape only uses cells 1 to $p(|x|)$ for an input x. For the input tape, we only need cells 0 through $|x| + 1$, because the head does not go any further and an output tape is not needed, since we are interested only in decision problems. Therefore, there are $Y, N \in Q$, the accepting and rejecting states respectively. Let $r_1 = \{0, 1, 2, \ldots, |x| + 1\}$ and $r_2 = \{1, 2, \ldots, p(|x|)\}$.

- $t_1[i], t_2[j]$, for every $i \in r_1, j \in r_2$; $t_1[i]$ will correspond to the head for the first tape pointing at cell i and similarly for $t_2[j]$,
- $\sigma_1[a, i], \sigma_2[a, j]$, for every $a \in \Sigma$, $i \in r_1, j \in r_2$; $\sigma_1[a, i]$ will correspond to cell i in the first tape having the symbol a and similarly for $\sigma_2[a, j]$ and the second tape,
- $q[a]$, for every $a \in Q$; $q[a]$ means the machine is currently in state a.

We need the following formulas. Intuitively, a state in a model for ϕ corresponds to a configuration of our Turing machine. q ensures there is exactly one state at every configuration; σ that there is exactly one symbol at every position of every tape; t that for each tape the head is located at exactly one position; σ' ensures that the only symbols that can change from one configuration to the next are the ones located in a position the head points at; ac ensures we never reach a rejecting state (therefore the machine accepts); st starts the computation at the starting configuration of the machine; finally, d ensures for each configuration that the next one is given by the transition function. Then, if $com = q \wedge \sigma \wedge t \wedge \sigma' \wedge ac \wedge d$,

$$\phi = st \wedge com \wedge x :_1 com$$

$$q = \left(\bigvee_{a \in Q} q[a] \right) \wedge \bigwedge_{\substack{a, b \in Q, \\ a \neq b}} \neg (q[a] \wedge q[b])$$

$$\sigma = \bigwedge_{\substack{j \in \{1, 2\}, \\ i \in r_j}} \left[\left(\bigvee_{a \in \Sigma} \sigma_j[a, i] \right) \wedge \bigwedge_{\substack{a, b \in \Sigma, \\ a \neq b}} \neg (\sigma_j[a] \wedge \sigma_j[b]) \right]$$

$$t = \bigwedge_{j \in \{1, 2\}} \left[\left(\bigvee_{i \in r_j} t_j[i] \right) \wedge \bigwedge_{\substack{i, k \in r_j \\ i \neq k}} \neg (t_j[i] \wedge t_j[k]) \right]$$

$$\sigma' = \bigwedge_{\substack{j\in\{1,2\},\\ i,i'\in r_j,\\ i\neq i',\\ a\in\Sigma}} [(t_j[i] \wedge \sigma_j[a,i']) \to x{:}_2\,\sigma_j[a,i']]$$

$ac = \neg q[N]$,

$st = \phi_{c_0}$, where ϕ_{c_0} describes the initial configuration of the machine,

$$d = \bigwedge_{\substack{(a,i_1,i_2)\in E\times\Sigma\times\Sigma,\\ j_1\in r_1,\\ j_2\in r_2}} \left[\begin{array}{l} q[a] \wedge \sigma_1[i_1,j_1] \wedge \sigma_2[i_2,j_2] \wedge t_1[j_1] \wedge t_2[j_2] \longrightarrow \\ x{:}_2\,(q[a_1] \wedge \sigma_2[k_1,j_2] \wedge t_1[j_1 + m_1] \wedge t_2[j_2 + m_2]) \end{array} \right]$$

where $(a_1, k_1, m_1, m_2) = \delta(a, i_1, i_2)$.

For every configuration c of the Turing machine, there is a formula that describes it. This formula is the conjunction of the following and from now on it will be denoted as ϕ_c: $q[a]$, if a is the state of the machine in c; $t_1[i]$ and $t_2[j]$, if the first tape's head is on cell i and the second tape's head is on cell j; $\sigma_1[a_1, i_1], \sigma_2[a_2, i_2]$, if $i_1 \in r_1, i_2 \in r_2$ and a_1 is the symbol currently in cell i_1 of the first tape and a_2 is the symbol currently in cell i_2 of the second tape. Then, st is ϕ_{c_0}, where c_0 is the initial configuration for the machine on input x.

Claim: If for some model $\mathcal{M}, w \models \phi$ and for some u, wR_1u and $u \models \phi_c$ and c_1 is the next configuration from c, then there is some w, uR_1u_1, such that $u_1 \models \phi_{c_1}$. From this claim, it immediately follows that if ϕ is satisfiable, then the Turing machine accepts its input. We now prove the claim. Because of formulas q, σ, t, in every state v, such that wR_1v, there is exactly one ϕ_c satisfied. There is some state u_1, (because of seriality of R_2) such that wR_2u_1 and if $u_1 \models \phi_a$, then because of d, a will differ from c in all respects δ demands; furthermore, because of σ', a differs only in the ways δ demands. Therefore, $a = c_1$.

On the other hand, assuming that the Turing machine accepts x, given its computation path for x, we can construct model $\mathcal{M} = (W, R_1, R_2, \mathcal{E}_1, \mathcal{E}_2, \mathcal{V})$ for ϕ. W is the set of configurations in the computation tree; let R_2 be minimal such that if a is a configuration and b its next configuration, then aR_2b; let R_1 be the transitive closure of R_1. $\mathcal{E}_i(t, \psi) = W$ for all i, t, ψ. $\mathcal{V}$ is defined to be such that $\mathcal{M}, a \models \phi_a$ (every ϕ_a is a conjunction of propositional variables). Then, it is not hard to see that $\mathcal{M}, c_0 \models \phi$.   □

Notice that it is crucial that the second logic in the pair is JD and not JD4, as otherwise neither σ' nor d would have the desired effect. What JD offers relative to JD4 is the ability from every state to specify certain conditions (dictated by σ', d) that should hold at *exactly* every (the) next state. This could not happen if instead of JD the logic was JD4. Lemma 2 demonstrated this even further, as we can collapse all further states into one. On the other hand, it is necessary that the first logic of the pair has positive introspection, as we need its accessibility relation too be transitive. This way we can make statements that hold globally (in every state we will eventually encounter if we follow an accessibility relation). Other than that the logic can either have factivity, consistency, or neither: it inherits consistency from JD anyway and factivity does not affect much – if anything, it makes statements of the form $s{:}_1\,\psi$ even more globally true.

Acknowledgments. The author is grateful to Sergei Artemov and Stathis Zachos for their support and encouragement.

References

1. Achilleos, A.: A complexity question in justification logic. Journal of Computer and System Sciences 80(6), 1038–1045 (2014)
2. Achilleos, A.: Modal logics with hard diamond-free fragments. CoRR, abs/1401.5846 (2014)
3. Achilleos, A.: On the complexity of two-agent justification logic. Technical Report TR–2014003, CUNY Ph.D. Program in Computer Science (January 2014)
4. Artemov, S.: Operational modal logic. Technical Report MSI 95–29, Cornell University (December 1995)
5. Artemov, S.: Explicit provability and constructive semantics. Bulletin of Symbolic Logic 7(1), 1–36 (2001)
6. Artemov, S.: Justification logic. In: Hölldobler, S., Lutz, C., Wansing, H. (eds.) JELIA 2008. LNCS (LNAI), vol. 5293, pp. 1–4. Springer, Heidelberg (2008)
7. Artemov, S.: The logic of justification. The Review of Symbolic Logic 1(4), 477–513 (2008)
8. Artemov, S., Kuznets, R.: Logical omniscience as a computational complexity problem. In: Heifetz, A. (ed.) TARK, pp. 14–23 (2009)
9. Brezhnev, V.N.: On explicit counterparts of modal logics. Technical Report CFIS 2000–05, Cornell University (2000)
10. Bucheli, S., Kuznets, R., Studer, T.: Justifications for common knowledge. Journal of Applied Non-Classical Logics 21(1), 35–60 (2011)
11. Demri, S.: Complexity of simple dependent bimodal logics. In: Dyckhoff, R. (ed.) TABLEAUX 2000. LNCS (LNAI), vol. 1847, pp. 190–204. Springer, Heidelberg (2000)
12. Fischer, M.J., Ladner, R.E.: Propositional dynamic logic of regular programs. Journal of Computer and System Sciences 18(2), 194–211 (1979)
13. Fitting, M.: The logic of proofs, semantically. Annals of Pure and Applied Logic 132(1), 1–25 (2005)
14. Krupski, N.V.: On the complexity of the reflected logic of proofs. Theoretical Computer Science 357(1-3), 136–142 (2006)
15. Kuznets, R.: On the complexity of explicit modal logics. In: Clote, P.G., Schwichtenberg, H. (eds.) CSL 2000. LNCS, vol. 1862, pp. 371–383. Springer, Heidelberg (2000), Errata concerning the explicit counterparts of $\mathcal{D}$ and $\mathcal{D}4$ are published as [17]
16. Kuznets, R.: Complexity Issues in Justification Logic. PhD thesis, CUNY Graduate Center (May 2008)
17. Kuznets, R.: Complexity through tableaux in justification logic. In: Plenary Talks, Tutorials, Special Sessions, Contributed Talks of Logic Colloquium (LC 2008), Bern, Switzerland, pp. 38–39 (2008)
18. Kuznets, R.: Self-referentiality of justified knowledge. In: Hirsch, E.A., Razborov, A.A., Semenov, A., Slissenko, A. (eds.) CSR 2008. LNCS, vol. 5010, pp. 228–239. Springer, Heidelberg (2008)
19. Ladner, R.E.: The computational complexity of provability in systems of modal propositional logic. SIAM Journal on Computing 6(3), 467–480 (1977)

20. Mkrtychev, A.: Models for the logic of proofs. In: Adian, S., Nerode, A. (eds.) LFCS 1997. LNCS, vol. 1234, pp. 266–275. Springer, Heidelberg (1997)
21. Pacuit, E.: A note on some explicit modal logics. In: Proceedings of the 5th Panhellenic Logic Symposium, Athens, Greece. University of Athens (2005)
22. Renne, B.: Simple evidence elimination in justification logic. In: Girard, P., Roy, O., Marion, M. (eds.) Dynamic Formal Epistemology. Synthese Library, vol. 351, ch. 7, pp. 127–149. Springer (2011)
23. Spaan, E.: Complexity of modal logics. PhD thesis, University of Amsterdam (1993)
24. Yavorskaya (Sidon), T.: Interacting explicit evidence systems. Theory Comput. Syst. 43(2), 272–293 (2008)

Fair Allocation of Group Tasks According to Social Norms

Natasha Alechina[1], Wiebe van der Hoek[2], and Brian Logan[1]

[1] University of Nottingham, Nottingham, UK
{nza,bsl}@cs.nott.ac.uk
[2] University of Liverpool, Liverpool, UK
Wiebe.Van-Der-Hoek@liverpool.ac.uk

Abstract. We consider the problem of decomposing a group norm into a set of individual obligations for the agents comprising the group, such that if the individual obligations are fulfilled, the group obligation is fulfilled. Such an assignment of tasks to agents is often subject to additional social or organisational norms that specify permissible ways in which tasks can be assigned. An important type of social norms are 'fairness constraints', that seek to distribute individual responsibility for discharging the group norm in a 'fair' or 'equitable' way. We propose a simple language for this kind of fairness constraints and analyse the problem of computing a fair decomposition of a group obligation, both for non-repeating and for repeating group obligations.

1 Introduction

Norms have been widely proposed as a means of achieving coordination and guaranteeing desirable system-level properties in multi-agent systems (MAS). Much of the literature on normative MAS has focussed on obligations and prohibitions associated with roles in an organisational structure or directed to individual agents (see for example [12]). However, many norms apply to *groups* of agents rather than to an agent enacting a role, or a particular agent in a MAS. For example, the members of the programme committee for a workshop may have a collective obligation to review the papers submitted to the workshop, or the occupants of a shared apartment may have an obligation to keep the apartment clean (e.g., as part of the rental agreement). Such *group norms* specify a sequence of actions that should be performed by members of the group, leaving the details of how the norm is to be implemented to the members of the group themselves. In general, there will be many possible implementations of a group norm, i.e., assignments of agents to particular tasks. Each assignment gives rise to a set of individual obligations that specify what each agent should do in order to discharge the group obligation.

The assignment of agents to tasks specified by a group norm is often subject to additional social or organisational norms that specify permissible ways in which tasks can be assigned. An important type of social norms are 'fairness constraints', that seek to distribute individual responsibility for discharging the group norm in a 'fair' or 'equitable' way. For example, there may be a constraint that no single agent should be required to do all the work necessary to discharge the group norm, or that no agent should have to

N. Bulling et al. (Eds.): CLIMA XV, LNAI 8624, pp. 19–34, 2014.

do a particular task more than once a week, etc. The social norms codifying what counts as 'fair' vary from organisation to organisation. For example, in some computer science departments, all members of academic staff may be assigned teaching duties, while in other departments, more senior academics are not obliged to teach. A key problem in normative MAS with group norms is determining whether a particular task allocation is both *effective* (i.e., it discharges the group norm) and *fair*, in the sense of respecting the social norms or fairness constraints in force within the organisation of which the group is a part.

In this paper we make a first step towards defining the notion of a fair decomposition of a group obligation into individual obligations for agents in the group. We consider a group obligation to be a sequential or parallel composition of actions that have to be performed by the agents in the group, either once or repeated indefinitely (for example, the obligation to keep the household running involves repeated execution of the same sequence of cleaning, cooking etc. actions). We show how to specify agents' individual offers to contribute to a group norm, and analyse the problem of producing a set of individual obligations for the agents in the group, such that if those individual obligations are fulfilled, the group obligation is fulfilled. We propose a simple language for fairness constraints and analyse the problem of computing a fair implementation of a group obligation, for both non-repeating and repeating group obligations. We also address the notion of *minimality*: an implementation should not unnecessarily demand contributions from agents.

The structure of the paper is as follows. In section 2 we introduce the formal preliminaries, such as the formal language we use to talk about group obligations and the structures used to interpret the language. In section 3 we introduce the basic setting of non-repeating group obligations and prove that the problem of whether an implementation exists is NP-complete. We also analyse the problem of the existence of minimal and fair implementations. In section 4 we analyse similar problems for repeating group obligations. We place our work in the context of existing research in section 5 and discuss future work in section 6.

2   Formal Setting

Several approaches to norms have been proposed in the literature, including state-based norms (where norms are defined in terms of states that should or should not occur), e.g., [18], and event or action-based norms (where norms are defined in terms of what agents should or should not do), e.g., [14,10]. In this paper we take an action-based view of norms, in which norms are interpreted as specifying a sequence of actions (possibly containing gaps) that should occur, either once or repeatedly.[1]

We work in a propositional language of linear-time temporal logic. We assume that we have a set of propositional variables $Prop$ that in addition to 'normal' propositional

---

[1] State-based norms require a state of affairs to be achieved rather than particular actions to be executed. Grossi et al [15] argue that a complex action or plan may be seen as equivalent to an action of the form $\texttt{achieve}(\tau)$ where τ is a state of affairs. This means that action- and state-based norms can be considered equivalent on the assumption that there is a single agreed action or sequence of actions that achieves the desired state.

variables such as c for 'the room is clean' contain a special kind of variables of the form $\mathbf{done}(a, i)$ where a is a type of action from a set of actions Ac (where Ac includes the no-op action $\mathtt{skip}$) and i is the name of an agent coming from the set of agent names $Ag = \{1, \ldots n\}$. Intuitively, $\mathbf{done}(a, i)$ is true in a state if immediately before that state, agent i has performed action a.

The syntax of Linear Time Temporal Logic (LTL), see, e.g., [21], is defined as follows:

$$\phi, \psi := p \mid \neg\phi \mid \phi \wedge \psi \mid \bigcirc\phi \mid \phi\,\mathcal{U}\psi$$

where $p \in Prop$, $\bigcirc$ means next state, and $\mathcal{U}$ means until.

Definition 1. *A transition system for a set Ag of n agents and a set Ac of actions is a tuple $\langle S, R, V, s_I \rangle$, where*

- *S is a non-empty set of states;*
- *$R \subseteq Ac^n \times S \times S$ (for $\mathbf{a} = \langle a_1, \ldots, a_n \rangle \in Ac^n$, we will write $(s, s') \in R_{\mathbf{a}}$ instead of $(\mathbf{a}, s, s') \in R$);*
- *$V : S \times Prop \rightarrow \{true, false\}$ assigns a truth value to each proposition in each state;*
- *$s_I \in S$ is the initial state.*

In addition, the following conditions are satisfied:

1. existence of successor: *for each state there exists tuple of actions $\mathbf{a}$ such that $\exists s'((s, s') \in R_{\mathbf{a}})$*
2. individual determinacy: *if $(s', s) \in R_{\mathbf{a}}$ and $(s'', s) \in R_{\mathbf{b}}$ then for all i, $a_i = b_i$*
3. meaning of action propositions: *$V(s, \mathbf{done}(a_i, i)) = true$ iff $\exists s'((s', s) \in R_{\langle a_1, \ldots, a_i, \ldots, a_n \rangle})$.*

The first condition is a standard simplifying condition for temporal logics [21]. A transition system that does not satisfy it can easily be transformed into one where all states with no outgoing transitions have a self-loop that can be interpreted as a no-op $\mathtt{skip}$ action performed by each agent. (To be precise, to satisfy Condition (2), from the terminal state we add a $\mathtt{skip}$ link to a new state which has a $\mathtt{skip}$ link to itself.) Conditions (2) and (3) are related, and are imposed in order to be able to correctly interpret propositions of the form $\mathbf{done}(a_i, i)$ which mean that agent i has just executed action a_i. For each state there should therefore be a unique tuple of actions by all agents that produces it (note this is not the same as requiring that each state has a unique predecessor state). This is also a standard condition in agent logics, for example [11], that need to be able to express which action or event causes the current state. Again, it is easy to transform any transition system into a system that satisfies conditions (2) and (3), by unravelling it [5].

For example, consider the transition system on the left in Figure 1 (with a single agent 1). This system violates all of the conditions (1)–(3). We can transform it to a system on the right in Figure 1 that encodes the same information but has a successor for every state and allows us to make an assignment to action propositions $\mathbf{done}(a, 1)$ and $\mathbf{done}(b, 1)$. In this system, t_1 and t_2 have the same propositional assignment as s apart from the action propositions, and t_3 and t_4 have the same assignment again apart

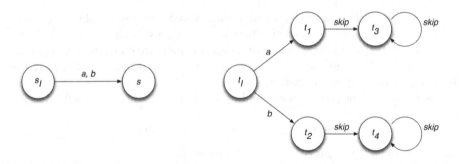

Fig. 1. A transition system that does not satisfy (1)-(3) (left) and the corresponding system that satisfies (1)-(3) (right)

from satisfying the action proposition **done**(skip, 1) where skip stands for the no-op action.

Given a transition system $M = (S, R, V, s_I)$, a *path* through M is a sequence $s_0, s_1, s_2, \ldots$ of states such that $(s_i, s_{i+1}) \in R_a$ for $i = 0, 1, 2, \ldots$. A *fullpath* is a maximal path (where every element in the sequence has a successor) and a *run* of M is a fullpath which starts from a state $s_I \in S$. We denote runs by $\rho, \rho', \ldots$, and the state at position i on ρ by $\rho[i]$.

The truth definition for formulas is given relative to a model, a run ρ and the state at position i on ρ:

$M, \rho, i \models p$ iff $V(\rho[i], p) = true$
$M, \rho, i \models \neg\phi$ iff $M, \rho, i \not\models \phi$
$M, \rho, i \models \phi \wedge \psi$ iff $M, \rho, i \models \phi$ and $M, \rho, i \models \psi$
$M, \rho, i \models \bigcirc\phi$ iff $M, \rho, i+1 \models \phi$
$M, \rho, i \models \phi\mathcal{U}\psi$ iff $\exists j \geq i$ such that $M, \rho, j \models \psi$ and $\forall k : i \leq k < j, M, \rho, k \models \phi$

Other boolean connectives are defined as usual, for example $\phi \rightarrow \psi := \neg(\phi \wedge \neg\psi)$. $\Diamond\phi$ (some time in the future) is defined as $\top\mathcal{U}\phi$, $\Box\phi$ (always in the future) is defined as $\neg\Diamond\neg\phi$. We use $\bigcirc^m$, $m \in \mathbb{N}$, to denote a sequence of $\bigcirc$ modalities of length m.

We say that a run ρ in a transition system $M = (S, R, V, s_I)$ satisfies ϕ $(M, \rho \models \phi)$ if $M, \rho, 0 \models \phi$. We say that M satisfies ϕ $(M \models \phi)$ if for all runs ρ in M, $M, \rho \models \phi$. A formula ϕ is valid if for all transition systems M, $M \models \phi$. A set of formulas Γ logically entails ϕ $(\Gamma \models \phi)$ if for every M and ρ, if M and ρ satisfy all formulas in Γ, then $M, \rho \models \phi$.

3   Non-repeating Norms

In this setting, a *group obligation* specifies a sequence of actions that should be performed collectively by a group of agents. Each step in the sequence specifies some actions that must be performed in parallel by the agents in the group. We allow actions that must be performed by more than one agent simultaneously, e.g., if two agents are necessary to move a table. The obligation specifies what must be done, and in which order; however it does not specify which actions should be performed by each agent in the group. For example a group of agents may be required to clean a room, where 'cleaning the room' is interpreted as "some agent has to vacuum the room and some agent has to do the dusting".

We assume that each agent in the group proposes one or more *individual contributions* to implementing the group norm. Each contribution specifies a set of actions the agent is prepared to perform in order to discharge the group norm. For example, an agent may specify that it is prepared to vacuum but not to dust. Where the group obligation specifies that the same action must be performed several times, we allow an agent's individual contribution to specify the maximum number of times the agent is prepared to perform the action. For example, if a group obligation when spending a week in a shared house involves cooking dinner each evening, an agent may specify that it is prepared to cook dinner at most twice during the week.

Before giving formal definitions of group norms and individual contribution schemes, we need some abbreviations. Let $\mathbf{hapd}(a_1\|\ldots\|a_m)$ (where $\{a_1,\ldots,a_m\}$ is a multiset of actions) stand for actions '$a_1,\ldots,a_m$ were executed in parallel'. This is definable as

$$\mathbf{hapd}(a_1\|\ldots\|a_m) = \bigvee_{i_1\neq\cdots\neq i_m} (\mathbf{done}(a_1,i_1) \wedge \ldots \wedge \mathbf{done}(a_m,i_m))$$

If $A = \{a\}$, we write $\mathbf{hapd}(a)$ for $\mathbf{hapd}(A)$. Moreover, $\mathbf{hapd}(\emptyset)$ is defined as *true*.

Let $\mathbf{haps}(A_1;\ldots;A_N)$ where each A_j is a multiset of actions connected by $\|$, stand for a sequence of parallel executions of actions in multisets A_j. This is definable as

$$\mathbf{haps}(A_1;\ldots;A_N) = \bigcirc(\mathbf{hapd}(A_1) \wedge \bigcirc(\mathbf{hapd}(A_2) \wedge \bigcirc(\ldots \bigcirc \mathbf{hapd}(A_N))\ldots))$$

where each A_i is in the scope of i nested $\bigcirc$ operators. In particular,

$$\mathbf{haps}(A_1;A_2) = \bigcirc(\mathbf{hapd}(A_1) \wedge \bigcirc\mathbf{hapd}(A_2))$$

Note that in this definition, the actions start 'tomorrow' rather than 'now', which is more or less an arbitrary decision, made for convenience.

Definition 2 (Non-repeating group norms). *Given $N \in \mathbb{N}$, a group norm η is defined as follows:*

$$\eta := \mathbf{haps}(A_1;\ldots;A_N)$$

Again, the obligation starts being executed 'tomorrow' rather than 'at some point in the future'. All formal results in the paper would hold if we used $\Diamond\mathbf{haps}(A_1;\ldots;A_N)$ instead.

Example 1. Two flatmates need to decide who contributes in which way to the duties of dusting (d), doing groceries (g), vacuum cleaning (v) and watering the plants (w) for the next week:

$$\eta = \mathbf{haps}(w\|g; d\|v; \emptyset; w; \emptyset; d; \emptyset)$$

That is, on Monday groceries and watering need to be done, on Tuesday, dusting and vacuuming, on Thursday the plants need to be watered again, and on Saturday dusting needs to be done. There are no constraints for Wednesday, Friday, and Sunday.

Note that $\emptyset$ means that no actions are *requireded* to be performed, so the agents can perform any action at this point in the sequence and still comply with the norm. In this paper, we are only concerned with obligations, and not with prohibitions on executing actions. We can extend the framework to prohibitions by using $\neg\mathbf{done}(a,i)$ expressions. It is also straightforward to extend the syntax of group norms to express 'twice a week' rather than 'on Monday and on Thursday' using disjunctions, but this increases the complexity of the norm decomposition problem, so we only consider the current (fixed order) setting. For the same reason, we do not consider conditional norms with deadlines. These can be easily expressed, but again at the cost of increased complexity.

We will use $\mathbf{do}(a,i)^m$ to indicate that i is prepared to perform a at most m times:

$$\mathbf{do}(a,i)^0 := \Box(\neg\mathbf{done}(a,i))$$

and

$$\mathbf{do}(a,i)^{m+1} := \Box(\mathbf{done}(a,i) \rightarrow \bigcirc\mathbf{do}(a,i)^m)$$

Definition 3 (Individual contribution schemes). *Given an agent i, an individual contribution scheme D_i is defined as $\bigvee C_i^j$ (with j ranging over disjuncts) where*

$$C_i^j := \bigwedge_{a_k \in Ac} \mathbf{do}(a_k,i)^{n_k^j}$$

We will refer to C_i^j as individual contribution offers *or simply offers.*

Sometimes we will treat D_i as a set and write $C_i^j \in D_i$ to mean that C_i^j is a disjunct in D_i.

Each C_i specifies a possible combination of actions i is prepared to contribute and does not refer to actions by other agents. For example, $\mathbf{do}(a,i)^2 \wedge \mathbf{do}(b,i)^1$ is an offer by agent i to execute action a at most twice and action b at most once.

Example 2 (Example 1 ctd). Consider the following offers by the agents:

$$D_1 = \mathbf{do}(d,1)^1 \wedge \mathbf{do}(g,1)^7 \wedge \mathbf{do}(v,1)^1 \wedge \mathbf{do}(w,1)^7$$
$$D_2 = \mathbf{do}(d,2)^0 \wedge \mathbf{do}(g,2)^1 \wedge \mathbf{do}(v,2)^0 \wedge \mathbf{do}(w,2)^0 \vee$$
$$\mathbf{do}(d,2)^1 \wedge \mathbf{do}(g,2)^0 \wedge \mathbf{do}(v,2)^0 \wedge \mathbf{do}(w,2)^1$$

The constraint $C_1^1 = D_1$ expresses that agent 1 does not mind doing the groceries and the watering, but is prepared to do the chores of dusting and vacuuming at most once. Agent 2 (let us call his constraints $C_2^1 \vee C_2^2$) is either (C_2^1) willing to do groceries once, or (C_2^2) he is willing to do dusting once and watering once.

Note that there is a gap between a group norm and the offers of the agents, in the sense that although the agents may offer to perform all the actions needed for the group norm, in order for the group norm to be discharged, the agents need to synchronise and commit to performing actions at particular times. An *implementation* of a group obligation is a set of *individual obligations* that particular agents should perform a subset of the actions specified in one of their individual contribution schemes (this is called a complete decomposition of the group obligation in [15]). Clearly an implementation should be effective, that is, if the agents discharge their individual obligations, the group norm is also discharged, and minimal, i.e., it should not create individual obligations unecessarily.

We introduce two types of individual obligation O_i. The first kind of obligation makes sense when an action that needs to be performed by an agent has to be performed in any case, regardless of whether the preceding actions have been performed.

Definition 4 (Unconditional individual obligation). *An unconditional obligation for i is a formula of the form* $\bigcirc^j \mathbf{done}(a, i)$.

$\bigcirc^j \mathbf{done}(a, i)$ is an obligation to perform a at step j (assuming steps are counted from 0).

The second kind of individual obligation is similar to those considered in [15]. They make sense for actions whose preconditions are created by the preceding actions. For example, where an agent is required to decorate a house and the action of decorating can only be carried out if other agents build the house first. In this case, it does not make sense to require the agent assigned to the decorating task to execute it unconditionally.

Definition 5 (Conditional individual obligation). *A conditional obligation for i is a formula of the form*

$$\mathbf{haps}(A_1; \ldots; A_m) \rightarrow \bigcirc^{m+1} \mathbf{done}(a, i)$$

That is, i has an individual obligation to do a if the group obligation $\mathbf{haps}(A_1; \ldots; A_m)$ is discharged.

An individual obligation O_i for agent i is a conjunction of unconditional and conditional individual obligations for i.

Given a tuple of individual obligations by agents in a group G (consisting of k agents), $O_G = \langle O_1, \ldots, O_k \rangle$, we will identify O_G with the conjunction of those O_i's. We say that O_G *respects* the individual offer C_i^j of agent i if $O_G \wedge C_i^j \not\models \bot$. Essentially this means that O_G does not require i to perform each action a more than the maximal number of times specified by C_i^j.

Definition 6 (Implementation of a norm). *Given a group norm η, a set of agents $G \subseteq Ag$ and their individual contributions $\{D_i \mid i \in G\}$, an implementation of η by G is a conjunction O_G of obligations O_i $(i \in G))$ such that*

$$\forall i \in G \, \exists C_i^j \in D_i : O_G \text{ respects } C_i^j \, \& \models O_G \rightarrow \eta$$

Note that the first action A_1 in any implementation of a group obligation $\mathbf{haps}(A_1; \ldots; A_N)$ can only have unconditional obligations corresponding to it. Note also that if O_G is an implementation of η, then O_G is logically equivalent to a conjunction of unconditional obligations.

Example 3 (Examples 1 and 2 ctd.). There is no implementation that implements η using the contributions C_1^1 and C_2^1, because on Tuesday both the dusting and the vacuuming would have to be performed by the same agent 1, which is impossible given

Definition 1 (condition 2): $\mathbf{done}(d, 1)$ and $\mathbf{done}(v, 1)$ cannot hold in the same state since d and v are different actions. On the other hand, we can assign all individual actions to agents consistently using C_1^1 and C_2^2: agent 1 is assigned g on Monday, v on Tuesday, w on Thursday, and d on Saturday. This is consistent with its offer C_1^1. Agent 2 is assigned w on Monday and d on Tuesday; this is consistent with its offer C_2^2. The individual obligation for agent 1 is

$$\bigcirc\mathbf{done}(g, 1) \wedge \bigcirc^2\mathbf{done}(v, 1) \wedge \bigcirc^4\mathbf{done}(w, 1) \wedge \bigcirc^6\mathbf{done}(d, 1)$$

and for agent 2 $\bigcirc\mathbf{done}(w, 2) \wedge \bigcirc^2\mathbf{done}(d, 2)$. Together both obligations entail η.

In order to compute individual obligations and hence an implementation of a group norm η, we also need an auxiliary notion of an assignment of agents to actions in η.

Definition 7 (Assignment). *An assignment of agents in $G \subseteq Ac$ to actions in $\eta = \mathbf{haps}(A_1; \ldots; A_N)$ is a function f that for every A_j in η assigns an agent $i \in G$ and a contribution C_i to every element a of A_j subject to the following constraints:*

C1 *if $f(A_j, a) = (i, C_i)$ for k different j (in other words, the agent is assigned to k different occurrences of a in η) then $\mathbf{do}(a, i)^m$ for $m \geq k$ is a conjunct in C_i;*

C2 *if $f(A_j, a) = (i, C_i)$ and $f(A_j, b) = (k, C_k)$ and $a \neq b$, then $i \neq k$ (only one action can be executed by the agent i in a single transition); and*

C3 *if $f(A_j, a) = (i, C_i)$ and $f(A_k, b) = (i, C_i')$, then $C_i = C_i'$ (only one offer by i is used by the assignment throughout).*

The following theorem will be useful for analysing the implementation of a norm as a computational problem.

Theorem 1. *Every assignment of agents to actions in η satisfying the conditions of Definition 7 gives rise to an implementation of η, and every implementation gives rise to such an assignment.*

Proof. Assume that we have an assignment f for a group norm $\eta = \mathbf{haps}(A_1; \ldots; A_N)$. By **C3**, for each agent i involved in the assignment, there is a single contribution C_i. Given the assignment, generate O_i as $\bigwedge_{f(A_j, a) = (i, C_i)} \bigcirc^j \mathbf{done}(a, i)$. Clearly $\bigwedge O_i$ respects C_i by **C1**. $\bigwedge_{i \in G} O_i$ is satisfiable by **C2**. Finally since f is an assignment, any run that satisfies $\bigwedge_{i \in G} O_i$ also satisfies η. Hence, $\bigwedge_i O_i$ is an implementation.

Now assume that we have an implementation $\bigwedge_{i \in G} O_i$ for $\eta = \mathbf{haps}(A_1; \ldots; A_N)$. We will show how to extract an assignment f for η from it. First of all, to satisfy **C3**, we assign only one contribution C_i with which O_i is consistent to every $i \in G$. Now we construct f for each of $A_1, \ldots, A_N$ in turn. Since $\bigwedge O_i \models \eta$ and $\eta \models \mathbf{haps}(A_1)$, there are enough conjuncts in $\bigwedge O_i$ to make sure $\mathbf{done}(a, i_j)$ holds for every $a \in A_1$ and there are enough different i_j to for every occurrence of a in A_1 (no agent is scheduled to perform more than one action in parallel since $\bigwedge O_i$ is satisfiable). We take some subset of those to assign to $f(A_1, a)$. Similarly in order for $\bigwedge O_i$ to entail $\mathbf{haps}(A_1; \ldots; A_{m+1})$ provided it entails $\mathbf{haps}(A_1; \ldots; A_m)$ there must be contributions in $\bigwedge O_i$ of agents promising to execute an action in A_{m+1} after $\mathbf{haps}(A_1; \ldots; A_m)$ (or in $m + 1$ timesteps unconditionally), and enough of them to entail $\mathbf{haps}(A_1; \ldots; A_{m+1})$. Assign some subset of those agents to actions in A_{m+1}.

Theorem 2. *Given a group norm η, a group of agents G, and agent contributions D_i for $i \in G$, the problem of whether an implementation of η by G exists is NP-complete.*

Proof. By Theorem 1, the problem of finding an implementation can be reduced to the problem of finding an assignment. For membership of NP, observe that an assignment can be guessed in time polynomial in the size of the group norm and checked that it satisfies the conditions **C1-C3** in time polynomial in the group norm and the set of agents' contributions. For NP-hardness, we reduce SAT to the problem of finding an assignment of agents to actions in a group norm. Let ϕ be a propositional formula in CNF containing n variables and k clauses. Without loss of generality, we assume that each clause is unique and none of them contains both p_i and $\neg p_i$ for some variable p_i. The corresponding group norm will be

$$\eta_\phi = c_1; \ldots; c_k$$

where c_j is an action corresponding to making the jth clause in ϕ true. Let G contain n agents, one for each propositional variable p_i in ϕ. Each agent i has two offers. Intuitively, the offer C_i^t corresponds to setting p_i to true and the offer C_i^f corresponds to setting p_i to false.

$$C_i^t = \bigwedge_{p_i \in c_j} \mathbf{done}(c_j, i), \quad C_i^f = \bigwedge_{\neg p_i \in c_j} \mathbf{done}(c_j, i)$$

Since we assume that each clause is unique, the agents offer to make each c_j true at most once. Now assume that we have a function f that assigns to clauses pairs (i, C_i^t) or (i, C_i^f). By **C3**, only one of C_i^t or C_i^f is used for each i in this assignment. Hence for each p_i where $i \in G$ (i was used in the assignment of agents), we can extract a unique assignment of a truth value *true* or *false* to p_i. Because of the way the offers were defined, this assignments of truth values to p_i for $i \in G$ will make all the clauses true.

3.1 Minimality

A natural and desirable property of an implementation of a group norm is that the agents are not obliged to do more than the norm requires.

Definition 8 (Minimality). *Let η be a group norm. Let $O_1, \ldots, O_k$ be individual obligations for agents in G, and $I = O_1 \wedge \cdots \wedge O_k$.*

- *I is a minimal implementation of η if it is an implementation of η and there is no implementation $I' = O_1' \wedge \cdots \wedge O_k'$ of η for which both $I \models I'$ and $I' \not\models I$.*
- *I is an i-minimal implementation of η if there is no obligation O_i' for i such that $(O_1 \wedge \cdots \wedge O_i' \wedge \ldots O_k)$ is an implementation of η for which both $O_i \models O_i'$ and $O_i' \not\models O_i$.*
- *I is an individually minimal implementation of η if it is an i-minimal implementation for every $i \in G$.*

Clearly, a minimal implementation I of η is individually minimal. In our setting, the opposite also holds:

Theorem 3. *Let* $I = O_1 \wedge \cdots \wedge O_k$ *be an implementation of a group norm* $\eta =$ **haps**$(A_1; \ldots; A_N)$ *by* G. *Then* I *is a minimal implementation iff* I *is an individually minimal implementation.*

Proof. The left to right direction is obvious, so consider $I = O_1 \wedge \cdots \wedge O_k$. Since it is an implementation of η, using Theorem 1 we can use an assignment f to write each individual obligation O_i in the following normal form:

$$O_i = \bigcirc(\gamma_{i_1} \wedge \bigcirc(\gamma_{i_2} \wedge \ldots \bigcirc \gamma_{i_N}) \ldots)$$

where each γ_{i_k} is of the form **done**(a, i) (i is required to do a at step k) or $\top$ (no requirement for i at step k), and there is a contribution C_i so that the number of times **done**(a, i) occurs for every a is consistent with C_i. Now let $\Gamma_j = \bigwedge_{i \leq n} \gamma_{i_k}$. It is not difficult to see that I is equivalent to

$$O = \bigcirc(\Gamma_1 \wedge \bigcirc(\Gamma_2 \wedge \ldots \bigcirc \Gamma_N) \ldots)$$

Now, if I is not minimal, there is a logically weaker implementation $I' = \bigcirc(\Gamma'_1 \wedge \bigcirc(\Gamma'_2 \wedge \ldots \bigcirc \Gamma'_N) \ldots)$. However, since no **done**(a, i) entails any **done**(a', i') unless $a = a'$ and $i = i'$, the implementation I' can only be weaker than I if there is some Γ_j and Γ'_j for which some $\Gamma_j \models$ **done**(a, i) while $\Gamma'_j \not\models$ **done**(b, i) for any action b (that is, Γ_j requires i to do a at step j, while Γ'_j does not impose a requirement on i at j). But then, O_i is not minimal, since replacing **done**(a, i) by $\top$ in O_i would be a weaker obligation for i, and hence I is not individually minimal.

Given the result above, it is clear that the problem of computing a minimal implementation is no harder than the problem of computing an implementation, since it is possible to check if an implementation (or rather the corresponding assignment) is individually minimal in polynomial time.

3.2 Fairness

Now we arrive at the main concern of this paper, that is how to define a notion of group norm implementation that agrees with the *social norms* accepted by the agents as a way to regulate the *fairness* of task assignments.

Some implementations of a group norm may be better than others from the point of view of the group's or the wider organisation's notion of fairness as captured in social norms. For example, fairness may require that all agents should contribute equally to the implementation of the group norm, or that agents with less experience are required to contribute less. LTL offers a natural setting to consider *fairness* constraints on implementations. By fairness constraints in this setting we do not mean just the notion of fairness as defined for processes in computer science (e.g., every request will be eventually granted). Instead we mean some additional constraints on possible implementations that reflect the organisation's view of what is reasonable to require from the agents. For example, it could be that the organisation does not consider it fair that the same agent performs an action a (for example, a work shift) twice in a row:

$$\square(\bigwedge_{i \in G}(\textbf{done}(a, i) \rightarrow \bigcirc \neg \textbf{done}(a, i)))$$

Another example is that each agent gets a rest from all chores every seventh day:

$$\Box(\bigwedge_{i \in G} (\neg \chi_i \vee \bigcirc \neg \chi_i \vee \ldots \vee \bigcirc^6 \neg \chi_i))$$

where $\chi_i = \bigvee_{a \in \{d,g,v,w\}} \mathbf{done}(a, i)$.

Definition 9 (Fair implementation). *Let ϕ be an LTL formula expressing a fairness constraint. An implementation of a group norm I is fair with respect to ϕ (or ϕ-fair) if $\models I \rightarrow \phi$.*

In other words, I is ϕ-fair if every run satisfying I also satisfies ϕ. Checking fairness of an implementation can be done by checking whether $I \wedge \neg\phi$ is satisfiable. Note that, since I essentially corresponds to a single finite run, it is possible to check whether it satisfies ϕ in polynomial time (rather than PSPACE as in the general LTL satisfiability problem).

If group norms are assumed to be fixed length sequences of actions, it arguably does not make sense to consider arbitrary LTL formulas as fairness constraints. In fact, most natural fairness constraints in human work allocation do not have the form 'everyone *eventually* gets a holiday' but 'everyone gets a holiday after working for n months'. For this reason, we propose to restrict the syntax of fairness constraints to talk about fixed finite patterns of actions.

Definition 10 (Fairness constraint). *An LTL formula ϕ is a fairness constraint if it is of the form $\Box\psi$, where ψ only contains $\bigcirc$ modalities.*

Examples of fairness constraints $\Box\psi$ are as follows, where N is a given number: (1) no agent i performs an action a twice in the next N steps, without another agent i performing it in between those occurrences; (2) agents $i_1, \ldots, i_m$ take perfect turns in all occurrences of action a; (3) if action a happens k times in the next N steps, then at least m different agents should be involved in their execution; (4) agent i is allowed to do something other than any of $a_1, \ldots, a_k$ at least once in every k steps; and (5) if i does a then j does it within k steps.

4   Repeating Norms

In the previous section, we looked at group norms that correspond to performing some group task/obligation once. In state-based terms, such norms correspond to achievement goals: a sequence of actions that must be executed in order to achieve a certain desirable state. In this section, we consider the case where a group norm relates, in state-based terms, to a maintenance goal: some condition needs to be maintained in perpetuity. In order to achieve this condition, some group task has to be executed periodically. For example, every week the agents in a household need to execute some combination of cleaning, shopping and cooking tasks: $A_1; \ldots; A_7$.

The norm itself requires them to iterate this sequence forever, which we write as $\mathbf{haps}(A_1; \ldots; A_7)^\infty$. We will refer to the number of sequentially composed actions in the repeated sequence in η as the cycle of η, $c(\eta)$ (in the example above, $c(\eta) = 7$).

An infinite repetition of a sequence $A_1; \ldots; A_N$ can be defined in LTL as follows:

$$\mathbf{haps}(A_1; \ldots; A_N)^\infty = \mathbf{haps}(A_1; \ldots; A_N) \wedge$$
$$\Box(\mathbf{haps}(A_1; \ldots; A_N) \to \bigcirc^N \mathbf{haps}(A_1; \ldots; A_N))$$

Definition 11 (Repeating group norm with cycle N). *A repeating norm with cycle N is an obligation to repeat $A_1; \ldots; A_N$ infinitely often:* $\eta = \mathbf{haps}(A_1; \ldots; A_N)^\infty$

The syntax for agent's individual contribution schemes is similar to Definition 3, apart from the addition of the norm cycle N: $\mathbf{do}(a, i)^{m,N}$ means that the agent offers to perform a at most m times in every $N = c(\eta)$. The most straightforward way to define this in LTL is to rule out all patterns of length N where the agent performings a more than m times, or, equivalently, to state that in every pattern of length N there are at least $N - m$ steps when the agent is *not* performing a. Let $\mathbf{K}^{m,N} = \{K \subseteq \{1, \ldots N\} \mid |K| = N - m\}$. Intuitively, this defines all possible combinations of a-free steps in a pattern of length N if the agent does a at most m times. Let $\mathbf{not}^K(a, i)$ for $k \in \mathbf{K}^{m,N}$ stand for $\bigwedge_{k \in K} \bigcirc^k \neg \mathbf{done}(a, i)$. This formula says that the agent does not do a on each of the time steps in K. Then $\mathbf{do}(a, i)^{m,N} = \bigvee_{K \in \mathbf{K}^{m,N}} \mathbf{not}^K(a, i)$ says that the agent does a at most m times in N steps. Finally, to make this apply not just to the first N steps but indefinitely, the offer is prefixed with a $\Box$:

Definition 12 (Individual contibution schemes for repeating norms). *Given an agent i, and a repeating norm η with cycle N, an individual contribution scheme D_i for η is defined as* $\bigvee C_i$ *where*

$$C_i^j := \bigwedge_{a_k \in Ac} \Box \mathbf{do}(a_k, i)^{n_k^j, N}$$

where $n_k^j \leq N$ for all k.

An unconditional obligation for agent i in a repeating norm setting is an obligation to perform an action a at step k in a cycle of length N.

Definition 13 (Unconditional individual obligation for repeating norms). *Given an agent i, and a repeating norm η with cycle N, an unconditional individual obligation for i with respect to η is a formula of the form*

$$\bigcirc^k \mathbf{done}(a, i) \wedge \Box(\mathbf{done}(a, i) \to \bigcirc^N \mathbf{done}(a, i))$$

where $k \leq N$.

A conditional obligation requires an agent to perform an action every time when the other agents have performed some actions.

Definition 14 (Conditional individual obligation for repeating norms). *Given an agent i, and a repeating norm η with cycle N, a conditional obligation for i is a formula of the form*

$$\Box(\mathbf{haps}(A_1; \ldots; A_m) \to \bigcirc^{m+1} \mathbf{done}(a, i))$$

where $m < N$.

An implementation of a repeating norm by a set of agents G is as before a conjunction of obligations $I = \bigwedge O_{i \in G}$ such that $\models I \rightarrow \eta$ and I is consistent with agent offers. A minimal implementation is defined as before, and the same type of fairness constraints as in the previous section can be applied to repeating norms.

A *single cycle assignment* of agents to actions in $\eta = \mathbf{haps}(A_1; \dots; A_N)^\infty$ is defined as an assignment for a non-repeating norm $\eta' = \mathbf{haps}(A_1; \dots; A_N)$. Clearly any single cycle assignment repeated every N steps gives rise to an implementation for a repeating norm. However for repeating norms it makes sense to consider implementations obtained by 'gluing' several different assignments together and repeating the resulting pattern. Repetition affects fairness in a non-trivial way. Considering the example fairness constraints in the previous section, we can see that 'gluing' together two (even identical) assignments satisfying fairness constraint (2) stated at the end of Section 3 may make the resulting implementation unfair (if the last occurrence of a in the implementation is done by i_k with $k < m$), and also two unfair implementations (not satisfying fairness constraint (5) in Section 3, for instance) may become fair when glued together.

A consequence of this is that when solving the problem of finding a ϕ-fair implementation of a repeating obligation η, it is not sufficient to consider only single cycle assignments. If none of those when repeated correspond to a fair implementation of η, this does not mean that η has no fair implementation. We may need to consider a combination of several assignments. For example, let $\phi = \square(\bigwedge_{i \in G}(\mathbf{done}(a, i) \rightarrow \bigcirc \neg \mathbf{done}(a, i)))$ and $\eta = \mathbf{haps}(a)^\infty$. The cycle of η is 1. Suppose there are two possible one cycle assignments for η, one where agent 1 does a, and another where agent 2 does a. If either of them alone is repeated, the resulting implementation is not fair: either all occurrences of action a are done by agent 1, or all of them are done by agent 2. Clearly, if we combine these two one cycle assignments or produce a one cycle assignment to an 'unravelling' of η of length two: $\eta^2 = \mathbf{haps}(a; a)^\infty$, we can produce an assignment that gives rise to a fair implementation: for example, the first a is done by agent 1 and the second by agent 2. However to solve the problem of finding a ϕ-fair implementation of a repeating norm η (if it exists) we need to know how long such an unravelling should get before we give up.

For $\eta = \mathbf{haps}(A_1; \dots; A_N)^\infty$, we will call

$$\eta^m = \mathbf{haps}(A_1; \dots; A_N; \ \dots \ ; A_1; \dots; A_N)^\infty \quad (m \text{ times})$$

an m-unravelling of η.

Theorem 4. *Let η be a group obligation with cycle N that has k different one cycle assignments $S_1, \dots, S_k$, and ϕ be a fairness constraint of modal depth d. If a ϕ-fair implementation of η exists, then there exists a ϕ-fair implementation of η based on the a single cycle assignment to an m-unravelling of η, where $m \leq max(k, k^{d/N+1})$.*

Proof. Let τ be an assignment corresponding to a fair implementation of η. Without loss of generality, we can assume that τ corresponds to a (possibly infinite) sequence of one cycle assignments for η, $S_{i_1}, \dots, S_{i_t}, \dots$. Given τ, we are going to construct a sequence of assignments of length m, that is, some sequence $\tau' = S'_1, \dots, S'_m$ (a single cycle assignment to η^m) that when repeated infinitely often, gives rise to a ϕ-fair implementation of η.

Note that τ (or any other assignment of agents to actions) corresponds to a description of a run in terms of action propositions. Observe that a run violates ϕ if it has a pattern of d consecutive states $s_1, \ldots, s_d$ that is a counterexample to ϕ. Clearly, τ desribes a run that does not contain such a counterexample sequence of states (since it corresponds to a fair implementation). Note also that none of single-cycle implementations of η that occur in τ contain such a sequence of states (otherwise τ would not satisfy ϕ).

Let us first consider a simpler case when $d < N$. Then the only way a sequence of single-cycle assignments $S_{j_1}, \ldots, S_{j_n}$ would violate ϕ is when there is a sequence on the 'joint' between two assignments S_{j_i} and $S_{j_{i+1}}$ that violates it. Let us build a sequence of assignments of length at most k that does not have such a violating joint. For convenience, let us say that S_{j_i} and $S_{j_{i+1}}$ *compose* if their concatenation does not contain a subsequence violating ϕ. To start building our sequence of length at most k, take the first assignments in τ, S_{j_1}. Clearly it composes with some other assignments, since τ does not violate ϕ. If S_{j_1} composes with itself (there is a subsequence in τ that has $S_{j_1}; S_{j_1}$, we are done: $\tau' = S_{j_1}$. Otherwise we consider the first two assignments in τ, $S_{j_1}; S_{j_2}$. If S_{j_2} composes with itself, we are done and $\tau' = S_{j_2}$, or if it composes with S_{j_1}, then $\tau' = S_{j_1}; S_{j_2}$. Otherwise we consider a 3-element prefix of τ. Note that eventually we are going to encounter S_{j_f} which composes with $S_{j_{f+1}}$ that already occurs in the prefix of the sequence (the maximal possible value for f is k, the total number of single-cycle implementations). Then we set τ' to be the subsequence of the current sequence that starts from the first occurrence of $S_{j_{f+1}}$ and continues until S_{j_f}. Clearly, τ' has length at most k and nowhere in the 'joints' of the single cycle implementations in τ' there is a counterexample to ϕ (including the joint of τ' to itself).

Now let $d \geq N$. Then a counterexample sequence $s_1, \ldots, s_d$ can span multiple single cycle assignments. Let $d \leq p \cdot N$ (p iterations of N are required to produce a counterexample to ϕ, so $p \leq (d/N) + 1$). Then we make a set of 'viable multi-cycle assignments' $Z_1, \ldots, Z_{k^p}$ of all p-sequences of single-cycle assignments occurring in τ. We treat them as we treated single cycle assignments S_i before, as the building blocks for τ'. Similarly to the previous construction, we are bound to start to encounter the same 'viable multi-cycle assignments' after k^p steps. So τ' is of length at most $k^{d/N+1}$.

This means that to construct a ϕ-fair implementation of η, we only need to consider assignments to sequences of actions of length $m \leq max(k, k^{d/N+1})$. This gives us an (exponential) algorithm for finding a ϕ-fair implementation of a repeating norm η (generate all possible one cycle assignments and then check all concatenations of them of length m for consistency with ϕ).

5   Related Work

Social laws have long been recognised as an important mechanism to facilitate coordination in multi-agent systems [9], and there exists an extensive literature on formal approaches to social laws and norms, for example [23,20,17,22,1,6,12,7,8,3]. Logics for social laws often build upon dynamic or temporal logics such as LTL, CTL, ATL and STIT. Most of this work specifies norms and their effects on the multi-agent system semantically by labelling certain transitions as forbidden (in the case of prohibitions) or labelling certain states as 'green' (good, or encouraged states) or 'red' (forbidden ones, see e.g. [19]). In this paper, we only model obligations (rather than prohibitions) and specify obligations in the object language.

Group norms have been studied in for example [2,15]. Our definition of non-repeating group norms is essentially the one from [15]. The emphasis of [15] is however on formalising synchronisation, and they abstract from the problem of computing individual obligations for a group norm. In [2] group norms are considered at a much more abstract level. In their framework, a group norm concerns making a state formula ϕ true, and the set of agents responsible for carrying out (an abstract STIT-like) action to achieve ϕ and the set of agents responsible for the violation are explicitly given as part of the norm. Our approach is closer to [15] in that the notion of agents responsible for the violation of a group norm given a particular implementation is definable from the set of individual obligations. An agent that does not fulfil an unconditional obligation is responsible for a violation, and an agent with a conditional obligation the condition of which has not been made true, is not responsible.

Team formation and coordination of joint actions has been extensively studied in Artificial Intelligence, for example [13,16,24]. However the emphasis of that work is on efficient and flexible team work rather than on fairness. An exception to this is the work in [4], where the authors consider the problem of repeatedly choosing actions (that could for example be actions of assigning jobs to people) in a fair way, where fairness has a decision theoretic interpretation based on minimising loss for worse-off beneficiaries of actions. The motivation of their work is very similar to our problem of finding a fair implementation of a repeated norm, but they have a specific notion of fairness and reduce the problem of fair selection of actions to an optimisation problem.

6   Conclusion

In this paper, we propose an approach to expressing and reasoning about implementations of group obligations and introduce the notion of fairness constraints. The approach is a first step in formalising these notions, and has a number of limitations. We model only obligations and do not consider prohibitions. In addition, the structure of group obligations is quite rigid: we do not consider obligations to perform some action m times during an interval of N days, instead we specify specific days on which those m actions have to be performed. We also consider only a restricted class of fairness constraints. Relaxing these limitations, and a more compact syntax for representing, for example, individual offers, are the subject of future work.

Acknowledgements. We thank the anonymous CLIMA 2014 referees for their insighful comments that helped to improve the paper.

References

1. Ågotnes, T., van der Hoek, W., Wooldridge, M.: Conservative social laws. In: Proc. 20th European Conference on Artificial Intelligence (ECAI 2012), pp. 49–54 (2012)
2. Aldewereld, H., Dignum, V., Vasconcelos, W.: We ought to; they do; blame the management! – a conceptualisation of group norms. In: Proc. 15th Int. Workshop on Coordination, Organisations, Institutions and Norms, COIN 2013 (2013)
3. Alechina, N., Dastani, M., Logan, B.: Reasoning about normative update. In: Proc. 23rd International Joint Conference on Artificial Intelligence, IJCAI 2013 (2013)

4. Balan, G.C., Richards, D., Luke, S.: Long-term fairness with bounded worst-case losses. Autonomous Agents and Multi-Agent Systems 22(1), 43–63 (2011)
5. Blackburn, P., de Rijke, M., Venema, Y.: Modal Logic, Cambridge Tracts in Theoretical Computer Science, vol. 53. Cambridge University Press (2001)
6. Boella, G., van der Torre, L.: Delegation of power in normative multiagent systems. In: Goble, L., Meyer, J.-J.C. (eds.) DEON 2006. LNCS (LNAI), vol. 4048, pp. 36–52. Springer, Heidelberg (2006)
7. Broersen, J., Mastop, R., Meyer, J.-J.C., Turrini, P.: A deontic logic for socially optimal norms. In: van der Meyden, R., van der Torre, L. (eds.) DEON 2008. LNCS (LNAI), vol. 5076, pp. 218–232. Springer, Heidelberg (2008)
8. Bulling, N., Dastani, M., Knobbout, M.: Monitoring norm violations in multi-agent systems. In: Proc. 12th International Conference on Autonomous Agents and Multiagent Systems (AAMAS 2013), pp. 491–498. IFAAMAS (2013)
9. Castelfranchi, C.: Modelling social action for AI agents. Artificial Intelligence 103(1-2), 157–182 (1998)
10. Cliffe, O., De Vos, M., Padget, J.: Specifying and reasoning about multiple institutions. In: Noriega, P., Vázquez-Salceda, J., Boella, G., Boissier, O., Dignum, V., Fornara, N., Matson, E. (eds.) COIN 2006. LNCS (LNAI), vol. 4386, pp. 67–85. Springer, Heidelberg (2007)
11. Cohen, P.R., Levesque, H.J.: Intention is choice with committment. Artificial Intelligence 42(2-3), 213–261 (1990)
12. Dastani, M., Grossi, D., Meyer, J.-J.C., Tinnemeier, N.: Normative multi-agent programs and their logics. In: Meyer, J.-J.C., Broersen, J. (eds.) KRAMAS 2008. LNCS, vol. 5605, pp. 16–31. Springer, Heidelberg (2009)
13. Decker, K., Lesser, V.: Designing a family of coordination algorithms. In: Proc. 1st International Conference on Multiagent Systems (ICMAS), pp. 73–80 (1995)
14. Esteva, M., de la Cruz, D., Sierra, C.: ISLANDER: an electronic institutions editor. In: Proc. of the 1st Int. Joint Conference on Autonomous Agents and Multiagent Systems (AAMAS 2002), pp. 1045–1052 (2002)
15. Grossi, D., Dignum, F.P.M., Royakkers, L.M.M., Meyer, J.-J.C.: Collective obligations and agents: Who gets the blame? In: Lomuscio, A., Nute, D. (eds.) DEON 2004. LNCS (LNAI), vol. 3065, pp. 129–145. Springer, Heidelberg (2004)
16. Grosz, B., Kraus, S.: Collaborative plans for complex group action. Artificial Intelligence 86(2), 269–357 (1996)
17. van der Hoek, W., Roberts, M., Wooldridge, M.: Social laws in alternating time: effectiveness, feasibility, and synthesis. Synthese 156(1), 1–19 (2007)
18. Hübner, J.F., Sichman, J.S., Boissier, O.: Developing organised multi-agent systems using the $\mathcal{M}OISE^+$ model: Programming issues at the system and agent levels. International Journal of Agent-Oriented Software Engineering 1(3/4), 370–395 (2007)
19. Lomuscio, A., Sergot, M.: Deontic interpreted systems. Studia Logica 75(1), 63–92 (2003)
20. Moses, Y., Tennenholtz, M.: Artificial social systems. Computers and AI 14(6), 533–562 (1995)
21. Schnoebelen, P.: The complexity of temporal logic model checking. In: Advances in Modal Logic 4, pp. 393–436. King's College Publications (2003)
22. Sergot, M.: Action and agency in norm-governed multi-agent systems. In: Artikis, A., O'Hare, G.M.P., Stathis, K., Vouros, G.A. (eds.) ESAW 2007. LNCS (LNAI), vol. 4995, pp. 1–54. Springer, Heidelberg (2008)
23. Shoham, Y., Tennenholtz, M.: On the synthesis of useful social laws for artificial agent societies. In: Proc. of the 10th National Conference on Artificial Intelligence (1992)
24. Tambe, M., Zhang, W.: Towards flexible teamwork in persistent teams: Extended report. Autonomous Agents and Multi-Agent Systems 3(2), 159–183 (2000)

A Conceptual Model for Situated Artificial Institutions

Maiquel de Brito[1], Jomi Fred Hübner[1], and Olivier Boissier[2]

[1] Federal University of Santa Catarina
Florianópolis, SC, Brazil
maiquel.b@posgrad.ufsc.br, jomi.hubner@ufsc.br
[2] Ecole Nationale Supérieure des Mines
FAYOL-EMSE, LSTI
F-42023 Saint-Etienne, France
Olivier.Boissier@emse.fr

Abstract. Artificial institutions have been proposed to regulate the acting of the agents in open multi-agent systems (MAS). They are composed of abstractions such as norms, roles, goals, etc. In this paper, we say that an artificial institution is situated when the whole regulation that it performs is based on facts occurring in the environment where agents act. The conceiving of situated institutions is challenging as it requires to situate all abstractions possibly involved in the MAS regulation considering their different natures, semantics, life cycles, etc. This work introduces a conceptual model of a situated artificial institution (SAI), structured along two axes: norms and constitutive rules. While norms are based on *status functions*, the constitutive rules allow a SAI model to clearly state the conditions for an element of the environment to carry a status function. From a first version of a SAI specification language based on this conceptual model, we discuss its features and illustrate its dynamics through examples.

Keywords: institutions, norms, status functions, constitutive rules, situatedness.

1 Introduction

Institutional abstractions, such as norms, roles, goals, missions, interaction scenes, etc, are suitable to conciliate the autonomy of the agents and the achievement of global goals in open and decentralized Multi-Agent Systems (MAS) where agents can act deviating from the system expectations [4,5,18,12]. These abstractions are gathered in the institutional dimension (or simply *institution*) that regulates the system, i.e., that enforces the agents to comply to the system expectations. The facts occurring in the environment affect the institutional regulation.[1] For instance, a norm is violated when some prohibited event takes place in the environment (e.g. a norm stating that one is prohibited to go through a red traffic light is violated only when one in fact crosses the red traffic light). Without such event, there is not violation. On the other hand, the

---

[1] The literature usually considers *environment* as the set of non-autonomous elements that are perceived and acted upon by the agents, where they act to achieve their goals [21,22,26]. We consider the environment from the institutional perspective, being composed also of the agents that act upon and perceive the non-autonomous elements.

N. Bulling et al. (Eds.): CLIMA XV, LNAI 8624, pp. 35–51, 2014.

environmental elements cannot ensure, themselves, the suitable behaviour of the agents. The fact of a norm being violated when one goes through a red traffic light is not related to the object *traffic light* itself. Rather, it is related to some institutional agreement or decision associating the norm fulfilment and violation to that object.[2]

Most of the existing institutional approaches are not concerned about the connection between facts in the environment and their consequences in the institution. Some of them leave to the agents the responsibility of informing norms violations, role adoptions, goal achievements, etc [17]. In this paper, however, we look for *situated institutions*, where the regulation is based on facts occurring in the environment so that it does not depend on agents informing norm violations, goal achievements, role adoptions, etc. A situated institution must have means to specify and to program how the environment affects the different institutional abstractions. Having such a situated institution allows the agents to reason about how to concretely act in the environment to comply with institutional expectations [1] without to handle the institutional platform [6]. Besides, it prevents that agents avoid institutional consequences of their actions [6].

Conceiving situated institutions is challenging as it requires to situate all abstractions possibly involved in the MAS regulation considering their different natures, semantics, life cycles, etc. For example, (i) if the institution contains norms, it is necessary to specify how the environmental elements affect norm activation, violation, fulfilment, etc, or (ii) if the institution contains roles, it is necessary to specify how the environmental elements affect role assignments and revocations, etc. Some related works propose to situate specific abstractions, such as norms in [9] or commitments in [10], ignoring the remainder ones. In this case, the situatedness specification explicitly defines which are the institutional abstractions affected by environmental facts. A drawback of this approach, however, is that the agents can only reason about a limited set of situated institutional abstractions. Other related works propose to link the environment to the institutional platform taking no account of the institutional abstractions that are situated [7,19,6]. Although these approaches allow to situate any institutional abstraction, they do not help the agents to reason about institutional consequences of their actions because the situatedness language does not explicitly define which are the institutional abstractions affected by the environment.

The difficulties related to linking environmental elements to different institutional abstractions lead us to investigate the very nature of the situatedness problem. While current related works, described in the Section 2, focus on the link between the environment and different institutional abstractions, this work aims to address the problem of institutional situatedness dealing with the very conception of the institution. The main contribution of this paper, described in the Section 3, is the proposal of a meta-model (henceforth *model*) named Situated Artificial Institutions (SAI) whose abstractions are conceived and arranged to allow the specification of institutions where the whole regulation is based on the environment. The name *Artificial Institution* is inspired by the work of Fornara et al. that advocates that the social dimension of an MAS is composed

---

[2] Although the behaviour of the agents may be regimented by the environmental elements (e.g. instead of using a traffic light, a physical barrier could block a lane when cars should not proceed), we are concerned with the cases where the compliance with the system expectations is a decision of the agents.

of other elements in addition to norms [13]. A language for specifying a SAI is proposed in the Section 4. In this paper we focus on the conceptual level of the proposed model, presenting its components and their arrangements. The dynamics of the model is informally explained through examples. The section 5 presents some discussions and perspectives based on this work.

2 Motivation

Institutional situatedness has been addressed by some related works in the multi-agent domain. From the perspective of situated institutions, i.e. institutions where the whole regulation is based on the environment, two important properties can be stated: *institutional semantics* and *institutional coverage*. Institutional semantics refers to the use of meaningful institutional concepts to specify situatedness. Models having institutional semantics allow the agents to reason about institutional effects of facts from the environment. Institutional coverage is related to the set of institutional abstractions that they can situate. Models having a wide institutional coverage allow to situate many (or perhaps any) institutional abstractions.

The approaches of [10] and [9] have *institutional semantics* as they allow to specify situatedness using institutional concepts. The model of [10] considers the specification of how the messages exchanged among the agents affect the life cycle of commitments. It uses concepts directly related to that abstraction, such as *conditional* commitment, *satisfied* commitment, *expired* commitment, etc. For example, the code excerpt (cex1) below specifies that (i) when an agent x sends an *offer* to y, a conditional commitment (C^c) is created between x and y and (ii) when x sends a *tell* to y informing that it has done q, then the commitment is satisfied (C^s). In [9] the proposed approach uses count-as rules to specify that specific states of the environment affect the life cycle of norms. In this case the situatedness specification is also done using meaningful institutional concepts related to norms, as it is possible to specify, for example, that a certain environmental state counts as a *norm violation*, which is a concept directly related to norms. In such approaches, agents are thus able to understand and reason on this institutional semantics, knowing perfectly what to do at the environmental level to produce effect at the institutional level. These approaches, however, have a limited *institutional coverage* because they only define situatedness for a limited set of institutional abstractions. Thus, they allow the agents to only reason about environmental facts affecting commitments [10] or norms [9].

$$1: \; offer(x,y,p,q,d_1,d_2) \Longrightarrow_{cr} \mathsf{C}^c(x,y,p,q,d_1,d_2)$$
$$2: \; tell(x,y,q) \wedge \mathsf{C}^c(x,y,p,q,d_1,d_2) \wedge \neg d1 \wedge q \Longrightarrow_{cr} \mathsf{C}^s(x,y,p,q,d_1,d_2)$$

(cex1)

The approaches of [7,19,6] consider that a situatedness interface observes the environment and, by interpreting the situatedness specification, produces informations about *what should happen* in the institution. It is assumed that the institutional platform takes such informations and changes its own state accordingly. Contrasting to the previously described works of [9,10], these models have a wide *institutional coverage*, as the provided informations can refer to any institutional abstraction. They address situatedness as a problem of interoperability between components of environment and institution. For example, the code (cex2) below, excerpted from [6], specifies that when the environment has the property *auction_status(closed)* the institution should have the property *play(Winner,Role)*. But that property does not have, in the situatedness specification, any institutional meaning. The property will have an institutional meaning when latter interpreted by the institutional platform. In its specific application, the property becomes true as soon as the platform detects that the agent *Winner* plays the role *Role*. But the institutional abstraction *role* is not part of the situatedness model. Thus, agents cannot reason about the institutional consequences of the situatedness specification of this example. They cannot infer that when the environment has the property *auction_status(closed)*, they will play a role, because *play(Winner,Role)* is just some information that will be sent to the institutional platform (which will then gives semantics to *play*).[3] As the consequence, if the property *play(Winner,Role)* is replaced by *meaninglessProp(x,y)*, the rule remains syntactically and semantically correct but the agents cannot say whether the rule still makes sense. Although these approaches have a wide coverage, they do not consider the institutional semantic, as institutional concepts do not belong to the situatedness model.

$$* \; \texttt{auction\_status(closed)}$$
$$\texttt{count} - \texttt{as play(Winner, Role)} \qquad\qquad (\text{cex2})$$
$$\texttt{in currentWinner(Winner)\& auction\_role(Art, Role).}$$

While the previously described approaches consider situatedness as a functional problem, where the environment affects the life cycle of the institution, the approach of [1], in line with [14,15,2], considers it as an ontological problem where the main concern is to relate the concepts used in the specification of norms to concrete elements from the environment. Although considering situatedness of norms, this approach has a wide institutional coverage as the use of similar rules could be applied to other institutional abstractions (e.g. roles, stating that the agent *bob* counts as a *teacher*). But the approach lacks of institutional semantics because the environmental elements are linked to the concepts in the norms but are not related to the semantics of such concepts. For example, for a norm stating that "*a* is obliged to *b*", it is possible to specify that "*j* counts as *a*" and "*k* counts as *b*". But it is possible also to specify that "*j* counts as *b*" and "*k* counts as *a*", that is wrong as *a* is an agent while *b* has a different nature. The rule stating that "*j* counts as *a*" does not take into account the nature of the element *j* that is linked to *a*.

We can observe that models that allow to specify situatedness using meaningful institutional concepts have a limited institutional coverage while models having a wide institutional coverage lack of institutional semantics. Thus, the current body of work in institutional situatedness does not allow to situate all institutional aspects relevant to the regulation of an MAS through institutional programming, i.e. using meaningful institutional concepts. Our work aims to contribute to fill this gap as it allows to specify the whole expected behaviour of the agents through status functions that can be

---

[3] Of course, if the agent also knows the institutional platform, it can infer the consequences of the environmental facts.

situated through constitutive rules. As status functions and constitutive rules are meaningful concepts in the proposed model, the specification of situatedness is part of the institutional specification.

3   Situated Artificial Institutions

As stated in the introduction, our Situated Artificial Institution (SAI) proposal aims to support the whole regulation of MAS based on environmental elements. This section presents our contribution, i.e. the SAI meta-model, describing it briefly in Section 3.1 and explaining its components in more details in Section 3.2. The dynamics of the model are beyond the scope of this paper and are briefly and informally explained along this section.

3.1   SAI Overview

A SAI is composed of norms, status functions and constitutive rules (Figure 1). Norms specify the expected behaviour of the agents. A norm, however, does not provide itself the situatedness of the institution because it does not refer directly to concrete environmental elements. The elements composing a norm (defining who must accomplish it, what must be achieved or avoided, etc) are status functions. The situatedness is achieved when the status functions are assigned to environmental elements through constitutive rules. For example, the norm "*the winner of an auction is obliged to pay its offer, otherwise it is fined*" makes sense in the institutional specification of an auction. The norm, however, does not specify aspects such as (i) what an agent should do to become the *winner* of the auction, (ii) what an agent must do to perform the *payment*, or (iii) how the *fine* is applied. In this scenario, winner, payment, and fine are all status functions: they are meaningful functions in the institution that the environmental elements cannot perform solely in virtue of their physical characteristics. Rather, the performing of the functions is the result of assignments through constitutive rules stating, for example, that a bank deposit counts as the payment of the offer. In a more concrete example, supposing that the environment has an automatic teller machine implemented by an artifact [21], an operation in such artifact could count as the payment.

The main inspiration for this idea is the social reality theory of John Searle [23,24]. According to that theory, the social reality where human people are immersed arises from the concrete world (i.e. the environment) based on some elements including *status functions*, *norms* and *constitutive rules*. Norms, referred by Searle as *deontic powers*, define the expected behaviour of the people in the society; status functions are functions that environmental elements perform independent of their physical virtues; constitutive rules constitute the status functions from the environment. For example, a constitutive rule can define that a small line of stones has the status function (or *counts as*) the boundary of a private property. Due to such assignment of status function, people have reasons to follow the norm that states that they are forbidden to get into the private property even though they are physically able to cross the line of stones. The ideas from Searle's work have inspired other works dealing with institutional situatedness. But those works take, in general, the idea that elements from the environment *count*

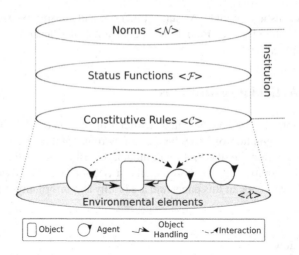

Fig. 1. A SAI composed by norms, status functions and constitutive rules regulates the agents acting in the environment

as elements in the institution without taking into account the conception of institution proposed by Searle. Our model is inspired both by the notion of *count as* and by the institutional view proposed by Searle.

3.2 SAI Meta-model

This section presents the conceptual meta-model of SAI, defining its fundamental elements and explaining their role in the model.

Definition 1. *A SAI is a tuple $\langle \mathcal{F}, \mathcal{N}, \mathcal{C} \rangle$, where $\mathcal{F}$ is a set of status functions, $\mathcal{N}$ is a set of norms, and $\mathcal{C}$ is a set of constitutive rules.*

Figure 1 shows a layered view of the components of SAI – norms, status functions and constitutive rules – that are explained in the sequel.

Status Functions in SAI Status functions are functions that the environmental elements may perform in the institution independent of their design aspects. Even if it is not possible to say that they are the main element of the model, it is possible to consider them as the *central* ones, and they are thus defined first since they are related to all the other elements.[4]

Definition 2. *In a SAI, $\mathcal{F} = \mathcal{A}_{\mathcal{F}} \cup \mathcal{E}_{\mathcal{F}} \cup \mathcal{S}_{\mathcal{F}}$, where (i) $\mathcal{A}_{\mathcal{F}}$ is the set of agent-status functions, (ii) $\mathcal{E}_{\mathcal{F}}$ is the set of event-status functions, and (iii) $\mathcal{S}_{\mathcal{F}}$ is the set of state-status*

---

[4] A *function*, in the context of status functions, does not have the usual mathematical sense of mapping elements from a domain to ones in a codomain. Rather, it is related to the performance of a function by some element.

functions. We consider that (i) agent-status functions are the status functions assignable to agents, (ii) event-status functions are the status functions assignable to events, and (iii) state-status functions are the status functions assignable to states.

We explicitly define the kind of elements that can carry a function considering the kind of status function present in the norm elements (as explained later). Thus, status functions can be assigned to:

- Agents: Agents may play functions in the institution that are not inherent to their design characteristics. For example, in a certain institution, an agent may have the function of auctioneer. But it has such function due to an institutional assignment. The agent may be implemented with expertise to be an auctioneer and may intend to be an auctioneer, but without the institutional assignment of the status function *auctioneer*, it will not be considered at the institutional level as playing that function.
- Events: the agents produce events when they act over objects in the environment and when they interact among themselves. These events may have a special meaning in an institution. For instance, the event corresponding to the utterance of "I offer $100,00" may have the status function of "bid" or "counter-proposal", depending on the institutional assignments.
- States: some states of the environment may get a meaning in the institution. For example, the state where "more than twenty people are inside a room at Friday 10am" may mean, in the institution, the minimum quorum for an auction.

Before to introduce norms, we introduce the status-function-formulas (sf-formulas), that are important to express the aims, conditions of applicability, consequences of noncompliance and deadlines of norms, as we will see later. A sf-formula $w_{\mathcal{F}} \in W_{\mathcal{F}}$ is a logical formula whose syntax is given by:

$$w_{\mathcal{F}} ::= s_{\mathcal{F}} | e_{\mathcal{F}} | \neg w_{\mathcal{F}} | w_{\mathcal{F}} \vee w_{\mathcal{F}} | w_{\mathcal{F}} \wedge w_{\mathcal{F}} | x \text{ is } f | \bot | \top$$

The proper semantic of the sf-formulas is defined later. Informally, a sf-formula $e_{\mathcal{F}}$ holds when something is carrying the event-status function $e_{\mathcal{F}}$ in the current state of the institution. For instance, when the speech act *offer($100)* is counting as a bid, the sf-formula *bid* is true (where $bid \in \mathcal{E}_{\mathcal{F}}$). The interpretation of $s_{\mathcal{F}}$ in sf-formulas is similar. Formulas using the operator *is* (e.g. bob *is* bidder) hold when something (bob) carries a status functions (bidder).

Norms in SAI Norms specify the expected behaviour of the agents acting in the system, by defining what they are obliged, prohibited, and permitted to do. Our definition of norms is inspired by the ADIC/ADICO sentences [8].

Definition 3. *A norm $n \in \mathcal{N}$ is a tuple $\langle a, d, i, c, o, \rho \rangle$ where:*

- $a \in \mathcal{A}_{\mathcal{F}}$ *is the attribute to whom the norm applies, i.e. it represents the agent that is obliged, prohibited, or permitted to do something;*
- $d \in \{obligation, prohibition, permission\}$ *is a deontic operator;*

- $i \in W_{\mathcal{F}}$ is the aim, i.e. the formula that should be true (when $d = obligation$) or false (when $d = prohibition$) to the norm be considered fulfilled;
- $c \in W_{\mathcal{F}}$ is a sf-formula conditioning the applicability of a norm;
- $o \in W_{\mathcal{F}}$ is a sf-formula expressing what should become true when the norm is violated;
- $\rho \in W_{\mathcal{F}}$ is a sf-formula expressing the condition before which the norm should be complied.

For example, when an auction is finished (c), the bidder (a) is obliged (d) to pay its offer (i) within two days (ρ), otherwise it will be fined (o). While most of the elements of norms are sf-formulas, the attribute a is an agent-status function because agents are the only elements that can act in order to fulfil or violate a norm.

Although the operational semantics of the model is beyond the scope of this paper, we informally explain how the elements of a norm are related to its dynamics: [5]

- a norm is active when the condition c holds;
- an active obligation is fulfilled if the aim i holds before ρ;
- an active prohibition is fulfilled if the aim i does not hold before ρ;
- an active obligation is violated if the aim i does not hold after ρ;
- an active prohibition is violated if the aim i holds before ρ;
- the consequence of the non-compliance of a norm takes place when o holds.

The element o is optional because we consider that norms can be specified without consequence for non-compliance.[6] Although the ADICO sentences consider that the Or-Else element must be backed by another norm [8], we consider that the consequence of norm violation can be also some institutional feedback at environmental level (i.e. the institution itself raises an event or a state change in the environment), as proposed by Piunti et al [19].

The norms are specified through status functions and their dynamic and management in the system is dependent on the assignments of status functions. These assignments are specified through the constitutive rules, that are explained below.

Constitutive Rules in SAI. The constitutive rules link the environment to the status functions. As status functions can be assigned to agents, events, and states from the environment, it is needed to represent these environmental elements.

Definition 4. *The elements of the environment that are relevant to the institutional regulation are represented by* $\mathcal{X} = \{\mathcal{A}_{\mathcal{X}}, \mathcal{E}_{\mathcal{X}}, \mathcal{S}_{\mathcal{X}}\}$ *where (i)* $\mathcal{A}_{\mathcal{X}}$ *is the set of agents possibly acting in the system, (ii)* $\mathcal{E}_{\mathcal{X}}$ *is the set of events that may happen in the environment, and (iii)* $\mathcal{S}_{\mathcal{X}}$ *is the set of possible properties used to describe the state of the environment.*

---

[5] We refer to an active norm whose deontic operator is an obligation as an *active obligation*. The same applies to prohibitions.

[6] An additional discussion about sanctions in norms can be found in [8].

It is important to observe that the set $\mathcal{X}$ is just a representation of the elements of the environment.[7] For example, when a SAI specification contains an event $e_\mathcal{X} \in \mathcal{E}_\mathcal{X}$, it does not mean that the event $e_\mathcal{X}$ has happened in the environment. Rather, it means that the designer of the institution assumes that $e_\mathcal{X}$ may happen.

From $\mathcal{X}$ we introduce also the environment-formulas (e-formulas), that are important to express the conditions under which the constitutive rules perform the assignments of status functions. An e-formula $w_\mathcal{X} \in W_\mathcal{X}$ is a logical formula defined as:

$$w_\mathcal{X} ::= s_\mathcal{X} | e_\mathcal{X} | \neg w_\mathcal{X} | w_\mathcal{X} \vee w_\mathcal{X} | w_\mathcal{X} \wedge w_\mathcal{X} | \bot | \top$$

Informally, an e-formula $e_\mathcal{X}$ holds when the event $e_\mathcal{X}$ happens in the environment. For instance, the e-formula *offer($100)* is true when the speech act *offer($100)* is performed by an agent. The interpretation of $s_\mathcal{X}$ in e-formulas is similar.

Having introduced the e-formulas, it is possible to define the constitutive rules.

Definition 5. $\mathcal{C}$ *is the set of constitutive rules of a SAI. A constitutive rule* $c \in \mathcal{C}$ *is a tuple* $\langle x, y, t, m \rangle$ *meaning that* $x \in \mathcal{F} \cup \mathcal{X} \cup \{\varepsilon\}$ *counts as (i.e. x has the status function)* $y \in \mathcal{F}$ *when the event* $t \in \mathcal{E}_\mathcal{F} \cup \mathcal{E}_\mathcal{X} \cup \{\varepsilon\}$ *has happened and while* $m \in W$ *holds (where* $W = W_\mathcal{F} \cup W_\mathcal{X}$).[8]

While in Searle's theory, the context of constitutive rules is true when generic circumstances c hold, we consider that the context is true (i) when some event t has happened and (ii) while m holds. A constitutive rule is read as x count-as y when t while m. In the case of $t = \varepsilon \wedge m = \top$, the constitutive rule is simply read as x count-as y since y is assigned to x in any circumstance.

The count-as relation performs the *constitution* of the status function y as follows:

– *Constitution by assignment of a status function y to an element x.* This kind of constitution applies to rules where $x \neq \varepsilon$. In this case, the status function y is assigned to an existing element x, that may be either a concrete element belonging to the environment or another status function. For example the rule $< bob, bidder, offer(10), auction\_running >$ is an example of assignment of status function to a concrete element: it means that the agent bob carries the status function of bidder after having uttered its offer and while the auction is running. An example of assignment of status function to another status function is the rule $< bidder, auction\_participant, \varepsilon, \varepsilon >$: it assigns the status function of *auction_participant* to the agents that have the status function of *bidder*.
– *Creation of freestanding status function.* This kind of constitution applies to rules where $x = \varepsilon$. In this case, there is not an element that carries the status function. Rather, the constitutive rules just state that the status function exists in a certain context. For example the rule $< \varepsilon, auction\_running, \varepsilon, \neg auction\_finished) >$ means that the property *auction_running* holds in the institution when the property *auction_finished* does not hold. In this case, there is not any property in

---

[7] It is beyond of the scope of this paper to deal in details with the environment. We just consider the elements of $\mathcal{X}$ as existing outside the institution, being available thanks to reliable interfaces.

[8] ε represents that the element is not present in the constitutive rule.

the environment that carries the status function of $auction\_running$. The idea of elements that exists in the institution but do not have a corresponding in the environment is recognized by Searle [23,24] and by other related authors [16,25,16].

Semantics of Formulas. While the previous sections just presents the sets $W_{\mathcal{F}}$ and $W_{\mathcal{X}}$ of formulas, this section explains their semantics.

The set of status functions assignments (i.e. the grounding of the status functions in the environment) is represented by $\mathcal{G} = \{\mathcal{A}_{\mathcal{G}}, \mathcal{E}_{\mathcal{G}}, \mathcal{S}_{\mathcal{G}}\}$ where (i) $< a_{\mathcal{F}}, a_{\mathcal{X}} >$ belongs to $\mathcal{A}_{\mathcal{G}}$ when the status function $a_{\mathcal{F}} \in \mathcal{A}_{\mathcal{F}}$ is assigned to an agent $a_{\mathcal{X}} \in \mathcal{A}_{\mathcal{X}}$, (ii) $< e_{\mathcal{F}}, e_{\mathcal{X}} >$ belongs to $\mathcal{E}_{\mathcal{G}}$ when the status function $e_{\mathcal{F}} \in \mathcal{E}_{\mathcal{F}}$ is assigned to an event $e_{\mathcal{X}} \in \mathcal{E}_{\mathcal{X}}$, (iii) $< s_{\mathcal{F}}, s_{\mathcal{X}} >$ belongs to $\mathcal{S}_{\mathcal{G}}$ when the status function $s_{\mathcal{F}} \in \mathcal{S}_{\mathcal{F}}$ is assigned to a property $s_{\mathcal{X}} \in \mathcal{S}_{\mathcal{X}}$, and (iv) $< s_{\mathcal{F}}, \varepsilon >$ belongs to $\mathcal{S}_{\mathcal{G}}$ when $s_{\mathcal{F}} \in \mathcal{S}_{\mathcal{F}}$ is a freestanding y existing in the institution.

Assuming that the history of a running system is given by a sequence of states, we use $\mathcal{G}^t = \{\mathcal{A}_{\mathcal{G}}^t, \mathcal{E}_{\mathcal{G}}^t, \mathcal{S}_{\mathcal{G}}^t\}$ to refer to the assignments of status functions in the tth state. The truth-value of a formula $w_{\mathcal{F}}$, considering the assignments $\mathcal{G}$ at the tth state of the execution of the system, is given by:

- $\mathcal{G}^t \models w_{\mathcal{F}}$ if $w_{\mathcal{F}} \in \mathcal{S}_{\mathcal{F}} \wedge \exists x :< w_{\mathcal{F}}, x >\in \mathcal{S}_{\mathcal{G}}^t$;
- $\mathcal{G}^t \models w_{\mathcal{F}}$ if $w_{\mathcal{F}} \in \mathcal{E}_{\mathcal{F}} \wedge \exists x :< w_{\mathcal{F}}, x >\in \mathcal{E}_{\mathcal{G}}^t$;
- $\mathcal{G}^t \models x$ is f if $f \in \mathcal{A}_{\mathcal{F}} \wedge\ < f, x >\in \mathcal{A}_{\mathcal{G}}^t$;
- $\mathcal{G}^t \models x$ is f if $f \in \mathcal{S}_{\mathcal{F}} \wedge\ < f, x >\in \mathcal{S}_{\mathcal{G}}^t$;
- $\mathcal{G}^t \models x$ is f if $f \in \mathcal{E}_{\mathcal{F}} \wedge\ < f, x >\in \mathcal{E}_{\mathcal{G}}^t$;

The satisfaction of $\perp$ (*false*), $\top$ (*true*), and boolean connectives runs as usual.

The evaluation of formulas in $W_{\mathcal{X}}$ is based on environmental elements. Considering Σ_e^t as the set of events occurring in the environment at the instant t and Σ_s^t as the state of the environmental properties at the instant t, the truth value of $w_{\mathcal{X}}$ at t is given by:

- $\Sigma^t \models w_{\mathcal{X}}$ if $w_{\mathcal{X}} \in \mathcal{S}_{\mathcal{X}} \wedge w_{\mathcal{X}} \in \Sigma_s^t$;
- $\Sigma^t \models w_{\mathcal{X}}$ if $w_{\mathcal{X}} \in \mathcal{E}_{\mathcal{X}} \wedge w_{\mathcal{X}} \in \Sigma_e^t$;

4   Language to Specify SAI

Besides the conceptual model presented in the Section 3, another contribution of this work is a language to specify SAI. The specification of a SAI, using the elements previously introduced, has two parts. The first one is the *normative specification*, that defines norms based on the status functions and state expressions, which are the elements that can be specified regardless of the environment. The second one is the *constitutive specification*, that defines the constitution of status functions from the environmental elements through constitutive rules, providing situatedness to the SAI. This twofoldness provides independence between normative and constitutive parts of the specification: the constitution of the status function may change without changing the norms. The opposite is also true: norms may change as long as the status functions stay the same.

The normative specification is written based on the syntax given in Figure 2 and defines the set of status functions ($\mathcal{F}$) and norms ($\mathcal{N}$) of the institution. The set $\mathcal{F}$ may have agent-, event-, and state-status functions. Norms follow the Definition 3: when the condition c is true, the norm becomes active and an agent carrying the status function a must to achieve or avoid (accordingly to the deontic operator d) the aim i before the deadline ρ, otherwise the consequence o becomes true.

$$
\begin{aligned}
normative\_spec &::= intitution\_id \ \mathcal{F} \ \mathcal{N} \\
institution\_id &::= \texttt{institution\_id:} \ inst\_name \ . \\
\mathcal{F} &::= \texttt{status\_functions:} \ \mathcal{A}_\mathcal{F}? \ \mathcal{E}_\mathcal{F}? \ \mathcal{S}_\mathcal{F}? \\
\mathcal{N} &::= \texttt{norms:} \ norm+ \\
\mathcal{A}_\mathcal{F} &::= \texttt{agents:} \ a_\mathcal{F}(, a_\mathcal{F}) * . \\
\mathcal{E}_\mathcal{F} &::= \texttt{events:} \ e_\mathcal{F}(, e_\mathcal{F}) * . \\
\mathcal{S}_\mathcal{F} &::= \texttt{states:} \ s_\mathcal{F}(, s_\mathcal{F}) * . \\
norm &::= id: \ c: \ a \, d \, i \ (\texttt{until} \ \rho)? \ (\texttt{else} \ o)?. \\
c &::= w_\mathcal{F} \\
a &::= a_\mathcal{F} \\
d &::= \texttt{obliged|prohibited|permitted} \\
i &::= w_\mathcal{F} \\
\rho &::= w_\mathcal{F} \\
o &::= w_\mathcal{F} \\
inst\_name &::= atom \\
id &::= atom \\
w_\mathcal{F} &::= s_\mathcal{F}|e_\mathcal{F}|\neg w_\mathcal{F}|w_\mathcal{F} \vee w_\mathcal{F}|w_\mathcal{F} \wedge w_\mathcal{F}|x \ \textbf{is} \ f|\bot|\top \\
a_\mathcal{F} &::= atom \\
e_\mathcal{F} &::= predicate \\
s_\mathcal{F} &::= predicate
\end{aligned}
$$

Fig. 2. Grammar of the normative specification

The constitutive specification, written based on the syntax given in Figure 3, models the set $\mathcal{C}$ of the constitutive rules of the SAI. In order to keep independence between normative and constitutive specifications, a constitutive specification refers to the normative specification that it is constituting through the element $normative\_id$. Each constitutive rule (*const_rule* in the grammar) has an identifier (*id*). Besides, the rules have the operator `count-as`, that performs the constitution of the status function identified in the y. Notice that the elements related to the context of the constitutive rule (t and m) are optional. Constitutive rules follow the Definition 5: the element x carries the status function y after the happening of the event t while m holds.

4.1 Example

As the formal semantics of the aforedescribed language is beyond the scope of this paper, we use an example to illustrate its dynamics. The Figure 4 shows a normative

$$const\_model ::= intra\_inst\_id\ C$$
$$normative\_id ::= \text{institution\_id} : instit\_id\ .$$
$$C ::= \text{constitutive\_rules:}\ const\_rule+$$
$$const\_rule ::= id : count\_as\_stat\ t?\ m?\ .$$
$$count\_as\_stat ::= ((a_{\mathcal{F}}|a_{\mathcal{X}})\ \text{count-as}\ a_{\mathcal{F}})\ |$$
$$((e_{\mathcal{F}}|e_{\mathcal{X}})\ \text{count-as}\ e_{\mathcal{F}})\ |$$
$$((s_{\mathcal{F}}|s_{\mathcal{X}})?\ \text{count-as}\ s_{\mathcal{F}})$$
$$t ::= \text{when}\quad e_{\mathcal{F}}|e_{\mathcal{X}}$$
$$m ::= \text{while}\ w$$
$$instit\_id ::= atom$$
$$w ::= w_{\mathcal{X}}|w_{\mathcal{F}}$$
$$w_{\mathcal{X}} ::= s_{\mathcal{X}}|e_{\mathcal{X}}|\neg w_{\mathcal{X}}|w_{\mathcal{X}} \vee w_{\mathcal{X}}|w_{\mathcal{X}} \wedge w_{\mathcal{X}}|\bot|\top$$

Fig. 3. Grammar of the constitutive specification

specification of SAI related to an auction scenario. The lines 3-9 define the status functions. Agents may have the function of *auctioneer*, *bidder*, *current_winner* (the agent that has placed the best offer before the finish of the auction) and *winner*. An agent may have more than one status function (e.g. the winner is also a bidder). The following event-status functions are defined for this scenario: (i) *to_pay*, that refers to the payment for an offer, (ii) *to_fine_winner*, that refers to the event of fining the winner when it does not pay its offer and (iii) *to_bid*, that refers to the performance of a bid. Finally, the state-status functions *auction_running* and *auction_finished* are defined to represent the two phases of an auction while the state-status function *current_value* points to the value of the best bid during the auction.

The normative specification defines three norms. The norm 1 states that when the auction is finished, the winner is obliged to pay its offer and, otherwise, it is fined with a fixed value. The norm 2 states that when the auction is running, bidders are permitted to bid. The norm 3 states that when the event *to_fine_winner* happens, the winner is obliged to pay its offer before a new auction starts.[9] As explained before, the norms do not refer to any specific environmental element: the sets of norms and status functions do not specify what *constitutes* finished auction, winner, payment, bidder, etc.

The constitutive specification (Figure 5) defines the constitution for the scenario. We explain here some rules of the constitutive specification. The rule 1 specifies that an agent has the status function of auctioneer when it has uttered a propose for an auction if there is not another auctioneer, and the agent keeps this function until the auction is finished.[10] By the rule 2, an auction is running until it is finished. By the rule 3 any agent (except the auctioneer) is a bidder while the auction is running. The rule 4 specifies that the auction is finished when the auctioneer says "The auction is finished". Notice that such phrase only finishes the auction if it is said by the agent that carries the status function of auctioneer. If the phrase is said by another agent, there is not any change

---

[9] Identifiers starting with an uppercase letter or the underscore (_) are variables.

[10] The negation is handled using the *closed world assumption*, where something that cannot be proved as true is considered false[20].

```
1    institution_id : auctionInst.
2
3    status_functions:
4       agents:
5          auctioneer, bidder, current_winner, winner.
6       events:
7          to_pay(Value), to_fine_winner(Value), to_bid.
8       states:
9          auction_running, auction_finished, current_value.
10   norms:
11      1: auction_finished:
12             winner obliged to_pay(current_value) else to_fine_winner(100).
13      2: auction_running:
14             bidder permitted to_bid .
15      3: to_fine_winner(Value):
16             winner obliged to_pay(Value) until auction_ready.
```

Fig. 4. Normative specification of the auction scenario

in the institutional state. The rule 5 specify that the utterance of an offer by an agent having the status function of bidder means, in the institution, a bid. The rule 6 assigns the status function *current_winner* to the agent that says "I offer..." when the auction is running, if the agent has the status function of *bidder*, and if the offered value is greater than the last offered value. The rule 7 states that the value offered by a bidder becomes the current value of the auction if it is greater that the last current value.

Discussion of the Example. The agents can use the specifications of the figures 4 and 5 to reason about how to act in the system. For example, by the constitutive rule 3, an agent knows when it is considered a bidder and, thus, by the constitutive rule 5 and the norm 2, it knows when it can to bid and how to act to perform the bid (i.e. uttering an *offer*). Similarly, by the rule 8 the agents know what constitutes the winner, by the constitutive rule 9, they know how the constituted winner must act to comply with the norm 1.

The twofold specification provides independence between the normative specification and the environment. The original constitutive specification could be, for instance, replaced by another one where the bids are done through the operation *doOffer* of an electronic artifact. In this case, the rules 5-7 of the Figure 5 would be replaced by the ones of the Figure 6. Similarly, the bids could be done both through telling the offers and through the electronic artifact. In this case, the rules 5-7 of the Figure 6 should be added to the constitutive specification of the Figure 5.

The example of the Figure 5 shows, with rules 2 and 4, a status function assignment of type "freestanding Y" [23]. In this case, a status function becomes true in the institution, but there is not a concrete element that carries such function.

In the normative specification (Figure 4), the *or-else* element of the norm 1 is the same event that activates the norm 3. There is here a norm attachment. When the norm 1 is violated, the institution expects that the event to_fine_winner is produced in the environment. When such event happens, the norm 3 is activated. Notice that the norm 3 is activated when the event to_fine_winner occurs in the environment rather than when institution detects the violation of the norm 1.

```
1    institution_id   : auctionInst.
2
3    constitutive rules:
4        1: Agent count-as auctioneer
5              when propose(Agent, auction)
6              while ((not _ is auctioneer) | (Agent is auctioneer)) &
7                    not auction_finished
8        2: count-as auction_running
9              while not auction_finished.
10       3: Agent count-as bidder
11             while (not Agent is auctioneer) &
12                   auction_running.
13       4: count-as auction_finished
14             when tell(Agent, "The auction is finished")
15             while Agent is auctioneer.
16       5: offer(Agent,Value) count-as to_bid
17             while auction_running & Agent is bidder.
18       6: Agent count-as current_winner
19             when offer(Agent,Value)
20             while Agent is bidder &
21                   (not (Current is current_value & Current>Value))&
22                   auction_running.
23       7: Value count-as current_value
24             when offer(Agent,Value)
25             while Agent is bidder &
26                   (not (Current is current_value & Current>Value))&
27                   auction_running.
28       8: Agent count-as winner
29             while Agent is current_winner &
30                   auction_finished.
31       9: sendDepositRecipt count-as to_pay.
32      10: sendFineWarning(Agent,Value) count-as to_fine_winner(Value)
33             while Agent is winner.
```

Fig. 5. Constitutive specification of the auction scenario

```
1    institution_id   : auctionInst.
2               ...
3               ...
4               ...
5        5: doOffer(Agent,Value) count-as to_bid
6              while auction_running.
7        6: Ag count-as current_winner
8           when doOffer(Agent,Value)
9           while Agent is bidder &
10               (not Current is current_value & Current>Value)&
11               auction_running.
12       7: Value count-as current_value
13          when doOffer(Agent,Value)
14          while Agent is bidder &
15               (not Current is current_value & Current>Value)&
16               auction_running.
```

Fig. 6. Constitutive rules for bid through electronic artifact

5   Discussion and Future Work

The problem motivating this paper is the conceiving of institutions where the whole regulation is based on environmental elements. Considering this problem, we propose the conceptual meta-model of Situated Artificial Institution (SAI). A SAI is composed of norms, status functions and constitutive rules. If the whole expected behaviour is defined through norms and norms are composed of status functions, which are constituted from the environment through constitutive rules, then the whole institutional regulation is based on environmental elements. The main advantages of such conception are (i) the possibility of to design an institution where situatedness is part of the model and (ii) the possibility of the agents to reason about how to concretely act in compliance with all institutional expectations. This conception is an adaptation, from a particular point of view, of Searle's theory, which claims that a system of status functions, norms (or deontic powers), and constitutive rules supports the whole human social reality. In human societies such system is (i) *internal*, as people have particular representations of the social reality, i.e. they do not necessarily reason in terms of status functions, norms, etc, and (ii) *implicit*, as it is built on top of people's mental states (that believe, for instance, that a certain man is the king). In the proposed model, status functions, norms and constitutive rules compose a system (i) *explicit*, as it is properly specified through institutional concepts and (ii) *external*, as it is persisted outside the agents mind.[11]

Norms and status functions allow to specify the expected behaviour of the agents abstracting from concrete agents and other environmental elements that will compose the system. This is important in open MAS, where these elements are not necessarily known at design time [3,27]. Different from our proposal, other models consider different abstractions to this high level representation of the MAS regulation. For example, roles represent behaviour patterns for the agents, organizational goals represent actions and states that agents should produce, interaction scenes define ordered actions to be followed by the agents to achieve some goal, etc. Status functions, on their turn, are in a different abstraction level, as they are just abstract representations to (i) agents that act in the system, (ii) events occurring in the environment and (iii) states that hold in the environment. Status functions can be viewed as an abstraction of the concrete environment on top which norms are specified. An investigation about how the system of status functions and norms can support more complex social abstractions (roles, goals, scenes, etc) is a future work.

While the system of status functions and norms allows to abstract all elements related to the system regulation, the constitutive rules relate this abstract level to the environment. The use of status functions as a well defined and limited set of abstractions of elements under institutional regulation enables someone to clearly define how the whole institution is situated. Instead of situating a large (or even undefined) set of complex institutional abstractions, we situate just status functions. As the norms are composed of status functions that are explicitly related to the environment, agents can use the institutional specification to reason about how their concrete actions lead to violations and fulfilments of norms.

---

[11] A discussion of explicitness and externality in institutional models is found in [11].

The elements of SAI allow the specification of institutions in two phases. Firstly, the norms that govern the institution are defined in terms of status functions. At this point of the design, there is not relation between institution and environment. In a further step, constitutive rules connect status functions to the environment, defining the concrete elements that carry status functions and are present in the institutional norms. With this arrangement, there is an independence between normative and constitutive elements of the institution. This independence may seem conflicting to our initial assumption that, in SAI, all basic elements are situated. But that assumption remains, as status functions are conceived to be situated (or constituted) and a possible unsituated status function is related to the particular specification of an institution rather than to the SAI model. With proposed arrangement of SAI elements, the model has itself sufficient elements to specify the constitution of institutional elements. This is coherent with our concept of institution as a set of mechanisms regulating a system: the definition of the constitution of the institutional elements is directly related to the regulating tasks. This is also coherent with Searle's view of institutions arising from the constitution of the institutional elements.

This work addresses the theoretical aspects of SAI. As future work, we plan to explore additional theoretical aspects related to the model, such as (i) the operational semantics of the proposed language, (ii) the verification of the consistency among norms, status functions and constitutive rules, (iii) investigations about how other proposed institutional abstractions fit on SAI, and (iv) how the SAI regulation concretely affects the environment. We plan also to address more practical points as (i) the implementation of an interpreter for the normative and constitutive programs, (ii) the modelling of a SAI based on a real institutional scenario, and (iii) the integration of SAI in an MAS platform. A deeper work on agents reasoning about SAI is also planned to the future.

Acknowledgments. The authors are grateful for the support given by CAPES (grant number CAPES-PVE 7608136) and CNPq (grant number 140261/2013-3). The authors thank Rafael Bordini, Jerusa Marchi, José E. R. Cury, and A. C. Rocha Costa for the valuable discussions related to this work.

References

1. Aldewereld, H., Álvarez-Napagao, S., Dignum, F., Vázquez-Salceda, J.: Making norms concrete. In: van der Hoek, W., Kaminka, G.A., Lespérance, Y., Luck, M., Sen, S. (eds.) Proc. 9th International Conference on Autonomous Agents and Multiagent Systems, pp. 807–814
2. Aldewereld, H., Alvarez-Napagao, S., Dignum, F., Vázquez-Salceda, J.: Engineering Social Reality with Inheritance Relations. In: Aldewereld, H., Dignum, V., Picard, G. (eds.) ESAW 2009. LNCS, vol. 5881, pp. 116–131. Springer, Heidelberg (2009)
3. Aldewereld, H., Dignum, V.: OperettA: Organization-oriented development environment. In: Dastani, M., El Fallah Seghrouchni, A., Hübner, J., Leite, J. (eds.) LADS 2010. LNCS, vol. 6822, pp. 1–18. Springer, Heidelberg (2011)
4. Artikis, A., Pitt, J., Sergot, M.: Animated specifications of computational societies. In: Proceedings of the First International Joint Conference on Autonomous Agents and Multiagent Systems: Part 3, AAMAS 2002, pp. 1053–1061. ACM, New York (2002)
5. Boissier, O., Hübner, J.F., Sichman, J.S.: Organization Oriented Programming: From Closed to Open Organizations. In: O'Hare, G.M.P., Ricci, A., O'Grady, M.J., Dikenelli, O. (eds.) ESAW 2006. LNCS (LNAI), vol. 4457, pp. 86–105. Springer, Heidelberg (2007)

6. de Brito, M., Hübner, J.F., Bordini, R.H.: Programming institutional facts in multi-agent systems. In: Aldewereld, H., Sichman, J.S. (eds.) COIN 2012. LNCS, vol. 7756, pp. 158–173. Springer, Heidelberg (2013)
7. Campos, J., López-Sánchez, M., Rodríguez-Aguilar, J.A., Esteva, M.: Formalising Situatedness and Adaptation in Electronic Iinstitutions. In: Hübner, J.F., Matson, E., Boissier, O., Dignum, V. (eds.) COIN 2008. LNCS, vol. 5428, pp. 126–139. Springer, Heidelberg (2009)
8. Crawford, S.E.S., Ostrom, E.: A Grammar of Institutions. The American Political Science Review 89(3), 582–600 (1995)
9. Dastani, M., Grossi, D., Meyer, J.-J.C., Tinnemeier, N.: Normative Multi-agent Programs and Their Logics. In: Meyer, J.-J.C., Broersen, J. (eds.) KRAMAS 2008. LNCS, vol. 5605, pp. 16–31. Springer, Heidelberg (2009)
10. Dastani, M., van der Torre, L., Yorke-Smith, N.: Monitoring interaction in organisations. In: Aldewereld, H., Sichman, J.S. (eds.) COIN 2012. LNCS, vol. 7756, pp. 17–34. Springer, Heidelberg (2013)
11. Dignum, V., Aldewereld, H., Dignum, F.: On the Engineering of Multi Agent Organizations. In: Weyns, D., Müller, J.P. (eds.) 12th International Workshop on Agent-Oriented Software Engineering (AOSE@AAMAS 2011), pp. 53–65 (2011)
12. Esteva, M., Rosell, B., Rodriguez-Aguilar, J.A., Arcos, J.L.: Ameli: An agent-based middleware for electronic institutions (2004)
13. Fornara, N., Viganò, F., Verdicchio, M., Colombetti, M.: Artificial institutions: a model of institutional reality for open multiagent systems. Artificial Intelligence and Law 16(1) (2008)
14. Grossi, D., Aldewereld, H., Vázquez-Salceda, J., Dignum, F.: Ontological aspects of the implementation of norms in agent-based electronic institutions. Computational & Mathematical Organization Theory 12(2-3), 251–275 (2006)
15. Grossi, D., Meyer, J.-J.C., Dignum, F.: Counts-as: Classification or Constitution? An Answer Using Modal Logic. In: Goble, L., Meyer, J.-J.C. (eds.) DEON 2006. LNCS (LNAI), vol. 4048, pp. 115–130. Springer, Heidelberg (2006)
16. Hindriks, F.: But where is the university? Dialectica 66(1), 93–113 (2012)
17. Hübner, J.F., Boissier, O., Kitio, R., Ricci, A.: Instrumenting multi-agent organisations with organisational artifacts and agents. Autonomous Agents and Multi-Agent Systems 20(3), 369–400 (2009)
18. Piunti, M.: Designing and Programming Organizational Infrastructures for Agents situated in Artifact-based Environments. PhD thesis, Universit á di Bologna (2009)
19. Piunti, M., Boissier, O., Hübner, J.F., Ricci, A.: Embodied organizations: a unifying perspective in programming agents, organizations and environments. In: MALLOW (2010)
20. Reiter, R.: On closed world data bases. In: Logic and Data Bases, pp. 55–76 (1977)
21. Ricci, A., Piunti, M., Viroli, M.: Environment programming in multi-agent systems: an artifact-based perspective. Autonomous Agents and Multi-Agent Systems 23(2), 158–192 (2011)
22. Russell, S., Norvig, P.: Artificial Intelligence: A Modern Approach, 2nd edn. Prentice-Hall, Englewood Cliffs (2003)
23. Searle, J.: The Construction of Social Reality. Free Press (1995)
24. Searle, J.: Making the Social World: The Structure of Human Civilization. Oxford University Press (2009)
25. Smith, B., Searle, J.: The Construction of Social Reality: An Exchange. American Journal of Economics and Sociology 62(1), 285–309 (2003)
26. Weyns, D., Omicini, A., Odell, J.: Environment as a first-class abstraction in multiagent systems. Autonomous Agents and Multi-Agent Systems 14(1), 5–30 (2007)
27. Zambonelli, F., Jennings, N.R., Wooldridge, M.J.: Organizational abstractions for the analysis and design of multi-agent systems. In: Ciancarini, P., Wooldridge, M.J. (eds.) AOSE 2000. LNCS, vol. 1957, pp. 235–251. Springer, Heidelberg (2001)

Evolving Bridge Rules
in Evolving Multi-Context Systems

Ricardo Gonçalves, Matthias Knorr, and João Leite

CENTRIA & Departamento de Informática, Faculdade Ciências e Tecnologia
Universidade Nova de Lisboa, Portugal

Abstract. In open environments, agents need to reason with knowledge from various sources, represented in different languages. Managed Multi-Context Systems (mMCSs) allow for the integration of knowledge from different heterogeneous sources in an effective and modular way, where so-called bridge rules express how information flows between the contexts. The problem is that mMCSs are essentially static as they were not designed to run in a dynamic scenario. Some recent approaches, among them evolving Multi-Context Systems (eMCSs), extend mMCSs by allowing not only the ability to integrate knowledge represented in heterogeneous KR formalisms, but at the same time to both react to, and reason in the presence of commonly temporary dynamic observations, and evolve by incorporating new knowledge. These approaches, however, only consider the dynamics of the knowledge bases, whereas the dynamics of the bridge rules, i.e., the dynamics of how the information flows, is neglected. In this paper, we fill this gap by building upon the framework of eMCSs by further extending it with the ability to update the bridge rules of each context taking into account an incoming stream of observed bridge rules. We show that several desirable properties are satisfied in our framework, and that the important problem of consistency management can be dealt with in our framework.

1 Introduction

In *Open Multi-Agent Systems*, the paradigm for knowledge representation and reasoning (KRR) is rapidly changing from one where each agent has its own monolithic knowledge base written in some language into one where each agent has to deal with several external heterogeneous sources of knowledge, possibly written in different languages (see, e.g.,[1,22,25] and references therein). These sources of knowledge include the large number of available ontologies and rule sets, as well as the norms and policies published by the *institutions*, the information communicated by other agents, to name only a few.

Each agent needs to be able to deal with such distributed sources of knowledge, taking into account the interactions and possible flows of information between them. For example, the agent may use inferences drawn from some ontology to justify the conclusions drawn from some rules in another knowledge base; or the agent may use some piece of information published by some other agent

N. Bulling et al. (Eds.): CLIMA XV, LNAI 8624, pp. 52–69, 2014.

to infer that some action it is about to undertake will not violate some norm published by some institution. Unlike approaches that aim to integrate several knowledge bases to obtain a common view of the system, our focus is on how a particular agent can integrate several knowledge bases to obtain its own view of the system. One consequence of our focus is that no coordination between agents is involved since the way knowledge bases are combined, how they interact, and how information flows between them, is internal, and ultimately private, to the agent in question.

Two common ways of integrating heterogeneous knowledge exist, namely either relying on hybrid languages (e.g., [20,27], and [24] with its reasoner NoHR [23]), to which other languages can be translated, or modular approaches (e.g., [9,14]) in which different formalisms and knowledge bases are considered as modules, and means are provided to model the flow of information between them. Among the latter, Multi-Context Systems (MCSs) [9,19,28] are particularly general and have gained some attention by agent developers [7,12,29].

MCSs consist of a set of contexts, each of which is a knowledge base in some KR formalism, such that each context can access information from other contexts using so-called bridge rules. Such non-monotonic bridge rules add their head to the context's knowledge base provided the queries (to other contexts) in the bodies are successful. Managed Multi-Context Systems (mMCSs) were introduced in [10] to extend MCSs by allowing operations, other than simple addition, to appear in the heads of bridge rules. This allows mMCSs to properly deal with the problem of consistency management within contexts.

A recent challenge for KR languages is the shift from static scenarios which assume a one-shot computation, usually triggered by a user query, to open and dynamic scenarios where there is a need to react and evolve in the presence of incoming information. Examples include EVOLP [2], Reactive ASP [17,16], C-SPARQL [6], Ontology Streams [26] and ETALIS [4], to name only a few.

Whereas mMCSs are quite general and flexible to address the problem of integration of different KR formalisms, they are essentially static in the sense that the contexts do not evolve to incorporate the changes in the dynamic scenarios. In such scenarios, new knowledge and information is dynamically produced, often from several different sources – for example a stream of raw data produced by some sensors, new ontological axioms written by some user, newly found exceptions to some general rule, etc.

To address this issue, two recent frameworks, evolving Multi-Context Systems (eMCSs) [21] and reactive Multi-Context Systems (rMCSs) [8,15,11] have been proposed sharing the broad motivation of designing general and flexible frameworks inheriting from mMCSs the ability to integrate and manage knowledge represented in heterogeneous KR formalisms, and at the same time be able to incorporate knowledge obtained from dynamic observations.

Whereas some differences set eMCSs and rMCSs apart, namely regarding how observations are handled, and the kind of state transitions that can be made, both focus only on the dynamics of the context's knowledge bases, thus not allowing the bridge rules of the contexts to change. However, as the world evolves, it is also quite natural that the way in which information flows between contexts be subject to change. For example, as bridge rules represent how contexts are accessed, and their knowledge used, changes in the level of trust of these contexts can lead to changes in the way their knowledge is used, i.e., changes in the bridge rules that appeal to those contexts. Even if not triggered by issues such as trust, we may simply want to change the bridge rules, e.g., by adding exceptions to existing ones. To address this drawback, we should allow the initial set of bridge rules to undergo change, at runtime, triggered by the observation of new bridge rules, which act as updates to the previous ones. This update naturally needs to go beyond the simple addition of the new rules since consistency between new and previously existing bridge rules needs to be ensured.

In this paper we fill this gap by presenting an extension to eMCSs, called bridge-rule evolving Multi-Context Systems (beMCSs), which combines the ability to both react to, and reason in the presence of commonly temporary dynamic observations, and evolve by incorporating new knowledge, inherited from eMCS, with the ability to update the bridge rules of each context, taking into account an incoming stream of observed bridge rules. We show that our framework satisfies several desirable properties and how the important problem of consistency management can be dealt with.

The remainder of this paper is structured as follows. After introducing the main concepts regarding mMCSs, we define beMCSs and prove some properties of the framework. Then, we discuss consistency management. We conclude with discussing related work and possible future directions.

Example 1 (Running example). Throughout this paper, we will illustrate some of our concepts using the scenario of an airport, where there is an agent responsible for its security.[1] Such an agent should build its knowledge based on existing knowledge distributed across several heterogeneous knowledge sources. First of all, the agent should have access to an airport ontology, which describes airport concepts, e.g., terminals, gates, etc., to avoid creating and maintaining its own. Another important component is that of the security norms, usually published by a national authority, that describe what is obligatory, permitted and forbidden with respect to airport security. As in any true multi-agent system, the agent should have a model of every other relevant agent, e.g., other security agents working in cooperation. Here, such models are meant to be the idealization the security agent has about the other agents based on observations about and communication with them. In this scenario, the security agent will have to react and evolve given incoming streams of information, e.g., provided by sensors (e.g., passengers arriving to the airport, images from cameras, etc.) or from other agents, but it should also be able to change its specification regarding how all this information flows between contexts and is combined.

---

[1] This example is partially inspired by an example presented in [25].

2   Preliminaries: Managed Multi-Context Systems

Following [9], a Multi-Context System (MCS) consists of a collection of components, each of which contains knowledge represented in some *logic*, defined as a triple $L = \langle \mathbf{KB}, \mathbf{BS}, \mathbf{ACC} \rangle$ where $\mathbf{KB}$ is the set of well-formed knowledge bases of L, $\mathbf{BS}$ is the set of possible belief sets, and $\mathbf{ACC} : \mathbf{KB} \rightarrow 2^{\mathbf{BS}}$ is a function describing the semantics of L by assigning to each knowledge base a set of acceptable belief sets. We assume that each element of $\mathbf{KB}$ and $\mathbf{BS}$ is a set, and we define $F = \{s : s \in kb \wedge kb \in \mathbf{KB}\}$.

In addition to the knowledge base in each component, *bridge rules* are used to interconnect the components, specifying what knowledge to assert in one component given certain beliefs held in the components of the MCS. Bridge rules in MCSs only allow adding information to the knowledge base of their corresponding context. In [10], an extension of MCSs, called managed Multi-Context Systems (mMCSs), is introduced in order to allow other types of operations to be performed on a knowledge base. For that purpose, each context of an mMCS is associated with a *management base*, which is a set of operations that can be applied to the possible knowledge bases of that context. Given a management base OP and a logic L, let $OF = \{op(s) : op \in OP \wedge s \in F\}$ be the *set of operational formulas* over OP and L. Each context of an mMCS gives semantics to operations in its management base using a *management function* over a logic L and a management base OP, $mng : 2^{OF} \times \mathbf{KB} \rightarrow (2^{\mathbf{KB}} \setminus \{\emptyset\})$, i.e., $mng(Op, kb)$ is the (non-empty) set of possible knowledge bases that result from applying the operations in Op to the knowledge base kb. We assume that $mng(\emptyset, kb) = \{kb\}$.

Let $L = \langle L_1, \dots, L_n \rangle$ be a sequence of logics and OP_i a management base. We denote by OF_i the set of operational formulas over OP_i and L_i. Then a *bridge rule* σ for L_i and OP_i over L, $1 \leq i \leq n$, is a rule of the form $op(s) \leftarrow a_1, \dots, a_k, \mathbf{not}\ a_{k+1}, \dots, \mathbf{not}\ a_n$, where $op(s) \in OF_i$, and, for each $1 \leq i \leq n$, a_i is of the form $(r{:}b)$ where $r \in \{1, \dots, n\}$ and b is a belief formula of L_r. Given a bridge rule σ of the above form, the head and the body of σ are defined as $H(\sigma) = op(s)$ and $B(\sigma) = \{a_1, \dots, a_k, \mathbf{not}\ a_{k+1}, \dots, \mathbf{not}\ a_n\}$, respectively. As we will specify below, intuitively, the operational formula in the head will be applied to the knowledge base using mng if all elements in the body are in accordance with the beliefs held in the corresponding contexts r.

Putting all the above together, a *managed Multi-Context System* (mMCS) is a sequence $M = \langle C_1, \dots, C_n \rangle$, where each C_i, $1 \leq i \leq n$, called a *managed context*, is defined as $C_i = \langle L_i, kb_i, br_i, OP_i, mng_i \rangle$ where

- $L_i = \langle \mathbf{KB}_i, \mathbf{BS}_i, \mathbf{ACC}_i \rangle$ is a logic
- $kb_i \in \mathbf{KB}_i$
- OP_i is a management base
- br_i is a set of bridge rules for L_i and OP_i over $\langle L_1, \dots, L_n \rangle$
- mng_i is a management function over L_i and OP_i.

For the sake of readability, we consider a slightly restricted version of mMCSs where each $\mathbf{ACC}_i$ is a function and not a set of functions as for logic suites [10].

Example 2 (Ctd.). We now briefly sketch an mMCS for the airport scenario as outlined in Sect. 1. The idea is not to present a full detailed description of the mMCS, but rather to describe parts of the example which will help us illustrating our approach. We present a simplified modeling of the airport security agent using an mMCS with five contexts, one for each relevant entity: the airport ontology, the normative entity, the security agent, and two other agents, agent A and agent B, which work in cooperation with the security agent. The airport ontology is a Description Logic (DL) [5] context, since DLs are well-suited for hierarchical information. Both the normative institution and the security agent are modeled by Logic Programming (LP) [18] contexts, since LP is well-suited to represent rule-based languages. For simplicity, we also assume that the representation of information the security agent has about the other two agents is modeled by a context in classical logic. We now present part of the configuration of the knowledge bases of the five contexts and refer for the (standard) definitions of their logics to [13] and [10]. The knowledge base of the ontology context includes taxonomic information based on usual airport vocabulary, such as *Onboard, Flight, Passenger.* The set of taxonomic axioms, usually denoted the TBox of the ontology, contains, for example, the axiom $\exists$ *Onboard.*$\top \sqsubseteq$ *Passenger,* stating that someone onboard is a passenger. Besides the hierarchical information in the TBox, with a more static nature, the ontology can also have more dynamic data, in this case about flights, airlines, etc., usually denoted the ABox of the ontology. The ABox contains, for example, *Flight(KM101)* and *Onboard(John,KM101).*

The knowledge base of the normative context contains the LP rules:

$$TakeOffNotAllowed(f) \leftarrow Flight(f), IntDest(f), Onboard(x,f), \textbf{not } HasPassport(x)$$
$$HasPassport(x) \leftarrow Passenger(x), Passport(p), Carries(x,p)$$

The first rule states that an international flight is not allowed to take off if there is someone onboard which is not known to carry a passport. The second rule defines when a passenger has a passport.

The knowledge base of the security agent includes the rule

$$Investigate(f) \leftarrow BoardingProblem(f), \textbf{not } UnderInvestigation(f)$$

stating that the agent should investigate a flight for which there is a boarding problem and it is not known that the flight is already being investigated (by another agent). The knowledge bases of agents A and B contain the formula *Investigating(f)* whenever they are investigating flight f. Then, as we will see later, *UnderInvestigation(f)* will be added to the knowledge base of the security agent's context via bridge rules whenever *Investigating(f)* is believed true in the context of either agent A or agent B.

For an mMCS $M = \langle C_1, \ldots, C_n \rangle$, a *belief state of M* is a sequence $S = \langle S_1, \ldots, S_n \rangle$ such that each S_i is an element of $\textbf{BS}_i$. For a bridge literal $(r\!:\!b)$, $S \models (r\!:\!b)$ if $b \in S_r$ and $S \models \textbf{not}\,(r\!:\!b)$ if $b \notin S_r$; for a set of bridge literals B, $S \models B$ if $S \models L$ for every $L \in B$. We say that a bridge rule σ of a context C_i is *applicable given a belief state S of M* if S satisfies $B(\sigma)$. We can then define

$app_i(S)$, the set of heads of bridge rules of C_i which are applicable in S, by setting $app_i(S) = \{H(\sigma) : \sigma \in br_i \wedge S \models B(\sigma)\}$.

Equilibria are belief states that simultaneously assign an acceptable belief set to each context in the mMCS such that the applicable operational formulas in bridge rule heads are taken into account. Let $M = \langle C_1, \ldots, C_n \rangle$ be an mMCS and $S = \langle S_1, \ldots, S_n \rangle$ a belief state of M. Then, S is an *equilibrium* of M if, for every $1 \le i \le n$, we have $S_i \in \mathbf{ACC}_i(kb)$ for some $kb \in mng_i(app_i(S), kb_i)$.

3 Evolving Bridge Rules

Evolving Multi-Context Systems (eMCSs) [21] admit so-called *observation contexts* whose knowledge bases are constantly changing over time according to the observations made, similar, e.g., to streams of data from sensors.[2] As outlined in Sect. 1, such eMCSs do not consider potential changes in the bridge rules that may be the result of simple observations, a learning process of the agent itself or indicated by the programmer at runtime. In this section, we introduce beMCSs, that extend eMCSs by also allowing that each context receives an incoming stream of sets of such bridge rules, which is meant to incrementally update the set of bridge rules of the context. For that purpose, rather than first recalling eMCSs and then presenting its extension beMCSs, we present the combined formalism beMCSs right away and point out concrete differences when discussing the formalization of updating bridge rules.

Following [21], regarding the observations made by the observation contexts, these will also affect the other contexts by means of the bridge rules. As we will see, such effect can either be instantaneous and temporary, i.e., limited to the current time instant, similar to (static) mMCSs, where the body of a bridge rule is evaluated in a state that already includes the effects of the operation in its head, or persistent, but only affecting the next time instant. To achieve the latter, we extend the operational language with a unary meta-operation *next* that can only be applied on top of operations.

Definition 1. *The* evolving operational language *over a management base OP and a logic L is defined as* $eOF = OF \cup \{next(op(s)) : op(s) \in OF\}$.

The idea of observation contexts is that each such context has a language describing the set of possible observations of that context, along with its current observation. The elements of the language of the observation contexts can then be used in the body of bridge rules to allow contexts to access the observations. Formally, an *observation context* is a tuple $O = \langle \Pi_O, \pi \rangle$ where Π_O is the *observation language* of O and $\pi \subseteq \Pi_O$ is its *current observation*.

We can now adapt beMCSs from eMCSs.

Definition 2. *A beMCS is a sequence* $M_e = \langle C_1, \ldots, C_n, O_1, \ldots, O_\ell \rangle$, *such that each* $O_j = \langle \Pi_{O_j}, \pi_j \rangle$, $j \in \{1, \ldots, \ell\}$, *is an* observation context, *and each* evolving context C_i, $i \in \{1, \ldots, n\}$, *is defined as* $C_i = \langle L_i, kb_i, br_i, OP_i, mng_i \rangle$ *where*

---

[2] For simplicity of presentation, discrete steps in time are considered.

- $L_i = \langle \mathbf{KB}_i, \mathbf{BS}_i, \mathbf{ACC}_i \rangle$ *is a logic*
- $kb_i \in \mathbf{KB}_i$
- br_i *is a set of bridge rules of the form*
$$H(\sigma) \leftarrow a_1, \ldots, a_k, \mathbf{not}\ a_{k+1}, \ldots, \mathbf{not}\ a_n \qquad (1)$$
  such that $H(\sigma) \in eOF_i$, *and each* a_i, $i \in \{1, \ldots, n\}$, *is either of the form* $(r\!:\!b)$ *with* $r \in \{1, \ldots, n\}$ *and* b *a belief formula of* L_r, *or of the form* $(r@o)$ *with* $r \in \{1, \ldots, \ell\}$ *and* $o \in \Pi_{O_r}$
- OP_i *is a management base*
- mng_i *is a management function over* L_i *and* OP_i.

We denote by $\mathbf{BR}_i$ the set of possible bridge rules of the form (1) for C_i.

Let $M_e = \langle C_1, \ldots, C_n, O_1, \ldots, O_\ell \rangle$ be a beMCS. As for mMCSs, the notion of *belief state for* M_e is defined as a sequence $S = \langle S_1, \ldots, S_n \rangle$ such that, for each $1 \leq i \leq n$, we have $S_i \in \mathbf{BS}_i$.

The notion $app_i(S)$ of the set of heads of bridge rules of C_i which are applicable in a belief state $S = \langle S_1, \ldots, S_n \rangle$, cannot be directly transferred from mMCSs to beMCS since bridge rule bodies can now contain atoms of the form $(r@o)$, whose satisfaction depends on the current observation.

The satisfaction of bridge literals of the form $(r\!:\!b)$ carries over from mMCSs. The satisfaction of bridge literal of the form $(r@b)$ depends on the current observations, i.e., we have that $S \models (r@o)$ if $o \in \pi_r$ and $S \models \mathbf{not}\ (r@o)$ if $o \notin \pi_r$. As before, for a set B of bridge literals, we have $S \models B$ if $S \models L$ for every $L \in B$.

We say that a bridge rule σ of a context C_i is *applicable given a belief state* S for M_e if $S \models B(\sigma)$. Then, given a belief state S for M_e and a set br of bridge rules for M_e, we can define $app(S, br) = \{H(\sigma) : \sigma \in br$ and $S \models B(\sigma)\}$, the set of heads of bridge rules in br which are applicable given S.

Recall that the heads of bridge rules in a beMCS are more expressive than in an mMCS, since they may be of two types: those that contain *next* and those that do not. As already mentioned, the former are to be applied to the current knowledge base and not persist, whereas the latter are to be applied in the next time instant and persist. Therefore, we distinguish these two subsets of $app(S, br)$ by setting:

Definition 3. *Let* $M_e = \langle C_1, \ldots, C_n, O_1, \ldots, O_\ell \rangle$ *be a beMCS,* br *a set of bridge rules with* $br \subseteq \bigcup_i \mathbf{BR}_i$, *and* S *a belief state for* M_e. *Then, consider the sets:*

- $app^{next}(S, br) = \{op(s) : next(op(s)) \in app(S, br)\}$
- $app^{now}(S, br) = \{op(s) : op(s) \in app(S, br)\}$

This definition is a generalization of Def. 3 [21] to arbitrary sets of bridge rules. Nevertheless, for the set of bridge rules of a context C_i, br_i, we can use the notation $app_i^{next}(S)$ and $app_i^{now}(S)$ as in [21] to denote, respectively, $app^{next}(S, br_i)$ and $app^{now}(S, br_i)$.

Note that we can easily model a scenario where we want an effect to be instantaneous and persistent. This can be achieved using two bridge rules with identical body, one with and one without *next* in the head.

Example 3 (Ctd.). We now sketch a beMCS modeling the airport security agent. Let $M_e = \langle C_1, C_2, C_3, C_4, C_5, O_1 \rangle$ be composed of five evolving contexts C_1, C_2,

C_3, C_4 and C_5, corresponding to the airport ontology, the normative entity, the security agent, agent A, and agent B, respectively, whose knowledge bases are partially given in Example 2. The observation context, O_1, now models incoming information arriving to the system, which allows each context, through its bridge rules, to react and evolve given such observations. For simplicity, we consider just one observation context, which is responsible for monitoring flight gates, and omit here more sophisticated observations, e.g., readings of electronic passports, images from cameras, etc. The language of O_1 contains elements such as *enterPlane(John,1234)*, stating that *John* has just entered the plane with identification *1234*.

The ontology context C_1 contains the following bridge rule:

$$next(add(Onboard(x,f))) \leftarrow 1@EnterPlane(x,p), 1: Assigned(p,f)$$

stating that if it is observed that a person enters a plane which is assigned to a flight, then this person is onboard that flight. Note the use of *next* in the head of the rule to guarantee that *Onboard(x,f)* is persistently added to the ontology.

The normative context C_2 contains the following bridge rules, importing the relevant information from the ontology context C_1:

$$upd(Flight(f)\leftarrow) \leftarrow 1: Flight(f)$$
$$upd(Onboard(x,f)\leftarrow) \leftarrow 1: Onboard(x,f)$$

Note that, to not duplicate information already in the ontology, the above rules only import information temporarily to C_2, without using the operator *next*.

The security agent context C_3 has the following bridge rules:

$$upd(UnderInvestigation(f)\leftarrow) \leftarrow 4: Investigating(f)$$
$$upd(UnderInvestigation(f)\leftarrow) \leftarrow 5: Investigating(f)$$

stating that some flight is under investigation if some of the other agents is already investigating it. Note that these rules are not meant to be persistent, since whenever *Investigating(f)* does not hold for the other agents, *UnderInvestigation(f)* should immediately not hold for the security agent.

The context of agent A, C_4, has an empty set of bridge rules, and the context of agent B, C_5, contains the following bridge rules:

$$add(goHelpSA) \leftarrow 3: NeedHelp$$
$$add(goHelpA) \leftarrow 4: NeedHelp$$

stating that agent B should help any of the other agents that asked for help.

Similar to equilibria in mMCS, the (static) equilibrium is defined to incorporate instantaneous effects based on $app_i^{now}(S)$ alone.

Definition 4. *Let* $M_e = \langle C_1, \ldots, C_n, O_1, \ldots, O_\ell \rangle$ *be a beMCS. A belief state* $S = \langle S_1, \ldots, S_n \rangle$ *for* M_e *is a* static *equilibrium of* M_e *iff for each* $1 \leq i \leq n$, *there exists some* $kb \in mng_i(app_i^{now}(S), kb_i)$ *such that* $S_i \in \mathbf{ACC}_i(kb)$.

To assign meaning to a beMCS evolving over time we consider sequences of belief states, evolving belief states, each referring to a subsequent time instant.

Definition 5. *Let M_e be a beMCS. An* evolving belief state *of size s for M_e is a sequence $\mathcal{S} = \langle S^1, \ldots, S^s \rangle$ where each S^j, $1 \leq j \leq s$, is a belief state for M_e.*

So far, apart from the generalization in Def. 3, the notions for eMCSs and beMCSs coincide. Next, we discuss how to update a beMCS, which unlike for eMCSs requires considering how to update bridge rules.

To be able to update the knowledge bases and the sets of bridge rules of the evolving contexts, we need the following notation. Given an evolving context C_i, a knowledge base $k \in \mathbf{KB}_i$ and a set of bridge rules $b \subseteq \mathbf{BR}_i$, we denote by $C_i[k, b]$ the evolving context in which kb_i and br_i are replaced by k and b respectively, i.e., $C_i[k, b] = \langle L_i, k, b, OP_i, mng_i \rangle$. For an observation context O_i, given a set $\pi \subseteq \Pi_{O_i}$ of observations for O_i, we denote by $O_i[\pi]$ the observation context in which its current observation is replaced by π, i.e., $O_i[\pi] = \langle \Pi_{O_i}, \pi \rangle$.

To enable beMCSs to react to incoming observations and evolve, an observation sequence defined in the following has to be processed. The idea is that, at each time instant, we have two types of observations. On the one hand, we have a set of observations for each observation context O_i, which is meant to replace its current observation. On the other hand, we have a set of bridge rules for each evolving context C_i, which is meant to update the set of bridge rules br_i of C_i.

Recall from the Introduction that there are two main motivations for updating the set of bridge rules of a context. One the one hand, we may want to substitute an existing rule with a more recent one, since, based for example on a change of trust, we may want to change the sources of information in a rule. On the other hand, we may want to add exceptions to existing rules. Given such motivations, and since the bridge rules in a beMCS, as in the case of mMCSs, are similar to logic programming rules, we build the updates of bridge rules upon the work done in updates of logic programs, namely on Dynamic Logic Programs (DLP) [3]. In this approach, the use of default negation in the head of rules is fundamental to allow explicit rejection of rules and also the introduction of exceptions to existing rules. Therefore, to update the set of bridge rules of a context C_i we consider more expressive bridge rules, which allow default negation in the head. Formally, for each $1 \leq i \leq n$, we consider $e\mathbf{BR}_i$, the set of *evolving bridge rules* for C_i, defined as $e\mathbf{BR}_i = \mathbf{BR}_i \cup \{\mathbf{not}\ H(\sigma) \leftarrow B(\sigma) : \sigma \in \mathbf{BR}_i\}$.

We can now define the notion of observation sequence for a beMCS.

Definition 6. *Let $M_e = \langle C_1, \ldots, C_n, O_1, \ldots, O_\ell \rangle$ be a beMCS. An* observation sequence *for M_e is a sequence $Obs = \langle \mathcal{O}^1, \ldots, \mathcal{O}^m \rangle$, where, for each $1 \leq j \leq m$, $\mathcal{O}^j = \langle o^j, obr^j \rangle$, is an* instant observation *containing observations $o^j = \langle o_1^j, \ldots, o_\ell^j \rangle$ such that, for each $1 \leq i \leq \ell$, $o_i^j \subseteq \Pi_{O_i}$, and observed bridge rules $obr^j = \langle obr_1^j, \ldots, obr_n^j \rangle$ such that, for each $1 \leq i \leq n$, $obr_i^j \subseteq e\mathbf{BR}_i$.*

Our aim now is to show how, given an observation sequence $\mathcal{O}$, the beMCS M_e is able to react and evolve. As mentioned before, the observation contexts evolve by replacing their set of current observations according to the observation sequence. We still need to define how the bridge rules of each evolving context are updated given an observation sequence. Our goal is to define for each context C_i the set $Upd(S, br, B)$ of possible updates of a set $br \subseteq \mathbf{BR}_i$ of bridge rules by a sequence $B = \langle obr_i^1, \ldots, obr_i^k \rangle$ of sets of evolving bridge rules with $obr_i^j \subseteq e\mathbf{BR}_i$ for $1 \leq j \leq k$, given the belief state S for M_e. The idea is to combine two update mechanisms, both building upon the notion of rejected bridge rule: one is based on the existence of an explicit conflict between an operation and its default negation in the head of bridge rules; the other is based on an implicit notion of inconsistency between operational formulas, which depends on each context.

To define update operators based on conflicts which arise due to the use of default negation in the head of rules we follow the ideas of DLP [3]. The intuition is that a rule σ is rejected in state S if there is a more recent rule which is applicable in S, and whose head is the default negation of the head of σ. Formally, let M_e be a beMCS, S a belief state for M_e, and $B = \langle obr_i^1, \ldots, obr_i^k \rangle$ a sequence of sets of evolving bridge rules of some evolving context C_i of M_e, i.e., each $obr_i^j \subseteq e\mathbf{BR}_i$. We can then define $ExpRej(S, \langle obr_i^1, \ldots, obr_i^k \rangle)$, the sequence of sets of bridge rules that result from B by removing the rules explicitly rejected by a more recent rule, by setting $ExpRej(S, \langle obr_i^1, \ldots, obr_i^k \rangle) = \langle Br^1, \ldots, Br^k \rangle$ such that, for each $1 \leq j \leq k$, we have $Br^j = (obr_i^j \cap \mathbf{BR}_i) \setminus Rej^j$ where

$$Rej^j = \{\sigma \in obr_i^j : \text{there is } \sigma' \in obr_i^{j'} \text{ with } j' > j \text{ such that}$$
$$H(\sigma') = \mathbf{not} \; H(\sigma) \text{ and } S \models B(\sigma')\}.$$

Example 4 (Ctd.). Continuing the airport example, suppose that the security agent no longer trusts agent A. In that case he wants to cancel the existing rule, and still investigate a flight even though agent A is already investigating it. In that case, he can update its set of bridge rules with the evolving bridge rule:

$$\mathbf{not} \; upd(UnderInvestigation(f)\leftarrow) \leftarrow 4\!:\!Investigating(f)$$

In this case, whenever $Investigating(f)$ is true in C_4 this more recent bridge rule rejects the initial one, and therefore the security agent does not update its knowledge base with the LP fact $UnderInvestigation(f)\leftarrow$.

We now focus on the notion of update of bridge rules based on a notion of implicit inconsistency between operational formulas. This makes sense since the language of the heads of bridge rules is so general and potentially quite expressive. Therefore, besides the explicit notion of rejected bridge rule mentioned above, we also consider a notion of rejected bridge rule based on a notion of inconsistency over operational formulas, which depends on each evolving context. More precisely, we assume that, for each evolving context C_i of M_e, there is a relation $Inc_i : \mathbf{BS}_i \times 2^{OF_i}$. The intuitive idea is that $\langle S_i, Op \rangle \in Inc_i$ if Op is an inconsistent set of operational formulas w.r.t. S_i. This notion of inconsistent set of operations depends on each context. Interesting examples include the case in which there is a conflict between two contrary operations, for example adding and removing, $add(p)$ and $rm(p)$. We can also have conflicts with the same operation, for example addition of two complementary literals, $add(p)$ and $add(\neg p)$.

Just as a last example, let C_i be a Classical Logic (CL) context and suppose that $OP_i = \{add\}$ where add is simple addition. We could then define Inc_i based on whether, for a set of operational formulas Op, the set $\{\varphi : add(\varphi) \in Op\}$ is consistent in CL. Given such definition, we have, for every S_i, for example that $\langle S_i, \{add(a \Rightarrow b), add(a), add(\neg b)\}\rangle \in Inc_i$.

Note that, contrarily to the above examples, there are cases where conflicts depend on the belief state. Take, for example, the case of Logic Programming (LP). The notion of conflict between LP rules depends on the belief state.

We assume that the notion of operational inconsistency satisfies the following natural condition. Given a belief state S, for all $1 \leq i \leq n$, we assume that the set $Inc_i^S = \{Op : \langle S_i, Op \rangle \in Inc_i\}$ is an upper set of the partially ordered set $\langle 2^{OF_i}, \subseteq \rangle$, i.e., if $\langle S_i, Op \rangle \in Inc_i$ and $Op \subseteq Op'$, then $\langle S_i, Op' \rangle \in Inc_i$.

Let br_1 and br_2 be two sets of bridge rules of a context C_i. Our aim is to define the possible sets of bridge rules that result from updating br_1 with br_2. For that, as we said, we define a notion of rejected rule based on operational inconsistency. Given a belief state S of M_e, we define $Rej(S, br_1, br_2)$, the set of sets of rejected bridge rules, as:

$$Rej(S, br_1, br_2) = \{b \subseteq br_1 : app^{now}(S, b \cup br_2) \in Inc_i^S \text{ or}$$
$$app^{next}(S, b \cup br_2) \in Inc_i^S\}.$$

When updating a set of rules br_1 by a set of rules br_2 we are interested in minimizing the set of rejected rules of br_1. Therefore, we consider the set $MinRej(S, br_1, br_2)$ of all minimal elements of $Rej(S, br_1, br_2)$.

Using the set of minimal set of rejected bridge rules, we can define, for a belief state S of M_e, the set of sets of acceptable bridge rules given S as:

$$Acpt(S, br_1, br_2) = \{b \subseteq br_1 : b' \not\subseteq b \text{ s.t. } \forall b' \in MinRej(S, br_1, br_2)\}.$$

The set $Acpt(S, br_1, br_2)$ is the set of all subsets of br_1 which can be consistently added to br_2 in the context of state S. As usual, when updating a set of rules br_1 by a set of rules br_2 we are interested in maximizing the set of elements of br_1 in the final result. Therefore, we define $MaxAcpt(S, br_1, br_2)$ as the set of maximal elements of $Acpt(S, br_1, br_2)$, i.e., those $b \in Acpt(S, br_1, br_2)$ for which there is no $b' \in Acpt(S, br_1, br_2)$ such that $b \subset b'$.

Example 5 (Ctd.). Recall that the context of agent B, C_5, has two bridge rules, denoted here by σ_1 and σ_2, which are meant to react to the fact that the other agents asked for help, and let $br_1 = \{\sigma_1, \sigma_2\}$. Now imagine that, for some reason (efficiency, design decision, etc.), agent B cannot help both agents at the same time. For incorporating this information, he can consider an update of br_1 by the set $br_2 = \{add(\neg(goHelpSA \wedge goHelpA)) \leftarrow 3 : NeedHelp, 4 : NeedHelp\}$. Suppose also that C_5 has the following natural inconsistency relation: for every belief state S, $\langle S_5, Op \rangle \in Inc_5$ if the set $\{p : add(p) \in Op\}$ is inconsistent in CL. Then, taking $Op = \{add(goHelpSA), add(goHelpA), add(\neg(goHelpSA \wedge goHelpA))\}$ we have, for every S, that $\langle S_5, Op \rangle \in Inc_5$. We can easily check that $MinRej(S, br_1, br_2) = \{br_1\}$. This implies that $MaxAcpt(S, br_1, br_2) =$

$\{\{\sigma_1\}, \{\sigma_2\}\}$, meaning that the possible updates of br_1 by br_2 should contain σ_1 or σ_2, but not both.

We now extend the notion of $MaxAcpt$ to sequences of sets of bridge rules:

$$MaxAcpt(S, \langle br^1, \ldots, br^k \rangle) = \{br_k : \text{ there exists } \langle b^1, \ldots, b^k \rangle \text{ satisfying}$$
$$- b^1 = br^1$$
$$- b^{j+1} = br^{j+1} \cup b \text{ where } b \in MaxAcpt(S, br^j, br^{j+1})\}.$$

The following result states the connection between the set of all maximal sets of accepted bridge rules and the set of all minimal sets of rejected rules.

Proposition 1. *Let $b \subseteq br_1$ such that $b \in MaxAcpt(S, br_1, br_2)$. Then we have that $br_1 \setminus (\bigcup MinRej(S, br_1, br_2)) \subseteq b$.*

We can now define $Upd(S, br, \langle br^1, \ldots, br^k \rangle)$ the set of possible results of updating the set br of bridge rules by the sequence $S = \langle br^1, \ldots, br^k \rangle$ of sets of evolving bridge rules. The idea is to combine the two update mechanisms described above: rejection based on conflict between an operation and its default negation, and rejection based on the operational inconsistency relation Inc_i.

Formally, given a set br of bridge rules of C_i, a sequence $B = \langle br^1, \ldots, br^k \rangle$ of sets of evolving bridge rules of C_i, and S a belief state of M_e, we can define the set $Upd(S, br, B)$ of possible results of updating br by the sequence B as:

$$Upd(S, br, B) = MaxAcpt(S, ExpRej(S, \langle br, br^1, \ldots, br^k \rangle)).$$

One basic property that we need to guarantee is that, when updating by a sequence of sets of bridge rules, the most recent bridge rules are always contained in every possible result of the update. The following result states this property, taking into account that bridge rules with default negation in the head cannot appear in the result of an update.

Proposition 2. *Let S be a belief state of M_e, br a set of bridge rules of C_i, and $B = \langle br_i^1, \ldots, br_i^k \rangle$ a sequence of sets of evolving bridge rules of C_i. Then, for every $b \in Upd(S, br, B)$, we have that $(br_i^k \cap \mathbf{BR}_i) \subseteq b$.*

Now that we have defined how the observation contexts and the sets of bridge rules evolve, we can define the notion of evolving equilibrium of a beMCS $M_e = \langle C_1, \ldots, C_n, O_1, \ldots, O_\ell \rangle$ given an observation sequence $Obs = \langle \mathcal{O}^1, \ldots, \mathcal{O}^m \rangle$ for M_e. The intuitive idea is that, given an evolving belief state $\mathcal{S} = \langle S^1, \ldots, S^s \rangle$ for M_e, in order to check if $\mathcal{S}$ is an evolving equilibrium, we need to consider a sequence of beMCSs, $M^1, \ldots, M^s$, representing a possible evolution of M_e according to the observations in Obs, such that S^j is a static equilibrium of M^j. For each M^j the sets of current observations of the observation contexts are exactly their corresponding elements π_i^j in $\mathcal{O}^j$. For each of the evolving contexts C_i, its knowledge base in M^j is obtained from the one in M^{j-1} by applying the operations in $app_i^{next}(S^{j-1})$. Moreover the set of bridge rules of each evolving context is updated using $Upd(S^j, br_i, \langle obr_i^1, \ldots, obr_i^j \rangle)$.

Definition 7. *Let $M_e = \langle C_1, \ldots, C_n, O_1, \ldots, O_\ell \rangle$ be a beMCS, $\mathcal{S} = \langle S^1, \ldots, S^s \rangle$ an evolving belief state of size s for M_e, and $Obs = \langle \mathcal{O}^1, \ldots, \mathcal{O}^m \rangle$ an observation sequence for M_e such that $m \geq s$. Then, $\mathcal{S}$ is an evolving equilibrium of size s of M_e given Obs iff, for each $1 \leq j \leq s$, S^j is a static equilibrium of $M^j = \langle C_1[k_1^j, b_1^j], \ldots, C_n[k_n^j, b_n^j], O_1[o_1^j], \ldots, O_\ell[o_\ell^j] \rangle$ where, for each $1 \leq i \leq n$,*

$$- \ b_i^j \in Upd(S^j, br_i, \langle obr_i^1, \ldots, obr_i^j \rangle)$$

and k_i^j is defined inductively as follows:

$$- \ k_i^1 = kb_i$$
$$- \ k_i^{j+1} \in mng_i(app^{next}(S^j, b_i^j), k_i^j).$$

Note that the set of bridge rules of a context can change from one time instant to the other even if no bridge rule of that context is observed. This happens because the set of updates depends also on the current state. For a simple example, let $\sigma_1 = (add(p) \leftarrow)$ be a bridge rule of a context in a beMCS, and suppose that at time 1 the rule $\sigma_2 = (\mathbf{not}\ add(p) \leftarrow 1 : \mathbf{not}\ q)$ is observed, which can be seen as an exception for the original rule. Suppose that q is not true in context C_1 at time 1. Then, both rules are applicable and their heads are conflicting, leading to the rejection of the first rule. Suppose that in the next time instant no bridge rule is observed, but q is true. Then, since the second rule is not applicable, the rules are not conflicting. Therefore, σ_1 is not rejected and it is now part of the set of bridge rules of C_1.

We now prove some properties of the notion of evolving equilibrium. In Def. 7, the size of the observation sequence is assumed to be greater or equal than the size of the evolving belief state. The intuition is that an equilibrium may also be defined for only a part of the observation sequence. As a consequence, any subsequence of an evolving equilibrium is still an evolving equilibrium.

Proposition 3. *Let M_e be a beMCS and $Obs = \langle \mathcal{O}^1, \ldots, \mathcal{O}^m \rangle$ an observation sequence for M_e. If $\mathcal{S} = \langle S^1, \ldots, S^s \rangle$ is an evolving equilibrium of size s of M_e given Obs, then, for each $1 \leq j \leq s$, and every $j \leq k \leq m$, $\langle S^1, \ldots, S^j \rangle$ is an evolving equilibrium of size j of M_e given the observation sequence $\langle \mathcal{O}^1, \ldots, \mathcal{O}^k \rangle$.*

It is not hard to see that an mMCS is a particular case of a beMCS with no observation context, the heads of bridge rules do not contain the operator *next*, and there are no updates to the bridge rules.

Proposition 4. *Let $M = \langle C_1, \ldots, C_n \rangle$ be an mMCS. Then, $S = \langle S_1, \ldots, S_n \rangle$ is an equilibrium of M iff $\mathcal{S} = \langle S \rangle$ is an evolving equilibrium of size 1 of M for some observation sequence $Obs = \langle \mathcal{O}^1, \ldots, \mathcal{O}^m \rangle$ for M with $m \geq 1$ and such that, for every $1 \leq i \leq n$, we have that $obr_i^1 = \emptyset$.*

4   Inconsistency Management

Inconsistency management is an important topic for frameworks that aim at integrating knowledge from different sources and has been extensively studied for MCSs and mMCSs [13,10]. In [21], inconsistency management for eMCSs is investigated, and it is shown that essential notions and results carry over from static mMCSs to dynamic eMCSs. In this section, we adapt these results from eMCSs to beMCSs and can confirm that the same favorable characteristics hold.

For the case of mMCSs, three forms of inconsistency are considered: *nonexistence of equilibria*, *local inconsistency*, and *operator inconsistency* [10]. The first form has been extensively studied for MCSs [13] and is also termed global inconsistency, while the second one deals with inconsistent belief sets potentially occurring in an equilibrium provided the contexts in the considered mMCS admit such a notion. The third form aims at detecting conflicts between operations in the heads of bridge rules.

We start by introducing the notion of (global) consistency.

Definition 8. *Let M_e be a beMCS and $Obs = \langle \mathcal{O}^1, \ldots, \mathcal{O}^m \rangle$ an observation sequence for M_e. Then, M_e is consistent with respect to Obs if it has an evolving equilibrium of size m given Obs.*

From Prop. 3, we immediately obtain that if there is a subsequence of Obs such that the considered beMCS is inconsistent, then the beMCS is also inconsistent for the entire sequence (and vice-versa).

Corollary 1. *Let M_e be a beMCS and let $Obs = \langle \mathcal{O}^1, \ldots, \mathcal{O}^m \rangle$ be an observation sequence for M_e. Then, M_e is consistent w.r.t. Obs iff M_e is consistent w.r.t. $\langle \mathcal{O}^1, \ldots, \mathcal{O}^j \rangle$ for every $1 \leq j \leq m$.*

We now focus on two notions that together are sufficient to ensure consistency. The first one focuses on the existence of an acceptable belief set for each knowledge base. Formally, an evolving context C_i in a beMCS M_e is *totally coherent* iff, for every $kb \in \mathbf{KB}_i$, $\mathbf{ACC}_i(kb) \neq \emptyset$. The second notion focuses on cycles between bridge rules. Let $B = \langle b_1, \ldots, b_n \rangle$ a tuple of sets of evolving bridge rules, one for each evolving context C_i of M_e, i.e., each $b_i \subseteq e\mathbf{BR}_i$. The idea is to describe cycles between the bridge rules that essentially may cause inconsistency. Formally we write $ref_r(i, j)$ iff r is a bridge rule of b_i and $(j:b)$ occurs in the body of r. Let $r_1, \ldots, r_k \in \bigcup_{1 \leq i \leq n} b_i$, then we say that $(r_1, \ldots, r_k)$ forms a cycle iff $ref_{r_1}(i_1, i_2), \ldots, ref_{r_{k-1}}(i_{k-1}, i_k)$, and $ref_{r_k}(i_k, i_1)$ hold. Then $B = \langle b_1, \ldots, b_n \rangle$ is *acyclic* if no such cycles exist. We can show the following.

Proposition 5. *Let $M_e = \langle C_1, \ldots, C_n, O_1, \ldots, O_\ell \rangle$ be a beMCS and $Obs = \langle \mathcal{O}^1, \ldots, \mathcal{O}^m \rangle$ an observation sequence for M_e. Then, if $B = \langle b_1, \ldots, b_n \rangle$ is acyclic, where, for each $1 \leq i \leq n$, $b_i = br_i \cup (\bigcup_{j \leq m} obr_i^j)$, then M_e is consistent with respect to Obs.*

A similar property holds for mMCSs, indicating that the extension to beMCSs as such does not decrease the likelihood of existence of evolving equilibria.

An adequate treatment of local inconsistency was one of the motivations for the introduction of mMCSs, and this is also the case in beMCSs with incoming observations that also should be subject to consistency management. As described in [10], we need to assume that each context has a notion of *inconsistent belief state*, which usually exists or is easily definable. Assuming such notion, a knowledge base $kb_i \in \mathbf{KB}_i$ of a context C_i is said to be *consistent* if $\mathbf{ACC}_i(kb_i)$ does not contain an inconsistent belief set. A management function mng_i of a context C_i is said to be *locally consistency preserving (lc-preserving)*, if for every set $Op_i \subseteq OF_i$ and consistent knowledge base $kb_i \in \mathbf{KB}_i$, we have that every element of $mng_i(Op_i, kb_i)$ is a consistent knowledge base.

Definition 9. *Let M_e be a beMCS and $Obs = \langle \mathcal{O}^1, \ldots, \mathcal{O}^m \rangle$ an observation sequence for M_e. Then, M_e is said to be* locally consistent *with respect to Obs if every evolving equilibrium $S = \langle S^1, \ldots, S^s \rangle$ of M_e with respect to Obs is such that, for each $1 \leq j \leq s$, all belief sets in S^j are consistent.*

Recall that observations are subject to consistency management in each context. If the management functions are lc-preserving, then consistent observations do not make a consistent beMCS inconsistent.

Proposition 6. *Let $M_e = \langle C_1, \ldots, C_n, O_1, \ldots, O_\ell \rangle$ be a beMCS such that, for each C_i, kb_i is consistent and mng_i is lc-preserving. Then, for every observation sequence Obs for M_e, we have that M_e is locally consistent with respect to Obs.*

Since we are assuming the existence of a notion of inconsistent set of operators for each context of a beMCS, we end this section by briefly studying this form of inconsistency. We extend to sets of bridge rules the notion of inconsistent set of operational formulas, as introduced in Sect. 3.

Definition 10. *Let $M_e = \langle C_1, \ldots, C_n, O_1, \ldots, O_\ell \rangle$ be a beMCS, and S a belief state for M_e. A set $br \subseteq e\mathbf{BR}_i$ of evolving bridge rules of C_i is* inconsistent *with respect to S if $app^{now}(S, br) \in Inc_i^S$ or $app^{next}(S, br) \in Inc_i^S$. A set of bridge rules is* consistent *with respect to S if it is not inconsistent with respect to S.*

The following proposition guarantees the desirable property that a set of bridge rules resulting from an update with respect to a sequence of consistent sets of bridge rules is itself consistent.

Proposition 7. *Let $M_e = \langle C_1, \ldots, C_n, O_1, \ldots, O_\ell \rangle$ be a beMCS, and $Obs = \langle \mathcal{O}^1, \ldots, \mathcal{O}^m \rangle$ an observation sequence for M_e, and $S = \langle S^1, \ldots, S^s \rangle$ an evolving equilibrium of M_e given Obs. If each set of bridge rules in Obs is consistent with respect to S^s then, for each $1 \leq i \leq n$, we have that every element of $Upd(S^s, br_i, \langle br_i^1, \ldots, br_i^s \rangle)$ is consistent with respect to S^s.*

5   Related and Future Work

In this paper we introduced beMCS, and extension of evolving Multi-Context Systems (eMCS) [21] to allow not only the evolution of the knowledge bases of the contexts, but also of their sets of bridge rules. Closely related to eMCSs is the framework of reactive Multi-Context Systems (rMCSs) [8,15,11] inasmuch as both aim at extending mMCSs to cope with dynamic observations. The main difference between and eMCSs and rMCSs is that eMCSs have the meta operator *next* that allows for a clear separation between persistent and non-persistent effects, and also the specification of transitions based on the current state.

Another framework closely related to beMCSs is that of evolving logic programs EVOLP [2] which deals with updates of generalized logic programs, and the two frameworks of reactive ASP, one implemented as a solver *oclingo* [17] and one described in [8]. Whereas EVOLP employs an update predicate that is similar in spirit to the *next* predicate of our beMCSs, and uses the update semantics of Dynamic Logic Programming in a way that is similar to how conflicts between bridge rules dealt with in beMCSs, it does not deal with distributed heterogeneous knowledge, neither do both versions of Reactive ASP.

Regarding future work, an important non-trivial topic is the study of the notion of minimal change within an evolving equilibrium. Whereas minimal change may be desirable to obtain more coherent evolving equilibria, there are also arguments against adopting a one-size-fits-all approach embedded in the semantics. Different contexts, i.e., KR formalisms, may require different notions of minimal change, or even require to avoid it – e.g., suppose we want to represent some variable that can non-deterministically take one of two values at each time instant: minimal change could force a constant value.

Also interesting is to study how to perform AGM style belief revision at the (semantic) level of the equilibria, as in Wang et al [34], though different since knowledge is not incorporated in the contexts.

Another important issue open for future work is a more fine-grained characterization of updating bridge rules (and knowledge bases) in light of the encountered difficulties when updating rules [30,31,33] and the combination of updates over various formalisms [31,32].

Finally, we may also consider the generalization of the notions of minimal and grounded equilibria [9] to beMCSs to avoid, e.g., self-supporting cycles introduced by bridge rules, or the use of preferences to deal with several evolving equilibria a beMCS can have for the same observation sequence.

Acknowledgments. We would like to thank the referees for their comments, which helped improve this paper considerably. Matthias Knorr and João Leite were partially supported by FCT under project "ERRO – Efficient Reasoning with Rules and Ontologies" (PTDC/EIA-CCO/121823/2010). Ricardo Gonçalves was supported by FCT grant SFRH/BPD/47245/2008 and Matthias Knorr was also partially supported by FCT grant SFRH/BPD/86970/2012.

References

1. Alberti, M., Gomes, A.S., Gonçalves, R., Leite, J., Slota, M.: Normative systems represented as hybrid knowledge bases. In: Leite, J., Torroni, P., Ågotnes, T., Boella, G., van der Torre, L. (eds.) CLIMA XII 2011. LNCS, vol. 6814, pp. 330–346. Springer, Heidelberg (2011)

2. Alferes, J.J., Brogi, A., Leite, J., Moniz Pereira, L.: Evolving logic programs. In: Flesca, S., Greco, S., Leone, N., Ianni, G. (eds.) JELIA 2002. LNCS (LNAI), vol. 2424, pp. 50–61. Springer, Heidelberg (2002)

3. Alferes, J., Leite, J., Pereira, L., Przymusinska, H., Przymusinski, T.: Dynamic logic programming. In: Cohn, A., Schubert, L., Shapiro, S. (eds.) KR, pp. 98–111. Morgan Kaufmann (1998)

4. Anicic, D., Rudolph, S., Fodor, P., Stojanovic, N.: Stream reasoning and complex event processing in ETALIS. Semantic Web 3(4), 397–407 (2012)

5. Baader, F., Calvanese, D., McGuinness, D.L., Nardi, D., Patel-Schneider, P.F. (eds.): The Description Logic Handbook: Theory, Implementation, and Applications. Cambridge University Press (2003)

6. Barbieri, D., Braga, D., Ceri, S., Valle, E., Grossniklaus, M.: C-SPARQL: a continuous query language for RDF data streams. Int. J. Semantic Computing 4(1), 3–25 (2010)

7. Benerecetti, M., Giunchiglia, F., Serafini, L.: Model checking multiagent systems. J. Log. Comput. 8(3), 401–423 (1998)

8. Brewka, G.: Towards reactive multi-context systems. In: Cabalar, P., Son, T.C. (eds.) LPNMR 2013. LNCS, vol. 8148, pp. 1–10. Springer, Heidelberg (2013)

9. Brewka, G., Eiter, T.: Equilibria in heterogeneous nonmonotonic multi-context systems. In: AAAI, pp. 385–390. AAAI Press (2007)

10. Brewka, G., Eiter, T., Fink, M., Weinzierl, A.: Managed multi-context systems. In: Walsh, T. (ed.) IJCAI, pp. 786–791. IJCAI/AAAI (2011)

11. Brewka, G., Ellmauthaler, S., Pührer, J.: Multi-context systems for reactive reasoning in dynamic environments. In: Schaub, T., Friedrich, G., O'Sullivan, B. (eds.) ECAI. IOS Press (to appear, 2014)

12. Dragoni, A., Giorgini, P., Serafini, L.: Mental states recognition from communication. J. Log. Comput. 12(1), 119–136 (2002)

13. Eiter, T., Fink, M., Schüller, P., Weinzierl, A.: Finding explanations of inconsistency in multi-context systems. In: Lin, F., Sattler, U., Truszczynski, M. (eds.) KR. AAAI Press (2010)

14. Eiter, T., Ianni, G., Lukasiewicz, T., Schindlauer, R., Tompits, H.: Combining answer set programming with description logics for the semantic web. Artif. Intell. 172(12-13), 1495–1539 (2008)

15. Ellmauthaler, S.: Generalizing multi-context systems for reactive stream reasoning applications. In: Jones, A.V., Ng, N. (eds.) ICCSW. OASICS, vol. 35, pp. 19–26. Schloss Dagstuhl - Leibniz-Zentrum fuer Informatik, Germany (2013)

16. Gebser, M., Grote, T., Kaminski, R., Obermeier, P., Sabuncu, O., Schaub, T.: Stream reasoning with answer set programming: Preliminary report. In: Brewka, G., Eiter, T., McIlraith, S.A. (eds.) KR. AAAI Press (2012)

17. Gebser, M., Grote, T., Kaminski, R., Schaub, T.: Reactive answer set programming. In: Delgrande, J.P., Faber, W. (eds.) LPNMR 2011. LNCS, vol. 6645, pp. 54–66. Springer, Heidelberg (2011)

18. Gelfond, M., Lifschitz, V.: Classical negation in logic programs and disjunctive databases. New Gen. Comput. 9(3/4), 365–386 (1991)

19. Giunchiglia, F., Serafini, L.: Multilanguage hierarchical logics or: How we can do without modal logics. Artif. Intell. 65(1), 29–70 (1994)

20. Gonçalves, R., Alferes, J.J.: Parametrized logic programming. In: Janhunen, T., Niemelä, I. (eds.) JELIA 2010. LNCS, vol. 6341, pp. 182–194. Springer, Heidelberg (2010)

21. Gonçalves, R., Knorr, M., Leite, J.: Evolving multi-context systems. In: Schaub, T., Friedrich, G., O'Sullivan, B. (eds.) ECAI. IOS Press (to appear, 2014)

22. Homola, M., Knorr, M., Leite, J., Slota, M.: MKNF knowledge bases in multi-context systems. In: Fisher, M., van der Torre, L., Dastani, M., Governatori, G. (eds.) CLIMA XIII 2012. LNCS, vol. 7486, pp. 146–162. Springer, Heidelberg (2012)

23. Ivanov, V., Knorr, M., Leite, J.: A query tool for $\mathcal{EL}$ with non-monotonic rules. In: Alani, H., et al. (eds.) ISWC 2013, Part I. LNCS, vol. 8218, pp. 216–231. Springer, Heidelberg (2013)

24. Knorr, M., Alferes, J., Hitzler, P.: Local closed world reasoning with description logics under the well-founded semantics. Artif. Intell. 175(9-10), 1528–1554 (2011)

25. Knorr, M., Slota, M., Leite, J., Homola, M.: What if no hybrid reasoner is available? Hybrid MKNF in multi-context systems. J. Log. Comput. (2013)

26. Lécué, F., Pan, J.: Predicting knowledge in an ontology stream. In: Rossi, F. (ed.) IJCAI. IJCAI/AAAI (2013)

27. Motik, B., Rosati, R.: Reconciling description logics and rules. J. ACM 57(5) (2010)

28. Roelofsen, F., Serafini, L.: Minimal and absent information in contexts. In: Kaelbling, L., Saffiotti, A. (eds.) IJCAI, pp. 558–563. Professional Book Center (2005)

29. Sabater, J., Sierra, C., Parsons, S., Jennings, N.R.: Engineering executable agents using multi-context systems. J. Log. Comput. 12(3), 413–442 (2002)

30. Slota, M., Leite, J.: On semantic update operators for answer-set programs. In: Coelho, H., Studer, R., Wooldridge, M. (eds.) ECAI. Frontiers in Artificial Intelligence and Applications, vol. 215, pp. 957–962. IOS Press (2010)

31. Slota, M., Leite, J.: Robust equivalence models for semantic updates of answer-set programs. In: Brewka, G., Eiter, T., McIlraith, S.A. (eds.) KR. AAAI Press (2012)

32. Slota, M., Leite, J.: A unifying perspective on knowledge updates. In: del Cerro, L.F., Herzig, A., Mengin, J. (eds.) JELIA 2012. LNCS, vol. 7519, pp. 372–384. Springer, Heidelberg (2012)

33. Slota, M., Leite, J.: The rise and fall of semantic rule updates based on SE-models. TPLP (to appear, 2014)

34. Wang, Y., Zhuang, Z., Wang, K.: Belief change in nonmonotonic multi-context systems. In: Cabalar, P., Son, T.C. (eds.) LPNMR 2013. LNCS, vol. 8148, pp. 543–555. Springer, Heidelberg (2013)

Enumerating Extensions on Random Abstract-AFs with ArgTools, Aspartix, ConArg2, and Dung-O-Matic

Stefano Bistarelli[1,2,*], Fabio Rossi[1], Francesco Santini[1,2,**]

[1] Dipartimento di Matematica e Informatica, Universitá of Perugia, Italy
{bista,rossi,francesco.santini}@dmi.unipg.it
[2] Istituto di Informatica e Telematica (IIT-CNR), Pisa, Italy
{stefano.bistarelli,francesco.santini}@iit.cnr.it

Abstract. We compare four different implementations of reasoning tools dedicated to Abstract Argumentation Frameworks. These systems are ArgTools, ASPARTIX, ConArg2, and Dung-O-Matic. They have been tested over three different models of randomly-generated graph models, corresponding to the Erdős-Rényi model, the Kleinberg small-world model, and the scale-free Barabasi-Albert model. This first comparison is useful to study the behaviour of these reasoners over networks with different topologies (including small-world ones): we scale the number of arguments to check the limits of today's systems. Such results can be used to guide further improvements, specifically ConArg2, which we recently developed, and tested for the first time in this work.

1 Introduction

Due to the widespread of multi-agent systems and Web 2.0, we can certainly claim that *Argumentation Theory* is arising all around us. Almost all social platforms support digital debate among the community members: everyday's examples are social networks, e-commerce websites, digital fora/magazines, where it is possible to debate about news, products, or just friends' statements.

An *Abstract Argumentation Framework* (*AAF*), or System, as introduced in a seminal paper by Dung [13], is simply a pair $\langle A, R \rangle$ consisting of a set A whose elements are called arguments and of a binary relation R on A, called "attack" relation. An abstract argument is not assumed to have any specific structure but, roughly speaking, an argument is anything that may attack or be attacked by another argument. The sets of arguments (or *extensions*) to be considered are then defined under different semantics, which are related to varying degrees of scepticism or credulousness. Argumentation has become an important subject of research in Artificial Intelligence and it is also of interest in several disciplines, such as Logic, Philosophy and Communication Theory (see [5] and [24, Ch. 1]).

---

* The author is supported by MIUR-PRIN "Metodi logici per il trattamento dell'informazione".

** The author is supported by MIUR PRIN "Security Horizons".

N. Bulling et al. (Eds.): CLIMA XV, LNAI 8624, pp. 70–86, 2014.

One of the main issues for any theory of argumentation is the selection of acceptable sets of arguments, based on the way arguments interact. Intuitively, an acceptable set of arguments must be in some sense coherent (no attacks among its arguments, i.e., *conflict-free*) and strong enough (for instance, able to defend itself against all attacking arguments, i.e., *admissible*).

The main goal of this paper is to better understand how efficiently such semantics can be computed at the state of the art of modern Abstract Argumentation reasoners, in terms of argument networks with different properties and size. Therefore, we test four tools whose main objective is the pure computation of such semantics, i.e., ArgTools, ASPARTIX, ConArg2 (our tool, tested in this paper for the first time), and Dung-O-Matic (see Sec 4.1). We consider three different randomly-generated graph models, thus assembling a variegate benchmark for this kind of testing. These networks are respectively generated according to Erdős-Rényi, Kleinberg, and Barabasi-Albert principles (see Sec. 4.2). We have not considered interaction graphs from the "real-world" due to the current lack of benchmarks extracted from real discussions. This will be part of the extensive future work we plan to investigate by elaborating on our tool and these tests (see Sec. 7). Note that we use three different random models in our testbed, since a clear definition of the topological properties behind real AAFs is not yet identified by the literature (see Sec. 7).

Existent and future applications exploiting AAFs need to efficiently behave and scale over large networks of arguments. In fact, in non-trivial discussions it is not hard to find 50-100 arguments at least, especially if we consider "hot topics" automatically extracted from on-line fora, or discussion groups. When we make these digital tribunes correspond to well-known social networks [20], as *Twitter*[1] [19] or *Facebook*[2] [27], but also to more structured debate-friendly tools, as *DebateGraph*[3] or *Debate.org*[4], then the number of arguments can further increase.[5] Obtaining a more efficient computation of AAF semantics will lead us to have more performant higher-level reasoners on top of these tools, which can in turn be used in broader applications related to, for instance, Law, Medicine and e-Democracy [24, Ch. 3, Pt. 5].

This work extends [7] and it is organized as follows: in Sec. 2 we briefly introduce AAFs, while in Sec. 3 we summarise the related work on reasoning tools. In Sec. 4 we define our benchmark environment, by describing adopted networks and tools. Afterwards, in Sec. 5 we show the results we obtained with our tests, and we discuss the charts trying to give some general considerations and guidelines. Section 6 shows the constraint-based models we have adopted to implement some of the basic semantics, i.e., conflict-free, admissible, complete, and stable. Finally, Sec. 7 presents ideas about future work.

---

[1] http://twitter.com

[2] http://www.facebook.com

[3] http://debategraph.org

[4] http://www.debate.org

[5] As an example, the "Anthropogenic Climate Change" map in DebateGraph stores 1.190 arguments.

2   Preliminaries

In this section we briefly summarise the background information related to classical AAFs [13]. We focus on the basic definitions of an AAF, and on the extension-based semantics that will be tested in the comparison (see Sec 5).

Definition 1. *An Abstract Argumentation Framework (AAF) is a pair $F = \langle A, R \rangle$ of a set A of arguments and a binary relation $R \subseteq A \times A$, called the attack relation. $\forall a, b \in A$, aRb (or, $a \rightarrowtail b$) means that a attacks b. An AAF may be represented by a directed graph (an interaction graph) whose nodes are arguments and edges represent the attack relation. A set of arguments $S \subseteq A$ attacks an argument a, i.e., $S \rightarrowtail a$, if a is attacked by an argument of S, i.e., $\exists b \in S.b \rightarrowtail a$.*

The notion of defence [13] is fundamental to AAFs.

Definition 2. *Given an AAF, $F = \langle A, R \rangle$, an argument $a \in A$ is defended (in F) by a set $S \subseteq A$ if for each $b \in A$, such that $b \rightarrowtail a$, also $S \rightarrowtail b$ holds. Moreover, for $S \subseteq A$, we denote by S_R^+ the set $S \cup \{b \mid S \rightarrowtail b\}$.*

The "acceptability" of an argument [13], defined under different semantics, depends on its membership to some sets, called *extensions*: such semantics characterise a collective "acceptability". In Def. 3 we report only those semantics of interest in our study, i.e., that are implemented by all the compared tools (see Sec. 4.1). Respectively, *adm, com, stb, prf, ide, gde*, and *sem*, stand for admissible, complete, stable, preferred, ideal, grounded, and semi-stable semantics. The intuition behind these semantics is outside the scope of this work (e.g., see [24, Ch. 3]).

Definition 3. *Let $F = \langle A, R \rangle$ be an AAF. A set $S \subseteq A$ is conflict-free (in F), denoted $S \in cf(F)$, iff there are no $a, b \in S$, such that $(a, b), (b, a) \in R$. For $S \in cf(F)$, it holds that*

- $S \in adm(F)$, if each $a \in S$ is defended by S;
- $S \in com(F)$, if $S \in adm(F)$ and for each $a \in A$ defended by S, $a \in S$ holds;
- $S \in stb(F)$, if foreach $a \in A \backslash S$, $S \rightarrowtail a$, i.e., $S_R^+ = A$;
- $S \in prf(F)$, if $S \in adm(F)$ and there is no $T \in adm(F)$ with $S \subset T$;
- $S = ide(F)$, if $S \in X = \{U \mid adm(U) \wedge \forall T \in prf(F).U \subseteq T\}$, and S is maximal w.r.t. set inclusion in X;
- $S = gde(F)$ if $S \in com(F)$ and there is no $T \in com(F)$ with $T \subset S$;
- $S \in sem(F)$, if $S \in adm(F)$ and there is no $T \in adm(F)$ with $S_R^+ \subset T_R^+$.

We recall that for each AAF, F, $stb(F) \subseteq sem(F) \subseteq prf(F) \subseteq com(F) \subseteq adm(F)$ holds, and that for each of the considered semantics σ (except stable) $\sigma(F) \neq \emptyset$ holds. Moreover, in case an AAF has at least one stable extension, its stable and semi-stable extensions coincide. Finally, $gde(F)$ and $ide(F)$ are always unique, and $gde(F), ide(F) \in com(F)$.

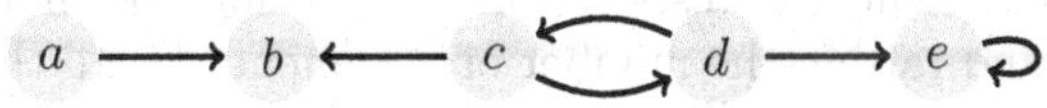

Fig. 1. An example of AAF

An argument $a \in A$ is *skeptically* justified iff $\forall E \in \sigma(F).a \in E$, and *credulously* justified iff $\exists E \in \sigma(F).a \in E$.

Consider the $F = \langle A, R \rangle$ in Fig. 1, with $A = \{a, b, c, d, e\}$ and $R = \{(a, b), (c, b), (c, d), (d, c), (d, e), (e, e)\}$. We have that $stb(F) = sem(F) = \{\{a, d\}\}$, and $gde(F) = ide(F) = \{a\}$. The admissible sets of F are $\emptyset, \{a\}, \{c\}, \{d\}, \{a, c\},$ $\{a, d\}$, and $prf(F) = \{\{a, c\}, \{a, d\}\}$. Complete extensions are $\{a\}, \{a, c\}, \{a, d\}$.

3   Related Work and Comparison

To the best of our knowledge, the performance results presented in [9,10,15,16] are the first ones proposed on medium-large problems, and [9,10] are the first ones using random networks showing small-world properties. Besides the tools we compare in this paper (see Sec. 4.1 for their description), in this section we report the other main systems in literature. We consider only the reasoners whose main goal is the solution of extension-based semantics (see Sec. 2).

In [15,16] the authors randomly generate graphs ranging from 20 to 110 arguments. They use two parameterized methods for generating the attack relation. The first generates arbitrary graphs and inserts for any pair (a, b) an attack from a to b with a given probability p (i.e., similarly to Erdős-Rényi). The other method generates AAFs with a $n \times m$ grid structure. They consider two different neighbourhoods, one connecting arguments vertically and horizontally, and one that additionally connects the arguments diagonally. Such a connection is a mutual attack with a given probability p and in only one direction otherwise. The probability p is chosen between 0.1 and 0.4. The authors generate AAFs with 60-200/25-500 arguments for a total of 4.800/2.948 tests; in addition, they set a timeout of 300 seconds (we adopt the same timeout in our tests).

Two more tools are, *i)* the *Counter-Example Guided Argumentation Reasoning Tool* (for short, *CEGARTIX*) [16], which relies on iterative calls to SAT a solver (as *Minisat*[6]), and *ii)* the *Dynamic Programming Argumentation Reasoning Tool* (*dynPARTIX*) [15], which is based on tree decompositions and dynamic programming. Note that both CEGARTIX and dynPARTIX are oriented to the solution of the skeptical and credulous acceptance under different semantics: this is why they do not appear in our comparison, since we only consider tools able to enumerate all the extensions under a given semantics.

One more mapping of AAFs to *Constraint Satisfaction Problems* (*CSPs*) [25] (as we do in our implementation of ConArg2, see Sec. 4.1) is shown in [2], but we are not aware of any available implementation.

---

[6] http://minisat.se

In this paper we extend the tests in [9,10], by using one more graph model, i.e., Erdős-Rényi, and raising the number of arguments for all the three models, in order to stress them up to the point there they are not able to solve any problem instance within a given timeout of 300 seconds. In addition, we provide for the first time a comparison among four independently-developed reasoners. We adopt different graph models, while in [16,15] the tests are executed over a single model, whose characteristics are not related to any social graph model (we justify the study of social networks in Sec. 4.2).

4   Tools and Graphs

We organise the content into two subsections: Section 4.1 presents a description of the four reasoning tools we used in our comparison, while Sec. 4.2 describes the random graphs we generated as benchmark.

4.1   Tools

ArgTools[7] is a very recent C++ collection of labelling-based algorithms [22] for enumerating extensions of an AAF with recursive attacks (*AFRA*). In [22] the authors present implemented algorithms for listing extensions by labelling attacks along with arguments. Such algorithms are concerned with enumerating all extensions of an AAF under different semantics: preferred, stable, complete, semi stable, stage, ideal and grounded. Since an AAF is a special case of AFRA, the developed algorithms also list extensions of an AAF. The input format adheres to ASPARTIX.

The **ASPARTIX**[8] system [17] is a tool for computing acceptable extensions for a broad range of formalisations of Dung's AFs and generalisations, such as value-based AFs [4] or preference-based [1]. *ASPARTIX* relies on a fixed disjunctive *Datalog* program which takes an instance of an argumentation framework as input, and uses an Answer-Set solver for computing the type of extension specified by the user. ASPARTIX is able to solve admissible, stable, complete, grounded, preferred, semi-stable, ideal, stage, cf2, resolution-based grounded and stage2 extensions. ASPARTIX has been improved with the *metasp*[9] optimization front-end for the ASP-package gringo/claspD[10], which provides direct commands to filter answer sets satisfying certain subset-minimality (or -maximality) constraints. We have included ASPARTIX in the comparison since it represents the state of the art of ASP-based solvers [26].

ConArg2[11] [9,10] is a reasoner based on the *Java Constraint Programming* solver[12] (JaCoP), a Java library that provides a *Finite Domain Constraint Pro-*

---

[7] http://sourceforge.net/projects/argtools/files/

[8] http://www.dbai.tuwien.ac.at/proj/argumentation/systempage/

[9] http://www.cs.uni-potsdam.de/wv/metasp/

[10] http://potassco.sourceforge.net

[11] http://www.dmi.unipg.it/bista/tt/conarg/

[12] http://www.jacop.eu

gramming paradigm [25]. The tool comes with a graphical interface, which visually shows all the obtained extensions for each problem. ConArg is able to solve also the weighted and coalition-based problems presented in [8,11]. Moreover, it can import/export AAFs with the same text format of ASPARTIX. Recently, we have extended the tool to its second version, i.e., ConArg2 (freely downloadable from the same webpage of ConArg), in order to improve its performance: we implemented all the models in Gecode[13], which is an open, free, and efficient C++ environment where to develop constraint-based applications. We have also dropped the graphical interface, having a textual output only. So far, ConArg2 finds all conflict-free, admissible, complete, stable, grounded, preferred, semi-stable and ideal extensions (see Def. 3).

Dung-O-Matic[14] is an Abstract Argument computation engine implemented by the *javaDungAF* class. Dung-O-Matic supports Dung's Argumentation Frameworks and several of their semantics, as admissible, complete, eager, grounded, ideal, preferred, semi-stable, and, finally stable one. javaDungAF is currently just a couple of java classes. Source code and documentation are available to download. For each of the proposed extensions, the tool implements a different algorithm presented in the literature; for instance, the grounded semantics is computed with the original algorithms presented by Dung in [13]. We have included Dung-O-Matic in the comparison because all the implemented extensions come from ad-hoc algorithms recently designed and proposed in the literature.

4.2   Graphs

Due to the lack of a well-established benchmark in the Argumentation literature, we randomly generate directed-graphs that we let correspond to AAFs: nodes are arguments, and directed edges are attacks.

To generate random graphs we adopted two different libraries. The first one is the *Java Universal Network/Graph Framework* (*JUNG*[15]), which is a Java software library for the modeling, generation, analysis and visualization of graphs. With JUNG we generate *Barabasi-Albert* [3] and *Kleinberg* [21] graphs. The second library we use is *NetworkX*[16], and it consists of a Python software package for the creation, manipulation, and study of the structure, dynamics, and functions of complex networks. With NetworkX we generate *Erdős-Rényi* [18] graphs. We use two different libraries because with JUNG we are able to randomly generate directed Barabasi and Kleinberg graphs, while NetworkX does not cover Kleinberg networks at all, and only provides undirected Barabasi graphs. On the other side, NetworkX offers Erdős-Rényi networks (not present in JUNG).

In order to test tools over sensibly wide AAFs, our attention has mainly turned to random networks with small-world features, as Kleinberg, or Barabasi-Albert (which is also a scale-free model [3]). Big hub-nodes in scale-free networks are

---

[13] http://www.gecode.org
[14] http://www.arg.dundee.ac.uk/?page_id=279
[15] http://jung.sourceforge.net
[16] http://networkx.github.io

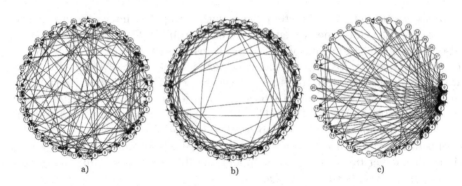

Fig. 2. An example of *a)* an Erdős-Rényi, *b)* a Kleinberg, and *c)* a Barabasi-Albert graph, all with 40 nodes (Kleinberg with 36)

responsible for the so-called small-world phenomenon, where most nodes can be reached from every other by a small number of hops. An example of each of these graphs is represented in Fig. 2. At least three big hub-nodes are easily detectable in the Barabasi-Albert graph in Fig. 2c. Figure 2b depicts the typical grid-like structure of Kleinberg graphs, with few long-distance connections. At last, the Erdős-Rényi model (see Fig. 2a) does not generate local clustering and does not account for the formation of hubs: this model is the least indicated to represent social patterns among the three models. Nevertheless, we have included it in this study for the sake of completeness.

We are not aware of any study matching AAFs to a precise graph model (or several models, depending on the kind of the discussion, e.g., persuasion or negotiation-oriented). The justification behind using this kind of graphs is that several works in the Argumentation literature investigate AAFs extracted from social networks [20] as Facebook [27] and Twitter [19].

In the following we detail the three graph models. In the **Erdős-Rényi** model [18] a graph is constructed by randomly connecting n nodes. Each edge is included in the graph with probability p independent from every other edge. Clearly, as p increases from 0 to 1, the model becomes more and more likely to include graphs with more edges. To create our benchmark we adopt $p = c \cdot log(n)/n$ (with c empirically set to 2.5), which ensures the connectedness of such graphs. We require all the graphs in the benchmark to be connected, since we suppose a discussion to dynamically evolve by adding each time an argument in order to challenge a different former argument.

Kleinberg [21] adds a number of directed long-range random links to an $n \times n$ lattice network (vertices as nodes of a grid, undirected edges between any two adjacent nodes). Links have a non-uniform distribution that favours edges to close nodes over more distant ones. In the implementation provided by JUNG, each node u has four local connections, one to each of its neighbors, and in addition 1 or more long range connection to some node v, where v is chosen randomly according to probability proportional to d^θ where d is the lattice distance between u and v and θ is the clustering exponent. In our generation we set $\theta = 0.9$, in order to have a high clustering coefficient.

In the generation of **Barabasi-Albert** graphs [3] through the JUNG libraries, at each time step a new vertex is created and connected to existing vertices according to the principle of "preferential attachment" [3], whereby vertices with higher degree have a higher probability of being selected for attachment. At a given step, the probability p of creating an edge between an existing vertex v and the newly added vertex is $p = (degree(v) + 1)/(|E| + |V|)$. $|E|$ and $|V|$ are, respectively, the number of edges and vertices currently in the network. Thus, p is not an input parameter. Scale-free networks are widely observed in natural and human-made systems, including the Internet, the World Wide Web, citation networks, and social networks.

5   Tests and Discussion

The results have been collected on an Intel(R) Core(TM) i7 CPU 970 @3.20GHz (6 cores, 2 threads per core), and 16GB of RAM. For all the tools, the output has been redirected to */dev/null*, and the standard error to file. To test ASPARTIX we used gringo 3.0.5 and claspD 1.1.4 (with metasp optimisation) on preferred and semi-stable semantics, and DLV build "BEN/Dec 16 2012 gcc 4.6.1" on the ideal semantics (since it is the only offered option). We used gringo/claspD (no metasp optimisation, since the available ASPARTIX models do not work with it) even with the admissible, complete, stable, and grounded semantics, but only on Kleinberg and Erdős-Rényi models: the performance on the Barabasi-Albert model seems not to benefit from this enhancement. To implement ConArg2 we used Gecode 4.0, and for Dung-O-Matic we used Java "1.6.0_18" launched with 64Mbyte of stack and 4Gbyte of heap. We set a timeout of 300 seconds for all the four systems. All the obtained extensions have been cross-checked to verify the four systems find the same results.

From Fig. 3a to Fig. 5a we show the results for finding all the admissible, complete, stable, preferred, ideal, grounded, and semi-stable extensions respectively. Since ArgTools does not implement the admissible semantics, Fig 4a reports a comparison only among the other four tools. The other six semantics are in common with all the four considered tools. In each figure we report the results over each of the three different random-graph models (see Sec. 4.2): the x axis report the number of arguments (we test 100 graphs given each number of arguments), on the left y axis we report the average (on 100 AAFs) CPU time needed to compute the successful instances (i.e., considering only the extensions found within the 300sec. timeout), and the right y axis shows the number of unsolved instances.

For each tool we tested $2,800$ AAFs on the Barabasi-Albert model (400 AAFs for each semantics), $3,200$ on Kleinberg (400 for stable, admissible, grounded, ideal, 300 for complete, 600 for preferred, 700 for semi-stable), and $2,800$ AAFs on the Erdős-Rényi model (400 AAFs for each semantics). Therefore, we executed a total of $8,800$ tests for ASPARTIX, ConArg2, and Dung-O-Matic, and $8,400$ for ArgTools, since the admissible semantics is not implemented.

Table 1. The best solvers on each graph and extension, with respect to the average time performance (and number of unsuccessful search-instances) in Fig. 3, Fig. 4, and Fig. 5: (A)SPARTIX, (C)onArg2, (D)ung-O-Matic, and Arg(T)ools

	adm	com	stb	prf	ide	gde	sem
Barabasi-Albert	C	A/C	A/C	C/T	C	C	C/T
Kleinberg	C	C	C	A	T	C/D/T	C
Erdős-Rényi	A/C	A	A/C	A	C	A/D/T	A

Table 1 summarises the tests showing the winner for each extension. Dung-O-Matic (D) works well with the grounded semantics, meaning that the polynomial algorithm is often better than representing the problem in a declarative way. With all the other problems, however, Dung-O-Matic is often not able to solve the instances within the timeout. For what concerns the other three tools, we can see that ConArg2 (C) works very well with Barabasi-Albert networks, being the best solver on all the semantics, together with ASPARTIX (A) on complete and stable, and ArgTools (T) on preferred and semi-stable. ConArg2 also works efficiently on Kleinberg graphs, but worse than ASPARTIX on the preferred semantics, and worse than ArgTools on the ideal one; on the grounded semantics ConArg2, Dung-O-Matic, and ArgTool show similar performance. Finally, higher-level semantics in Erdős-Rényi graphs are usually solved better by ASPARTIX, except the ideal one, where ConArg2 performs better, and the admissible and stable semantics (where both solvers works similarly).

In the following we report some general considerations on the tests, not considering a specific reasoner:

- First, we would like to point out that the graph model sensitively impacts on the performance of the tool: for instance, Barabasi-Albert networks are easier to be solved (with ConArg2 in particular) since the number of nodes can be raised to thousands still solving the problem. On the other end, it is possible to only work with Kleinberg graphs with less than one hundred nodes (except for grounded extensions). Erdős-Rényi stays in the middle. Therefore, it is really important to discover the structure of real AAFs, before developing the proper technology to work on them. This point represents the main result of this paper: our goal is just to show that there is no absolute winner (Tab. 1 proves this), and each reasoner has its own advantages and disadvantages, and, of course, margins of improvement. Tools could be also merged together with the purpose to catch each one's best results on different graph-models.
- A possible conjecture is that, among all the models shown in this paper, some classical debate-schemes are more likely to resemble Barabasi-Albert graphs: such *evolving* networks change as a function of time, similarly to a debate where new arguments appear and attack previous ones.

  Moreover, like other kinds of social or natural phenomena [3], Barabasi-Albert's preferential attachment explains big hubs receiving many attacks,

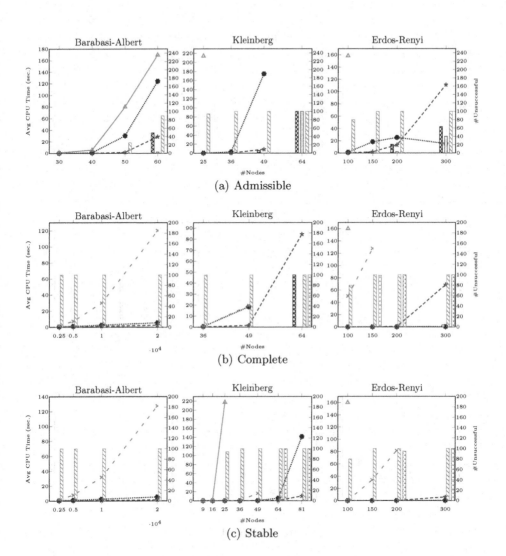

(a) Admissible

(b) Complete

(c) Stable

Fig. 3. ASPARTIX (··•··), ConArg2 (-*-), Dung-O-Matic (—▲—), ArgTools (-*-),
and their respective number of unsolved instances within 300sec.: #Unsucc. ASPAR-
TIX (▨▨), ConArg2 (▨▨), Dung-O-Matic (▨▨), and ArgTools (▨▨).

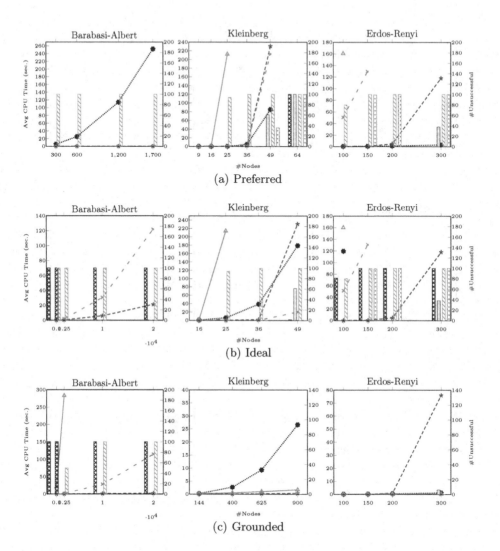

Fig. 4. ASPARTIX (⋯•⋯), ConArg (-⋆-), Dung-O-Matic (—▲—), ArgTools (-×-), and their respective number of unsolved instances within 300sec.: #Unsucc. ASPARTIX (▨), ConArg2 (▨), Dung-O-Matic (▨), and ArgTools (▨).

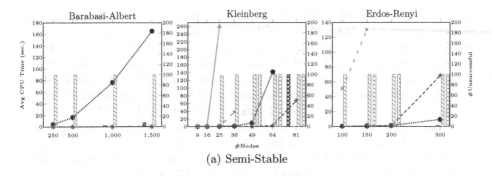

(a) Semi-Stable

Fig. 5. ASPARTIX (⋯•⋯), ConArg (-•-), Dung-O-Matic (─▲─), ArgTools (-×-), and their respective number of unsolved instances within 300sec.: #Unsucc. ASPARTIX (▨), ConArg2 (▨), Dung-O-Matic (▨), and ArgTools (▨).

since they represent the most debatable arguments in the opponent's reasoning. Other forms of topologies to be investigated in the future are plain trees power-law trees[17]: this random-model follows the same preferential-attachment law as the Barabasi-Albert model, the only difference is that it generates trees instead of graphs, thus $|R| = |A| - 1$. Trees are frequently used topologies in Argumentation: for instance, dynPARTIX [15] makes use of the tree-width score of a graph, which measures the "tree-likeness" of a graph.

6   Minizinc Models

In this section we give a few hints on how we developed ConArg2. At the beginning, we used *MiniZinc*[18], which is a medium-level constraint modelling language. It is high-level enough to express most constraint problems easily, but low-level enough that it can be mapped onto existing solvers easily and consistently. *FlatZinc* is a low-level solver input language that is the target language for MiniZinc. It is designed to be easy to translate into the form required by a solver. Several existing solvers can be directly interfaced to Flatzinc, such as The ECLiPSe Constraint Programming System, SICStus Prolog, the JaCoP constraint solver, MinisatID, of course all the solvers in the (G12) MiniZinc distribution, and Gecode.

In Fig. 6 we report the complete Minizinc code to find (and print on the screen) all the conflict-free, admissible, complete, and stable extensions. The adjacency matrix represents the attacks between any two arguments in the considered (directed) AAF. We are able automatically import this data structure from a text file, in order to automate the tests. A solution is represented by

---

[17] http://networkx.github.io/documentation/latest/reference/generated/
networkx.generators.random_graphs.random_powerlaw_tree.html

[18] http://www.minizinc.org

the `arguments` array of boolean values, which assigns a values to all the arguments in an AAF (i.e., [`1..node`]): a `true` value means that the assigned argument belongs to a solution. Afterwards, in Fig. 6 we define two classes of constraints (see [9] for a formal definition), expressing conflict-free and stable properties in the solution. Their definition is quite straightforward: conflict-free constraints state that, if a attacks b, then one of the two must not be taken in a solution (i.e., `arguments[a] == false` ∨ `arguments[b] = false`). Admissible constraints enforce an argument c to be defended from b by an argument a, in case c is taken in an extension. Complete constraints are used in combination with admissible ones: the first one in Fig. 6 imposes that not-attacked arguments (b) belong to a complete extension, while the following constraint ensures that all defended arguments c that are not in conflict with any already taken argument a (`adjMatrix[a,c] != 1` ∧ `adjMatrix[c,a] != 1`), must be part of any complete extension. Stable constraints force any not-taken b (i.e., `not arguments[b]`) to be attacked by at least one argument a (i.e., `arguments[a]`). This implementation has been formally given already in [9,2].

In Fig. 6 the solver is executed to find all the possible solutions, looking across the entire search tree (i.e., `complete` search). With only `solve satisfy;` instead, we search for one solution of the problem: this can be used to verify the existence of at least one extension of a given semantics (see Sec. 2). The first three parameters of `bool_search` are $i)$ the set of problem variables, $ii)$ the strategy of variable selection during search, and $iii)$ the strategy of variable assignment during search. Typically, finite domain solvers use depth-first search and try to assign variables one by one, backtracking to a different value in case of a partial solution violating some constraint.

Note that we can easily change the code in Fig. 6 in order to solve the credulous or skeptical justification of an argument a_i: by adding the line `constraint arguments[i]=true;` we search for all the stable extensions containing a_i. If we use `solve satisfy;`, we can positively answer when a_i is credulously accepted, while if it does not return any solution, a_i is not credulously accepted. Dually, if we impose `constraint arguments[i]=false;`, in case a solution is returned then a_i is not skeptically accepted.

We have first formulated this model in Minizinc in order to have a general support where to test different solvers in the future, e.g. SAT solvers, as *MinisatID*[19]. However, we passed to an implementation in native Gecode to look for performance improvement. Even if these specific hard-problems are boolean, we opt for a constraint solver, instead of a SAT solver, because we would like to have a comprehensive framework where to also implement the weighted problems presented in [8,14] (and already implemented in the JaCoP version of ConArg). Moreover, *labelling-based* semantics in Argumentation [24, Ch. 1]), differently from extension-based ones (see Def. 3), assign each argument to more that just two yes/no labels, e.g., {*in*, *out*, *undecided*}.

---

[19] http://dtai.cs.kuleuven.be/krr/software/minisatid

```
\% Declarations and definitions
int: nnode;
array [1.. nnode,1.. nnode] of int: adjMatrix;
set of int: argumentsRange = 1..nnode;
array [1..nnode] of var bool: arguments;

nnode =5;
adjMatrix = [| 0, 1, 0, 0, 0
             | 0, 0, 0, 0, 0
             | 0, 1, 0, 1, 0
             | 0, 0, 1, 0, 1
             | 0, 0, 0, 0, 1 |];

/* Uncomment Admissible = Admissible extensions
   Uncomment Admissible + Complete = Complete extensions
   Uncomment Stable = Stable extensions */

\% Conflict-free constraints
constraint forall(a,b in argumentsRange where adjMatrix[a,b] == 1)
    (arguments[a] = false \/ arguments[b] = false);

\% Admissible constraints
\% constraint forall(b,c in argumentsRange where adjMatrix[b,c] == 1)
    (arguments[c] -> exists (a in argumentsRange where adjMatrix[a,b]
       == 1)(arguments[a]));

\% Complete constraints
\% constraint forall(b in argumentsRange )( if sum(a in argumentsRange where
    adjMatrix[a,b] == 1)(adjMatrix[a,b]) == 0 then arguments[b] else
       true endif);
\% constraint forall(a,b in argumentsRange where adjMatrix[a,b] == 1)
    (arguments[a] -> forall (c in argumentsRange where adjMatrix[b,c]
       == 1)((adjMatrix[a,c] != 1 /\ adjMatrix[c,a] != 1 /\
          sum(d in argumentsRange where adjMatrix[d,c] == 1)
             (adjMatrix[d,c]) == 1) -> arguments[c]));

\% Stable constraints
\% constraint forall(b in argumentsRange ) ((not arguments[b]) -> exists
    (a in argumentsRange where adjMatrix[a,b] == 1)(arguments[a]));

\% Search (annotated)
solve :: bool_search(arguments, input_order, indomain_max, complete)
    satisfy;

\% Output format
output [show(arguments[a]) ++ " " | a in argumentsRange ];
```

Fig. 6. The complete Minizinc code to find all the extensions (following the conflict-free, admissible, complete, or stable semantics) on the example in Fig. 1, represented in `adjMatrix`. Since only conflict-free constraints are uncommented, as it is the above code finds all conflict-free extensions. It is necessary to uncomment other lines to solve different semantics.

However, after some preliminary tests using Minizinc and different underlying solvers, we implemented ConArg2 by coding in native Gecode. The two main reasons are that, to feed a solver with the Flatzinc representation of a Minizinc model we need a further (delaying) translation step in the middle, and also due to the opportunity to better tune the search algorithm and its heuristics. For lower-order extensions, our Gecode models follow the Minizinc models in Fig. 6. With higher-order extensions instead, which in this paper are preferred, ideal and semi-stable extensions, we externally elaborate on the results provided by Gecode on their lower counterpart. For instance, to find all preferred extensions we search for all admissible extensions using the Gecode library, and then we scan them to satisfy maximal inclusion. Therefore, since max/min inclusion property is not represented with constraints at the moment, we reckon that ConArg2 has wide margins of improvement (see also Sec. 7) for the performance shown in Fig. 4a (preferred), Fig. 4b (ideal), Fig. 4c (grounded), and Fig. 5a (semi-stable): as we can appreciate from Tab. 1, on Erdős-Rényi and Kleinberg, ConArg2 behaves worse than the competitors.

7   Future Work

The main goal of the paper is to provide a first comparative study on how efficiently state-of-the-art reasoners on extension-based semantics behave, and how much they can be stressed: this sets a current limit to the size of AAFs they can be applied to. The testbed has been created by using three different random graph-models. Due to the lack of certain AAF-topologies in the literature, we have explored different models with the purpose to be as more objective as possible. Real argument-maps collected in DebateGraph seem to point towards graphs with few outgoing edges for each node, and few hubs with many incoming attacks. For this reason we believe that, at least in such scenario of community-oriented debating platform, the Barabasi-Albert model (or power-law trees) proves to be the more appropriate model. However, since DebateGraph maps are not simple AAFs, but include different relationships among nodes, we leave such topology study to successive works.

The results in Sec. 5 point us along several interesting lines. First of all, we plan to extend ConArg2 to solve weighted problems [8], and the hard problems implemented in CEGARTIX and dynPARTIX (e.g., the credulous or skeptical acceptance of an argument in preferred extensions) in order to have a comparison with these tools. We have recently evaluated ConArg2 and dynPARTIX on the stable semantics in [6]. To do so, we also plan to design and implement specific search-heuristics (using Gecode) in order to improve the performance with higher-order extensions (e.g., preferred), so to better manage e.g. maximality of set inclusion, and compare it to other solutions as the work in [12] or [23]. Note that these heuristics can be inspired by or tuned on a specific graph model. Finally, we would like to test the tools over AAFs extracted from real debates, for instance using [19]. Related, but on a different perspective, we would like to study the topology of real AAFs, in order to match them to specific (social) graph-models and improve the performance with real data.

References

1. Amgoud, L., Cayrol, C.: Inferring from inconsistency in preference-based argumentation frameworks. J. Autom. Reasoning 29(2), 125–169 (2002)
2. Amgoud, L., Devred, C.: Argumentation frameworks as constraint satisfaction problems. In: Benferhat, S., Grant, J. (eds.) SUM 2011. LNCS, vol. 6929, pp. 110–122. Springer, Heidelberg (2011)
3. Barabasi, A.L., Albert, R.: Emergence of scaling in random networks. Science 286(5439), 509–512 (1999)
4. Bench-Capon, T.J.M.: Persuasion in practical argument using value-based argumentation frameworks. J. Log. Comput. 13(3), 429–448 (2003)
5. Bench-Capon, T.J.M., Dunne, P.E.: Argumentation in artificial intelligence. Artif. Intell. 171(10-15), 619–641 (2007),
http://dx.doi.org/10.1016/j.artint.2007.05.001
6. Bistarelli, S., Rossi, F., Santini, F.: Benchmarking hard problems in random abstract AFs: The stable semantics. In: Proceedings of the Fifth International Conference on Computational Models of Argument. FAIA. IOS Press (to appear, 2014)

7. Bistarelli, S., Rossi, F., Santini, F.: Comparing three abstract argumentation reasoning-tools over three graph models. In: ECAI 2014 - 21st European Conference on Artificial Intelligence. Frontiers in Artificial Intelligence and Applications. IOS Press (to appear, 2014)
8. Bistarelli, S., Santini, F.: A common computational framework for semiring-based argumentation systems. In: ECAI 2010 - 19th European Conference on Artificial Intelligence. Frontiers in Artificial Intelligence and Applications, vol. 215, pp. 131–136. IOS Press (2010)
9. Bistarelli, S., Santini, F.: Conarg: A constraint-based computational framework for argumentation systems. In: Proceedings of the 2011 IEEE 23rd International Conference on Tools with Artificial Intelligence, ICTAI 2011, pp. 605–612. IEEE Computer Society, Washington, DC (2011),
   http://dx.doi.org/10.1109/ICTAI.2011.96
10. Bistarelli, S., Santini, F.: Modeling and solving afs with a constraint-based tool: Conarg. In: Modgil, S., Oren, N., Toni, F. (eds.) TAFA 2011. LNCS, vol. 7132, pp. 99–116. Springer, Heidelberg (2012),
    http://dx.doi.org/10.1007/978-3-642-29184-5_7
11. Bistarelli, S., Santini, F.: Coalitions of arguments: An approach with constraint programming. Fundam. Inform. 124(4), 383–401 (2013)
12. Cerutti, F., Dunne, P.E., Giacomin, M., Vallati, M.: Computing preferred extensions in abstract argumentation: A SAT-based approach. In: Black, E., Modgil, S., Oren, N. (eds.) TAFA 2013. LNCS, vol. 8306, pp. 176–193. Springer, Heidelberg (2014)
13. Dung, P.M.: On the acceptability of arguments and its fundamental role in non-monotonic reasoning, logic programming and n-person games. Artif. Intell. 77(2), 321–357 (1995)
14. Dunne, P.E., Hunter, A., McBurney, P., Parsons, S., Wooldridge, M.: Weighted argument systems: Basic definitions, algorithms, and complexity results. Artif. Intell. 175(2), 457–486 (2011)
15. Dvořák, W., Morak, M., Nopp, C., Woltran, S.: dynPARTIX - A dynamic programming reasoner for abstract argumentation. In: Tompits, H., Abreu, S., Oetsch, J., Pührer, J., Seipel, D., Umeda, M., Wolf, A. (eds.) INAP/WLP 2011. LNCS (LNAI), vol. 7773, pp. 259–268. Springer, Heidelberg (2013)
16. Dvořák, W., Järvisalo, M., Wallner, J.P., Woltran, S.: Complexity-sensitive decision procedures for abstract argumentation. Artif. Intell. 206, 53–78 (2014),
    http://dx.doi.org/10.1016/j.artint.2013.10.001
17. Egly, U., Gaggl, S.A., Woltran, S.: Answer-set programming encodings for argumentation frameworks. Argument & Computation 1(2), 147–177 (2010)
18. Erdős, P., Rényi, A.: On the evolution of random graphs. Bull. Inst. Internat. Statist. 38(4), 343–347 (1961)
19. Gabbriellini, S., Torroni, P.: Large scale agreements via microdebates. In: AT. CEUR Workshop Proceedings, vol. 918, pp. 366–377. CEUR-WS.org (2012)
20. Gabbriellini, S., Torroni, P.: Arguments in social networks. In: Proceedings of the 2013 International Conference on Autonomous Agents and Multi-agent Systems, AAMAS 2013, pp. 1119–1120. International Foundation for Autonomous Agents and Multiagent Systems, Richland (2013),
    http://dl.acm.org/citation.cfm?id=2484920.2485100
21. Martel, C., Nguyen, V.: Analyzing Kleinberg's (and other) small-world models. In: Proceedings of the ACM Symposium on Principles of Distributed Computing, PODC 2004, pp. 179–188. ACM, New York (2004),
    http://doi.acm.org/10.1145/1011767.1011794

22. Nofal, S., Atkinson, K., Dunne, P.E.: Algorithms for argumentation semantics: Labeling attacks as a generalization of labeling arguments. Journal of Artificial Intelligence Research 49, 635–668 (2014)
23. Nofal, S., Atkinson, K., Dunne, P.E.: Algorithms for decision problems in argument systems under preferred semantics. Artif. Intell. 207, 23–51 (2014)
24. Rahwan, I., Simari, G.R.: Argumentation in Artificial Intelligence, 1st edn. Springer Publishing Company, Incorporated (2009)
25. Rossi, F., van Beek, P., Walsh, T.: Handbook of Constraint Programming (Foundations of Artificial Intelligence). Elsevier Science Inc., New York (2006)
26. Toni, F., Sergot, M.: Argumentation and answer set programming. In: Balduccini, M., Son, T.C. (eds.) Logic Programming, Knowledge Representation, and Nonmonotonic Reasoning. LNCS, vol. 6565, pp. 164–180. Springer, Heidelberg (2011), http://dx.doi.org/10.1007/978-3-642-20832-4_11
27. Toni, F., Torroni, P.: Bottom-up argumentation. In: Modgil, S., Oren, N., Toni, F. (eds.) TAFA 2011. LNCS, vol. 7132, pp. 249–262. Springer, Heidelberg (2012), http://dx.doi.org/10.1007/978-3-642-29184-5_16

Automated Planning of Simple Persuasion Dialogues

Elizabeth Black, Amanda Coles, and Sara Bernardini

Department of Informatics, King's College London, UK
firstname.surname@kcl.ac.uk

Abstract. We take a simple form of non-adversarial persuasion dialogue in which one participant (the *persuader*) aims to convince the other (the *responder*) to accept the *topic* of the dialogue by asserting sets of beliefs. The responder replies honestly to indicate whether it finds the topic to be acceptable (we make no prescription as to what formalism and semantics must be used for this, only assuming some function for determining acceptable beliefs from a logical knowledge base). Our persuader has a *model* of the responder, which assigns probabilities to sets of beliefs, representing the likelihood that each set is the responder's actual beliefs. The beliefs the persuader chooses to assert and the order in which it asserts them (i.e. its *strategy*) can impact on the success of the dialogue and the success of a particular strategy cannot generally be guaranteed (because of the uncertainty over the responder's beliefs). We define our persuasion dialogue as a *classical planning problem*, which can then be solved by an automated planner to generate a strategy that maximises the chance of success given the persuader's model of the responder; this allows us to exploit the power of existing automated planners, which have been shown to be efficient in many complex domains. We provide preliminary results that demonstrate how the efficiency of our approach scales with the number of beliefs.

1 Introduction

Argument dialogues are an established agreement technology; they provide a principled way of structuring rational interactions between participants (machine or human) who argue about the validity of certain claims in order to resolve their conflicting information, competing goals, incompatible intentions or opposing views of the world [16]. Such dialogues are typically defined by the *moves* that can be made and rules to determine which moves are permissible at any point in the dialogue. Much existing work in the field focusses on defining argument dialogues that allow achievement of a particular goal; for example, to persuade the other participant to accept some belief [19] or to agree on some action to achieve a shared goal [3]. However, successful achievement of a participant's dialogue goal normally depends on the *strategy* it employs to determine which of the permissible moves to make during the dialogue; the development of effective argument dialogue strategies is thus an important area of active research [23].

We consider a simple non-adversarial persuasion dialogue in which the *persuader* asserts beliefs with the aim of convincing the *responder* to accept the dialogue *topic*. Success depends on the beliefs the persuader chooses to assert and the order in which it asserts them (its *strategy*); this is informed by the persuader's (uncertain) *model* of the responder (i.e. its beliefs about the responder's beliefs). Our proposal is general in that it

N. Bulling et al. (Eds.): CLIMA XV, LNAI 8624, pp. 87–104, 2014.

allows for any logical formalism and semantics to be used to determine the acceptability of claims; the beliefs asserted may be logical formulas or abstract arguments.

We define the persuader's choice of beliefs to assert as a *classical planning problem*; this allows us to use an automated planner to search for an optimal strategy given the persuader's model of the responder. Our preliminary results show that a planner can find an optimal strategy for a problem where there are 8 beliefs the persuader can assert and 2^8 possible sets of responder beliefs it considers in 70.22 seconds (32.54 seconds to find the strategy, 37.68 seconds to prove it optimal). We discuss how we might adapt our encoding of the planning problem and the search strategy of the planner to improve the scalability.

2   Simple Persuasion Dialogues

In our simple persuasion dialogues, the persuader aims to convince the responder to accept the topic of the dialogue by asserting beliefs. We make no prescription as to which semantics the responder must use to reason about the acceptability of beliefs. We assume only a finite logical language $\mathcal{L}$ and some function for determining the set of *acceptable* claims given some knowledge base of $\mathcal{L}$.

Definition 1. *We assume a function* Acceptable $: \wp(\mathcal{L}) \rightarrow \wp(\mathcal{L})$ *which, for a knowledge base* $\Phi \subseteq \mathcal{L}$, *returns the set of* **acceptable claims** *of* Φ *such that:*

$$\text{Acceptable}(\Phi) = \{\alpha \in \mathcal{L} \mid \alpha \text{ is acceptable given } \Phi \text{ under the chosen acceptability} \\ semantics\}$$

The examples in our paper use a simple argumentation formalism with Dung's grounded semantics [5] to determine the acceptability of beliefs (which we define later). There are, however, many formalisms and associated acceptability semantics that may be used to instantiate Definition 1, some examples are: logic-based deductive argumentation [2], abstract argumentation [5], assumption-based argumentation [6], defeasible logic programming [9], ASPIC+ [15], classical logic.

Each dialogue participant has a set of *beliefs*, which is a subset of $\mathcal{L}$. We assume some *common knowledge*, which is a subset of the intersection of the participants' beliefs and is known by the persuader to be part of the responder's beliefs. The persuader has a *model* of the responder, which is a function that assigns a probability to subsets of $\mathcal{L}$, representing how likely the persuader believes it is that the responder's beliefs are that set ([11] considers how such a model might be constructed). Our framework thus allows for the case where the persuader believes the responder has beliefs the persuader itself does not believe, but assumes that the persuader is aware of all the beliefs the responder may hold.

This proposal allows us to capture situations where the persuader is an expert who aims to convince the responder to accept a certain belief. For example, the persuader may be a medical expert aiming to convince a patient that they ought to give up smoking, where the common knowledge contains the patient-specific information such as their age and medical history and the expert's model of the patient captures the beliefs it has about the patient's preferences and values. Based on this model, the expert must select knowledge to assert to the patient that will convince them to accept that they ought to give up smoking based on the information specific to their circumstances.

We define a *simple persuasion situation* by the persuader's and responder's beliefs, the common knowledge, the persuader's model of the responder and the topic of the dialogue. The set of *possible responder belief sets* refers to those sets of beliefs that the persuader believes may be the responder's beliefs (each of which contain the common knowledge, which is known by the persuader to be part of the responder's beliefs). We assume that the persuader's model is accurate in the sense that it assigns a non-zero probability to the responder's actual set of beliefs.

Definition 2. *A* **simple persuasion situation** *is a tuple* $\langle \Sigma^P, \Sigma^R, \Omega, \mathsf{m}, T \rangle$ *where:*

- $\Sigma^P \subseteq \mathcal{L}$ *is the* **persuader's beliefs***;*
- $\Sigma^R \subseteq \mathcal{L}$ *is the* **responder's beliefs***;*
- $\Omega \subseteq \Sigma^P \cap \Sigma^R$ *is the* **common knowledge***;*
- $\mathsf{m} : \wp(\mathcal{L}) \to [0,1]$ *is the* **persuader's model of the responder** *such that*
  (a) $\sum_{\Phi \subseteq \mathcal{L}} \mathsf{m}(\Phi) = 1$,
  (b) for all Φ *such that* $\mathsf{m}(\Phi) > 0$, $\Omega \subseteq \Phi$, *and*
  (c) $\mathsf{m}(\Sigma^R) > 0$;
- $T \in \mathcal{L}$ *is the* **topic** *of the dialogue.*

The **possible responder belief sets** *given a particular model of the responder* m *is denoted* $\mathsf{PossRespBels}(\mathsf{m})$ *where:* $\mathsf{PossRespBels}(\mathsf{m}) = \{\Phi \mid \mathsf{m}(\Phi) > 0\}$.

The two participants take it in turn to make moves to one another. The persuader asserts subsets of its beliefs, not asserting beliefs it knows to be part of the common knowledge and not repeating beliefs previously asserted. After each asserting move made by the persuader, the responder replies honestly with a yes or no move, indicating whether it finds the topic of the dialogue to be acceptable given the union of its beliefs and those beliefs that the persuader has asserted thus far in the dialogue. If the responder makes a yes move, then the dialogue terminates successfully. We thus define a *well-formed simple persuasion dialogue* as follows.

Definition 3. *A* **well-formed simple persuasion dialogue** *of a simple persuasion situation* $\langle \Sigma^P, \Sigma^R, \Omega, \mathsf{m}, T \rangle$ *is a sequence of moves* $[P_1, R_1, \ldots, P_n, R_n]$ *such that:*

1. $P_1 = \{T\}$,
2. *for all* i *such that* $1 < i \leq n$:
   (a) $P_i \subseteq \Sigma^P \setminus \Omega$,
   (b) for all j *such that* $1 < j < i$, $P_j \cap P_i = \emptyset$;
3. *for all* i *such that* $1 \leq i < n$:
   (a) $R_i = \mathsf{no}$,
   (b) $T \notin \mathsf{Acceptable}(\Sigma^R \cup P_2 \cup \ldots \cup P_i)$;
4. $R_n \in \{\mathsf{yes}, \mathsf{no}\}$,
5. $R_n = \mathsf{yes}$ *iff* $T \in \mathsf{Acceptable}(\Sigma^R \cup P_2 \cup \ldots \cup P_n)$.

If $R_n = \mathsf{yes}$, *the dialogue is* **successful***. If* $R_n = \mathsf{no}$, *the dialogue is* **unsuccessful***.*

The persuader has a choice of beliefs it can assert at each point in the dialogue (determined by its *strategy*), while the responder's moves are determined by its beliefs and those asserted by the persuader. A *strategy* for the persuader is simply a sequence of non-intersecting subsets of its beliefs.

Definition 4. *A **strategy** for a persuader with beliefs Σ^P, for a dialogue with topic T where the common knowledge is Ω is a sequence $[P_1, P_2, \ldots, P_{n-1}, P_n]$ such that:*

1. *$P_1 = \{T\}$,*
2. *for all i such that $1 < i \leq n$:*
   (a) $P_i \subseteq \Sigma^P \setminus \Omega$,
   (b) for all j such that $1 < j < i$, $P_j \cap P_i = \emptyset$.

A strategy thus corresponds to a sequence of persuader moves in a simple persuasion dialogue. We give some examples in the following section.

2.1 Simple Persuasion Dialogue Examples

To illustrate our simple persuasion dialogues, we must first specify the acceptability semantics with which we instantiate Definition 1; for this, we define an argumentation formalism to which we apply the grounded semantics of Dung [5]. The argumentation formalism we define allows us to concisely present some examples; we make no claims about the appropriateness of its properties. Recall that any semantics for determining the set of acceptable claims given some knowledge base of a logical language can be used with our proposal; this is only one such example and the argumentation formalism we present can be replaced with an established formalism (e.g. [2,5,6,9,15]).

We use a simple propositional language $\mathcal{L}$ that is constructed from a set of propositional atoms $\{a, b, c, \ldots\}$; α is a strong literal iff α is an atom or of the form $\neg\beta$ where β is an atom and $\neg$ represents strong classical negation; α is a weak literal iff α is of the form $\sim\beta$ where β is a strong literal and $\sim$ represents negation as failure; α is a wff of $\mathcal{L}$ iff α is a strong literal or α takes the form of a rule $\phi_1 \wedge \ldots \wedge \phi_n \rightarrow \psi$ where ψ is a strong literal and each $\phi_1, \ldots, \phi_n$ is either a strong or weak literal.[1]

An *argument* constructed from a knowledge base of $\mathcal{L}$ has a *support* and a *claim* such that: (1) the support is a subset of the knowledge base; (2) the claim is either a strong literal that appears as the support or is the head of a rule in the support; (3) for every rule in the support of the argument, every strong literal that appears in its body is either the head of another rule in the support or is itself a member of the support; (4) the support is consistent; and (5) the support is a minimal set satisfying (1-4).

Definition 5. *An **argument** constructed from a knowledge base $\Delta \subseteq \mathcal{L}$ is a tuple (Γ, γ) where Γ is the **support** and γ is the **claim** such that γ is a strong literal from $\mathcal{L}$ and:*

1. *$\Gamma \subseteq \Delta$;*
2. *either $\Gamma = \{\gamma\}$ or there exists $\phi_1 \wedge \ldots \wedge \phi_n \rightarrow \gamma \in \Gamma$;*

---

[1] Note that the symbols $\wedge$ and $\rightarrow$ are not being used here to represent classical conjunction or implication, but rather represent meta-relations between sets of literals.

3. *for every* $\alpha_1 \wedge \ldots \wedge \alpha_n \rightarrow \beta \in \Gamma$, *for every* $i \in \{1, \ldots, n\}$ *such that* α_i *is a strong literal, either* $\alpha_i \in \Gamma$ *or there exists* $\phi_1 \wedge \ldots \wedge \phi_m \rightarrow \alpha_i \in \Gamma$;

4. *if* $\Phi = (\{\psi \in \Gamma \mid \psi \text{ is a strong literal}\} \cup \{\beta \mid \text{there exists } \alpha_1 \wedge \ldots \wedge \alpha_n \rightarrow \beta \in \Gamma\})$, *then*

   (a) $\Phi \nvdash \bot$, *and*

   (b) *if there exists* $\alpha_1 \wedge \ldots \wedge \alpha_n \rightarrow \beta \in \Gamma$ *such that* $\sim \psi \in \{\alpha_1, \ldots, \alpha_n\}$, *then* $\psi \notin \Phi$;

5. Γ *is minimal under set inclusion.*

We denote **the set of all arguments that can be constructed from** Δ *as* $\mathsf{Args}(\Delta)$.

An argument $A1$ *attacks* an argument $A2$ if either: the claim of $A1$ is the negation of the claim of $A2$, the claim of $A1$ is the negation of something that has been derived by negation of failure to support $A2$, or the claim of $A1$ is the negation of something that appears as the head of a rule that is part of the support of $A2$.

Definition 6. *An argument* (Γ_1, γ_1) **attacks** *an argument* (Γ_2, γ_2) *iff either:*

- $\gamma_1 = \neg \gamma_2$,
- *there exists a rule* $\alpha_1 \wedge \ldots \wedge \alpha_n \rightarrow \beta \in \Gamma_2$ *such that* $\sim \gamma_1 \in \{\alpha_1, \ldots, \alpha_n\}$, *or*
- *there exists a rule* $\alpha_1 \wedge \ldots \wedge \alpha_n \rightarrow \beta \in \Gamma_2$ *such that* $\gamma_1 = \neg \beta$.

The *argument framework* of a particular knowledge base represents the set of all arguments that can be constructed and the attack relations between those arguments.

Definition 7. *The* **argument framework** *of a knowledge base* $\Delta \subseteq \mathcal{L}$, *denoted* $\mathsf{AF}(\Delta)$, *is the tuple* $(\mathcal{A}, \mathcal{R})$ *where:*

1. $\mathcal{A} = \mathsf{Args}(\Delta)$,
2. $\mathcal{R} = \{(A_1, A_2) \mid A_1, A_2 \in \mathcal{A} \text{ and } A_1 \text{ attacks } A_2\}$.

We apply the grounded semantics [5] to determine the acceptable claims of an argument framework. To define the grounded semantics, we follow Caminada's labelling approach [4], which assigns exactly one label from $\{\mathtt{in}, \mathtt{out}, \mathtt{undecided}\}$ to each argument in an argument graph such that the *reinstatement labelling* conditions given in the definition below hold. The *grounded labelling* is the unique labelling that meets the reinstatement labelling conditions and minimises the number of arguments labelled as $\mathtt{in}$, which are those arguments that are acceptable under the grounded semantics.

Definition 8. *Let* $(\mathcal{A}, \mathcal{R})$ *be an argument framework. A* **reinstatement labelling** *of* $(\mathcal{A}, \mathcal{R})$ *is an assignment of exactly one label from* $\{\mathtt{in}, \mathtt{out}, \mathtt{undecided}\}$ *to each of the arguments in* $\mathcal{A}$ *such that the following conditions hold.*

1. *An argument is labelled as* $\mathtt{in}$ *iff every argument that attacks it is labelled as* $\mathtt{out}$.
2. *An argument is labelled as* $\mathtt{out}$ *iff there is no argument that attacks it and is labelled as* $\mathtt{in}$.

The **grounded labelling** *of an argument framework* $(\mathcal{A}, \mathcal{R})$ *is the reinstatement labelling of* $(\mathcal{A}, \mathcal{R})$ *that minimises the number of arguments labelled as* $\mathtt{in}$.

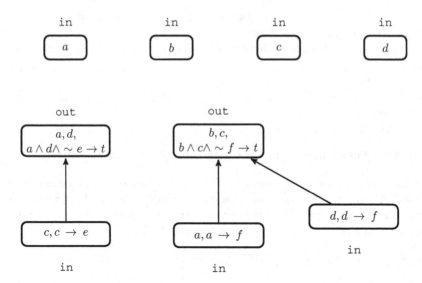

Fig. 1. The argument framework constructed from the knowledge base given in Example 1. For brevity, nodes are labelled only with the support of the argument they correspond to. The directed edges represent the attacks between arguments and nodes are annotated with the grounded labelling.

We can now define the acceptable claims of a particular knowledge base Δ as those that appear as the claim of an argument that can be constructed from Δ and are labelled as in in the grounded labelling of the argument framework constructed from Δ.

Definition 9. *Let* $\Delta \subseteq \mathcal{L}$ *be a knowledge base such that* $\mathsf{AF}(\Delta) = (\mathcal{A}, \mathcal{R})$. *A wff* $\alpha \in \mathcal{L}$ *is* **acceptable** *given* Δ *iff there exists an argument* $(\Phi, \alpha) \in \mathcal{A}$ *such that* (Φ, α) *is labelled* in *in the grounded labelling of* $(\mathcal{A}, \mathcal{R})$.

Example 1. Consider the knowledge base $\Delta = \{a, b, c, d, a \wedge d \wedge \sim e \rightarrow t, b \wedge c \wedge \sim f \rightarrow t, c \rightarrow e, a \rightarrow f, d \rightarrow f\}$. The argument framework $\mathsf{AF}(\Delta)$ is shown in Figure 1. Thus we see that $\mathsf{Acceptable}(\Delta) = \{a, b, c, d, e, f\}$.

Now we have defined a mechanism for determining the acceptable claims from some knowledge base of $\mathcal{L}$, we present some examples of well-formed persuasion dialogues where Definition 1 is instantiated with the definition of acceptable claims from Definition 9.

Example 2. Consider a persuader with beliefs Σ^P, common knowledge Ω, model of the responder m, for a dialogue with topic t where:

- $\Sigma^P = \{a, b, c\} \cup \Omega$;
- $\Omega = \{a \wedge d \wedge \sim e \rightarrow t, b \wedge c \wedge \sim f \rightarrow t, c \rightarrow e, a \rightarrow f, d \rightarrow f\}$;
- $\mathsf{m}(\{c\} \cup \Omega) = \mathsf{m}(\{d\} \cup \Omega) = 0.4$, $\mathsf{m}(\{a, c\} \cup \Omega) = 0.2$ and for all other $\Phi \subseteq \mathcal{L}$, $\mathsf{m}(\Phi) = 0$.

There are three possible responder belief sets to consider: $\{c\} \cup \Omega$, $\{d\} \cup \Omega$, $\{a, c\} \cup \Omega$.

- If $\Sigma^R = \{c\} \cup \Omega$, some examples of well-formed simple persuasion dialogues are: $D1 = [\{t\}, \text{no}, \{a, b\}, \text{no}]$; $D2 = [\{t\}, \text{no}, \{b\}, \text{yes}]$.
- If $\Sigma^R = \{d\} \cup \Omega$, some examples of well-formed simple persuasion dialogues are: $D3 = [\{t\}, \text{no}, \{a, b\}, \text{yes}]$; $D4 = [\{t\}, \text{no}, \{b\}, \text{no}, \{a\}, \text{yes}]$.
- If $\Sigma^R = \{a, c\} \cup \Omega$, some examples of well-formed simple persuasion dialogues are: $D1 = [\{t\}, \text{no}, \{a, b\}, \text{no}]$; $D5 = [\{t\}, \text{no}, \{b\}, \text{no}, \{a\}, \text{no}]$.

We consider two corresponding strategies for this persuader: $S1 = [\{t\}, \{a, b\}]$; $S2 = [\{t\}, \{b\}, \{a\}]$.

- If the persuader follows strategy $S1$ and $\Sigma^R = \{c\} \cup \Omega$ or $\Sigma^R = \{a, c\} \cup \Omega$, dialogue $D1$ will result; if $\Sigma^R = \{d\} \cup \Omega$, dialogue $D3$ will result.
- If the persuader follows strategy $S2$ and $\Sigma^R = \{c\} \cup \Omega$, dialogue $D2$ will result; if $\Sigma^R = \{d\} \cup \Omega$, dialogue $D4$ will result; if $\Sigma^R = \{a, c\} \cup \Omega$, dialogue $D5$ will result.

If the persuader in Example 2 follows strategy $S1$, it will be successful if the responder's beliefs are $\{c\} \cup \Omega$ but not if they are $\{d\} \cup \Omega$ or $\{c, d\} \cup \Omega$. If the persuader follows strategy $S2$, it will be successful if the responder's beliefs are either $\{d\} \cup \Omega$ (as in dialogue $D4$) or $\{c\} \cup \Omega$ (in which case the responder would terminate the dialogue successfully after the persuader moves $\{b\}$, as in dialogue $D2$). Thus the persuader should prefer $S2$ over $S1$.

We see then that there may be multiple possible responder belief sets given which a particular strategy will lead to success. We define the *probability of success* of a strategy (given the persuader's model of the responder) as the sum of the probabilities assigned by the persuader's model to each possible responder belief set under which that strategy leads to success.

Definition 10. *The **probability of success** of the strategy $[P_1, P_2, \ldots, P_{n-1}, P_n]$ for a persuader whose model of the responder is* m, *for a dialogue with topic T and common knowledge Ω is $\sum_{\Psi \in \Phi} \text{m}(\Psi)$ where:*

$$\Phi = \{\Sigma^R \mid \text{there exists } m \text{ such that } 1 \leq m \leq n \text{ and}$$
$$[P_1, \text{no}, P_2, \text{no}, \ldots, P_{m-1}, \text{no}, P_m, \text{yes}]$$
$$\text{is a well-formed simple persuasion dialogue of } \langle \Sigma^P, \Sigma^R, \Omega, \text{m}, T \rangle \}$$

Example 3. Continuing Example 2, the probability of success of $S1$ is 0.4, the probability of success of $S2$ is 0.8.

An *optimal strategy* for a persuader (given its model of the responder) is one that maximises the probability of success. In the next section we show how we can represent the persuader's choice of moves to make in a simple persuasion dialogue as a classical planning problem so that we can use an automated planner to search the space of possible strategies to find one that maximises the probability of success.

3   Representing Simple Persuasion Dialogues as a Planning Problem

In this section we describe how the simple persuasion dialogue can be modelled as a classical planning problem, which can then be solved by an automated planner to generate a strategy for the persuader. A classical planning problem consists of four components: an initial state, I, describing the current state of the world; a desired goal condition, G; an optimisation metric M; and the set of actions, A, which determine the state transitions that can be made. Each action in A has preconditions, which must be true in a state S for it to be applicable, and effects that occur when it is applied allowing the generation of a new state S'. A solution to a planning problem is a *plan*: an ordered sequence of actions (each of which is applicable in sequence) that transforms I into a state that satisfies G.

We formally define our model of the planning problem later, but first we discuss some high-level issues. The major challenge in representing our persuasion dialogue as a classical planning problem is that the initial state is not known: that is, the persuader does not know which of the possible responder belief sets hold. We might desire a plan that will convince the responder regardless of which of the possible belief sets it holds; in the planning literature such a plan is known as a *conformant plan*. Many approaches to solving conformant planning problems have been proposed, the most closely related to our work is that of compiling conformant planning into classical planning and then using a classical planner to solve the problem [1].

Whilst conformant planning is sufficient in the case where there exists a sequence of actions that will achieve the goal no matter which of the possible initial states actually hold, this is not always the case in our simple persuasion dialogues (as we see in Example 2 and later in our experimental analysis). Instead what we seek is the plan that maximises the probability of success. In a sense we are seeking the 'most conformant' plan, the one that is most likely to result in the responder being convinced, but accept that it is not possible to guarantee success. This problem is related to that considered in [22]; whilst [22] considers a general solution to this type of planning problem, our compilation is made more efficient by exploiting particular properties of this problem, specifically that we do not need to consider possible initial states any further once the responder is convinced from these states.

3.1   Overview of Model

To aid in understanding the formal model of our planning problem we give a brief overview here, making use of a small example. The actions that the persuader can perform are to `assert` a belief or to pass the turn to the responder (we refer to this action as `responder-turn`). We allow the persuader to make multiple assertions before the responder makes a response; this is simply a way of modelling the fact that the persuader can assert multiple beliefs simultaneously. Since the first move the persuader must make is fixed (it must assert the topic) a plan to determine the persuader's strategy always starts with a `responder-turn` (this action must be included since the persuader does not know what move the responder will make); similarly a plan must always end with a `responder-turn`.

Example 4. Following from Example 2, the strategy $S1$ is captured by the plan

(responder-turn) (assert a) (assert b) (responder-turn)

and the strategy $S2$ is captured by the plan

(responder-turn) (assert b) (responder-turn) (assert a) (responder-turn)

At each state in a simple persuasion plan (i.e. after each action is made), we can consider the formulas the responder is reasoning with to determine whether it finds the topic acceptable, i.e. the union of its beliefs and the beliefs asserted so far by the persuader; we refer to this set as the **responder's reasoning set**. Although the persuader does not know what this set is in a particular state, since we assume that the responder's beliefs are one of the possible responder belief sets, the persuader does know that the responder's reasoning set is a member of the following set (where m is the persuader's model of the responder): $\{\Phi \cup \Psi \mid \Phi$ are the beliefs asserted so far and $\Psi \in$ PossRespBels(m)$\}$.

The general idea is to monitor in each state during planning, given the beliefs that have been asserted so far and the persuader's model of the responder: (a) the probability that the responder's reasoning set is each of the possible sets that may occur (i.e. $\{\Phi \cup \Psi \mid \Phi \subseteq \Sigma^P$ and $\Psi \in$ PossRespBels(m)$\}$), and (b) the probability that the responder will terminate the dialogue successfully either in the current state or some previous state of the plan (i.e. the probability of success of the plan).

Table 1 shows how the two strategies discussed in Example 2 are evaluated by our approach. We see that there are 12 possible sets that may occur as the responder's reasoning set. Let us consider strategy $S1$. In the initial state, the responder's reasoning set is simply its beliefs (as the persuader has not yet asserted anything) and so (according to the persuader's model of the responder) there is a 0.4 probability that the responder's reasoning set is $\{c\} \cup \Omega$, a 0.4 probability that it is $\{d\} \cup \Omega$, and a 0.2 probability that it is $\{a, c\} \cup \Omega$. Since none of these sets cause the responder to find the topic acceptable (and so the responder is sure to make a no move), after the first (responder-turn) action these probabilities stay the same.

After the (assert a) action, if the responder's reasoning set had been $\{c\} \cup \Omega$ or $\{a, c\} \cup \Omega$ in the previous state it would now be $\{a, c\} \cup \Omega$, thus the probability assigned to $\{c\} \cup \Omega$ is now 0 and the probability assigned to $\{a, c\} \cup \Omega$ is now 0.6. If the responder's reasoning set had been $\{d\} \cup \Omega$ in the previous state it would now be $\{a, d\} \cup \Omega$, thus the probability assigned to $\{d\} \cup \Omega$ is now 0 and the probability assigned to $\{a, d\} \cup \Omega$ is 0.4.

After the (assert b) action, if the responder's reasoning set had been $\{a, c\} \cup \Omega$ in the previous state it would now be $\{a, b, c\} \cup \Omega$, thus the probability assigned to $\{a, c\} \cup \Omega$ is now 0 and the probability assigned to $\{a, b, c\} \cup \Omega$ is now 0.6. If the responder's reasoning set had been $\{a, d\} \cup \Omega$ in the previous state it would now be $\{a, b, d\} \cup \Omega$, thus the probability assigned to $\{a, d\} \cup \Omega$ is now 0 and the probability assigned to $\{a, b, d\} \cup \Omega$ is 0.4.

If the responder's reasoning set is $\{a, b, d\} \cup \Omega$, then it will find the topic acceptable and terminate the dialogue successfully, thus we increase the probability of success in the state after the final (responder-turn) action by 0.4 (the probability that the

Table 1. For Example 2, at each state during planning, shows the updates to: (a) the probabilities assigned to the sets that may occur as the responder's reasoning set and (b) the probability of success

	Probability responder's reasoning set is:												Probability of success
	$\{c\}\cup\Omega$	$\{d\}\cup\Omega$	$\{a,c\}\cup\Omega$	$\{a,d\}\cup\Omega$	$\{b,c\}\cup\Omega$	$\{b,d\}\cup\Omega$	$\{a,b,c\}\cup\Omega$	$\{c,d\}\cup\Omega$	$\{a,b,d\}\cup\Omega$	$\{a,c,d\}\cup\Omega$	$\{b,c,d\}\cup\Omega$	$\{a,b,c,d\}\cup\Omega$	
Strategy $S1$:													
Initial state	0.4	0.4	0.2	0	0	0	0	0	0	0	0	0	0
(responder-turn)	0.4	0.4	0.2	0	0	0	0	0	0	0	0	0	0
(assert a)	0	0	0.6	0.4	0	0	0	0	0	0	0	0	0
(assert b)	0	0	0	0	0	0	0.6	0	0.4	0	0	0	0
(responder-turn)	0	0	0	0	0	0	0.6	0	0	0	0	0	0.4
Strategy $S2$:													
Initial state	0.4	0.4	0.2	0	0	0	0	0	0	0	0	0	0
(responder-turn)	0.4	0.4	0.2	0	0	0	0	0	0	0	0	0	0
(assert b)	0	0	0	0	0.4	0.4	0.2	0	0	0	0	0	0
(responder-turn)	0	0	0	0	0	0.4	0.2	0	0	0	0	0	0.4
(assert a)	0	0	0	0	0	0	0.2	0	0.4	0	0	0	0.4
(responder-turn)	0	0	0	0	0	0	0.2	0	0	0	0	0	0.8

responder's reasoning set in the previous state was $\{a,b,d\}\cup\Omega$) and set the probability assigned to $\{a,b,d\}\cup\Omega$ to 0 (as, if the plan were to continue after this point, the responder could no longer be reasoning with this set, as if it had been it would have ended the dialogue successfully). The probability of success of the plan that captures Strategy $S1$ is thus 0.4.

The effect of an `asssert` action is to update the probabilities assigned to the possible responder's reasoning sets (i.e. those with a non-zero probability), as a consequence of the asserted belief being added to these sets. The effect of a `responder-turn` move is to update the probability of success assigned to the plan when a possible responder reasoning set would cause the topic to be acceptable, and to assign the probability associated with that set to zero. In the following section we formally define the conditions and effects of these two actions and specify how a planning problem instance is constructed from a simple persuasion situation.

3.2   Formal Model of the Simple Persuasion Planning Problem

To represent our simple persuasion dialogues as a planning problem, we use PDDL2.1 [8], a standard language for encoding the information required by automated planners (i.e. the actions that can be performed, the initial situation, the goal and the optimisation metric). PDDL2.1 allows the use of typed objects, predicates and functions to define the preconditions and effects of actions. We define two types of object: the `wff` type

Table 2. Predicates and functions used to define the actions `assert` and `responder-turn`

(can-assert ?w — wff)	True if ?w is a persuader's belief that has not yet been asserted
(acceptable ?sow — setOfWffs)	True if the topic is acceptable given ?sow
(add ?w — wff ?sow1 ?sow2 — setOfWffs)	True if the adding ?w to the set ?sow1 gives the new set ?sow2
(belief-asserted)	Flag to ensure that the persuader asserts at least one belief each turn
(initial-move)	Flag to ensure the first action of a plan is a (responder-turn)
(responder-moved)	Flag to ensure the last action of a plan is a (responder-turn)
(prob-resp-reasoning-with ?sow — setOfWffs)	Function that assigns probabilities to the sets that may occur as the responder's reasoning set
(prob-of-success)	Function that updates the probability of success of a plan

is used to capture wff of $\mathcal{L}$; the `setOfWffs` type is used to capture sets of wff of $\mathcal{L}$. The predicates and functions used to define our actions are given in Table 2 (variables in PDDL2.1 begin with a ? and are annotated with their type). Recall that we take the initial state to be where the persuader has opened the dialogue by asserting the topic (as all simple persuasion dialogues start in this manner), thus a plan must always start with a (responder-move) action. A plan must also always end with a (responder-move) action, to allow the persuader to consider the responder's possible responses.

We now define how a planning problem instance is constructed for a simple persuasion situation; this determines the initial state that the planner must plan from.

Definition 11. *For a persuader with beliefs* Σ^P, *for a dialogue with common knowledge* Ω, *topic* T, *where its model of the responder is* m *we construct a* **planning problem instance** *as follows:*

- *for every belief* $\alpha \in \Sigma^P$, *there is an equivalent* `wff` *object:* α;
- *for every set of beliefs* $\Upsilon \in \{\Phi \cup \Psi \mid \Phi \subseteq \Sigma^P \text{ and } \Psi \in \text{PossRespBelSets(m)}\}$ *(i.e. for every set that may occur as the responder's reasoning set), there is an equivalent* `setOfWffs` *object:* Υ;
- *for all* $\alpha \in \Sigma^P$, (can-assert α) *is true* ;
- (acceptable Φ) *is true if and only if* $T \in \text{Acceptable}(\Phi)$;
- (belief-asserted) *is true (since we assume we are in the state where the persuader has asserted the topic);*
- (initial-move) *is true;*
- (responder-moved) *is not true;*
- *for all* $\Upsilon \in \{\Phi \cup \Psi \mid \Phi \subseteq \Sigma^P \text{ and } \Psi \in \text{PossRespBelSets(m)}\}$:
  - *if* $\Upsilon \in \text{PossRespBelSets(m)}$,
    (= (prob-resp-reasoning-with Υ) x) *where* $x = \text{m}(\Upsilon)$;

- *otherwise*
  $(= (\texttt{prob-resp-reasoning-with}\ \Upsilon)\ 0);$
- $(= (\texttt{prob-of-success})\ 0)$;
- *the goal is* (responder-moved);
- *the optimisation metric is to maximise* (prob-of-success).

The PDDL2.1 definition of our actions is shown in Figure 2. The persuader can assert a wff object ?w as long as it can assert ?w (i.e. it has not asserted it already) and it is not the initial move. The main effect of an asssert action is to update the probabilities assigned to the sets that can occur as the responder's reasoning set. For each set ?sow1 that was assigned a non-zero probability p in the previous state, asserting the belief ?w has the effect of setting the probability assigned to ?sow1 to zero and increasing the probability assigned to ?sow1 $\cup$ {?w} (i.e. ?sow2) by p (so that if ?w is already a member of ?sow1, the probability assigned to ?sow1 does not change).

A responder-turn action can be made as long as a belief has been asserted (so two or more responder-turn actions cannot occur in sequence). The main effect of a responder-turn action is to update the probability of success assigned to the plan. For each of the possible responder's reasoning sets ?sow that was assigned a non-zero probability p in the previous state, if that set causes the responder to find the topic acceptable, responder-turn has the effect of increasing the probability of success by p and setting the probability assigned to ?sow to zero.

Given this formal model of our planning problem, a planner can search for a plan that maximises the probability of success. In the following section we present some preliminary results that explore the efficiency of the automated planning process.

3.3 Experimental Results

We used the planner Metric-FF [12,13] to generate plans for our model. The combination of features required by the model means that this is the most appropriate planner: standard ('STRIPS') planners support only conjunctions in preconditions, whereas we require quantification and conditional effects[2]. We also require numeric fluents, the values of prob-resp-reasoning-with, and optimisation based on a metric function. In fact, because the updates to the values of prob-resp-reasoning-with and prob-of-success are state-dependent, Metric-FF is not able to optimise our problem off-the-shelf; however, we implemented a simple wrapper which allows us to use Metric-FF to perform the optimisation as follows[3]. The wrapper first calls Metric-FF to solve the problem with the goal:

```
(and (responder-moved)
     (> (prob-of-success) 0)
)
```

---

[2] In theory it is possible to compile these away to create a STRIPS representation, with the possibility of using different planners, we leave this to future work.

[3] This wrapper, our formal model of the planning problem and some example problem instances can be downloaded from http://www.inf.kcl.ac.uk/staff/lizblack/automated-planning-simple-persuasion.html.

```
(:action assert
 :parameters (?w - wff)
 :precondition (and (not (initial-move))
                    (can-assert ?w))
 :effect (and (belief-asserted)
              (not (responder-moved))
              (not (can-assert ?w))
              (forall (?sow1 ?sow2 - setOfWffs)
                      (when (and (> (prob-resp-reasoning-with ?sow1) 0)
                                 (add ?w ?sow1 ?sow2))
                            (and (increase (prob-resp-reasoning-with ?sow2)
                                           (prob-resp-reasoning-with ?sow1))
                                 (assign (prob-resp-reasoning-with ?sow1) 0))
                      )
              )
         )
)

(:action responder-turn
 :parameters ()
 :precondition (belief-asserted)
 :effect (and (not (belief-asserted))
              (not (initial-move))
              (responder-moved)
              (forall (?sow - setOfWffs)
                      (when (and (> (prob-resp-reasoning-with ?sow) 0)
                                 (acceptable ?sow))
                            (and (increase (prob-of-success)
                                           (prob-resp-reasoning-with ?sow))
                                 (assign (prob-resp-reasoning-with ?sow) 0))
                      )
              )
         )
)
```

Fig. 2. The PDDL2.1 definition of the two actions used to model simple persuasion dialogues as a planning problem: assert and responder-turn

If a plan exists to solve the problem (i.e. if there is a strategy that has a greater than 0 probability of success), Metric-FF will return some such plan. The wrapper then updates the problem instance so that the goal is now

```
(and (responder-moved)
     (> (prob-of-success) X)
)
```

where X is the probability of success of the plan returned by Metric-FF in the previous step, and calls Metric-FF to solve the problem again with the new goal. This process continues until the planner reports that the problem is unsolvable with a probability of success higher than the last plan found; we know therefore that the previous plan found by the planner is optimal.

For our experiments we generated problem instances with #beliefs possible beliefs that the persuader can assert. The possible responder belief sets are all the elements of the power set of the persuader's beliefs, to which we have assigned equal probability (so we assume the persuader believes that the responder's beliefs are some subset of its own but has no *a priori* beliefs about which is more likely and is not aware of any common knowledge). Each possible set of beliefs was randomly determined to make the topic acceptable with probability θ. Our first set of experiments scaled #beliefs, while keeping $\theta = 0.3$. The second set of experiments set #beliefs to 8 and varied θ. For each parameter setting we generated a single problem instance and recorded: the time taken to find the optimal plan, the cumulative time taken to find the optimal plan *and* prove it optimal, the number of runs of the planner required to find the optimal plan and prove it optimal, the probability of success of the optimal plan. All experiments were run on a 3GHz machine with a memory limit of 27GB. Results of both experiments are shown in Table 3.

Note that what we are evaluating here is the time taken to find an optimal plan, not the time taken to generate the problem instance. Generating the problem instance is not trivial; in particular, determining the sets that make the topic acceptable is typically costly (depending on the acceptability semantics chosen to instantiate Definition 1, an existing implementation such as ASPARTIX [7] could be used for this). We expect that the work done in generating the problem instance can be reused for other problem instances, and will explore this in future work.

Our experiments show that we can optimally solve problems with up to 2^9 possible responder belief sets; problems of this size are very difficult for humans to solve even close to optimally, and this shows real benefits of automation. Scalability does remain a challenge, however; in particular memory usage seems to be the bigger concern than time. The size of the problem, and the search space, grows exponentially with the number of persuader beliefs that can be asserted; the number of possible responder belief sets also grows exponentially with the number of persuader beliefs and reasoning about all of these is challenging. We plan to work on more efficient encodings that will allow significantly greater scalability. We also expect improved performance for problems where there are fewer possible responder belief sets.

Our first experiment shows that planning gets more difficult as the space of possible solutions increases, but the overall time remains reasonable for problems with up to 8

Table 3. Shows: seconds to find the optimal plan (`findOptPlan`); seconds to find the optimal plan *and* prove it optimal (`proveOpt`); number of runs of planner to prove plan optimal (`#runs`; probability of success of the optimal plan (`probSucc`). Top part of table shows results for first experiment (where we varied the number `#beliefs` of persuader beliefs and the probability that a set causes the topic to be acceptable was fixed as 0.3); bottom part of table shows results for second experiment (where we varied the probability that a set causes the topic to be acceptable and the number `#beliefs` of persuader beliefs was fixed as 8) and gives the percentage `%acceptable` of the 2^8 possible responder belief sets that were determined to make the topic acceptable as we varied the probability θ that a set causes the topic to be acceptable.

#beliefs	1	2	3	4	5	6	7	8	9			
findOptPlan	< 0.1	< 0.1	< 0.1	< 0.1	< 0.1	< 0.1	1.3	32.54	1220.09			
proveOpt	< 0.1	< 0.1	< 0.1	< 0.1	< 0.1	0.16	2.46	70.22	2464.46			
#runs	3	3	6	6	8	12	20	30	34			
probSucc	1	1	1	0.81	1	0.94	0.80	0.94	0.97			
%acceptable	49.6	25.8	23.1	17.6	15.6	13.3	11.3	9.4	4.3	3.5	2.7	1.2
findOptPlan	5.76	15.71	48.41	33.65	20.97	20.71	9.26	19.16	5.22	4.77	8.69	3.17
proveOpt	14.69	54.67	73.02	68.7	49.89	49.46	32.61	39.77	8.41	7.47	10.86	4.14
#runs	24	31	28	30	32	25	20	17	11	17	17	11
probSucc	1	0.85	0.72	0.82	0.79	0.80	0.76	0.75	0.24	0.23	0.23	0.26

persuader beliefs. In general the most time consuming step is the final run to prove the solution optimal; finding the optimal solution often takes less than half as long as proving it optimal, a future direction is to scale to larger problems by finding solutions that have a certain probability of success but are not necessarily optimal. The difficulty of the problem clearly depends on *which* sets cause the topic to be acceptable; this is currently assigned randomly by our problem generator, we control only the proportion of such sets. We intend to run experiments where acceptability status of sets is determined from the underlying logic, to investigate whether this improves performance.

Results of our second experiment support what might be expected. If a large percentage of the possible sets make the topic acceptable then planning is relatively quick because solutions are abundant; so, although the planner might run many times, it is relatively easy to find a solution that improves on the previous one quickly. As the number of belief sets that make the topic acceptable becomes low, it is harder to find solutions to the planning problem as there are fewer, but (because the number is so low) search space pruning is more powerful as the planner can recognise early during plan generation that a plan cannot lead to a better state and prune it without further exploring. There is somewhat of a phase transition between these two extremes, at approximately 10-25% of belief sets acceptable, where neither of these advantages prevails. Variation in the results appears because of the random assignment of acceptable sets by our problem generator, which impacts on the the difficulty of the problem.

4   Related Work

Recent works on argument dialogue strategy [3,10,21] also use a *model* of the other participant. The dialogue of [3] allows participants to agree on some action to achieve a shared goal. The authors provide a strategy that requires a certain model of the other participant's preferences and depends on a particular argumentation formalism, whilst a strategy generated by our approach maximises the chance of success taking into account the uncertainty over the responder's beliefs and we allow for any reasoning mechanism.

Different tactics for making concessions in argumentation-based negotiation are presented in [10], which use a model of the other participant's (perhaps distinct) defeat relation over the arguments that can be used to support or attack offers; here we instead use a model of the responder's beliefs, and assume its mechanism for determining the acceptability of claims is known to the persuader. In case this mechanism is argument based, our approach can account for the construction by the responder of new arguments by combining its existing beliefs with those asserted by the persuader; this is not possible in [10], which does not consider the structure of arguments.

In [21], a variation of the minimax algorithm is used with a recursive model of the opponent to determine dialogue strategy in an adversarial abstract persuasion setting. Uncertainty over the opponent model is also allowed for in [21]. The authors present results regarding the effectiveness of their approach (i.e. whether the strategy leads to success) but do not present results regarding the efficiency of their algorithm; we consider the time taken to find a guaranteed optimal strategy (albeit in a simpler non-adversarial setting). The experiments in [21] assume 10 arguments distributed between the two agents, which is comparable to the size of problem we have shown our approach to be efficient for. Whilst we assume that the persuader is aware of all beliefs the responder may believe, [21] uses *virtual arguments* to allow the for the case where the responder has beliefs that the persuader is unaware of; this is something we will consider adopting in our model.

The application of the minimax algorithm to dialogical argumentation is also considered in [14], which proposes a general framework for specifying argument dialogue systems using propositional executable logic; this allows a finite state machine to be generated, which represents all possible dialogues from a particular initial state. Such a finite state machine can then be analysed with the minimax algorithm to determine an optimal strategy for a participant, although this requires certain knowledge of the other participant's private state. Efficiency results are also given in [14]; these are better than the results we achieve here but we are considering a set of possible initial states (i.e. the different possible responder belief sets) while [14] considers a situation in which the persuader and responder beliefs are known. It will be interesting to explore more closely the relationship between our approach and [14].

In [17] and in [18], argument-based negotiation is considered as a planning problem. Each of these proposals allow plans of arguments specific to negotiation to be generated, where the arguments that can be generated are specified by the domain; our approach is more general than this, since our domain does not depend on a particular argumentation formalism, and so could also be used to determine a persuasive line of argument within a negotiation context.

Finally, [20] also considers the generation of a persuasive line of argument as a planning problem. The focus of that work is on generating natural language discourse; it is concerned with eloquence and style of language, as well as the logical structure of arguments, whilst we consider only the acceptability of logical formulas.

5 Discussion

Our proposal allows an automated planner to find an optimal strategy for a simple persuasion dialogue; a key advantage is that it is general in the sense that it does not prescribe the logical formalism and semantics for determining acceptability of claims, allowing for both abstract and structured argumentation, as well as other non-argumentation based formalisms. Our preliminary results show that the efficiency of the planner does not scale well beyond 8 persuader beliefs; however, we expect a significant improvement when we reduce the number of possible responder belief sets considered.

The major obstacle to scalability in our current approach is that we are not exploiting any knowledge about the responder belief sets that we know are either not possible or not likely. Whilst the current model allows reasoning with these as zero probability states, it does not reduce the size of the task. We intend to explore more efficient encodings of the planning problem to allow exploitation of such knowledge, and also to consider exclusion of unlikely possible responder belief states to further improve scalability. Better exploitation of the native ability of planners to handle sets, through the explicit reasoning over beliefs as individual entities rather than as black-box sets, is also an avenue to improve performance. Finally, we intend to investigate how the search algorithms and heuristics of the planner itself can be modified to allow better performance in this particular domain, or indeed what inspiration we can gain from this problem for improving general planning strategies across different types of problems.

Our optimisation metric currently only considers the success of the dialogue. We could also consider that the persuader may have some preferences regarding the beliefs it shares with the responder. By assigning values to each belief that represent how willing the persuader is to make it known to the responder, we could adapt our optimisation metric to also take into account the beliefs the persuader has had to share.

We intend to model more complex types of argument dialogue as planning problems. In particular, we are interested in the case where both participants are making assertions with the aim of achieving their individual (and potentially conflicting) dialogue goals. The dynamic and uncertain nature of these dialogues presents interesting challenges for classical planning; nevertheless, we believe this work demonstrates the feasibility of using automated planners to generate strategies for such dialogues.

References

1. Albore, A., Palacios, H., Geffner, H.: Compiling uncertainty away in non-deterministic conformant planning. In: Proc. of 19th European Conf. on Artificial Intelligence, pp. 465–470 (2010)
2. Besnard, P., Hunter, A.: A logic-based theory of deductive arguments. Artificial Intelligence 128(1-2), 203–235 (2001)

3. Black, E., Atkinson, K.: Choosing persuasive arguments for action. In: Proc. of 10th Int. Conf. on Autonomous Agents and Multiagent Systems, pp. 905–912 (2011)
4. Caminada, M.: On the issue of reinstatement in argumentation. In: Fisher, M., van der Hoek, W., Konev, B., Lisitsa, A. (eds.) JELIA 2006. LNCS (LNAI), vol. 4160, pp. 111–123. Springer, Heidelberg (2006)
5. Dung, P.M.: On the acceptability of arguments and its fundamental role in nonmonotonic reasoning, logic programming and n-person games. Artificial Intellegence 77, 321–357 (1995)
6. Dung, P.M., Kowalski, R.A., Toni, F.: Dialectic proof procedures for assumption-based, admissible argumentation. Artificial Intelligence 170(2), 114–159 (2006)
7. Egly, U., Gaggl, S.A., Woltran, S.: ASPARTIX: Implementing argumentation frameworks using answer-set programming. In: Garcia de la Banda, M., Pontelli, E. (eds.) ICLP 2008. LNCS, vol. 5366, pp. 734–738. Springer, Heidelberg (2008)
8. Fox, M., Long, D.: PDDL2.1: An extension to PDDL for expressing temporal planning domains. J. of Artificial Intelligence Research 20, 61–124 (2003)
9. García, A.J., Simari, G.R.: Defeasible logic programming an argumentative approach. Theory and Practice of Logic Programming 4(1-2), 95–138 (2004)
10. Hadidi, N., Dimopoulos, Y., Moraitis, P.: Tactics and concessions for argumentation-based negotiation. In: Proc. of the 4th Int. Conf. on Computational Models of Argument, pp. 285–296 (2012)
11. Hadjinikolis, C., Siantos, Y., Modgil, S., Black, E., McBurney, P.: Opponent modelling in persuasion dialogues. In: Proc. of the 23rd Int. Joint Conf. on Artificial Intelligence, pp. 164–170 (2013)
12. Hoffmann, J.: The Metric-FF planning system: Translating "ignoring delete lists" to numeric state variables. J. of Artificial Intelligence Research 20, 291–341 (2003)
13. Hoffmann, J., Nebel, B.: The FF planning system: Fast plan generation through heuristic search. J. of Artificial Intelligence Research 14, 253–302 (2001)
14. Hunter, A.: Analysis of dialogical argumentation via finite state machines. In: Liu, W., Subrahmanian, V.S., Wijsen, J. (eds.) SUM 2013. LNCS, vol. 8078, pp. 1–14. Springer, Heidelberg (2013)
15. Modgil, S., Prakken, H.: A general account of argumentation with preferences. Artificial Intelligence 195, 361–397 (2013)
16. Modgil, S., Toni, F., Bex, F., Bratko, I., Chesñevar, C.I., Dvořák, W., Falappa, M.A., Fan, X., Gaggl, S.A., García, A.J., González, M.P., Gordon, T.F., Leite, J., Možina, M., Reed, C., Simari, G.R., Szeider, S., Torroni, P., Woltran, S.: The added value of argumentation. In: Ossowski, S. (ed.) Agreement Technologies, pp. 357–403. Springer, Netherlands (2013)
17. Monteserin, A., Amandi, A.: Argumentation–based negotiation planning for autonomous agents. Decision Support Systems 51(3), 532–548 (2011)
18. Panisson, A.R., Farias, G., Freitas, A., Meneguzzi, F., Vieira, R., Bordini, R.H.: Planning interactions for agents in argumentation-based negotiation. In: Proc. of 11th Int. Workshop on Argumentation in Multi-Agent Systems (2014)
19. Prakken, H.: Formal systems for persuasion dialogue. The Knowledge Engineering Review 21(02), 163–188 (2006)
20. Reed, C., Long, D., Fox, M.: An architecture for argumentative dialogue planning. In: Gabbay, D.M., Ohlbach, H.J. (eds.) FAPR 1996. LNCS, vol. 1085, pp. 555–566. Springer, Heidelberg (1996)
21. Rienstra, T., Thimm, M., Oren, N.: Opponent models with uncertainty for strategic argumentation. In: Proc. of the 23rd Int. Joint Conf. on Artificial Intelligence (2013)
22. Taig, R., Brafman, R.I.: Compiling conformant probabilistic planning problems into classical planning. In: Proc. of 23rd Int. Conf. on Automated Planning and Scheduling (2013)
23. Thimm, M.: Strategic argumentation in multi-agent systems. In: Künstliche Intelligenz, Special Issue on Multi-Agent Decision Making (in press, 2014)

Empirical Evaluation of Strategies
for Multiparty Argumentative Debates

Dionysios Kontarinis[1], Elise Bonzon[1], Nicolas Maudet[2], and Pavlos Moraitis[1]

[1] LIPADE, Université Paris Descartes, France
dionysios.kontarinis@parisdescartes.fr,
{elise.bonzon,pavlos}@mi.parisdescartes.fr
[2] LIP6, Université Pierre et Marie Curie, France
nicolas.maudet@lip6.fr

Abstract. Debating agents have often different areas of expertise and conflicting opinions on the subjects under discussion. They are faced with the problem of deciding how to contribute to the current state of the debate in order to satisfy their personal goals. We focus on target sets, that specify minimal changes on the current state of the debate allowing agents to satisfy their goals, where changes are the addition and/or deletion of attacks among arguments. In this paper, we experimentally test a number of strategies based on target sets, and we evaluate them with respect to different criteria, as the length of the debate, the happiness of the agents, and the rationality of the result.

1 Introduction

In recent years, the study of the collective aspects of argumentation (which can now be increasingly experienced on-line [1]), has seen a surge of interest in AI. Such settings raise new challenges for argumentation theory [2]. The object constructed by a group of agents is a *weighted argumentation system* [3], where a natural interpretation of the weights attached to an edge is that it reflects the number of agents who have committed to a given attack, or the aggregated expertise of those agents [4], as we shall also assume here. New semantics have been proposed to account for the social nature of argumentation and its specific use in a context where votes can be cast on top of arguments (and relations among them), either sticking to the framework initially set up by Dung [5], see *e.g.* [6], or departing from it [7,8].

Debates in online settings are incrementally built, with agents adding new arguments, attacks, and casting new votes in response to the opinion voiced by others. In practice such debates may be (more or less flexibly) regulated, to ensure that they remain focused, and that some fairness is guaranteed among the different agents. One thing that is missing though is a study of the dynamics of debates regulated by such protocols: it is not clear how strategies used by agents would change the outcome of debates. In [9] a very simple dynamic is investigated, based on a direct notion of relevance inspired by [10], and it is shown that in the absence of coordination and with a myopic behavior, agents can actually play against their own interest, leading to undesirable results. This justifies the fact that some "guidance" might be useful to agents, without assuming though any sort of explicit coordination among agents. Recently, the notion of *target*

N. Bulling et al. (Eds.): CLIMA XV, LNAI 8624, pp. 105–122, 2014.

sets has been proposed in the litterature [11,12]. Roughly speaking, a target set specifies the minimal (sets of) moves which would achieve the argumentative goal of a given side of the debate, *provided the debate remains in its current state*. The intuition is that agents should be better off focusing their moves on target sets. One challenge though is that target sets may prescribe more than one move for agents to play, and that it is impossible to assume that agents will have the opportunity to completely "control" a target set.

In this paper we experimentally investigate how well strategies based on target sets behave. We study a number of dynamics, of increasing complexity, where the notion of target set is thoroughly exploited. Our experimental results show in particular that the use of these sophisticated strategies provides an advantage to the side using it, and that it shortens the length of debates.

The rest of this paper is as follows. Section 2 provides the necessary background, introducing the different elements composing the "gameboard" of the debate. Section 3 recalls the definition of target sets. Section 4 presents a protocol, and Section 5 presents a study of different strategies of increasing complexity, based on this notion of target sets. These strategies are experimentally compared in Section 6. Section 7 concludes.

2 Argumentative Debates Featuring Conflicting Expert Opinions

The aim of this work is to study argumentative debates among expert agents. We consider an arbitrary number of participating agents, each of them having a private argumentation system. For the sake of simplicity we assume that all agents have the same set of arguments, but they can disagree on the validity of the attacks between those arguments. Each argument concerns a finite set of topics, and the agents are experts on a subset of these topics. The debate is about the status (wrt a given semantics) of a single argument, called $issue$. The agents vote on the attacks involved in the computation of the status of the issue, on a specific common system called Gameboard. The objective of each agent is to have the status of the issue in his private argumentation system be the same as the status of the issue on the Gameboard, at the end of the debate.

2.1 Modelling the Participants

A finite set of agents, denoted Ag, take part in a debate. Each agent $i \in Ag$ has a private Dung argumentation system [5], where the exact structure of the arguments is unspecified. All agents share the same set of arguments A, but they may disagree on the attacks between them. For this reason we introduce the notion of **master argumentation system** which contains all attacks on which the agents agree, as well as all attacks on which they disagree. The attacks on which the agents agree are called fixed (or undeniable). Private argumentations systems of agents inherit fixed attacks appearing in the master AS. More formally:

Definition 1. *An **argumentation system (AS)** is a pair $\langle A, R \rangle$ of a set A of arguments and a binary relation R on A called the **attack relation**. $\forall a, b \in A$, aRb (or $(a, b) \in R$) means that a **attacks** b.*

Given a **master argumentation system** $AS = \langle A, R \rangle$ *and* $R^* \subseteq R$ *a set of* **fixed attacks***, an agent* $i \in Ag$ *is equipped with a private argumentation system denoted* $AS_i = \langle A, R_i \rangle$*, such that* $R_i \subseteq R$ *and* $R^* \subseteq R_i$*. Attacks in* $R \setminus R^*$ *are called* **debated attacks***.*

In Dung's framework, the *acceptability of an argument* depends on its membership to some sets, called extensions. These extensions characterize collective acceptability. Several *semantics for acceptability* have been defined in [5]. In what follows, we concentrate on the notion of *grounded semantics*, which can be defined as follows:

Definition 2. *Let* $AS = \langle A, R \rangle$ *and* $C \subseteq A$*. The set* C *is* **conflict-free** *iff* $\nexists a, b \in C$ *such that* aRb*.* C **defends** *an argument* a *iff* $\forall b \in A$ *such that* bRa*,* $\exists c \in C$ *such that* cRb*.* C *is a* **grounded extension** *of* AS *iff* C *is the least fixed point of the characteristic function of* AS *(*$F: 2^A \to 2^A$ *with* $F(C) = \{a \mid C \text{ defends } a\}$*).*

Intuitively, a *grounded extension* contains all arguments which are not attacked, as well as the arguments which are defended (directly or not) by non-attacked arguments. There always exists a unique grounded extension which, however, might be the empty set. Thus, all the debating agents know, at every time of the debate, which arguments are accepted and which are not. We shall denote by $Gr(AS)$ the grounded extension of the system AS.

Example 1. Let a master system $AS = \langle A, R \rangle$, with $A = \{a, b, c, d\}$, $R = \{(a, b), (b, c), (d, c)\}$ and $R^* = \{(b, c)\}$. This system can be represented as follows, where fixed attacks are represented by thick arrows, and debated attacks by simple arrows.

Let three agents, such that $AS_1 = \langle A, R_1 \rangle$, with $R_1 = \{(a, b), (b, c)\}$; $AS_2 = \langle A, R_2 \rangle$, with $R_2 = \{(b, c), (d, c)\}$ and $AS_3 = \langle A, R_3 \rangle$, with $R_3 = \{(b, c)\}$. We have $Gr(AS_1) = \{a, c, d\}$, $Gr(AS_2) = \{a, b, d\}$ and $Gr(AS_3) = \{a, b, d\}$.

Each argument is associated with a set of keywords specifying which topics this argument is about. This is common practice in systems like the ones in [2,4]. We assume that there is a fixed set of topics, denoted T, and every argument concerns a subset of T.

Definition 3. *Let* T *be the set of topics. The set of* **topics of an argument** $a \in A$ *is given by function* $top(a) \subseteq T$*. The set of* **topics of an attack** $(a, b) \in R$ *is given by function* $top(a, b) = top(a) \cup top(b) \subseteq T$*. The* **expertise of agent** $i \in Ag$ *is given by* $exp(i) \subseteq T$*.*

2.2 Modelling the Gameboard

Inspired from [9], we use a central structure called gameboard (GB in short). The gameboard stores all the opinions expressed by the agents during the debate and aggregates them, giving rise to a single argumentation system, which will allow us to draw the debate's conclusions. An essential element in the debates we consider, is that agents may disagree on the existence of some attacks. Thus, an agent can vote either for, or against the existence of an attack. The role of the GB is to gather and aggregate all the votes cast during the debate. Moreover, the voters' relevant expertise will play a crucial role in determining the result of the aggregation. In the rest of the paper, we assume that $AS = \langle A, R \rangle$ is a master argumentation system, $R^\star$ is the set of fixed attacks, T a set of topics, and Ag is a set of agents, such that $\forall i \in Ag$, $AS_i = \langle A, R_i \rangle$.

Definition 4. *A **vote**, also called a **move**, is a tuple $\langle (a, b), s, i \rangle$ where $(a, b) \in R \setminus R^\star$ is the debated attack[1] concerned by the vote, $s \in \{-1, +1\}$ is the sign of the vote, and $i \in Ag$ is the voter.*

A positive vote by an agent means that he supports that the attack does hold, while a negative vote means that he supports the opposite.

Let $(a, b) \in R \setminus R^\star$, then $eval(a, b)$ is the **evaluation vector of** (a, b). This vector contains $|top(a, b)|$ elements.

Definition 5. *Let $(a, b) \in R \setminus R^\star$ with $top(a, b) = \{t_1, \ldots, t_n\}$. The evaluation vector of (a, b) is denoted $eval(a, b) = \langle v_{t_1}, \ldots, v_{t_n} \rangle$. The value $v_{t_i} \in \mathbb{Z}$, $\forall t_i \in top(a, b)$, depends on the voters' expertise in t_i. Whenever a vote $\langle (a, b), s, i \rangle$ is cast by agent i, then the vector $eval(a, b) = \langle v_{t_1}, \ldots, v_{t_n} \rangle$ is updated into:*
$\langle v_{t_1} + s \times |\{t_1\} \cap exp(i)|, \ldots, v_{t_n} + s \times |\{t_n\} \cap exp(i)| \rangle$.

Example 1, cont. Let $T = \{t_1, t_2, t_3, t_4\}$, with $top(a) = \{t_1, t_2, t_3\}$, $top(b) = \{t_2\}$, $top(c) = \{t_2, t_3\}$, $top(d) = \{t_4\}$. Also, let $exp(1) = \{t_1, t_2\}$, $exp(2) = \{t_2, t_3\}$ and $exp(3) = \{t_1, t_4\}$. Initially, no votes have been cast on any attack belonging to the master AS. Agent 1 votes for attack (a, b). We then have, as $top(a, b) = \{t_1, t_2, t_3\}$ and $exp(1) = \{t_1, t_2\}$, that $eval(a, b) = \langle 1, 1, 0 \rangle$. Next, agent 2 votes against attack (a, b) and for attack (d, c). We then have $eval(a, b) = \langle 1, 0, -1 \rangle$ and $eval(d, c) = \langle 1, 1, 0 \rangle$. Finally, agent 3 votes also against (a, b). We have $eval(a, b) = \langle 0, 0, -1 \rangle$.

Given an evaluation vector $eval(a, b)$, we can decide whether attack (a, b) should be accepted or rejected. We underline that there exist various methods to obtain such a verdict, given an evaluation vector. Here we use a simple method taking into account all the elements of an evaluation vector and using a simple sum.

Definition 6. *Let $(a, b) \in R \setminus R^\star$ and let $eval(a, b) = \langle v_{t_1}, \ldots, v_{t_n} \rangle$ be its evaluation vector. The **verdict on** (a, b), denoted $verdict(a, b) \in \{true, false\}$ is computed as follows: $verdict(a, b) = true$ iff $\sum_{i=1}^{n} v_{t_i} > 0$, $verdict(a, b) = false$, otherwise.*

In other words, the verdict on an attack is positive if the aggregated relevant expertise of agents having voted for the attack is strictly greater than the aggregated relevant expertise of agents having voted against it. Otherwise, the verdict on the attack is negative.

Let us now see how a gameboard is defined. Its main feature is a set containing the evaluation vectors of all the possible attacks.

---

[1] We assume that the agents cannot vote on the attacks which are fixed in the master system.

Definition 7. *A* **gameboard** *is a triplet* $GB = \langle A, R, Eval \rangle$*, where* A *is the set of arguments shared by all agents,* R *is the set of attacks and* $Eval$ *is the set of evaluation vectors of* $R \setminus R^\star$.

Let $AS_{GB} = \langle A, R_{GB} \rangle$ be **the argumentation system of the** GB, such that $R_{GB} = \{(a, b) \in R \setminus R^\star \mid verdict(a, b) = true\} \cup R^\star$.

Example 1, cont. Let the gameboard $GB = \langle A, R, Eval \rangle$ with the function $Eval$ defined as previously. We have $verdict(a, b) = false$ and $verdict(d, c) = true$. This gameboard can be represented as follows:

$$a\,\{t_1, t_2, t_3\} \qquad b\,\{t_2\} \qquad\qquad c\,\{t_2, t_3\} \qquad\qquad d\,\{t_4\}$$
$$\langle 0, 0, -1 \rangle \qquad\qquad\qquad\qquad \langle 1, 1, 0 \rangle$$

Fixed attacks are represented by thick arrows, attacks with true verdict by simple arrows, and attacks with false verdict by dashed arrows. The argumentation system $AS_{GB} = \langle A, R_{GB} \rangle$ contains thus only the fixed attacks and the debated attacks with true verdict.

$$a \qquad\qquad b \qquad\qquad c \qquad\qquad d$$

2.3 Merged System

When participating to the debate, agents are assumed truthful, and they cannot vote for (resp. against) an attack if they think that it does not (resp. does) hold. Certainly, absolute truthfulness is not often encountered in real-life debates, but it is an assumption preventing the agents from stating anything that may help them in the debate. A more refined approach, left for future work, would be to define a set of beliefs (in our case attacks) upon which an agent is able to lie, if he considers it favorable at some point. This kind of situation has already been studied by Rahwan et al [13]. In this work, they introduced a formal argumentation theory, namely ArgMD, in which an agent may hide an argument or lie about arguments.

On the other hand, we allow agents to *not* express their opinion on some attacks, because that could harm their purpose, or make them disclose information they wish to hide. This is related to the notion of *dishonest arguments*, that has been studied by Caminada in [14] and by Sakama in [15]. We thus need a way to compare the results obtained in our debates with a collective view of the argumentation systems of the agents. We rely on two different notions. The first one is the notion of *merged* argumentation system [16]. In the specific case we discuss here, it turns out that a meaningful way to merge is to take the vote of all agents on all attacks in $R \setminus R^\star$.

Definition 8. *Let* $AS = \langle A, R \rangle$ *be a master AS and* Ag *be a set of agents. The* **merged argumentation system** *is* $AS^M_{Ag} = \langle A, R^M \cup R^\star \rangle$ *where* $R^M \subseteq R$ *and* $a R^M b$ *iff* $verdict(a, b) = true$ *when all the agents in* Ag *have voted on* (a, b).

Another notion which can be useful for analyzing the collective view of the debate is the one of *happiness*: we could want to see a majority of agents satisfied at the end of the debate, in the sense that they agree with the status of a specific argument, called *issue of the debate*.

Definition 9. *Let Ag be a set of agents and let, $\forall i \in Ag$, AS_i denote i's private AS. Also, let $c \in A$ be an argument called* issue of the debate. *The* **majority result** *is denoted* $majIn(c) \Leftrightarrow |\{i \in Ag \mid c \in Gr(AS_i)\}| \geq |Ag|/2$, *and it is denoted* $majOut(c) \Leftrightarrow |\{i \in Ag \mid c \notin Gr(AS_i)\}| > |Ag|/2$.

Note that ties for the majority are broken in favour of the agents who want to see the issue in the grounded extension.

3   Focus on Minimal Changes

At this point we turn our attention to possible strategic considerations of agents in this type of debates. What are the attacks of the gameboard on which the voting agents should focus and try to add/remove? The aim of the analysis that follows is to provide insight on how to vote in order to achieve a goal. We will focus on target sets [11,12], which represent the minimal change on an argumentation system, achieving an argumentative goal.

A target set is a minimal set of *actions* on an argumentation system allowing to achieve a given goal. Please note beforehand that an action is *not* the same notion as a vote on the gameboard: here we assume that an action *changes* the verdict of some attacks, whereas a vote on the gameboard does not necessarily do the same (as an agent does not always have a sufficiently high expertise). Thus, we focus, on the following definition, on the verdict of the attacks in the gameboard, and not on the exact value of the eval functions.

Definition 10. *Let $GB = \langle A, R, Eval \rangle$ be the gameboard at a given time. An* **action** *on GB is a set of* **atoms** $m = \{((x, y), s) \mid (x, y) \in (R \setminus R^\star), s \in \{+, -\}\}$, *such that* $\forall((x, y), +) \in m$, $verdict(x, y) = false^2$, *and* $\forall((x, y), -) \in m$, $verdict(x, y) = true$.

The **resulting GB** *after playing an action m, is denoted* $\Delta(GB, m) = \langle A, R, Eval^m \rangle$, *such that* $\forall(x, y) \in R \setminus R^\star$:

1. $verdict^m(x, y) = true$ *iff either* $verdict(x, y) = true$ *and* $((x, y), -) \notin m$, *or* $((x, y), +) \in m$.
2. $verdict^m(x, y) = false$ *iff either* $verdict(x, y) = false$ *and* $((x, y), +) \notin m$, *or* $((x, y), -) \in m$.

Here is an example showing how an action modifies a system.
Example 1, cont. We take the same gameboard GB as defined previously. If we play the action $m = \{((a, b), +), ((d, c), -)\}$ on GB, we obtain the following system $\Delta(GB, m)$:

---

^{2} That is, $Eval(x, y)$ is such that $verdict(x, y) = false$.

$a \{t_1, t_2, t_3\}$ $b \{t_2\}$ $c \{t_2, t_3\}$ $d \{t_4\}$

In order to define the notion of target set, we first need to provide the definition of the goal of a debate.

Definition 11. *Let GB be a gameboard, $AS_{GB} = \langle A, R_{GB} \rangle$ be its system, and $d \in A$ be the issue. The* **goal** g_d^+ *(resp. g_d^-) is* **satisfied** *in GB iff $d \in Gr(AS_{GB})$ (resp. $d \notin Gr(AS_{GB})$).*

Definition 12. *Let GB be a gameboard and let g be a goal. m is a* **successful action** *on GB for goal g iff g is satisfied in the resulting gameboard $\Delta(GB, m)$. We denote $\mathbb{M}(GB, g)$ the set of all successful actions on GB for goal g. m is a* **target set on GB** *for goal g iff m is a minimal (w.r.t. $\subseteq$) element of $\mathbb{M}(GB, g)$. We denote $\mathbb{T}(GB, g)$ the set of all target sets on GB for goal g.*

In [12] we studied the evolution of target sets when changes occur on a system (that is, when an action is done). We have shown that if an agent plays an action which does not contain any atom of any target set, then the target sets of the new gameboard will "grow", and it will become harder (or at least not easier) to satisfy the goal under consideration. On the other hand, if an agent plays in a target set, then that target set will "shrink", regardless of what happens to other target sets. In that sense, at least one "path" towards the satisfaction of the goal becomes shorter, while this is not the case if we do not play on any target set.

However, as we will show in Section 5, at some point during a debate, an agent may be better off playing a move outside target sets, as this may incite his opponents to play a move which will backfire. We will also propose different strategies with which agents can choose their moves, focusing on target sets, and we will experimentally test them.

4   A Debate Protocol

In this section we define a specific debate protocol. The agents focus on the status (under the grounded semantics) of a single argument $d \in A$, which is the issue of the debate. The goal of an agent $i \in Ag$ is therefore to have the issue's status be the same, on the GB and in his private system, at the end of the debate. We can therefore distinguish two groups of agents: the agents of the group PRO (resp. CON) who have (resp. do not have) the issue in the grounded extension of their systems. An advantage of using grounded semantics is that the grounded extension is easy to calculate and it is always unique. Therefore, every agent is either PRO or CON, and at every point of the debate the issue is either accepted or rejected.

The protocol proceeds in timesteps. Let $GB^t = \langle A, R, Eval^t \rangle$ denote the gameboard at timestep t. At $t = 0$, we have $GB^0 = \langle A, R, Eval^0 \rangle$, with $\forall (a, b) \in R \setminus R^\star$, $Eval^0(a, b) = \langle 0, \ldots, 0 \rangle$. Recall that attacks in $R^\star$ are fixed in the system, and cannot be modified (so, they are not associated to any evaluation vector), whereas attacks in any $R' \subseteq (A \times A) \setminus R$ cannot be added. In order to ensure the termination of our protocol, we assume that an agent cannot vote on the same attack twice. To account for this, each agent $i \in Ag$ is equipped with a set $HV_i^t \subseteq R$ which contains all the attacks agent i has voted on, until timestep t. The protocol is defined by the following:

- **Participants**: A finite set of agents Ag, each one being either PRO or CON, according to his opinion on the issue's status.
- **Turntaking**: Round-robin. The token is given to each agent, in turn, and comes back to the first agent once all agents have played.
- **Permitted moves**: Agent i at timestep t can either:
  - Vote on $\langle (a, b), +, i \rangle$, if $(a, b) \in R_i \setminus R^\star$ and $(a, b) \notin HV_i^t$
  - Vote on $\langle (a, b), -, i \rangle$, if $(a, b) \in R \setminus R_i$ and $(a, b) \notin HV_i^t$
  - Play a **pass move** (giving the token to the next agent).
- **Stopping condition**: $|Ag|$ pass moves have been played in a row.
- **Winning condition**: Once the debate has stopped, all PRO (resp. CON) agents win iff the issue belongs (resp. does not belong) to the grounded extension of the argumentation system of AS_{GB}.

5   Strategies

When having the token, an agent can vote on any of the attacks under discussion, but which one should he choose? In general, a *strategy* states, for each agent, what move should be uttered next in the course of the debate. When a strategy returns a single move, we say it is *deterministic*. Depending on the information required to take this decision, we can distinguish different kind of strategies:

- *(k)-history-based strategies*: the strategy selects moves based on the last k moves uttered in the debate, noted *h(k)-strategies*. For instance:
  "If someone just attacked argument a, I will try to defend it."
- *(k)-state-based strategies*: the strategy selects moves based on the last k states of the gameboard, noted *s(k)-strategies*. For instance:
  "If $a \in Gr(AS_{GB})$, then I will utter the attack (d, a)."

We say that a strategy s has a richer information basis than a strategy s' (noted $s \rhd s'$) when it uses more information to select the next moves. Observe that, for a round t, both *h(t)-strategies* and *s(t)-strategies* are fully expressive, since they can capture the whole history of the debate so far. Note also that *h(k)-strategies*, based on

$$[GB^t, GB^{t-1}, GB^{t-2}, \ldots, GB^{t-k}]$$

could as well be expressed as a strategy based on the single state GB^{t-k}, together with the k last moves. Also, when $t > t'$, a t-state-based strategy has a richer information basis than a t'-history-based-strategy. Finally, for the same k, state-based and history-based strategies are incomparable: for instance, a strategy based on the last state of the gameboard may capture intuitively more information than a strategy based on the last move, but it misses the information of what was the last move uttered.

In what follows, we study a natural class of *s(1)-strategies*, as we define strategies based on the computation of the target sets of the last GB. We also make the assumption that all agents from one side (PRO or CON) use the same strategy. This facilitates the analysis, but constitutes of course a simplification. Moreover, we assume that the agents cannot disclose their private argumentation systems. Thus, agents do not have any knowledge on the other agents' private systems. As said before, the analysis of target sets and their properties leads us naturally to think that agents would profit from focusing on attacks of target sets, as it is the fastest and most economical way to achieve a goal.

5.1 Lack of Dominance and Equilibrium Guarantees

Dominance. One may wonder whether "playing within target sets" is a dominant strategy, that is, whether agents can never be better off playing a different strategy, whatever the strategy of the other party is. Note first that "playing within target sets" does not constitute a single strategy, but instead a class of strategies, in fact a subclass of $s(1)$-*strategies*. So when say "a dominant strategy", we abuse language and mean *any* strategy belonging to this class. This turns out to be a too demanding notion, because the strategy of the other player can be of any kind, in particular, it may be such that moves played outside a target set will precisely be the moves required to lead to a winning result.

This may be illustrated in the following scenario:

Example 1, cont. Assume that we are in the beginning of the debate, and no moves have been played yet. Let the gameboard be $GB^0 = \langle A, R, Eval^0 \rangle$. We have $eval(a, b) = \langle 0, 0, 0 \rangle$, so $verdict(a, b) = false$, and $eval(d, c) = \langle 0, 0, 0 \rangle$, so $verdict(d, c) = false$. Now, we add a new argument e in A (referring to topic t_2), as well as the attack (b, e) in R, with $eval(b, e) = \langle 0 \rangle$, so $verdict(b, e) = false$. This new gameboard is represented as follows:

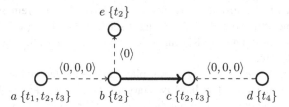

Agent 1, who belongs to PRO, focuses on target set $\{((a, b), +)\}$, as adding (a, b) will make c accepted. However, it is impossible for him alone to impose the attack (a, b), as both agents 2 and 3 will disagree on its existence.

But now suppose that an agent of the CON team (eg. agent 2) is very picky on the issue of the (new) argument e, and he has a strategy which says: "If e is attacked, then I will defend e"[3]. Of course this strategy is not directly focused on the topic of the debate (which is c), but this kind of rhetorical move is common in real-life argumentation. In this case, agent 1 has an incentive to play move $((b, e), +)$ (provided that he is able to), and lure agent 2 in responding with $((a, b), +)$. This way, thus not focusing always on target sets, agent 1 can eventually make c accepted and win the debate.

---

[3] For the sake of simplicity, let us assume that here agent 2 may violate his truthfulness.

Symmetric Equilibrum. The previous example showed that not focusing on target sets may in some cases lure the other group to make a "bad" move. Of course this relies on the rather artificial construction consisting of an agent playing a somewhat irrational strategy. We may then ask whether a weaker property can be guaranteed: is it the case that, *if the other agent follows a strategy consisting of playing within target sets*, then agents of the other side will not have an incentive to play differently, ie. whether this constitutes a symmetric equilibrium. The following example, shows that this is not the case either.

Example 2. Four agents have the following argumentation systems (we assume for the sake of simplicity that the arguments concern the same topic, and that all agents are expert on this topic):

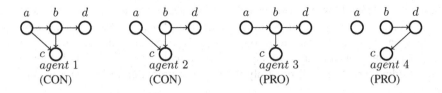

The dialogue's issue is argument c. We have $CON = \{a_1, a_2\}$, $PRO = \{a_3, a_4\}$. If both teams of agents play only in the targets sets, agents in PRO cannot win: at the beginning of the debate, agents in CON have two target sets $\{((b, c), +)\}$ and $\{((a, c), +)\}$. If they vote on (a, c), agents in PRO will be able to remove that attack (by voting twice if it is necessary). The remaining target set for CON will then be $\{((b, c), +)\}$. Once CON agents vote on (b, c), agents in PRO will have two target sets: $\{((b, c), -)\}$ and $\{((a, b), +)\}$. Assume that a_4 votes against (b, c). Then agents in CON can vote again to reinstate it. Agents in PRO have then one remaining target set: $\{((a, b), +)\}$. Once this vote is cast, the target set for CON is $\{((a, b), -)\}$. a_2 votes against (a, b), and the agents in PRO cannot do anything else. In this case, PRO agents cannot win the debate.

Assume now that agents in PRO do not play only in the target sets. As previously, at the beginning, agents in CON have two target sets, $\{((b, c), +)\}$ and $\{((a, c), +)\}$. Once again, they can vote on (a, c) but these votes will be removed by agents in PRO. Once CON agents vote on (b, c), assume that a_4 votes on (b, d). The target set for CON is empty (as their goal is satisfied). a_4, for the PRO team, can play once more, so he chooses to add (d, c), and then to remove (b, c). The group CON has now two target sets, $\{((a, b), +)\}$ and $\{((b, c), +)\}$. Assume that a_1 votes for (a, b). Agents in PRO have now two target sets, $\{((a, b), -)\}$ and $\{((d, c), -)\}$. If a_3 votes against (d, c), agents in CON will have one target set, $\{((a, b), -), ((b, c), +)\}$. Assume that a_2 votes against (a, b), and after everybody passes, he votes again for (b, c). a_3 can now vote for (a, b). Agents in CON cannot do anything else, as a_2 has already voted against (a, b) once. PRO wins the debate.

All in all, playing in target sets looks intuitively like a good strategy, but it seems difficult to obtain theoretical guarantees. This leads us to study it experimentally.

5.2   Strategies Based on Target Sets

Here we define 5 strategies, from the simpler to the more complex, mainly focusing on target sets. Strategy 0 is the exception, as it is a *random strategy*, which will allow us to assert that playing in the target sets is useful. We remind that, at any timestep, an agent is winning (resp. losing) the debate if the status of a given issue is the same (resp. is not the same) both in his private system and in the argumentation system associated to the GB. Note that when there are no available moves for an agent (we remind that an agent cannot vote on the same attack twice), that agent obligatorily passes.

Strategy 0: This is a random strategy, where (1) if the agent is winning, then he plays pass. (2) otherwise, he votes randomly on an attack on the gameboard.

Strategy 1: The idea of this strategy is to allow only agents who are not satisfied by the current state of the gameboard to vote. Moreover, these agents can only vote if they can change the status of the issue (and thus, if they can change the verdict of an attack belonging to a target set of cardinality 1).[4] More precisely: (1) if the agent is winning, then he plays pass. (2) otherwise, the agent can only vote on an attack if this vote allows to change the status of the issue.

Strategy 2: This strategy improves the previous one by allowing agents to vote on a target set of cardinality greater than 1: an agent can vote on an attack if he can change its verdict, but this vote does not have to change the status of the issue. More precisely: (1) if the agent is winning, then he plays pass. (2) otherwise, the agent can only vote on an attack if this attack belongs to a target set, and if this vote allows to change the verdict on this attack.

Strategy 3: This strategy allows an agent to vote on an attack belonging to a target set, even if he cannot change the verdict on this attack. More precisely: (1) if the agent is winning, then he plays pass. (2) otherwise, the agent can vote on any attack belonging to a target set (towards changing the verdict).

Strategy 4: This strategy improves the previous one by allowing a winning agent to play a move which renders the goal of the other team more difficult to be reached. More precisely: (1) if the agent is winning, then he can vote on an attack which belongs to a target set for the goal of the other team and "reinforce" it.[5] (2) otherwise, the agent can vote on any attack belonging to a target set (towards changing the verdict).

As we can have several target sets, and several actions in a target set, an agent can have several possible votes for each of these strategies. We thus introduce three heuristics to help an agent to choose which vote to cast.

5.3   Heuristics

An agent can compute a set of possible votes, using any of the above strategies. Then, he can either randomly choose a vote among them, or use a more subtle heuristic. We have defined three heuristics which can be used for filtering the initial set of possible votes.

---

[4] Note that this strategy is the one studied in [9].

[5] And thus making it more difficult for the other team to change the verdict on this attack.

- **Heuristics A:** the agent randomly chooses a possible vote.
- **Heuristics B:** the agent filters out all possible votes on non-minimal (wrt. cardinality) target sets [6]. Then, he randomly chooses a vote.
- **Heuristics C:** the agent filters out all possible votes on non-minimal (wrt. cardinality) target sets. If he can change the verdict of an attack among the remaining ones, he filters-out all the attacks he cannot change. Then, he randomly chooses a vote.

5.4 Strategy and Debate Profiles

Coupling a strategy with a heuristics gives us a specific **strategy profile**. As Strategy 0 does not use target sets, it can not be coupled with any heuristics. Also, in Strategy 1 an agent can only vote on an attack if it belongs to a target set of cardinality 1 and he can change its verdict, so it does not make any sense to associate Strategy 1 with heuristics B or C. In the same way, in Strategy 2 an agent can only vote on an attack if he can change its verdict, so it does not make sense to couple Strategy 2 with heuristics C. We thus have the following strategy profiles to consider (the number indicates the strategy type and the capital letter the heuristics): $SP = \{0, 1, 2A, 2B, 3A, 3B, 3C, 4A, 4B, 4C\}$.

We assume that the agents of the same group (PRO or CON) are using the same strategy profile during a debate. This is done in order to draw more easily conclusions on how the strategy profiles fare against each other. We can thus introduce the notion of **debate profile**. A debate profile is defined as a couple (SP_{PRO}, SP_{CON}) with $SP_{PRO}, SP_{CON} \in SP$. It indicates that all agents in the PRO (resp. CON) group are using the strategy profile SP_{PRO} (resp. SP_{CON}). Since there are 10 strategy profiles, there exist $10 \times 10 = 100$ different debate profiles. In the following, we first examine Strategy 0, and then we turn our attention to the 9 other strategy profiles which use target sets (thus on their corresponding $9 \times 9 = 81$ debate profiles).

6 Experimental Results - Discussion

We have implemented in Java the debate framework presented in the previous sections and performed a number of experiments.

6.1 Generating Debate Configurations

In order to perform an important number of debates, our program is able to generate different *debate configurations*. A configuration consists on three elements: the set of all topics, a master argumentation system AS, and a set of agents with their private systems and their expertise. In our experiments we made the following choices:

Topics: We have $|T| = 6$ topics.

---

[6] For example, if an agent can vote on two attacks, the first being in a target set of cardinality 1, and the second in a target set of cardinality 2, then he will filter out the second option.

Master argumentation system: Every generated argumentation graph contains $|A| = 20$ arguments, each one randomly attached to one or two topics. The graph has a density of attacks equal to 0.1. Among the attacks, 10 are debated, and thus belong into $R \setminus R^\star$.[7] Finally, the issue is randomly chosen among the arguments in A.

Agents: Each debate involves 10 agents. Each of them is expert in one, two, or three topics randomly chosen. The AS_i of each agent includes all the attacks in $R^\star$, whereas each debated attack in $R \setminus R^\star$ belongs to R_i with a 50% probability.

6.2 The Debates

A number of configurations were randomly generated, using the above parameter values. When the difference in the number of agents in groups PRO and CON was important, the debates were trivial, as the majority easily won. The impact of the groups' size difference is now studied in more detail: we randomly generated 10 configurations for each combination of PRO and CON cardinalities (so, 10 configurations with 9 PRO and 1 CON agents (denoted 9/1), then 10 configurations with 8 PRO and 2 CON agents (denoted 8/2), and so on (7/3, 6/4, 5/5, 4/6, 3/7, 2/8, 1/9)). This amounts to 90 different configurations in total. Each configuration was tested with all 81 debate profiles focusing on target sets (see Section 5.4), and for every debate profile, the debate was repeated 10 times. [8] So in total we have 9x10x81x10=72900 debates focusing on target sets.

The next histogram summarizes the percentage of agreement between the debates' results and the majority results for each combination of PRO/CON agents.

As it can be seen, when a group contains the vast majority of the agents (8 or 9 out of 10), the debate's result almost always agrees with the majority result. This is the reason why we filtered out cases of near-unanimity, and we kept only the configurations where the combination of PRO/CON agents was 3/7, 4/6, 5/5, 6/4 or 7/3. As a result, we focused on 50 configurations. As previously stated, all 81 debate profiles were tested for each configuration, and for every debate profile, the debate was repeated 10 times.

Another interesting element of the histogram is that the column of 7/3 (resp. 6/4) is bigger than the column of 3/7 (resp. 4/6). Furthermore, the column of 5/5 is also relatively big (in most debates, PRO wins [9]). Apparently, the random configurations for which balanced teams of agents were (randomly) generated, slightly favor the PRO group, as far as winning the debate is concerned. This is verified in what follows, and it merits a deeper study in the future.

6.3 Analysis of the Results

As said above, we shall first examine the behaviour of the random Strategy, and then we shall focus on the remaining 81 debate profiles which focus on target sets.

---

[7] We chose a small number of debated attacks, as this element causes an overhead in the computations of target sets.

[8] As the agents randomly choose their moves among a set of possible moves, the results of these 10 debates may still differ.

[9] We remind that in case of 5/5, PRO is by default considered to be the majority.

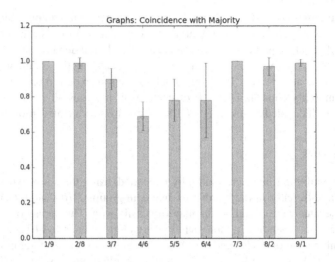

Fig. 1. Histogram showing the coincidence of the debates' results with the majority results, for configurations having different compositions of PRO/CON agents

For the analysis of the results and the evaluation of the strategies and debate profiles, we considered three criteria:

- **Debate length**: the average number of rounds in the debate.
- **Happiness**: the percentage of coincidence between the debate's result and the majority result. Its interest is better understood from the perspective of the debate's central authority. For example, if the central authority chooses a strategy profile for both PRO and CON (eg. the same one), then it may wish to know which one would help the majority, and which one would offer more chances to the minority.
- **Rationality**: the percentage of coincidence between the result of the debate and the merged result.

We also want to find the "best" strategies, meaning the strategies which maximize a group's chances to win the debate.

The Random Strategy Profile. We begin our analysis with the random strategy profile. As far as the maximization of a group's winning chances are concerned, the random strategy profile did not fare worse than the quite simple strategy profiles 1 and 2X. The reason is that its drawback (the fact that agents playing random attacks could harm their own group), was balanced by the drawback of profiles 1 and 2X, which can "block" a group normally able to change an attack by casting two or more votes (because in 1 and 2X, the first voter will be prohibited from casting his vote).

On the other hand, we expected that the winning percentage of a group would increase, if instead of the random profile, he used the elaborated profiles 3X and 4X. This was indeed verified, as the winning percentage always increased, up to 25% in some cases (although less in others). We also conjecture that the more attacks the GB has, the worse the results will be for the random profile, compared to 3X and 4X. It seems logical to assume that the more attacks there are on the GB, the more harmful it is for a group to randomly play attacks, some of which may backfire.

A key disadvantage of the random profile is that, if a group uses it, then the number of rounds of the debate explodes. In most cases, when one group adopted the random profile, the number of rounds increased by a factor of 10 (eg. from 25 rounds, into 250 rounds). Remember that in the profiles focusing on target sets, if an agent has no move in a target set, he plays pass. This is not the case in the random profile, where a group can play a lot of "dummy" moves before achieving its goal.

On a positive side, if a group uses the random strategy, then the percentage of agreement with the merged outcome is quite high (in almost all cases we tested that percentage was bigger than 90%). Naturally, the reason behind this, is that that group using the random profile will cast a lot more votes during the debate, and as a result, the GB will resemble more to the merged system. This was even clearer when both groups used the random profile, when that percentage went up to 97.6%.

Concluding, the fact that the number of rounds increases dramatically when a group uses the random strategy, as well as the fact that it fares worse (as far as winning the debate is concerned) than strategies 3X and 4X, lead us to not include the random profile in the following tests, where we just compare the 9 strategy profiles focusing on target sets.

Strategies Based on Target Sets. We now turn our attention to the 9 strategy profiles focusing on target sets and their corrsponding 81 debate profiles.

Each of the four graphics contains information on *all* debate profiles focusing on target sets. The top left shows the percentage of PRO wins (for every profile), the top right shows the average number of rounds of the debates, the bottom left shows the percentage of agreement between the results of the debates and the merged results, and the bottom right shows the percentage of agreement between the results of the debates and the majority results.

Let us first consider the criterion of *debate length* (top-right). The lowest number of rounds is found when both agents use strategy 4. A small number of rounds is also obtained in profiles (1,4X), (4X,1) (where $X \in \{A, B, C\}$) and (1,1). For the latter, the reason is that there are cases where a group cannot vote on an attack because no single agent can change it (and thus the debate stops). For profiles (4X,4Y) the reason debates are short is that agents are not forced to play (useless) pass-moves, as they can reinforce attacks on the GB while they are winning. This is not possible with profiles (3X,3Y) which give the longest debates. Note that agents using the strategy profiles 4X have incentive to give more information than with the other strategy profiles. That can be seen as a disadvantage for agents who wish to hide information. A last remark on debate length: If we concentrate only on rounds which do not contain pass moves (let us call them *no-pass rounds*), then the results of strategy profiles 3X and 4X are inversed. Strategy profiles 4X lead to more no-pass rounds, than profiles 3X (eg. (4C,4C) leads in average to 11.97 no-pass rounds, while (3C,3C) leads in average to 10.36 no-pass rounds). We clearly see that when profiles 3X are used, many rounds involve pass moves, and this is the reason why profiles 3X have the biggest total number of rounds.

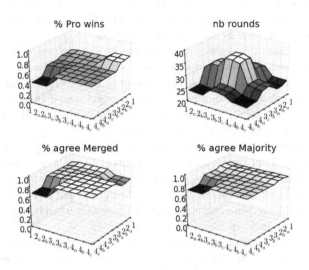

Fig. 2. Top-Left: Percentage of wins by PRO. Top-Right: Number of rounds of the debates. Bottom-Left: Percentage of agreement with the merged result. Bottom-Right: Percentage of agreement with the majority result. PRO strategies are shown on the left side, and CON strategies on the right side of every graphic.

Let us now focus on *rationality* (bottom-left). The most "rational" outcomes (closer to the results of the merged system) are obtained when both groups use one of the strategies: 3A, 3B, 3C, 4A, 4B, 4C (the percentage of agreement being 0.88). The only cases where the results of the debates are farther from the merged results are when a group uses strategy profile 4X and the other group uses strategy profile 1 or 2X. So, we pull away from the merged result when a group uses the most advanced strategy (4X), while the other a simple one (1 or 2X). The smallest agreement is 0.66, at profile (1,4X).

Similar results are obtained when we focus on *happiness* (bottom-right). Almost all profiles give a similar value of agreement with the majority (about 0.85). However, when PRO uses strategies 1, or 2X, and CON uses 4X, the debate's result starts to move away from the majority's opinion (its minimum value is 0.7).

Regarding the strategy which is most likely to win a debate, the most elaborated strategies 3 and 4 provide a clear advantage. PRO's best chance to win is when the profile (4X,1) is used (0.75 percentage of PRO winning). Similarly, CON's best chance to win is in profile (1,4X) (0.38 of PRO winning). In general, no matter what strategy a group is using, the other group increases its winning percentage if it uses strategy 3 or 4, instead of the simpler 2 and 1 (1 being the worst choice). It is also quite clear, as mentioned before, that PRO win more debates than CON, something apparently related to the nature of the randomly generated master systems from which balanced PRO/CON groups are generated.

Finally, some remarks on the heuristics. Heuristics C which focuses on the smallest target sets, and prefers moves able to add/remove an attack, was expected to lead to the quickest debates. This was verified, although its results were not significantly better than the results of the simpler heuristics B and A. For example, the debate profile (4C,4C) lead to 23.88 rounds in average, while the profile (4A,4A) lead to 24.81. Also, the debate profile (3C,3C) lead to 35.29 rounds in average, while the profile (3A,3A) lead to 36.29. We conjecture that, when heuristics C is used instead of B or A, the decrease in the number of rounds is small, due to the fact that the randomly generated systems do not contain many target sets, and these target sets do not have great differences in size. We expect that in the case of master systems with target sets of considerably different sizes, heuristics C will lead to a more significant decrease in the number of rounds, compared to heuristics B and A.

To conclude, a general observation is that the more sophisticated strategy profiles (3X and 4X) are the best choices for the agents who want to win the debate. Their main difference lies on the average number of rounds, and on the amount of information disclosed during the debate. Surprisingly, the simpler strategy profiles (1 and 2X) offer an interesting alternative, provided that the debate's central authority can ensure that both groups will use a simple strategy profile, and that no group will switch into using a sophisticated one. It is worth noting that, in the above experiments, the probability that the winner is the same, when either profile (1,1) or profile (3C,3C) is used, was almost 95%. Finally, the use of heuristics C shortens the length of the debates, though more tests are needed in order to evaluate its impact.

7 Conclusion

We have presented a framework, where debating agents vote on attacks, focusing on a single argument. The agents' relevant expertise plays an important role on the aggregation of the votes. Some interesting properties of target sets, presented in [12], motivated us to define debate strategies focusing on them. A number of strategies and heuristics (of varying complexity) were proposed. We performed a number of experiments and drew conclusions on the strategies, using as criteria the probability of winning, the debate's length, its rationality and the agents' happiness. We also verified our intuition on the best strategies and studied the heuristics' contribution. There are many interesting directions for future research: the relation between the master system (number of arguments, debated attacks, cycles) and the debate's results, as well as the relation between different agent group compositions (eg. with low or high intra-group similarity) and the debate's results. Also, studying debates where the agents' systems may change during the debate looks promising, but challenging.

Acknowledgement. This work benefited from the support of the project AMANDE ANR-13-BS02-0004 of the French National Research Agency (ANR).

References

1. Scheuer, O., Loll, F., Pinkwart, N., McLaren, B.: Computer-supported argumentation: A review of the state of the art. International Journal of Computer-Supported Collaborative Learning 5, 43–102 (2010)
2. Toni, F., Torroni, P.: Bottom-up argumentation. In: Modgil, S., Oren, N., Toni, F. (eds.) TAFA 2011. LNCS, vol. 7132, pp. 249–262. Springer, Heidelberg (2012)
3. Dunne, P.E., Hunter, A., McBurney, P., Parsons, S., Wooldridge, M.: Weighted argument systems: Basic definitions, algorithms, and complexity results. Artif. Intell. 175(2), 457–486 (2011)
4. Kontarinis, D., Bonzon, E., Maudet, N., Moraitis, P.: Picking the right expert to make a debate uncontroversial. In: Proc. of COMMA 2012, pp. 486–497 (2012)
5. Dung, P.M.: On the acceptability of arguments and its fundamental role in nonmonotonic reasoning, logic programming and n-person games. Artificial Intelligence 77(2), 321–358 (1995)
6. Coste-Marquis, S., Konieczny, S., Marquis, P., Ouali, M.: Weighted attacks in argumentation frameworks. In: Proc. of KR 2012 (2012)
7. Leite, J., Martins, J.: Social abstract argumentation. In: Proc. of IJCAI 2011, pp. 2287–2292 (2011)
8. Eğilmez, S., Martins, J., Leite, J.: Extending social abstract argumentation with votes on attacks. In: Black, E., Modgil, S., Oren, N. (eds.) TAFA 2013. LNCS, vol. 8306, pp. 16–31. Springer, Heidelberg (2014)
9. Bonzon, E., Maudet, N.: On the outcomes of multiparty persuasion. In: Proc. of AAMAS 2011, pp. 47–54 (May 2011)
10. Prakken, H.: Coherence and flexibility in dialogue games for argumentation. Journal of Logic and Computation 15, 347–376 (2005)
11. Boella, G., Gabbay, D.M., Perotti, A., van der Torre, L., Villata, S.: Conditional labelling for abstract argumentation. In: Modgil, S., Oren, N., Toni, F. (eds.) TAFA 2011. LNCS (LNAI), vol. 7132, pp. 232–248. Springer, Heidelberg (2012)
12. Kontarinis, D., Bonzon, E., Maudet, N., Moraitis, P.: On the use of target sets for move selection in multi-agent debates. In: Proc. of ECAI 2014 (to appear, 2014)
13. Rahwan, I., Larson, K., Tohmé, F.: A characterisation of strategy-proofness for grounded argumentation semantics. In: Proc. of IJCAI 2009, pp. 251–256 (2009)
14. Caminada, M.: Truth, lies and bullshit; distinguishing classes of dishonesty. In: Proc. of SS@IJCAI 2009, pp. 39–50 (2009)
15. Sakama, C.: Dishonest arguments in debate games. In: Proc. of COMMA 2012, pp. 177–184 (2012)
16. Coste-Marquis, S., Devred, C., Konieczny, S., Lagasquie-Schiex, M.C., Marquis, P.: On the Merging of Dung's Argumentation Systems. Artificial Intelligence 171, 740–753 (2007)

How to Build Input/Output Logic

Xin Sun

Faculty of Science, Technology and Communication,
University of Luxembourg, Luxembourg
xin.sun@uni.lu

Abstract. In this paper we analyze various derivation rules of input/output logic in isolation and define the corresponding semantics. We develop fixed point characterizations for input/output logic involving rules of cumulative transitivity and present new completeness proofs. A toolbox to build input/output logic is therefore created. We use this toolbox to correct a hasty mistake appeared in the work of applying input/output logic to constitutive norms.

Keywords: input/ouput logic, norms, fixed point, deontic logic.

1 Introduction

In the first volume of the handbook of deontic logic and normative systems [8], input/output logic [14–16, 18] appears as one of the new achievement in deontic logic in this century. Input/output logic takes its origin in the study of conditional norms. It is now an established logical framewor to model conditionals, especially but not exclusively in deontic logic. Unlike the modal logic framework [23], which usually uses possible world semantics, input/output logic adopts mainly operational semantics: a normative system is conceived in input/output logic as a deductive machine, like a black box which produces normative statements as output, when we feed it descriptive statements as input.

Such an operational treatment can be traced back to Alchourron and Bulygin [1]. Boella and van der Torre [3] extended input/output logic to reasoning about constitutive norms. Tosatto *et al.* [6] adapted it to represent and reason about abstract normative systems. For a comprehensive introduction to input/output logic, see Parent and van der Torre [18].

The procedure of operational semantics is divided into three stages. In the first stage, we have in hand a set of propositions (call it the input) as a description of the current state. We then apply logical operators to this set, say close the set by logical consequence. Then we pass this set to the deductive machine and we reach the second stage. In the second stage, the machine accepts the input and produces a set of propositions as output. In the third stage, we accept the output and apply logical operators to it.

On the proof-theoretical side, input/output logics are characterized by derivation rules about norms, which are represented by an ordered pair of formulas. Given a set of norms N, a derivation system is the smallest set of norms which extends N and is closed under certain derivation rules.

One feature of the existing work of input/output logic is: the derivation rules always work in bundles. For example in simple-minded input/output logic of Makinson and van

N. Bulling et al. (Eds.): CLIMA XV, LNAI 8624, pp. 123–137, 2014.

der Torre [14], the derivation system is decided by three rules: strengthening the input (SI), weakening the output (WO) and conjunction in the output (AND). When several derivation rules work together, the corresponding operational semantics will be rather complex, and insights of the machinery is therefore concealed. To achieve a deeper understanding on input/output logic, it is helpful to isolate every single rule and study them separately. This is the motivation of this paper.

In this paper we anatomize input/output logic. We take a close look at various rules in isolation and define the corresponding semantics. Not surprisingly, as long as we have semantics for single rules, we can use it as a toolbox to construct semantics for systems decided by multiple rules.

The structure of this paper is the following: we first review input/output logic in Section 2. Then we study a number of rules from Section 3 to 6. In Section 7 we use the result of this paper to correct a mistake of Boella and van der Torre [3]. We then discuss related work in Section 8. We conclude this paper with future work in Section 9. For the sake of readability, all complex proofs are given in the appendix.

2   Background

Let $\mathbb{P} = \{p_0, p_1, \ldots\}$ be a countable set of propositional letters and L be the propositional language built upon $\mathbb{P}$. Let $N \subseteq L \times L$ be a set of ordered pairs of formulas of L. We call N a normative system. A pair $(a, x) \in N$, call it a norm, is read as "given a, it ought to be x". N can be viewed as a function from 2^L to 2^L such that for a set A of formulas, $N(A) = \{x : (a, x) \in N \text{ for some } a \in A\}$.

Makison and van der Torre define the operations from out_1 to out_4 as follows:

- $out_1(N, A) = Cn(N(Cn(A)))$
- $out_2(N, A) = \bigcap\{Cn(N(V)) : A \subset V, V \text{ is complete}\}$
- $out_3(N, A) = \bigcap\{Cn(N(B)) : A \subseteq B = Cn(B) \supseteq N(B)\}$
- $out_4(N, A) = \bigcap\{Cn(N(V) : A \subseteq V \supseteq N(V)), V \text{ is complete}\}$

Here Cn is the classical consequence operator of propositional logic, and a set of formulas is complete if it is either maxi-consistent or equal to L. For each of these four operations, a throughput version that allows inputs to reappear as outputs is defined as $out_n^+(N, A) = out(N_{id}, A)$, where $N_{id} = N \cup \{(a, a) \mid a \in L\}$.

Input/output logics are given a proof theoretic characterization. We say that an ordered pair of formulas is derivable from a set N iff (a, x) is in the least set that extends $N \cup \{(\top, \top)\}$ and is closed under a number of rules. The following are the rules we need to define out_1 to out_4:

- SI (strengthening the input): from (a, x) to (b, x) whenever $b \vdash a$
- WO (weakening the output): from (a, x) to (a, y) whenever $x \vdash y$
- AND (conjunction of output): from (a, x) and (a, y) to $(a, x \wedge y)$
- OR (disjunction of input): from (a, x) and (b, x) to $(a \vee b, x)$
- CT (cumulative transitivity): from (a, x) and $(a \wedge x, y)$ to (a, y)
- ID (identity): from nothing to (a, a), for every $a \in L$.

The derivation system based on the rules SI, WO and AND is called $deriv_1$. Adding OR to $deriv_1$ gives $deriv_2$. Adding CT to $deriv_1$ gives $deriv_3$. The five rules together give $deriv_4$. Adding ID to $deriv_i$ gives $deriv_i^+$ for $i \in \{1, 2, 3, 4\}$. $(a, x) \in deriv(N)$ is used to denote the argument (a, x) is derivable from N using rules of derivation system $deriv$. In Makinson and van der Torre [14], the following soundness and completeness theorems are given:

Theorem 1 ([14]). *Given an arbitrary normative system N and a formula a,*

- *$x \in out_i(N, a)$ iff $(a, x) \in deriv_i(N)$, for $i \in \{1, 2, 3, 4\}$*
- *$x \in out_i^+(N, a)$ iff $(a, x) \in deriv_i^+(N)$, for $i \in \{1, 2, 3, 4\}$*

3   Rules of Input

In this section we investigate the following rules regulating the input:

- input equivalence (IEQ): from (a, x) and $a \dashv\vdash b$ to (b, x). Here $a \dashv\vdash b$ means $a \vdash b$ and $b \vdash a$.
- strengthening the input (SI): from (a, x) to (b, x) whenever $b \vdash a$.
- disjunction of the input (OR): from (a, x) and (b, x) to $(a \vee b, x)$.

IEQ is a basic rule in the logic of constitutive norms [11]. SI is involved in all input/output logics of Makinson and van der Torre. OR is valid in out_2 and out_4. OR is called sure-thing reasoning in Horty [10]. It is heavily used in daily life and on the technical side, it is the most interesting rule among those rules of input. The derivation systems decided by rules of input are defined as follows:

Definition 1. *Let $D_{ie}(N)$ $[D_{si}(N), D_{or}(N)]$ be closure of N under the rule IEQ [SI, OR].* [1]

That is, $D_{ie}(N)$ is the smallest set of norms such that $N \subseteq D_{ie}(N)$ and $D_{ie}(N)$ is closed under the IEQ rule, and similarly for $D_{si}(N)$ and $D_{or}(N)$.

Now our task is to construct the semantics corresponding to those derivation systems. For the convenience of notation, we let $C_e(A) = \{b \in L | \exists a \in A, a \dashv\vdash b\}$, for a set $A \subseteq L$. Moreover, we call a set A disjunctive if it satisfies the following: for all $x \vee y \in A$, either $x \in A$ or $y \in A$. The following is the definition of semantics corresponding to the rules of input.

Definition 2. *For a set of norms N and a formula a, we define $O^{ie}(N, a) = N(C_e(\{a\}))$, $O^{si}(N, a) = N(Cn(a))$, $O^{or}(N, a) = \bigcap\{N(B) | a \in B, B \text{ is disjunctive}\}$.*

Theorem 2

1. *$(a, x) \in D_{ie}(N)$ iff $x \in O^{ie}(N, a)$.*
2. *$(a, x) \in D_{si}(N)$ iff $x \in O^{si}(N, a)$.*
3. *$(a, x) \in D_{or}(N)$ iff $x \in O^{or}(N, a)$.*

Remark 1. *The above result reveals that rules of input correspond to operations in the first stage: SI means to close the input by logical consequence; IEQ means to close the input by logical equivalence; OR ensures the input has to be extended to satisfy disjunctive property.*

---

[1] The closure of a set X under a rule R (resp. a set of rules $\mathfrak{R}$) is the smallest superset Y of X that is closed under R (resp. closed under $\mathfrak{R}$).

4   Rules of Output

In this section we investigate the following rules regulating the output:

- output equivalence (OEQ): from (a, x) and $x \dashv\vdash y$ to (a, y).
- weakening the output (WO): from (a, x) to (a, y) whenever $x \vdash y$.
- conjunction of the output (AND): from (a, x) and (a, y) to $(a, x \wedge y)$.

OEQ is a basic rule in the logic of constitutive norms [11]. WO and AND are involved in all input/output logics of Makinson and van der Torre. The derivation systems decided by rules of output are defined as follows:

Definition 3. *Let* $D_{oe}(N)$, $[D_{wo}(N), D_{an}(N)]$ *be closure of* N *under the rule* OEQ $[WO, AND]$.

For a set of propositional formulas $A \subseteq L$, let $C_s(A) = \{b \in L | \exists a \in A, a \vdash b\}$, $C_a(A) = \{x \in L : \text{there exist } x_1, \dots, x_n \in A, x \text{ is } x_1 \wedge \dots \wedge x_n\}$. The following is the definition of semantics corresponding to the rules of output. For simplicity of notation, $N(a)$ is short for $N(\{a\})$.

Definition 4. *For every set of norms* N *and formula* a, *we define* $O^{oe}(N, a) = C_e(N(a))$, $O^{wo}(N, a) = C_s(N(a))$, $O^{an}(N, a) = C_a(N(a))$.

Theorem 3.

1. $(a, x) \in D_{oe}(N)$ *iff* $x \in O^{oe}(N, a)$.
2. $(a, x) \in D_{wo}(N)$ *iff* $x \in O^{wo}(N, a)$.
3. $(a, x) \in D_{an}(N)$ *iff* $x \in O^{an}(N, a)$.

Proof. The proof is straightforward and left to readers.

Remark 2. *The above result reveals that rules of output correspond to operations in the third stage: WO means close the input by logical consequence,[2] OEQ means close the input by logical equivalence; AND ensures the output is closed under conjunction.*

5   Rules of Normative System

While rules of input and output affect the first stage and the third stage respectively, rules of normative system affect the second stage. We investigate three rules of the normative system:

- zero premise (Z): from nothing to $(\top, \top)$
- identity (ID): from nothing to (a, a), for every $a \in L$.
- conditioning (CD) from nothing to (a, b), for every $a, b \in L$ such that $a \vdash b$

Definition 5. $D_z(N)$ $[D_{id}(N), D_{cd}(N)]$ *is the closure of* N *by the rule* Z $[ID, CD]$.

---

[2] Here $O^{wo}(N, a) = C_s(N(a))$, not $Cn(N(a))$. The readers can verify that the rules adequate for $Cn(N(a))$ is WO+AND.

Definition 6. *For every set of norms N, let $N_z = N \cup \{(\top, \top)\}$, $N_{id} = N \cup \{(a, a) \mid a \in L\}$, $N_{cd} = N \cup \{(a, b) \mid a, b \in L, a \vdash b\}$. We define $O^z(N, a) = N_z(a)$, $O^{id}(N, a) = N_{id}(a)$, $O^{cd}(N, a) = N_{cd}(a)$.*

Theorem 4. *For every set of norms N and a norm (a, x),*

1. $(a, x) \in D_z(N)$ iff $x \in O^z(N, a)$.
2. $(a, x) \in D_{id}(N)$ iff $x \in O^{id}(N, a)$.
3. $(a, x) \in D_{cd}(N)$ iff $x \in O^{cd}(N, a)$.

Proof. The proof is trivial and safely left to the readers.

6   Cross-Stage Rules

In this section we investigate cross-stage rules, which affect more than one stage. Such rules typically have the form of transitivity. We discuss the following rules:

- plain transitivity (T): from (a, x) and (x, y) to (a, y)
- cumulative transitivity (CT): from $(a, x), (a \wedge x, y)$ to (a, y)
- mediated cumulative transitivity (MCT): from $(a, x'), x' \vdash x$ and $(a \wedge x, y)$ to (a, y)
- aggregative cumulative transitivity (ACT): from $(a, x), (a \wedge x, y)$ to $(a, x \wedge y)$

T is used in the input/output logic for constitutive norms [3]. CT is involved in $deriv_3$ and $deriv_4$. MCT and ACT are introduced by Stolpe [21] and Parent and van der Torre [19] respectively.

Definition 7. $D_t(N)$ *is the closure of n under the T rule.*

The corresponding semantics for $D_t(N)$ is defined in an inductive manner.

Definition 8. *For every set of norms N and formula a, we define $O^t(N, a) = \bigcup_{i=1}^{\infty} N_t^i(\{a\})$. Here for a set A, $N_t^i(A)$ is defined as follows:*

- $N_t^1(A) = N(A)$
- $N_t^{i+1}(A) = N(N_t^i(A))$

Theorem 5. $(a, x) \in D_t(N)$ iff $x \in O^t(N, a)$.

6.1   Fixed Point Approach

Concerning other cross-stage rules, on the one hand, it is difficult to define their corresponding semantics. On the other hand, we can use a fixed point approach to define systems containing cross-stage rules together with other rules. We start by giving a fixed point theoretic semantics for out_3 and out_3^+. Then we extend to Stople's mediated reusable input/output logic [21] and Parent and van der Torre's aggregative input/output logic [19].

Out$_3$ and out$_3^+$. Given a set N of norms and a set A of formulas, we define a function $f_A^N : 2^L \to 2^L$ such that $f_A^N(X) = Cn(A \cup N(X))$. It can be proved that f_A^N is monotonic with respect to the set theoretical $\subseteq$ relation, and $(2^L, \subseteq)$ is a complete lattice. Then by Tarski's fixed point theorem [22] there exists a least fixed point of f_A^N. The following proposition shows that the least fixed point can be constructed in an inductive manner.

Proposition 1. *Let B_A^N be the least fixed point of the function f_A^N. Then $B_A^N = \bigcup_{i=0}^{\infty} B_{A,i}^N$, where $B_{A,0}^N = Cn(A), B_{A,i+1}^N = Cn(A \cup N(B_{A,i}^N))$.*

Using the least fixed point, the semantics of out$_3$ and out$_3^+$ are reformulated as follows:

Theorem 6. *For a set of norms N and a formula a,*

1. *$(a, x) \in deriv_3(N)$ iff $x \in Cn(N(B_a^N))$.*
2. *$(a, x) \in deriv_3^+(N)$ iff $x \in Cn(N_{id}(B_a^{N_{id}}))$.*

Mediated Reusable Input/Output Logic. Input/output logic containing the rule of WO is not free from Ross paradox [20]. Stolpe [21] develops the mediated reusable input/output logic such that Ross paradox is avoided without damaging the power of WO. Stolpe achieve this by replacing WO and CT in $deriv_3$ by OEQ and MCT respectively.

Definition 9. (Proof system of mediated reusable input/output logic [21]) $D_{mr}(N)$ *is the smallest set of norms such that $N_z \subseteq D_{mr}(N)$ and $D_{mr}(N)$ is closed under the following rules: SI, OEQ, AND and MCT.*

The semantics of mediated reusable input/output logic is given by an inductive definition.

Definition 10. (Semantics of mediated reusable input/output logic [21]) *For every $N \subseteq L \times L, A \subseteq L, x \in O_{mr}(N, A)$ iff x is equivalent to a subset of $\bigcup_{i=0}^{\infty} A_i$ where*

- *$A_0 = N(Cn(a))$, and*
- *$A_{n+1} = A_n \cup N(Cn(A_n \cup \{a\}))$*

Theorem 7. (Completeness of mediated reusable input/output logic [21]) $(a, x) \in D_{mr}(N)$ *iff $x \in O_{mr}(N, a)$.*

Applying the fixed point approach and the previous result about the rule AND, OEQ and Z, we have the following equivalence result:

Theorem 8. $(a, x) \in D_{mr}(N)$ *iff $x \in C_{ae}^\top(N_z(B_a^{N_z}))$. Here $C_{ae}^\top(\bullet)$ is a logical operator called "contains $\top$ and closed under conjunction and equivalence". Formally, for a set of formulas A, $C_{ae}^\top(A) = \{a \in L | a \dashv\vdash \top \text{ or } \exists b_1, \ldots, b_n \in A \text{ such that } a \dashv\vdash b_1 \wedge \ldots \wedge b_n\}$.*

Proof. The proof is obtained by combining the proof of Theorem 4 and 6. Here we omit the details.

Aggregative Input/Output Logic. Parent and van der Torre [19] introduce aggregative input/output logic based on the following ideas: on one hand, deontic detachment or cumulative transitivity is fully in line with the tradition of deontic logic. For instance, the Danielsson-Hansson-Lewis semantics [7, 9, 13] for conditional obligation validates such a law. On the other hand, they also observe that potential counterexamples to deontic detachment may be found in the literature. Parent and van der Torre illustrate this with the following example, due to Broome [4, §7.4]:

> You ought to exercise hard everyday
> If you exercise hard everyday, you ought to eat heartily
> ?* You ought to eat heartily

Intuitively, the obligation to eat heartily no longer holds, if you take no exercise. Like the others, Parent and van der Torre claim that this counterexample suggests an alternative form of detachment, which keeps track of what has been previously detached. They therefore reject the CT rule, and they accept a weaker rule ACT. As a consequence WO is no longer accepted.

Definition 11. (Proof system of aggregative input/output logic [19]) $D_{ag}(N)$ *is the smallest set of norms such that* $N \subseteq D_{ag}(N)$ *and* $D_{ag}(N)$ *is closed under the following rules: SI, OEQ and ACT.*

Definition 12. (Semantics of aggregative input/output logic [19]) *For every* $N \subseteq L \times L$, $A \subseteq L$, $x \in O_{ag}(N, A)$ *iff there is finite* $N' \subseteq N$ *with* $N'(A) \neq \emptyset$ *such that* $\forall B = Cn(B)$, *if* $A \cup N'(B) \subseteq B$ *then* $x \dashv\vdash \bigwedge N'(B)$.

Parent and van der Torre define $x \in D_{ag}(N, A)$ iff there exist $a_1, \ldots, a_n \in A$ such that $(a_1 \wedge \ldots \wedge a_n, x) \in D_{ag}(N)$. The following completeness result is proved [19].

Theorem 9. (Completeness of aggregative input/output logic [19]) *Given an arbitrary normative system* N *and a set* A *of formulas,* $D_{ag}(N, A) = O_{ag}(N, A)$.

Applying the fixed point approach, we reformulate the semantics of aggregative input/output logic as follows:

Theorem 10. $(a, x) \in D_{ag}(N)$ *iff there exists finite* $N' \subseteq N$, *such that* $N'(A) \neq \emptyset$, $x \dashv\vdash \bigwedge N'(B_A^{N'})$.

Proof. Having those lemmas on B_a^N in the appendix (Lemma 4 to 8), the proof is routine.

7 Application: Input/Output Logic for Constitutive Norms

Constitutive norms are one of the traditional developments of normative reasoning discussed in the handbook of deontic logic. Boella and van der Torre [3] use a weak input/output logic, decided by rules of IEQ, OEQ, AND and T to reason about constitutive norms. However, we discover the semantics defined by Boella and van der Torre [3] is not sound with respect to the derivation system. In what follows, we first state the hasty mistake of Boella and van der Torre [3], then we use the previous results in this paper as a toolbox to build an alternative semantics which is a sound and complete.

Let $D_{BT}(N)$ be the smallest set of norms such that $N \subseteq D_{BT}(N)$, and $D_{BT}(N)$ is closed under the rules of IEQ, OEQ, AND and T. In Boella and van der Torre [3], the semantics for $D_{BT}(N)$ is defined as follows: given a set A of formulas, $O(N, A) = \{\wedge Y | Y \subseteq \bigcup_{i=0}^{\infty} O^i(N, A)\}$ is calculated as follows, assuming the replacements by logical equivalence:

- $O^0(N, A) = \emptyset$
- $O^{i+1}(N, A) = O^i(N, A) \cup \{y \mid (\wedge X, y) \in N, X \subseteq O^i(N, A)\}$.

This semantics is not sound with respect to $D_{BT}(N)$.[3] For an illustration, let $N = \{(p, q)\}$, where p and q are distinct propositional letters. Then $(p, q) \in D_{BT}(N)$. Following the definition of $O(N, A)$, we have $O^0(N, \{p\}) = \emptyset$. $O^1(N, \{p\}) = \emptyset \cup \{y \mid (\wedge X', y) \in N, X' \subseteq \emptyset\} = \{y \mid (\wedge \emptyset, y) \in N\} = \{y | (\top, y) \in N\} = \emptyset$. And similarly, $O^2(N, \{p\}) = O^3(N, \{p\}) = \ldots = \emptyset$. Therefore $O(N, \{p\}) = \emptyset$ and $q \notin O(N, \{p\})$. This shows that the semantics $O(N, A)$ is not sound for $D_{BT}(N)$. Using the results of this paper, an alternative sound and complete semantics for $D_{BT}(N)$ is defined as follows.

Definition 13. *For every set of norms N and formula a, let $O_{BT}(N, a) = \bigcup_{i=1}^{\infty} N_{BT}^i(\{a\})$. Here for a set of formulas A,*

- $N_{BT}^1(A) = C_{ae}(N(C_e(A)))$
- $N_{BT}^{i+1}(A) = C_{ae}(N_{BT}^i(A) \cup N(N_{BT}^i(A)))$.

with $C_{ae}(A) = \{b \in L \mid \exists a_1, \ldots, a_n \in A, a_1 \wedge \ldots \wedge a_n \Vdash b\}$.

C_{ae}, read as "closed under aggregation and equivalence", is a combination of C_e defined in Section 3 and C_a defined in Section 4. For convenience we will use $N_{BT}^i(a)$ to represent $N^i(\{a\})$.

Theorem 11. $(a, x) \in D_{BT}(N)$ *iff* $x \in O_{BT}(N, a)$.

8   Related Work

Input/output logic is reformulated by Bochman [2] to model production and causal reasoning. Bochman uses bimodel, which is an order pair of logically closed and consistent set of formulas, to interpret an ordered pair of formulas (a, x).[4] A production semantics is a set of bimodels. An ordered pair (a, x) is valid in a production semantics B iff for all $(U, V) \in B$, if $a \in U$ then $x \in V$.

Restrictions are imposed to production semantics. A production semantics B is inclusive if for all $(U, V) \in B$, $V \subseteq U$. B is a possible worlds semantics if for all $(U, V) \in B$, U, V are maximal consistent sets. For a set N of ordered pairs of formulas which contains $(\top, \top)$ and $(\bot, \bot)$, Bochman's production semantics is sound and complete for $deriv_1(N)$, inclusive production semantics is sound and complete for $deriv_3(N)$ and possible worlds semantics is sound and complete for $deriv_2(N)$.

---

[3] A reviewer proved that a sound and complete semantics can be obtained by simply define $O^0(N, A) = N(A)$. The proof is similar to the proof of Theorem 11.

[4] Bochman uses $a \Rightarrow x$ instead of (a, x). $a \Rightarrow x$ is read as "If a is true, then x is caused".

All of Bochman's production semantics validates at the same time IEQ, OEQ, SI, WO, and AND. Using the technical results of this paper, we can anatomize production semantics. For example, if we define a weak bimodel as a pair of consistent set of formulas which is closed under logical equivalence, and a weak production semantics is a set of weak bimodels. Then weak production semantics validates IEQ and OEQ, but neither SI nor WO. Things will get interesting for the weak production semantics which validate cross-stage rules. We leave this as a future work.

9   Conclusion and Future Work

In this paper we anatomize input/output logic. We analyze various derivation rules in isolation and define the corresponding semantics. We thus create a toolbox to build input/output logic. This toolbox is used to develop a new semantics for input/output logic on constitutive norms. We further develop fixed point characterizations for input/output logics involving rules of cumulative transitivity and present new completeness proofs.

Concerning future works, except the problem mentioned in the end of the related work section, we consider the following:

- all the input/output logics in this paper are based on propositional logic. Parent *et al.* [17] build input/output logic on intuitionistic logic. STIT logic is a tool preferred by many deontic logicians [10, 12]. It is worthy studying how to build input/output logic based on STIT logic.
- Norms, and more generally conditionals, can be interpreted using neighborhood semantics [5, 11]. How to compare the operational semantics of this paper to neighborhood semantics?

Acknowledgment. I thank Leender van der Torre and Xavier Parent for comments on the early version of this paper. I am grateful to the four anonymous reviewers of the CLIMA workshop for valuable comments.

References

1. Alchourron, C., Bulygin, E.: Normative Systems. Springer, Wien (1971)
2. Bochman, A.: A causal approach to nonmonotonic reasoning. Artificial intelligence 160(1-2), 105–143 (2004)
3. Boella, G., van der Torre, L.: A logical architecture of a normative system. In: Goble, L., Meyer, J.-J.C. (eds.) DEON 2006. LNCS (LNAI), vol. 4048, pp. 24–35. Springer, Heidelberg (2006)
4. Broome, J.: Rationality Through Reasoning. Wiley-Blackwell, West Sussex (2013)
5. Chellas, B.: Modal logic: an introduction. Cambridge University Press, Cambridge (1980)
6. Tosatto, S.C., Boella, G., van der Torre, L., Villata, S.: Abstract normative systems: Semantics and proof theory. In: Proceedings of the Thirteenth International Conference on Principles of Knowledge Representation and Reasoning, pp. 358–368 (2012)
7. Danielsson, S.: Preference and Obligation: Studies in the Logic of Ethics. Filosofiska Freningen, Uppsala (1968)

8. Gabbay, D., Horty, J., Parent, X., van der Meyden, R., van der Torre, L. (eds.): Handbook of Deontic Logic and Normative Systems. College Publications, London (2013)
9. Hansson, B.: An analysis of some deontic logics. Noûs, pp. 373–398 (1969)
10. Horty, J.: Agency and Deontic Logic. Oxford University Press, New York (2001)
11. Jones, A., Sergot, M.: A formal characterization of institutionalised power. Logic Journal of the IGPL 3, 427–443 (1996)
12. Kooi, B., Tamminga, A.: Moral conflicts between groups of agents. Journal of Philosophical Logic 37, 1–21 (2008)
13. Lewis, D.: Counterfactuals. Blackwell, Oxford (1973)
14. Makinson, D., van der Torre, L.: Input-output logics. Journal of Philosophical Logic 29, 383–408 (2000)
15. Makinson, D., van der Torre, L.: Constraints for input/output logics. Journal of Philosophical Logic 30(2), 155–185 (2001)
16. Makinson, D., van der Torre, L.: Permission from an input/output perspective. Journal of Philosophical Logic 32, 391–416 (2003)
17. Parent, X., Gabbay, D., van der Torre, L.: An intuitionistic basis for input/output logic. In: Hasson, S.O. (ed.) David Makinson on Classical Methods for Non-Classical Problems. Springer (2012)
18. Parent, X., van der Torre, L.: I/O logic. In: Horty, J., Gabbay, D., Parent, X., van der Meyden, R., van der Torre, L. (eds.) Handbook of Deontic Logic and Normative Systems, College Publications (2013)
19. Parent, X., van der Torre, L.: Put your parachute on, and jump out! Technical report (2014), to appear in Proceedings of DEON 2014
20. Ross, A.: Imperatives and logic. Theoria 7(5371) (1941)
21. Stolpe, A.: Normative consequence: The problem of keeping it whilst giving it up. In: van der Meyden, R., van der Torre, L. (eds.) DEON 2008. LNCS (LNAI), vol. 5076, pp. 174–188. Springer, Heidelberg (2008)
22. Tarski, A.: A lattice-theoretical fixpoint theorem and its applications. Pacific Journal of Mathematics 5(2), 285–309 (1955)
23. von Wright, G.: Deontic logic. Mind 60, 1–15 (1952)

Appendix

Theorem 2

1. $(a, x) \in D_{ie}(N)$ iff $x \in O^{ie}(N, a)$.
2. $(a, x) \in D_{si}(N)$ iff $x \in O^{si}(N, a)$.
3. $(a, x) \in D_{or}(N)$ iff $x \in O^{or}(N, a)$.

Proof. The case for the first two items are easy and left to the reader. Here we focus on the third item.

(left-to-right) Assume $(a, x) \in D_{or}(N)$, then either $(a, x) \in N$ or (a, x) is derived by the OR rule. The first case is easy to prove. Here we focus on the second case. If (a, x) is derived by the OR rule, then there exist $(b, x) \in D_{or}(N)$, $(c, x) \in D_{or}(N)$ and a is $b \vee c$. By induction hypothesis we know $x \in O^{or}(N, b)$ and $x \in O^{or}(N, c)$. Now for every B^* such that $a \in B^*$ and B^* is disjunctive, we have $b \vee c \in B^*$ since a is $b \vee c$. Note that B^* is disjunctive, so we further have either $b \in B^*$ or $c \in B^*$. If $b \in B^*$, then B^* is a disjunctive set that contains b. So we have $x \in O^{or}(N, b) = \bigcap\{N(B) : b \in B, B \text{ is a disjunctive set }\} \subseteq N(B^*)$. Hence $x \in N(B^*)$. If $c \in B^*$, we can similarly deduce $x \in N(B^*)$. Therefore no matter $b \in B^*$ or $c \in B^*$, we have $x \in N(B^*)$. Therefore $x \in O^{or}(N, a)$.

(right-to-left)[5] Suppose $(a, x) \notin D_{or}(N)$. We construct the set $B = a_0, \ldots, a_n$ by means of the following procedure (where $a_0 = a$).

- $i = 0$
- while a_i is of the form $a_i^1 \vee a_i^2$ do
  - if $(a_i^1, x) \notin D_{or}(N)$, let $a_{i+1} := a_i^1$, $elseleta_{i+1} := a_i^2$
  - $i := i + 1$

Clearly, the procedure terminates in view of the fact that a is a finite string. Note that (‡) for each $i \in \{1, \ldots, n\}$, $(a_i, x) \notin D_{or}(N)$. For a_0 this is so by our supposition. Suppose it holds for i. In case $a_{i+1} = a_i^1$, trivially $a_{i+1} \notin D_{or}(N)$. Suppose thus that $a_{i+1} = a_i^2$ and thus that $(a_i^1, x)2 \in D_{or}(N)$. If $(a_{i+1}, x) \in D_{or}(N)$ then by (OR), $(a_i, x) \in D_{or}(N)$ which contradicts the induction hypothesis. Thus $(a_{i+1}, x) \notin D_{or}(N)$.

Note also that by the construction B is a disjunctive set that contains a. By (‡), $x \notin N(B)$ and thus $x \notin O^{or}(N, a)$. $\qquad\square$

To prove the left to right direction of Theorem 5, we need the following lemmas:

Lemma 1. For all $i \geq 1$, if $A \subseteq B$ the $N_t^i(A) \subseteq N_t^i(B)$.

Proof. This follows immediately by induction and the fact that $N(A) \subseteq N(B)$ whenever $A \subseteq B$. $\qquad\square$

Lemma 2. For all $i, j \geq 1$, if $x \in N_t^i(a)$ and $y \in N_t^j(x)$, then $y \in N_t^{i+j}(a)$.

Proof. Suppose $x \in N_t^i(a)$ and $y \in N_t^j(x)$. Let $k = i + j$, then by the above lemma we have $y \in N_t^j(N_t^i(a)) = N_t^{i+j}(a)$. $\qquad\square$

Lemma 3. For all $i \geq 1$, if $x \in N_t^i(a)$ then $(a, x) \in D_t(N)$.

Proof. We prove by induction. If $i = 1$, then from $x \in N_t^1(a) = N(a)$ we can deduce $(a, x) \in N \subseteq D_t(N)$. Now for $i = k + 1$, if $x \in N_t^{k+1}(a)$, then $x \in N(N_t^k(a))$. Therefore there exist $y \in N_t^k(a)$, $(y, x) \in N$. By I.H. we have $(a, y) \in D_t(N)$ and then use the rule T we have $(a, x) \in D_t(N)$. $\qquad\square$

Theorem 5. $(a, x) \in D_t(N)$ iff $x \in O^t(N, a)$.

Proof. (left to right) Assume $(a, x) \in D_t(N)$, then either $(a, x) \in N$ or (a, x) is derived by the T rule. The first case is easy to prove. Here we just focus on the second case.

Assume $(a, y) \in D_t(N)$ and it is deduced by the T rule. Then there exist $(a, x) \in D_t(N)$ and $(x, y) \in D_t(N)$. By induction hypothesis we have $x \in O^t(N, a)$ and $y \in O(N, x)$. That is, $x \in \bigcup_{i=1}^{\infty} N_t^i(a)$ and $y \in \bigcup_{i=1}^{\infty} N_t^i(x)$. Therefore there exist

---

[5] This proof is due to an anonymous reviewer. The original proof is much complex than the current proof.

some i, j such that $x \in N_t^i(a)$ and $y \in N_t^j(x)$. Therefore we have $y \in N_t^{i+j}(a)$ by the Lemma 2. Hence $y \in \bigcup_{i=1}^{\infty} N_t^i(a)$ and $y \in O^t(N, a)$.

(right to left) Assume $x \in O^t(N, a)$, then $x \in \bigcup_{i=1}^{\infty} N_t^i(a)$. Then there exist some i, $x \in N_t^i(a)$. Now by Lemma 3 below we have $(a, x) \in D_t(N)$. $\qquad\square$

Now we start the proof of Theorem 6.

Proposition 1. Let B_A^N be the least fixed point of the function f_A^N. Then $B_A^N = \bigcup_{i=0}^{\infty} B_{A,i}^N$, where $B_{A,0}^N = Cn(A), B_{A,i+1}^N = Cn(A \cup N(B_{A,i}^N))$.

Proof. We first prove that $\bigcup_{i=0}^{\infty} B_{A,i}^N$ is a fixed point of f_A^N. We prove by showing the following:

1. $A \subseteq \bigcup_{i=0}^{\infty} B_{A,i}^N$: this is because $A \subseteq Cn(A) = B_{A,0}^N \subseteq \bigcup_{i=0}^{\infty} B_{A,i}^N$
2. $N(\bigcup_{i=0}^{\infty} B_{A,i}^N) \subseteq \bigcup_{i=0}^{\infty} B_{A,i}^N$: Let $x \in N(\bigcup_{i=0}^{\infty} B_{A,i}^N)$. Thus, there is an $a \in \bigcup_{i=0}^{\infty} B_{A,i}^N$ such that $(a, x) \in N$. Hence there exist $k \geq 0$ such that $a \in B_{A,k}^N$, which means that $x \in N(B_{A,k}^N) \subseteq B_{A,k+1}^N \subseteq \bigcup_{i=0}^{\infty} B_{A,i}^N$.
3. $Cn(\bigcup_{i=0}^{\infty} B_{A,i}^N) = \bigcup_{i=0}^{\infty} B_{A,i}^N$: the right-to-left direction is obvious; for the other direction: assume $x \in Cn(\bigcup_{i=0}^{\infty} B_{A,i}^N)$, then there exist $x_1, \ldots x_n \in \bigcup_{i=0}^{\infty} B_{A,i}^N$ such that $x_1 \wedge \ldots \wedge x_n \vdash x$. Therefore there exist k such that $x_1, \ldots x_n \in B_{A,k}^N$. Hence $x \in B_{A,k+1}^N \subseteq \bigcup_{i=0}^{\infty} B_{A,i}^N$.

With the above clauses in hand, we can prove that $f_A^N(\bigcup_{i=0}^{\infty} B_{A,i}^N) \subseteq \bigcup_{i=0}^{\infty} B_{A,i}^N$. For the other direction, we prove by induction on i that for every i, $B_{A,i}^N \subseteq f_A^N(\bigcup_{i=0}^{\infty} B_{A,i}^N)$. Here we omit the details.

So we have proved that $\bigcup_{i=0}^{\infty} B_{A,i}^N$ is a fixed point of f_A^N. To prove that it is the least fixed point, we can again prove by induction that for every i, $B_{A,i}^N \subseteq f_A^N(B)$, where B is a fixed point of f_A^N. Here we omit the details. $\qquad\square$

The following lemmas are needed to prove the left to right direction of Theorem 6.

Lemma 4. *For every* $A \subseteq L, N \subseteq L \times L, A \subseteq B_A^N$

Proof. By Proposition 1, the proof is trivial. $\qquad\square$

Lemma 5. *For every* $A \subseteq L, N \subseteq L \times L, B_A^N = Cn(B_A^N)$.

Proof. By the compactness of propositional logic and Proposition 1, the proof is easy. $\square$

Lemma 6. *For every* $a, b \in L, N \subseteq L \times L$, *if* $a \vdash b$ *then* $B_b^N \subseteq B_a^N$. *Here* B_a^N *is short for* $B_{\{a\}}^N$.

Proof. We will prove that for every i, $B_{b,i}^N \subseteq B_{a,i}^N$.
We prove by induction on i.
If $i = 0$, then $B_{b,0}^N = Cn(b) \subseteq Cn(a) \subseteq B_{a,0}^N$. Assume $i = k + 1$ and $B_{b,k}^N \subseteq B_{a,k}^N$. Then $B_{b,k+1}^N = Cn(\{b\} \cup N(B_{b,k}^N))$. From $B_{b,k}^N \subseteq B_{a,k}^N$ we deduce $N(B_{b,k}^N) \subseteq N(B_{a,k}^N)$. Now by the monotony of $Cn(\bullet)$ we know $Cn(\{b\} \cup N(B_{b,k}^N)) \subseteq Cn(\{a\} \cup N(B_{a,k}^N))$. Hence $B_{b,k+1}^N \subseteq B_{a,k+1}^N$.
So we have proved for every i, $B_{b,i}^N \subseteq B_{a,i}^N$. With this result in hand, we can easily deduce that $B_b^N \subseteq B_a^N$. $\qquad\square$

Lemma 7. *If* $x \in Cn(N(B_a^N))$, *then* $x \in B_a^N$.

Proof. By Proposition 1, it is easy to verify that $N(B_a^N) \subseteq B_a^N$ and $Cn(B_a^N) \subseteq B_a^N$ by Lemma 5. The result then follows. □

Lemma 8. *If* $x \in Cn(N(B_a^N))$, *then* $B_a^N = B_{a \wedge x}^N$.

Proof. By Lemma 6, $B_a^N \subseteq B_{a \wedge x}^N$. For the other direction, we need to prove that for every i, $B_{a \wedge x, i}^N \subseteq B_a^N$. We prove this by induction on i.

- Base step: Let $i = 0$, we then have $B_{a \wedge x, i}^N = Cn(a \wedge x)$. By Lemma 4 we have $a \in B_a^N$. By Lemma 7 we have $x \in B_a^N$. Then by Lemma 5 we have $a \wedge x \in Cn(B_a^N) = B_a^N$.
- Inductive step: Assume for $i = k$, $B_{a \wedge x, k}^N \subseteq B_a^N$. By I.H. and the monotonicity of N, $N(B_{a \wedge x, k}^N) \subseteq N(B_a^N)$. Thus, by the monotonicity of Cn and since $B_{a \wedge x, k+1}^N = Cn(\{a \wedge x\} \cup N(B_{a \wedge x, k}^N))$ we have $B_{a \wedge x, k+1}^N \subseteq Cn(\{a \wedge x\} \cup N(B_a^N))$. Since $x \in Cn(N(B_a^N))$ also $B_{a \wedge x, k+1}^N \subseteq Cn(\{a\} \cup N(B_a^N)) = B_a^N$. □

Lemma 9. *For all* i, *if* $b \in B_{a,i}^N$ *and* $(b, x) \in N$, *then* $(a, x) \in deriv_3(N)$

Proof. We prove by induction on i.

- Base step: Let $i = 0$. Then $b \in B_{a,0}^N = Cn(a)$. Hence $a \vdash b$. Therefore we can apply SI to $a \vdash b$ and (b, x) to derive (a, x).
- Inductive step: Assume for $i = k$, if $b \in B_{a,k}^N$ and $(b, x) \in N$, then $(a, x) \in deriv_3(N)$. Now let $b \in B_{a,k+1}^N$. Then $b \in Cn(\{a\} \cup N(B_{a,k}^N))$, and there exist $b_1 \ldots b_n \in N(B_{a,k}^N)$ such that $a \wedge b_1 \wedge \ldots \wedge b_n \vdash b$. Then apply SI to $(b, x) \in N$ and $a \wedge b_1 \wedge \ldots \wedge b_n \vdash b$ we have $(a \wedge b_1 \wedge \ldots \wedge b_n, x) \in deriv_3(N)$. Note that for each $i \in \{1, \ldots, n\}$, from $b_i \in N(B_{a,k}^N)$ we know there is $a_i \in B_{a,k}^N$ such that $(a_i, b_i) \in N$. Now by inductive hypothesis we have $(a, b_i) \in deriv_3(N)$. Then applying the AND rule we have $(a, b_1 \wedge \ldots \wedge b_n) \in deriv_3(N)$. From $(a, b_1 \wedge \ldots \wedge b_n) \in deriv_3(N)$ and $(a \wedge b_1 \wedge \ldots \wedge b_n, x) \in deriv_3(N)$ we can adopt the CT rule to derive $(a, x) \in deriv_3(N)$. □

Theorem 6. For a set of norms N and a formula a,

1. $(a, x) \in deriv_3(N)$ iff $x \in Cn(N(B_a^N))$.
2. $(a, x) \in deriv_3^+(N)$ iff $x \in Cn(N_{id}(B_A^{N_{id}}))$.

Proof. Here we focus on the case for $deriv_3$, the other case is similar.
(left to right) We prove by induction that for all $a \in L$, $(a, x) \in deriv_3(N)$ implies $x \in Cn(N(B_a^N))$.

- (Base step) Assume $(a, x) \in N$, then by Lemma 4 we have $a \in B_a^N$. Hence $x \in N(B_a^N) \subseteq Cn(N(B_a^N))$.
- Assume $(b, x) \in deriv_3(N)$ and it is derived at the last step by using SI from $(a, x) \in deriv_3(N)$ and $b \vdash a$. Then by inductive hypothesis we have $x \in Cn(N(B_a^N))$. By Lemma 6 we know $B_a^N \subseteq B_b^N$. Therefore we further have $N(B_a^N) \subseteq N(B_b^N)$, $Cn(N(B_a^N)) \subseteq Cn(N(B_b^N))$. Hence $x \in Cn(N(B_b^N))$.

– Assume $(a, x \land y) \in deriv_3(N)$ and it is derived at the last step by using AND from (a, x) and (a, y). Then by inductive hypothesis we have $x \in Cn(N(B_a^N))$ and $y \in Cn(N(B_a^N))$. Therefore $x \land y \in Cn(N(B_a^N))$.

– Assume $(a, y) \in deriv_3(N)$ and it is derived by using WO from $(a, x) \in deriv_3(N)$ and $x \vdash y$. Then by inductive hypothesis we have $x \in Cn(N(B_a^N))$. Since $x \vdash y$, we can prove that $y \in Cn(N(B_a^N))$.

– Assume $(a, y) \in deriv_3(N)$ and it is derived by using CT form $(a, x) \in deriv_3(N)$ and $(a \land x, y) \in deriv_3(N)$. Then by inductive hypothesis we have $x \in Cn(N(B_a^N))$ and $y \in Cn(N(B_{a \land x}^N))$. Then by Lemma 8 we have $B_a^N = B_{a \land x}^N$. Therefore $y \in Cn(N(B_a^N))$.

(right to left) Assume $x \in Cn(N(B_a^N))$, then there exist $x_1, \ldots, x_n \in N(B_a^N)$ such that $x_1 \land \ldots \land x_n \vdash x$. For each $i \in \{1, \ldots, n\}$, from $x_i \in N(B_a^N)$ we know there is $a_i \in B_a^N$ such that $(a_i, x_i) \in N$. From $a_i \in B_a^N$ we know there exists k such that $a_i \in B_{a,k}^N$. Now by Lemma 9 we know $(a, x_i) \in deriv_3(N)$. Then applying the AND rule we have $(a, x_1 \land \ldots x_n) \in deriv_3(N)$. Then by the WO rule we have $(a, x) \in deriv_3(N)$. □

To prove the left to right direction of Theorem 11, we need the following lemmas:

Lemma 10. *For all A, if $i \le j$ then $N_{BT}^i(A) \subseteq N_{BT}^j(A)$*

Proof. The proof is trivial and left to the readers. □

Lemma 11. *For all $i \ge 1$, if $A \subseteq B$ the $N_{BT}^i(A) \subseteq N_{BT}^i(B)$.*

Proof. We prove by induction. We focus on the inductive step. Assume $N_{BT}^i(A) \subseteq N_{BT}^i(B)$, consider $N_{BT}^{i+1}(A)$ and $N_{BT}^{i+1}(B)$. Note that $N_{BT}^{i+1}(A) = C_{ae}(N_{BT}^i(A) \cup N(N_{BT}^i(A)))$. By I.H. we have $N_{BT}^i(A) \subseteq N_{BT}^i(B)$. By the monotonicity of $N(\bullet)$ we have $N(N_{BT}^i(A)) \subseteq N(N_{BT}^i(B))$. Therefore $N_{BT}^i(A) \cup N(N_{BT}^i(A)) \subseteq N_{BT}^i(B) \cup N(N_{BT}^i(B))$. Therefore $C_{ae}(N_{BT}^i(A) \cup N(N_{BT}^i(A))) \subseteq C_{ae}(N_{BT}^i(B) \cup N(N_{BT}^i(B)))$ by the monotonicity of C_{ae}. That is, $N_{BT}^{i+1}(A) \subseteq N_{BT}^{i+1}(B)$. □

Lemma 12. *For all $i, j \ge 1$, for all sets A, $N_{BT}^i(N_{BT}^j(A)) \subseteq N_{BT}^{i+j}(A)$.*

Proof. We prove by induction on i.

If $i = 1$, then $N_{BT}^1(N_{BT}^j(A)) = C_{ae}(N(C_e(N_{BT}^j(A)))) = C_{ae}(N(N_{BT}^j(A)))$. $N_{BT}^{1+j}(A) = C_{ae}(N_{BT}^j(A) \cup N(N_{BT}^j(A)))$. By monotonicity of C_{ae} we have that $C_{ae}(N(N_{BT}^j(A))) \subseteq C_{ae}(N_{BT}^j(A) \cup N(N_{BT}^j(A)))$. Therefore $N_{BT}^1(N_{BT}^j(A)) \subseteq N_{BT}^{1+j}(A)$.

Now for the inductive step. Consider $N_{BT}^{i+1}(N_{BT}^j(A))$ and $N_{BT}^{i+1+j}(A)$. Note that $N_{BT}^{i+1}(N_{BT}^j(A)) = C_{ae}(N_{BT}^i(N_{BT}^j(A)) \cup N(N_{BT}^i(N^j(A))))$. And $N_{BT}^{i+1+j}(A) = C_{ae}(N_{BT}^{i+j}(A) \cup N(N_{BT}^{i+j}(A)))$. By I.H. we have $N_{BT}^i(N_{BT}^j(A)) \subseteq N_{BT}^{i+j}(A)$, and by the monotonicity of N we have $N(N_{BT}^i(N_{BT}^j(A))) \subseteq N(N_{BT}^{i+j}(A))$. Then we have $C_{ae}(N_{BT}^i(N_{BT}^j(A)) \cup N(N_{BT}^i(N_{BT}^j(A)))) \subseteq C_{ae}(N_{BT}^{i+j}(A) \cup N(N_{BT}^{i+j}(A)))$. That is, $N_{BT}^{i+1}(N_{BT}^j(A)) \subseteq N_{BT}^{i+1+j}(A)$. □

Lemma 13. *For all $i, j \geq 1$, if $x \in N_{BT}^i(a)$ and $y \in N_{BT}^j(x)$, then there exists some k such that $y \in N_{BT}^k(a)$*

Proof. Assume $x \in N_{BT}^i(a)$ and $y \in N_{BT}^j(x)$, then by Lemma 11 we have $y \in N_{BT}^j(N_{BT}^i(a))$. Now by the lemma above we have $y \in N_{BT}^{i+j}(a)$. $\qquad\square$

Lemma 14. *For all $i \geq 1$, if $x \in N_{BT}^i(a)$ and $y \in N_{BT}^i(a)$, then $x \wedge y \in N_{BT}^i(a)$*

Proof. The result easily follows by the definition of C_{ae}. Here we skip the details. $\quad\square$

To prove the right to left direction of Theorem 11, we need the following lemma.

Lemma 15. *For all $i \geq 1$, if $x \in N_{BT}^i(a)$ then $(a, x) \in D_{BT}(N)$.*

Proof. We prove by induction. If $i = 1$, from $x \in N_{BT}^1(a)$ we know $x \in C_{ae}(N(C_e(a)))$. Therefore there exist $x_1 \ldots x_m \in N(C_e(a))$ such that $x \vdash\!\!\!\vdash x_1 \wedge \ldots \wedge x_m$. From $x_1 \ldots x_m \in N(C_e(a))$ we can deduce that there exist $(a_1, x_1), \ldots, (a_n, x_m) \in N$ such that $a_1, \ldots, a_m \in C_e(a)$. Therefore $a \vdash\!\!\!\vdash a_1, \ldots, a \vdash\!\!\!\vdash a_m$. Now by IEQ we have $(a, x_1), \ldots, (a, x_m) \in D_{BT}(N)$. And by AND rule finite times we have $(a, x_1 \wedge \ldots \wedge x_m) \in D_{BT}(N)$. Then by OEQ we know $(a, x) \in D_{BT}(N)$.

Now for the inductive step. Assume $x \in N_{BT}^{i+1}(a)$, then $x \in C_{ae}(N_{BT}^i(a) \cup N(N_{BT}^i(A)))$. Therefore there exist $x_1, \ldots, x_m \in N_{BT}^i(a)$ and $y_1, \ldots, y_n \in N(N_{BT}^i(a))$ such that $x \vdash\!\!\!\vdash x_1 \wedge \ldots \wedge x_m \wedge y_1 \wedge \ldots \wedge y_n$. By I.H. we can deduce $(a, x_1), \ldots, (a, x_m) \in D_{BT}(N)$ from $x_1, \ldots, x_m \in N_{BT}^i(a)$. And from $y_1, \ldots, y_n \in N(N_{BT}^i(a))$ know there exist $a_1, \ldots, a_n \in N_{BT}^i(a)$ such that $(a_1, y_1), \ldots, (a_n, y_n) \in N$. By I.H. we can deduce $(a, a_1), \ldots, (a, a_n) \in D_{BT}(N)$ from $a_1, \ldots, a_n \in N_{BT}^i(a)$. Now by using the T rule n times we have $(a, y_1), \ldots, (a, y_n) \in D_{BT}(N)$. Then by using the AND rule we have $(a, x_1 \wedge \ldots \wedge x_m \wedge y_1 \wedge \ldots y_n) \in D_{BT}(N)$. Then by OEQ we have $(a, x) \in D_{BT}(N)$. $\qquad\square$

Theorem 11. $(a, x) \in D_{BT}(N)$ iff $x \in O_{BT}(N, a)$.

Proof. (left to right) Assume $(a, x) \in D_{BT}(N)$, then either $(a, x) \in N$, or (a, x) is derived by using at the last step one of the rules IEQ, OEQ, T and AND. Here we only deal with the last two cases. The other cases are easy and left to the reader.

Assume $(a, x) \in D_{BT}(N)$ and it is deduced by the T rule at the last step. Then there exist $(a, y) \in D_{BT}(N)$ and $(y, x) \in D_{BT}(N)$. By I.H. we have $y \in O_{BT}(N, a)$ and $x \in O_{BT}(N, y)$. That is, $y \in \bigcup_{i=1}^{\infty} N_{BT}^i(a)$ and $x \in \bigcup_{i=1}^{\infty} N_{BT}^i(y)$. Therefore there exist some i, j such that $y \in N_{BT}^i(a)$ and $x \in N_{BT}^j(y)$. Therefore we have $x \in N_{BT}^k(a)$ for some k by Lemma 13. Hence $x \in \bigcup_{i=1}^{\infty} N_{BT}^i(a)$. $x \in O_{BT}(N)$.

Assume $(a, x) \in D_{BT}(N)$ and it is deduced by the AND rule at the last step. Then there exist x_1, x_2 such that x is $x_1 \wedge x_2$ and $(a, x_1), (a, x_2) \in D_{BT}(N)$. By I.H. we have $x_1 \in \bigcup_{i=1}^{\infty} N_{BT}^i(a)$ and $x_2 \in \bigcup_{i=1}^{\infty} N_{BT}^i(a)$. Therefore for some m, n we have $x_1 \in N_{BT}^m(a)$ and $x_2 \in N_{BT}^n(a)$. Let $k = max\{m, n\}$, then by Lemma 10 we have $x_1, x_2 \in N_{BT}^k(a)$. Then by Lemma 14 we have $x_1 \wedge x_2 \in N_{BT}^k(a)$. That is, $x \in N_{BT}^k(a)$, $x \in \bigcup_{i=1}^{\infty} N_{BT}^i(a)$ and $x \in O_{BT}(N, a)$.

(right to left) Assume $x \in O_{BT}(N, a)$, then $x \in \bigcup_{i=1}^{\infty} N_{BT}^i(a)$. Then there exist some k, $x \in N_{BT}^k(a)$. Now by Lemma 15 we have $(a, x) \in D_{BT}(N)$. $\qquad\square$

The Problem of Judgment Aggregation in the Framework of Boolean-Valued Models

Daniel Eckert[1] and Frederik Herzberg[2,3]

[1] Institut für Finanzwissenschaft, Universität Graz, Austria
[2] Institut für Mathematische Wirtschaftsforschung, Universität Bielefeld, Germany
[3] Munich Center for Mathematical Philosophy,
Ludwig-Maximilians-Universität, Germany

Abstract. A framework for boolean-valued judgment aggregation is described. The simple (im)possibility results in this paper highlight the role of the set of truth values and its algebraic structure. In particular, it is shown that central properties of aggregation rules can be formulated as homomorphy or order-preservation conditions on the mapping between the power-set algebra over the set of individuals and the algebra of truth values. This is further evidence that the problems in aggregation theory are driven by information loss, which in our framework is given by a coarsening of the algebra of truth values.

1 Introduction and Motivation

One of the most elementary problems in multiagent systems is the problem of aggregating the distributed information coming from different sources. For collective decision making by autonomous software agents, the canonical version of this problem (which will be used in the following for the illustration of the more general aggregation framework) is, of course, the aggregation of the preferences that the individual agents express over a given set of alternatives (see e.g. [20], Chapter 12). In its almost ubiquitous form, this problem is given by a set A of alternatives (e.g. candidates) which has to be ranked by a set I of agents, based on the individual orderings of these alternatives. A preference is then a binary relation $P \subset A \times A$, which is typically assumed to be a linear order, i.e. an anti-symmetric, transitive and complete binary relation on the set of alternatives. For all alternatives $x, y \in A$, $(x, y) \in P$ then denotes the strict preference of x over y. Denoting by $L(A)$ the set of all linear orders on A, the problem of preference aggregation consists in finding a rule that assigns to each product, or profile, of individual preferences $\langle P_i \rangle_{i \in I} \in L(A)^I$ a collective preference $P \in L(A)$. As preference aggregation is the core problem of social choice theory, namely the classical Arrovian aggregation problem of the (im)possibility of constructing a social welfare function which assigns to each profile of individual preferences a collective preference relation and satisfies a set of normatively desirable properties, the significance of social choice theory as a fundamental tool for the study of multiagent systems has always been recognized [18], — especially so since the incorporation of computational issues in the new field

N. Bulling et al. (Eds.): CLIMA XV, LNAI 8624, pp. 138–147, 2014.

of computational social choice [4]. This significance of social choice theory has greatly been increased by the recent generalization of the classical Arrovian aggregation problem, culminating in the new field of judgment aggregation (for a survey see [14]). An essential feature of this generalization is the extension of the problem of aggregation from the aggregation of preferences to the aggregation of arbitrary information represented by individual "judgments" on a set of logically interconnected propositions (the agenda) expressed in some formal language (typically propositional logic), the truth values of which are to be collectively determined.

Especially, in order to also exploit the expressive power of first-order logic, it seems natural to use the potential of model theory which, broadly speaking, studies the relation between abstract structures and statements about them (for an introduction to model theory see [3]) and to analyse the problem of of aggregating judgments as the problem of aggregating the models that satisfy these judgments (see [11], following [13]). In a model theoretic perspective, the aggregation problem as it underlies Arrovian impossibility results can be related to the well known fact (see [1], p. 174) that a (direct) product of individual models (e.g. a profile of individual preference relations) may not share the first-order properties of its factor models (e.g. transitivity). For this reason the direct product construction is often modified by using another boolean algebra than $\mathbf{2} = \{0, 1\}$ and in particular the power-set algebra over the index set as an algebra of truth values (see e.g. [2]). This approach was first applied to social welfare functions in [19] as one of the many attempts to overcome Arrow's dictatorship result and is here extended to the problem of aggregating judgments in first-order logic. While the major body of the literature on judgment aggregation studies the (in)consistency between properties of the aggregation rule and properties of the agenda (for a survey see [6]), the significance of our simple (im)possibility results consists in stressing the importance of the set of truth values and its algebraic structure.[1] This significance is closely related to a property of order preservation of mappings between the power-set algebra over the set of individuals and the algebra of truth values.

The theory of boolean algebras can be seen as the natural method to analyse axiom systems in first-order predicate logic. The reason is that axiom systems under first-order predicate logic induce an algebraic structure on the set of well-formed formulae: The axiom system combined with the deduction rules of first-order logic induces a notion of provability, and the quotient of the set of well-formed formulae with respect to the equivalence relation of provable equivalence turns out to be a boolean algebra, called the Lindenbaum algebra.

---

[1] Among the relatively few many-valued extensions of judgment aggregation [17], [7], and [10] deserve to be noted. Closest in spirit to our (im)possibility results is, however, [8] which establishes a characterization of the possibility/impossibility boundary in the framework of t-norms.

2   Formal Framework and Results

Fix an arbitrary set A, and let $\mathcal{L}$ be a language consisting of constant symbols for all elements a of A as well as (at most countably many) predicate symbols P_n, $n \in \mathbf{N}$. We shall denote the arity of P_n by $\delta(n)$ (for all $n \in \mathbf{N}$).

In the case of preference aggregation, A is interpreted as the set of alternatives and the (unique) binary predicate symbol P denotes strict preference.

Let $\mathcal{S}$ be the set of atomic formulae in $\mathcal{L}$, and let $\mathcal{T}$ be the *boolean closure* of $\mathcal{S}$, i.e. the closure of $\mathcal{S}$ under the logical connectives $\neg$, $\wedge$, $\vee$.

Obviously, in the case of preference aggregation, $\mathcal{S} = \{P(x,y) : x, y \in A\}$.

The relational structure $\mathfrak{A} = \langle A, \langle R_n : n \in \mathbf{N} \rangle \rangle$ is called a *realisation of* $\mathcal{L}$ *with domain* A or an $\mathcal{L}$-*structure with domain* A if and only if the arities of the relations R_n correspond to the arities of the predicate symbols P_n and the relations are evaluated in A, that is if $R_n \subseteq A^{\delta(n)}$ for each n.

An $\mathcal{L}$-structure $\mathfrak{A}$ is a *model* of the theory T if $\mathfrak{A} \models \varphi$ for all $\varphi \in T$, i.e. if all sentences of the theory hold true in $\mathfrak{A}$ (with the usual Tarski definition of truth).

In the case of preference aggregation with linear preferences, T is the set of $\mathcal{L}$-sentences which axiomatize the class of linear orders, i.e.

$\forall x \neg P(x, x)$ (irreflexivity),

$\forall x \forall y \forall z [(P(x, y) \wedge P(y, z)) \to P(x, z)]$ (transitivity),

$\forall x \forall y (P(x, y) \vee P(y, x) \vee x = y)$ (completeness).

A boolean-valued model for $\mathcal{L}$ is a mapping which assigns to each $\mathcal{L}$-formula λ a truth value $\|\lambda\|$ in some arbitrary complete boolean algebra $\mathbf{B} = \langle B, \sqcup, \sqcap, ^*, 0_B, 1_B \rangle$ in such a way that boolean connectives and logical connectives commute:

$\|\neg\lambda\| = \|\lambda\|^*$; $\|\phi \vee \varphi\| = \|\phi\| \sqcup \|\varphi\|$; $\|\phi \wedge \varphi\| = \|\phi\| \sqcap \|\varphi\|$ (see [12]).

Boolean-valued models stand in a natural relation to products of models, like they play a role in aggregation theory. Indeed, in a model theoretic framework, a profile of individual judgments is nothing else than the direct product of the individual (factor) models, and this makes the power-set algebra over the index set of individuals a natural choice for a modification of the direct product construction and an alternative boolean valuation (see [1], p. 174f.)

Let Ω be the collection of models of T with domain A.

Let I be a (finite or infinite) set. Elements of I will be called *individuals*, elements of Ω^I will be called *profiles* and will be denoted by $\underline{\mathfrak{A}} := \langle \mathfrak{A} \rangle_{i \in I}$.

Thus, in the case of preference aggregation, Ω^I represents the set of all logically possible profiles of preferences.

For simplicity, let us assume for our preference aggregation example that $I = \{1, 2, 3\}$, $A = \{a, b, c\}$, and that the preferences of the individuals are given by the classical configuration of the Condorcet paradox, respectively

$\mathfrak{A}_1 \models P(a, b) \wedge P(b, c) \wedge P(a, c)$

$\mathfrak{A}_2 \models P(b, c) \wedge P(c, a) \wedge P(b, a)$

$\mathfrak{A}_3 \models P(c, a) \wedge P(a, b) \wedge P(c, b)$.

Remark 1. Observe that any such profile $\underline{\mathfrak{A}} \in \Omega^I$ as a mapping $I \to \Omega$ induces a map from the set of $\mathcal{L}$-formulae to the power-set algebra $P(I) =$

$\langle 2^I, \sqcup, \cap, \complement, \varnothing, I \rangle^2$, which maps every $\mathcal{L}$-formula λ to the coalition of all individuals whose models satisfy λ, i.e. $\{i \in I : \mathfrak{A}_i \models \lambda\}$.

Thus, e.g. in our simple preference aggregation example $\{i \in I : \mathfrak{A}_i \models P(a,c)\} = \{1\}$ and $\{i \in I : \mathfrak{A}_i \models P(a,b)\} = \{1,3\}$.

We now call a boolean-valued map f which assigns to each profile $\underline{\mathfrak{A}} \in \Omega^I$ and each formula λ a truth value $\|\lambda\|_f^{\mathfrak{A}}$ in some arbitrary complete boolean algebra $\mathbf{B} = \langle B, \sqcup, \sqcap, ^*, 0_B, 1_B \rangle$ a **boolean-valued aggregation rule** (BVAR) if and only if $\|\neg\lambda\|_f^{\mathfrak{A}} = \left(\|\lambda\|_f^{\mathfrak{A}}\right)^*$; $\|\phi \vee \varphi\|_f^{\mathfrak{A}} = \|\phi\|_f^{\mathfrak{A}} \sqcup \|\varphi\|_f^{\mathfrak{A}}$; $\|\phi \wedge \varphi\|_f^{\mathfrak{A}} = \|\phi\|_f^{\mathfrak{A}} \sqcap \|\varphi\|_f^{\mathfrak{A}}$ (see [12]).

If we now take for our preference aggregation example the power-set algebra $P(I)$ as an algebra of truth valuations,[3] we obtain a boolean-valued map F which assigns to each atomic formula the set of individuals in the models of which it holds true. Thus, e.g. $\|P(a,b)\|_F^{\mathfrak{A}} = \|\neg P(b,a)\|_F^{\mathfrak{A}} = \{1,3\}$, whereas $\|P(a,b) \wedge P(b,c)\|_F^{\mathfrak{A}} = \|P(a,c)\|_F^{\mathfrak{A}} = \{1\}$ and $\|P(a,b) \vee P(b,c)\|_F^{\mathfrak{A}} = \{1,2,3\}$.

The following properties are reformulations of standard conditions for judgment aggregation rules in the framework of BVARs.

In particular, the non-dictatorship condition can be expressed in the following way:

Definition 1. *A BVAR f is **non-dictatorial** if there exists no individual $i \in I$ such that for every $\mathcal{L}$-formula λ and every profile $\underline{\mathfrak{A}} \in \Omega^I$ $\mathfrak{A}_i \models \lambda \Rightarrow \|\lambda\|_f^{\mathfrak{A}} = 1_B$ (where 1_B the top element of the set of truth values).*

Obviously, non-dictatorship is only relevant if the set I consists of at least two individuals, which will be assumed throughout.

Intuitively, non-dictatorship in the framework of BVARs guarantees that there exists no individual who can ensure for her judgments the highest truth degree. On the other hand, the intuitively appealing Pareto principle requires that unanimous agreement be respected by a judgment aggregation rule:

---

[2] Wherein $\complement D = I \setminus D$ for all $D \subseteq I$.

[3] For another simple example which does not involve the power-set boolean algebra, consider a set of three agents $I = \{1,2,3\}$ facing a set of four different alternatives $A = \{a,b,c,d\}$. Suppose each of them linearly ranks the alternatives according to their own subjective preferences.

Let $\mathcal{L}$ be the first-order language consisting of four constants a,b,c,d and one relation symbol P, and let T be the theory of linear orders. Let Ω be the set of models of T with domain A. A profile is then simply a triple of linear orders on the set $\{a,b,c,d\}$, i.e. an element of Ω^I.

A particularly simple aggregation function is a map $f : \Omega^I \times \mathcal{L} \to 2$ which maps to each pair $\langle \underline{\mathfrak{A}}, \lambda \rangle$ of a profile $\underline{\mathfrak{A}} \in \Omega^I$ and an $\mathcal{L}$-formula λ the truth value which a majority of the agents assigns. In other words, for all $\underline{\mathfrak{A}} \in \Omega^I$ and all $\mathcal{L}$-formulae λ,

$$f(\underline{\mathfrak{A}}, \lambda) = \begin{cases} 1, & \#\{i \in I \ : \ \mathfrak{A}_i \models \lambda\} \geq 2, \\ 0, & \text{otherwise} \end{cases}$$

Verifying that this is a paretian, systematic and non-dictatorial boolean-valued aggregation function with values in $\{0,1\}$ is left as an exercise to the reader.

Definition 2. *A BVAR f is **paretian** if for every $\mathcal{L}$-formula λ and every profile $\mathfrak{A} \in \Omega^I$*
$$\{i \in I : \mathfrak{A}_i \models \lambda\} = I \Rightarrow \|\lambda\|_f^{\mathfrak{A}} = 1_B.$$

Central to aggregation problems are independence conditions of various strength:

Definition 3. *A BVAR f is **independent** if for every $\mathcal{L}$-formula λ and every pair of profiles $\mathfrak{A}, \mathfrak{A}' \in \Omega^I$*
$$\{i \in I : \mathfrak{A}_i \models \lambda\} = \{i \in I : \mathfrak{A}'_i \models \lambda\} \Rightarrow \|\lambda\|_f^{\mathfrak{A}} = \|\lambda\|_f^{\mathfrak{A}'}.$$

Definition 4. *A BVAR f is **neutral** if for every $\mathcal{L}$-formulae λ, λ' and every profile $\mathfrak{A} \in \Omega^I$*
$$\{i \in I : \mathfrak{A}_i \models \lambda\} = \{i \in I : \mathfrak{A}_i \models \lambda'\} \Rightarrow \|\lambda\|_f^{\mathfrak{A}} = \|\lambda'\|_f^{\mathfrak{A}}.$$

Definition 5. *A BVAR f is **systematic** if it is independent and neutral, i.e. if for every pair of $\mathcal{L}$-formulae λ, λ' and every pair of profiles $\mathfrak{A}, \mathfrak{A}' \in \Omega^I$*
$$\{i \in I : \mathfrak{A}_i \models \lambda\} = \{i \in I : \mathfrak{A}'_i \models \lambda'\} \Rightarrow \|\lambda\|_f^{\mathfrak{A}} = \|\lambda'\|_f^{\mathfrak{A}'}.$$

The property of systematicity might appear strong at first sight but it is well-known in the literature on judgment aggregation that it is implied by the independence property and a condition of logical richness known as total blockedness, i.e. if every formula is related to every other one by a sequence of conditional entailments.

The framework of BVARs allows to use the partial order structure $\langle P(I), \subseteq \rangle$ of the power-set algebra $P(I)$ over the set of individuals (the "coalition algebra"), respectively of the algebra of truth values $\langle \mathbf{B}, \sqsubseteq \rangle$ for the formulation of conditions on aggregation rules.[4] In particular, the monotonicity property can be formulated in a natural way as such an order preservation property:

Definition 6. *A BVAR f is **monotonic** if for every $\mathcal{L}$-formula λ and every pair of profiles $\mathfrak{A}, \mathfrak{A}' \in \Omega^I$*
$$\{i \in I : \mathfrak{A}_i \models \lambda\} \subsetneq \{i \in I : \mathfrak{A}'_i \models \lambda\} \Rightarrow \|\lambda\|_f^{\mathfrak{A}} \sqsubseteq \|\lambda\|_f^{\mathfrak{A}'}.$$

Monotonicity is known to be an important property of aggregation rules because it guarantees non-manipulability, i.e. the impossibility for any individual to increase the collectively assigned truth value of a formula by signalling its negation.

The conjunction of monotonicity and independence (known in the judgment aggregation literature as monotone independence, see [16]) can now be formulated as an order preservation property of the aggregation rule with respect to the partial orders of the coalition algebra and the algebra of truth values.

---

[4] Herein, $\sqsubseteq$ is the canonical partial order on the boolean algebra; it can be defined algebraically, for all $x, y \in B$, by

$$x \sqsubseteq y \Leftrightarrow x \sqcap y^* = 0_B$$

(or equivalently $x \sqsubseteq y \Leftrightarrow x \sqcap y = x$).

Proposition 1. *A BVAR f satisfies **monotone independence** (i.e. is monotonic and independent) if and only if for every pair of profiles $\mathfrak{A}, \mathfrak{A}' \in \Omega^I$ and every formula $\lambda \in \mathcal{T}$*

$$\{i \in I : \mathfrak{A}_i \models \lambda\} \subseteq \{i \in I : \mathfrak{A}'_i \models \lambda\} \Rightarrow \|\lambda\|_f^{\mathfrak{A}} \sqsubseteq \|\lambda\|_f^{\mathfrak{A}'} . \tag{1}$$

A natural BVAR F can now be defined by assigning to every $\mathcal{L}$-formula λ and every profile $\mathfrak{A} \in \Omega^I$ precisely the subset of individuals in whose models it holds true, i.e. $\|\lambda\|_F^{\mathfrak{A}} = \{i \in I : \mathfrak{A}_i \models \lambda\}$. Thus, the algebra of truth values is simply identified with the coalition algebra.

This construction immediately leads to the following possibility result:

Theorem 1. *The BVAR F is a neutral, paretian and non-dictatorial judgment aggregation rule which satisfies monotone independence.*

For a proof, see the Appendix; the easy verification for the case of our simple preference aggregation example being left to the reader.

The main interest of this simple boolean-valued construction consists in highlighting the implications for the aggregation problem of the structure of the set of truth values and the significance of the condition of order preservation with respect to the power-set algebra over the set of individuals and the algebra of truth values (for a deeper exploration of the relation between judgment aggregation rules and boolean algebra homomorphisms see [9]).

This significance is closely related to a property of homomorphisms of boolean algebras. [5] Note that systematicity (i.e. the conjunction of independence and neutrality) permits a decomposition of every BVAR as $h \circ F$. One can show that this h is a homomorphism and thus order-preserving, whence neutrality and independence already entail monotonicity.

By the **agenda richness condition** we mean that there are $\lambda, \mu \in \mathcal{S}$ such that T is consistent with each of $\lambda \wedge \mu$, $\neg\lambda \wedge \mu$ and $\lambda \wedge \neg\mu$.

In preference aggregation, this condition is satisfied if there are at least three alternatives $x, y, z \in A$ such that $\lambda = P(x, y)$ and $\mu = P(y, z)$.

Theorem 2. *Let the agenda richness condition be satisfied. A neutral and independent BVAR induces a homomorphism h_f of the coalition algebra $P(I) = \langle 2^I, \cup, \cap, \mathsf{C}, \varnothing, I \rangle$ to its co-domain, the boolean algebra of truth values $\mathbf{B} = \langle B, \sqcup, \sqcap, ^*, 0_B, 1_B \rangle$*

As we shall see presently, using the notion of the Lindenbaum algebra, Theorem 2 can be reformulated as an algebraic factorization result. Let $\vdash$ be the provability relation of classical first-order logic, let $T \subseteq \mathcal{L}$ be consistent (possibly empty), and let $\equiv$ denote provable equivalence given T (i.e., $\phi \equiv \psi$ if and

---

[5] A homomorphism of a boolean algebra B into a boolean algebra B' is a map $h : B \to B'$ which preserves the algebraic operations, i.e. such that for all $x, y \in B$, $h(x \sqcap y) = h(x) \sqcap h(y)$, $h(x \sqcup y) = h(x) \sqcup h(y)$, $h(x^*) = h(x)^*$. A homomorphism is always order-preserving with respect to the canonical partial orders of the corresponding boolean algebras.

only if both $T \cup \{\phi\} \vdash \psi$ and $T \cup \{\psi\} \vdash \phi$). The set of equivalence classes of $\mathcal{L}$-formulae under $\equiv$ is known as the *Lindenbaum algebra* and will be denoted $\mathcal{L}/_{\equiv}$. It is obvious that for every BVAR f, the map

$$H_f : \mathcal{L}/_{\equiv} \times \Omega^I \to B, \quad \langle [\lambda]_{\equiv}, \mathfrak{A} \rangle \mapsto \|\lambda\|_f^{\mathfrak{A}}$$

is well-defined. It is also clear that for every $\mathfrak{A} \in \Omega^I$, $H_f(\cdot, \mathfrak{A})$ is a homomorphism. Given any profile $\mathfrak{A} \in \Omega^I$, we then have the following commutative diagram or factorization:

$$
\begin{array}{ccc}
\mathcal{L}/_{\equiv} & \xrightarrow{H_F(\cdot,\mathfrak{A})} & P(I) \\
{\scriptstyle H_f(\cdot,\mathfrak{A})} \downarrow & \swarrow {\scriptstyle h_f} & \\
B & &
\end{array}
$$

Hence, every boolean-valued aggregation rule can be, for an arbitrary fixed profile, decomposed into a (a) a structure-preserving map from the set of $\mathcal{L}$-formulae (modulo provable equivalence) to the coalition algebra and (b) another structure-preserving map from the coalition algebra to the actual algebra of truth values. This latter step can be seen as a coarsening of the set of the algebra of truth values at the social level compared to the richness of "social valuations" of the formulae by the coalition algebra. The extreme case is the classical situation where the truth values at the social level are just binary.

Now there is a connection between the homomorphy among boolean algebras and the source of dictatorship in this classical case of binary social truth values, viz. the existence of an ultrafilter on the set of individuals.

Recall that a non-empty subset $F \subsetneq B$ of a boolean algebra B is a **(proper) filter** if and only if for all $x, y \in F$ and any $z \sqsupseteq x$, both $x \sqcap y \in F$ and $z \in F$ (*meet closure* and *successor closure*). A filter $U \subsetneq B$ is an **ultrafilter** if and only if it is *maximal* in the sense that there exists no filter F with $U \subsetneq F \subsetneq B$.[6] In the case of the power-set boolean algebra 2^I, a proper filter is a proper non-empty subset of 2^I which is closed under the intersection operation $\cap$ and the superset relation $\supseteq$; a proper filter U in 2^I is an ultrafilter if and only for every set $C \in 2^I$ either C or its complement $\complement C = I \setminus C$ is an element of U. It is well known that every ultrafilter on a finite set is the collection of all supersets of a singleton — the dictator —, and 2-valued homomorphisms have an ultrafilter as its shell (see e.g. [3]):

Lemma 1. *Let $g : B' \to B$ be a homomorphism between boolean algebras. Then the shell of g, i.e. the set $\{x \in B' : g(x) = 1_B\}$ is a filter. If B is the two-valued algebra $\mathbf{2} = \{0, 1\}$ of truth values, then the shell $g^{-1}\{1_B\}$ of g is an ultrafilter.*

With the help of such a purely algebraic result, we obtain in the BVAR framework a typical Arrow-style dictatorship result, as a simple corollary of the previous theorem:

---

[6] The maximality condition is equivalent to the so-called *ultrafilter property*: A filter U is an ultrafilter if and only if for all $x \in B$, either $x \in U$ or $x^* \in U$.

Corollary 1. *Let f be a neutral BVAR which satisfies monotone independence and has co-domain $\mathbf{2} = \{0,1\}$. If the set I of individuals is finite, then f is a dictatorship.*

It is thus the rigidity of the truth-value algebra at the social level which forces dictatorship results. This finding confirms the intuition behind the recent unification of probabilistic opinion pooling and judgment aggregation through the overarching concept of propositional attitudes [5]. In the former case, there is a continuum of possible propositional attitudes at the social level, allowing for a beautiful possibility result in terms of linear opinion pools [15], and in the latter case, only binary propositional attitudes are admissible, leading to dictatorial impossibility results [17].

3   Conclusion

We have thus described a framework for boolean-valued judgment aggregation. While the major body of the literature on judgment aggregation draws attention to inconsistencies between properties of the agenda and properties of the aggregation rule, the simple (im)possibility results in this paper highlight the role of the set of truth values and its algebraic structure. In particular, it is shown that central properties of aggregation rules can be formulated as homomorphy or order-preservation conditions on the mapping between the power-set algebra over the set of individuals and the algebra of truth values. This is further evidence that the problems in aggregation theory are driven by information loss, which in our framework is given by a coarsening of the algebra of truth values.

Appendix: Proofs

Proof (Proof of Proposition 1). (if part) a) Monotonicity of f can easily be seen from the fact that the antecedent of the property in formula (1) is just a weakening of the antecedent of the monotonicity property. b) Independence of f follows from the fact that in case $\{i \in I : \mathfrak{A}_i \models \lambda\} = \{i \in I : \mathfrak{A}'_i \models \lambda\}$, formula (1) requires both $\|\lambda\|_f^{\mathfrak{A}} \sqsubseteq \|\lambda\|_f^{\mathfrak{A}'}$ and $\|\lambda\|_f^{\mathfrak{A}'} \sqsubseteq \|\lambda\|_f^{\mathfrak{A}}$, and thus by the antisymmetry of the partial order $\sqsubseteq$ on B, $\|\lambda\|_f^{\mathfrak{A}} = \|\lambda\|_f^{\mathfrak{A}'}$. (only if part) Suppose f is monotonic and independent. If the antecedent in formula (1) is satisfied, then either $\{i \in I : \mathfrak{A}_i \models \lambda\} \subsetneq \{i \in I : \mathfrak{A}'_i \models \lambda\}$ or $\{i \in I : \mathfrak{A}_i \models \lambda\} = \{i \in I : \mathfrak{A}'_i \models \lambda\}$. In the former case, the monotonicity yields $\|\lambda\|_f^{\mathfrak{A}} \sqsubseteq \|\lambda\|_f^{\mathfrak{A}'}$, and in the latter case, so does the independence of f.

Proof (Proof of Theorem 1). By construction, F is neutral. Also, F satisfies monotone independence, since the antecedent and the consequent in formula (1) become identical if F is inserted for f. That F is both non-dictatorial and paretian can be verified easily by noting that $\|\lambda\|_F^{\mathfrak{A}} = 1_{P(I)} (= I)$ is tantamount to $\{i \in I : \mathfrak{A}_i \models \lambda\} = I$ (for every profile $\underline{\mathfrak{A}} \in \Omega^I$ and every formula λ).

Proof (Proof of Theorem 2). By the agenda richness, it is easy to see that

for every $D, E \subseteq I$ there is a profile $\mathfrak{D}$ such that
$$D = \{i \in I : \mathfrak{D}_i \models \lambda\} \text{ and } E = \{i \in I : \mathfrak{D}_i \models \mu\}. \tag{2}$$

Let $h_f(D) = \|\lambda\|_f^{\mathfrak{D}}$. Then, h_f (henceforth h for brevity) is well-defined — in the sense of being independent of the choice of $\mathfrak{D}$ and λ — because whenever $\{i \in I : \mathfrak{D}_i \models \lambda\} = D = \{i \in I : \mathfrak{D}_i' \models \lambda'\}$, the independence and neutrality (i.e., systematicity) of h ensures that $\|\lambda\|_f^{\mathfrak{D}} = \|\lambda\|_f^{\mathfrak{D}'} = \|\lambda'\|_f^{\mathfrak{D}'}$. Now, for every $D \subseteq I$, one can find (by our above abservation (2), applied to $\complement D$ instead of D) a profile $\mathfrak{C}$ such that $\complement D = \{i \in I : \mathfrak{C}_i \models \lambda\}$ whence $h(\complement D) = \|\lambda\|_f^{\mathfrak{C}}$. Now by Tarski's definition of truth, $\{i \in I : \mathfrak{D}_i \models \neg\lambda\} = \complement D = \{i \in I : \mathfrak{C}_i \models \lambda\}$. Since f is both neutral and independent (hence systematic), this entails $\|\neg\lambda\|_f^{\mathfrak{D}} = \|\lambda\|_f^{\mathfrak{C}}$. By our definition of a BVAR, this amounts to $\left(\|\lambda\|_f^{\mathfrak{D}}\right)^* = \|\lambda\|_f^{\mathfrak{C}}$, whence $h(D)^* = h(\complement D)$ for arbitrary $D \in 2^I$. In a similar vein, one can establish $h(D) \sqcap h(E) = h(D \cap E)$ for all $D, E \subseteq I$. Indeed, let $D, E \subseteq I$. Then there will (by (2)) be a profile $\mathfrak{D}$ such that

$$D = \{i \in I : \mathfrak{D}_i \models \lambda\}$$
$$E = \{i \in I : \mathfrak{D}_i \models \mu\}$$

and (by the consistency of $T \cup \{\lambda \wedge \mu\}$) another profile $\mathfrak{C}$ such that

$$D \cap E = \{i \in I : \mathfrak{C}_i \models \lambda \wedge \mu\},$$

whence

$$h(D \cap E) = \|\lambda \wedge \mu\|_f^{\mathfrak{C}}, \quad h(D) = \|\lambda\|_f^{\mathfrak{D}}, \quad h(E) = \|\mu\|_f^{\mathfrak{D}}.$$

Now by Tarski's definition of truth, $\{i \in I : \mathfrak{D}_i \models \lambda \wedge \mu\} = D \cap E = \{i \in I : \mathfrak{C}_i \models \lambda \wedge \mu\}$. Since f is independent, this entails $\|\lambda \wedge \mu\|_f^{\mathfrak{D}} = \|\lambda \wedge \mu\|_f^{\mathfrak{C}}$. By our definition of a BVAR, this amounts to $\|\lambda\|_f^{\mathfrak{D}} \sqcap \|\mu\|_f^{\mathfrak{D}} = \|\lambda \wedge \mu\|_f^{\mathfrak{C}}$, whence $h(D) \sqcap h(E) = h(D \cap E)$ for arbitrary $D, E \in 2^I$. By De Morgan's formulae in the boolean algebras B and 2^I as well as iterated application of the preservation of meets and complements by h one can now deduce that $h(D) \sqcup h(E) = h(D \cup E)$ for arbitrary $D, E \in 2^I$.[7] So, h preserves joins, too, and thus is a homomorphism.

Acknowledgements. We wish to thank Achim Jung for helpful comments on an earlier version of this paper.

---
[7]

$$h(D) \sqcup h(E) = (h(D)^* \sqcap h(E)^*)^* = (h(\complement D) \sqcap h(\complement E))^* = (h((\complement D) \cap (\complement E)))^*$$
$$= h(\complement((\complement D) \cap (\complement E))) = h(D \cup E).$$

References

1. Bell, J., Machover, M.: A Course in Mathematical Logic. North Holland, Amsterdam (1977)
2. Bell, J.: Set theory. Boolean-valued models and independence proofs, 3rd edn. Oxford Logic Guides, vol. 47. Clarendon Press, Oxford (2005)
3. Bell, J., Slomson, A.: Models and Ultraproducts. An Introduction. North Holland, Amsterdam (1969)
4. Brandt, F., Conitzer, V., Endriss, U.: Computational social choice. In: Weiss, G. (ed.) Multiagent Systems, 2nd edn., pp. 213–284. MIT Press, Cambridge (2013)
5. Dietrich, F., List, C.: The aggregation of propositional attitudes: Towards a general theory. Oxford Studies in Epistemology, vol. 3, pp. 215–234. Oxford University Press, Oxford (2010)
6. Dietrich, F., List, C.: Propositionwise judgment aggregation: the general case. Social Choice and Welfare 40, 1067–1095 (2013)
7. Dokow, E., Holzman, R.: Aggregation of non-binary evaluations. Advances in Applied Mathematics 45(4), 487–504 (2010)
8. Duddy, C., Piggins, A.: Many-valued judgment aggregation: characterizing the possibility/impossibility boundary. Journal of Economic Theory 148(2), 793–805 (2013)
9. Herzberg, F.: Judgment aggregators and Boolean algebra homomorphisms. Journal of Mathematical Economics 46(1), 132–140 (2010)
10. Herzberg, F.: Universal algebra and general aggregation: Many-valued propositional-attitude aggregators as MV-homomorphisms. Journal of Logic and Computation (to appear, 2014)
11. Herzberg, F., Eckert, D.: The model-theoretic approach to aggregation: Impossibility results for finite and infinite electorates. Mathematical Social Sciences 64, 41–47 (2012)
12. Jech, T.: Boolean-valued models. In: Monk, J., Bonnet, R. (eds.) Handbook of Boolean Algebras, vol. 3, pp. 1197–1211. North-Holland, Amsterdam (1989)
13. Lauwers, L., Van Liedekerke, L.: Ultraproducts and aggregation. Journal of Mathematical Economics 24(3), 217–237 (1995)
14. List, C., Puppe, C.: Judgment aggregation: A survey. In: Anand, P., Pattanaik, P., Puppe, C. (eds.) The Handbook of Rational and Social Choice: An Overview of New Foundations and Applications, pp. 457–482. Oxford University Press, Oxford (2009)
15. McConway, K.: Marginalization and linear opinion pools. Journal of the American Statistical Association 76(374), 410–414 (1981)
16. Nehring, K., Puppe, C.: Abstract Arrowian aggregation. Journal of Economic Theory 145(2), 467–494 (2010)
17. Pauly, M., van Hees, M.: Logical constraints on judgement aggregation. Journal of Philosophical Logic 35(6), 569–585 (2006)
18. Rossi, F., Venable, K., Walsh, T.: A short introduction to preferences: Between artificial intelligence and social choice. Synthesis Lectures on Artificial Intelligence and Machine Learning 5(4), 1–102 (2011)
19. Skala, H.: Arrow's impossibility theorem: Some new aspects. In: Gottinger, H., Leinfellner, W. (eds.) Decision Theory and Social Ethics. Reidel, Dordrecht (1978)
20. Woolridge, M.: An Introduction to MultiAgent Systems, 2nd edn. Wiley, Chichester (2009)

A Behavioral Hierarchy of Strategy Logic*

Fabio Mogavero, Aniello Murano, and Luigi Sauro

Università degli Studi di Napoli Federico II, Italy

Abstract. Starting from the seminal work introducing *Alternating Temporal Logic*, formalisms for *strategic reasoning* have assumed a prominent role in *multi-agent systems* verification. Among the others, *Strategy Logic* (SL) allows to represent sophisticated solution concepts, by treating agent strategies as *first-order objects*.

A drawback from the high power of SL is to admit *non-behavioral strategies*: a choice of an agent, at a given point of a play, may depend on choices other agents can make in the future or in counterfactual plays. As the latter moves are unpredictable, such strategies cannot be easily implemented, making the use of the logic problematic in practice.

In this paper, we describe a hierarchy of SL fragments as syntactic restrictions of the recently defined *Boolean-Goal Strategy Logic* (SL[BG]). Specifically, we introduce *Alternating-Goal Strategy Logic* (SL[AG]) that, by imposing a suitable alternation over the nesting of the Boolean connectives in SL[BG], induces two dual chains of sets of formulas, the *conjunctive* and *disjunctive* ones. A formula belongs to the level i of the conjunctive chain if it just contains conjunctions of atomic goals together with a unique formula belonging to the disjunctive chain of level $i - 1$. The disjunctive chain is defined similarly. We formally prove that classic and behavioral semantics for SL[AG] coincide. Additionally, we study the related model-checking problem showing that it is 2ExpTime-complete.

1 Introduction

In the *multi-agent system* domain, formalisms for *strategic reasoning* have assumed a prominent role in the specification, verification, and synthesis tasks [3, 12–17, 27, 29, 31]. A story of success in this field is Alternating Temporal Logic (ATL*, for short), introduced by Alur, Henzinger, and Kupferman [3]. Such a logic has the ability to express cooperation and competition among teams of agents in order to achieve robust temporal requirements, such as *fairness, liveness*, etc. This is made possible thanks to the fact that ATL* formally comes as a generalization of the well known branching-time temporal logic CTL* [8], where the existential and universal path quantifiers E and A are replaced with strategic modalities of the form ⟨⟨A⟩⟩ and [[A]], for a generic set A of *agents*. The simplicity of these modalities results in a *"friendly-use"* logic with an elementary complexity for the main related decision procedures. Indeed, both the

---

* Partially supported by the FP7 European Union project 600958-SHERPA, the Embedded System Cup Project B25B09090100007 (POR Campania FS 2007/2013, asse IV e asse V), and the OR.C.HE.S.T.R.A. MIUR PON project.

N. Bulling et al. (Eds.): CLIMA XV, LNAI 8624, pp. 148–165, 2014.

model-checking and the satisfiability problems are 2ExpTime-complete [3,28]. On the other hand, the use of strategic modalities in ATL* is restricted in such a way that the internal quantifications are just coupled in the strict $\exists\forall$ and $\forall\exists$ alternation. Moreover, and more important, agent strategies are only treated implicitly through these modalities, so they cannot be explicitly associated with any particular agent nor used by the same agent in different contexts. All these aspects give to ATL* a number of limitations when one tries to apply it to multi-agent system reasoning and games [1,9,11,20,30].

To overcome these difficulties and, thus, be able to describe sophisticated interactions among agent behaviors, new and more powerful logics have been recently introduced [4,6,7,18,24,32]. Among the others, *Strategy Logic* (SL), as it has been introduced in [23], allows to formalize important solution concepts by treating agent strategies as *first-order objects*. Intuitively, SL unpacks the ATL* modalities, allowing to explicitly declare the strategy profiles. Notably, strategies in SL represent general conditional plans that at each step prescribe an action on the base of the previous history. Then, by means of a binding operator, they can be liked to specific agents. This allows to reuse strategies or share them among different agents. With more details, SL makes use of the existential $\langle\!\langle x \rangle\!\rangle$ and the universal $[\![x]\!]$ strategic quantifications, which stand for *"there exists a strategy x"* and *"for all strategies x"*, respectively. Furthermore, it uses the *binding* operator (a, x) that allows to bind an agent a to the strategy associated with a variable x. Using these operators, key game-theoretic properties such as *Nash equilibria* and *sub-game perfect equilibria*, not expressible in ATL*, can be described in SL.

Apart from the expressive gain of SL with respect to ATL*, the finer-grained exploitation of agent strategies let to study and reveal intrinsic game-theoretic properties of the logics for strategic reasonings, never grasped before. The most important one is that SL allows to specify sentences that can be satisfied only by agent strategies that are *not behavioral* [19,21]. More specifically, in a determined history of a play, the value of a strategy may depend on what the other strategies will prescribe in the future or in other counterfactual plays. This means that, to choose an existential strategy, we need to know the entire structure of all universal strategies previously quantified. But this is in general unpredictable, as what we actually know is their value on the history of interest only. Clearly, using logics that admit non-behavioral strategies makes problematic their adoption in practical applications. Additionally, by allowing in SL such complicated strategies, we lose important model-theoretic properties and incur an increased complexity of related decision problems [19].

The quest for a behavioral semantics of SL has led to the definition of a settled family of syntactic restrictions [19]. Among the others, *Boolean-Goal Strategy Logic* (SL[bg], for short) encompasses sentences in a special prenex normal form having only a Boolean combination of temporal goals to handle at a time. For a goal, it is formally meant an SL formula of the form $\flat\psi$, where $\flat$ is a binding prefix of the type $(a_1, x_1), \ldots, (a_n, x_n)$ containing all the involved agents and ψ is a linear-time temporal logic formula, possibly expressed in LTL [26]. It has been shown that SL[BG] admits non-behavioral strategies and, to avoid this, it is enough to limit the Boolean combination of goals just to a conjunction or a disjunction of them [21]. The corresponding logics, named *Conjunctive-Goal Strategy Logic* (SL[CG], for short) and *Disjunctive-Goal Strategy Logic* (SL[DG], for short), respectively, are the maximal syntactic fragment of SL known so far to admit a behavioral semantics and with a model-checking problem to be 2EXPTIME-COMPLETE, as for ATL*. On the other hand, it is worth recalling that the exact complexity of the model-checking problem for SL[BG] is an open question and the best existing algorithm requires non-elementary time.

The positive results regarding SL[CG] and SL[DG] have left us with a conjecture in [21] that dealing with a fragment holding a behavioral semantics is a sufficient condition to ensure an elementary procedure for the related model-checking problem. This has stimulated us to introduce and study in this paper a whole hierarchy of syntactic behavioral fragments of SL[BG] and effectively show that the model-checking problem is elementary decidable. Precisely, we introduce *Alternating-Goal Strategy Logic* (SL[AG], for short) that, by imposing an opportune alternation over the nesting of Boolean connectives in SL[BG], induces two dual chains of behavioral classes of sentences, called *conjunctive-chain* and *disjunctive-chain*, of which SL[CG] and SL[DG] are just the base case. Analogously to the definition of classic dual hierarchies, each level i in a given chain is built recursively by making use of formulas at level $i - 1$ of the other one. With more details, a matrix of a given level in these two chains has as form either $\phi \wedge \bigwedge_i \flat_i \psi_i$ or $\phi \vee \bigvee_i \flat_i \psi_i$, where ϕ belongs to the level $i - 1$ of the dual chain. We grant the usefulness of SL[AG] by providing along the paper an example that requires a sentence belonging to the second level.

To give an idea of the shape that the internal matrix of an SL[AG] sentence can have, consider its parsing-tree along the Boolean connectives over goals. Such a tree has the property that, for each node, its labeling and the one of all its children but one coincide. This means that there is at most one path in the parsing-tree having an alternating interleaving of $\vee$ and $\wedge$ (this also provides an explanation for the name of the logic). Clearly, if such a path starts with $\wedge$, then the formula belongs to the conjunctive chain; otherwise, it belongs to the disjunctive one. Also, the length of the path determines the alternation level k of the class. Finally, observe that having in the parse-tree more than one node labeled differently from its father may already induce a sentence with a non-behavioral semantics [19, 21].

As a main result in this paper, we formally prove that classic and behavioral semantics for SL[AG] coincide. Additionally, we study the related model-checking problem showing that it is 2EXPTIME-COMPLETE, thus not harder than that for ATL*. The latter result also keeps alive the conjecture mentioned above.

From a technical point of view, the specific restrictions imposed to SL[AG] formulas allow to simplify the reasoning about strategies by reducing this to a step-by-step analysis about which action to perform in each moment. With this observation in mind, we reduce the the satisfiability checking of a generic SL[AG] sentence over a given structure to that for a suitably *One-Goal Strategy*

Logic (SL[1G], for short) sentence over an ad hoc built structure. SL[1G] is, as expected from the name, a logic in which no Boolean combinations among goals are allowed [19]. This logic has the benefit of sharing with ATL* several positive structural properties, as well as, it results to be the maximal fragment of SL known so far to have a decidable satisfiability problem.

Due to space limit, most of the concepts related to SL and proofs are sketched. We refer to [19, 20, 23] for more material, motivations, and examples. Also, for recent works in strategic reasoning, one can see [1, 2, 4, 5, 7, 9, 25, 32].

2 Strategy Logic

In this section we introduce *Strategy Logic* [23]. Along the paper we use basic notation that, being standard, we omit and refer to [19] for a formal definition.

2.1 Game Structure

We start formalizing the game-theoretic framework on which the proposed strategic reasoning is performed. First, we introduce multi-agent concurrent arenas that, roughly speaking, describe the game board and its moves, *i.e.*, the physical world where agents act. Formally, an arena is defined as follows.

Definition 1. *Arena.* - *A multi-agent concurrent* arena *is a tuple* $\mathcal{A} \triangleq \langle \text{Ag}, \text{Ac}, \text{St}, \text{tr} \rangle$, *where* Ag *is the finite set of* agents, *a.k.a. players,* Ac *is the set of* actions, *a.k.a. moves,* St *is the non-empty sets of* states, *a.k.a. positions. Assume* $\text{Dc} \triangleq \text{Ag} \rightharpoonup \text{Ac}$ *to be the set of* decisions, *i.e., partial functions describing the choices of an action by some agent. Then,* tr $: \text{Dc} \rightarrow (\text{St} \rightharpoonup \text{St})$ *denotes the* transition function *mapping every decision* $\delta \in \text{Dc}$ *to a partial function* $\text{tr}(\delta) \subseteq \text{St} \times \text{St}$ *representing a deterministic graph over the states.*

Informally, an arena can be seen as a generic *labeled transition graph*, where labels are agent decisions. However, in this work some conditions rule out how the transition function maps partial decisions to transitions. We preliminary introduce the set of decisions that trigger some transition in a given state $s \in \text{St}$:

$$\text{dc}(s) \triangleq \{\delta \in \text{Dc} : s \in \text{dom}(\text{tr}(\delta))\};$$

As first property, we require is absence of end-states, *i.e.*, $\text{dc}(s) \neq \emptyset$, for all $s \in \text{St}$. Then, we need to provide a meaning to incomplete decisions. Roughly speaking, agents not mentioned in a decision are non influential, that is $(s_1, s_2) \in \text{tr}(\delta)$ means that, in case the agents in $\text{dom}(\delta)$ act as prescribed, the system goes from s_1 to s_2, no matter what the other agents do. This requires the following condition to be satisfied: for all $s \in \text{St}$ and $\delta_1, \delta_2 \in \text{dc}(s)$, there exists an agent $a \in \text{dom}(\delta_1) \cap \text{dom}(\delta_2)$ such that $\delta_1(a) \neq \delta_2(a)$. Finally, we assume that, each active agent in in a state $s \in \text{St}$ is associated with a finite non-empty set of actions and all possible deriving combinations trigger some transition. First, the set of active agents in s and the relative associated actions are defined as follows:

$$\text{ag}(s) \triangleq \{a \in \text{Ag} : \exists \delta \in \text{dc}(s) \,.\, a \in \text{dom}(\delta)\},$$

$$\text{ac}(s, a) \triangleq \{\delta(a) \in \text{Ac} : \delta \in \text{dc}(s) \wedge a \in \text{dom}(\delta)\}.$$

Then, for all states s and decisions δ, if $\delta(a) \in \text{ac}(s, a)$, for all $a \in \text{ag}(s)$, we have that there is a decision $\delta' \in \text{dc}(s)$ such that $\delta' \subseteq \delta$ (equivalently, $\delta\lceil_{\text{dom}(\delta')} = \delta'$).

An arena $\mathcal{A}$ naturally induces a graph $\mathcal{G}(\mathcal{A}) \triangleq \langle \text{St}, Ed \rangle$, where the edge relation $Ed \triangleq \bigcup_{\delta \in \text{Dc}} \text{tr}(\delta)$ is obtained by rubbing out all labels on the transitions. A path $\pi \in \text{Pth}$ in $\mathcal{A}$ is simply a path in $\mathcal{G}(\mathcal{A})$. Similarly, the *order* $|\mathcal{A}| \triangleq |\mathcal{G}(\mathcal{A})|$ (resp., *size* $\|\mathcal{A}\| \triangleq \|\mathcal{G}(\mathcal{A})\|$) of $\mathcal{A}$ is the order (resp., size) of its induced graph. Finite paths also describe the possible evolutions of a play up to a certain point. For this reason, they are also called in the game-theoretic jargon *histories* and the corresponding set is denoted by $\text{Hst} \triangleq \{\rho \in \text{Pth} : |\rho| < \omega\}$.

A *strategy* is a function $\sigma \in \text{Str} \triangleq \text{Hst} \to \text{Ac}$ prescribing which action has to be performed given a certain history. Roughly speaking, a strategy is a generic conditional plan which specifies *"what to do"* but not *"who will do it"*. We say that a strategy σ is *coherent* w.r.t. an agent a (a-coherent) if in each possible evolution of the game either a is not influential or the action that σ prescribes is available to a. Formally, for each history $\rho = s_0 \cdots s_n$, either $a \notin \text{ag}(s_n)$ or $\sigma(\rho) \in \text{ac}(s_n, a)$. A (strategy) *profile* $\xi \in \text{Prf} \triangleq \text{Ag} \to \text{Str}$ specifies for each agent a coherent strategy. Given a profile ξ and an agent a, $\xi(a)(\rho)$ determines which action an agent a has chosen to perform on a history ρ. To identify, instead, the whole decision on ρ, we apply the flipping function $\widehat{\xi} : \text{Hst} \to \text{Dc}$.

A path π is *coherent* w.r.t. a profile ξ (ξ-coherent, for short) iff, for all $i \in [1, |\pi|[$, there exists a decision $\delta \in \text{dc}(\pi_{i-1})$ such that $\delta \subseteq \widehat{\xi}(\pi_{<i})$ (equivalently, $\widehat{\xi}(\pi_{<i})\lceil_{\text{dom}(\delta)} = \delta$) and $\pi_i = \text{tr}(\delta)(\pi_{i-1})$, *i.e.*, π_i is the successor of π_{i-1} produced by the agent decision $\widehat{\xi}(\pi_{<i})$ prescribed by the profile ξ on the history $\pi_{<i}$. In case π is infinite, we say that it is a ξ-*play*. Note that, given a state s, the determinism of the arena ensures that there exists exactly one ξ-play π starting in s. Such a play is called (ξ, s)-*play* and is denoted by $\text{play}(\xi, s)$.

As final remark, an arena is *turn-based* in case that for all states s, $|\text{ag}(s)| \leq 1$.

An arena corresponds in the jargon of Modal Logics to a frame representing the "naked" structure of a model without any connection to the logic. Clearly, to check formulas, we need to interpret the atomic propositions over the states of the arena. We call a *concurrent game structure* the resulting structure.

Definition 2. *Concurrent Game Structure.* - *A* concurrent game structure *is a tuple* $\mathcal{G} \triangleq \langle \mathcal{A}, \text{AP}, \text{ap}, s_I \rangle$, *where* $\mathcal{A} \triangleq \langle \text{Ag}, \text{Ac}, \text{St}, \text{tr} \rangle$ *is a multi agent concurrent arena,* AP *is finite non-empty sets of atomic propositions,* $s_I \in \text{St}$ *is a designated initial state, and* $\text{ap} : \text{St} \to 2^{\text{AP}}$ *is a labeling function that maps each state to the set of atomic propositions true in that state.*

As a running example, consider the arena $\mathcal{A}_S$ depicted in Figure 1. It represents a simple *scheduler system* in which two *processes*, P_1 and P_2, can require the access to a shared resource and an *arbiter* A is used to solve all conflicts that may arise. In particular, the arbiter can preempt a process owning the resource to allow the other one to access to it. The processes have three actions to interact with the system: r is used to request the resource from the system, when this is not yet owned, while f releases it, when this is not necessary anymore and d is a "do-nothing" action in the case it does not want to change the present state. The arbiter, from its side, has two actions to decide which process has to receive the resource: 1 for P_1 and 2 for P_2.

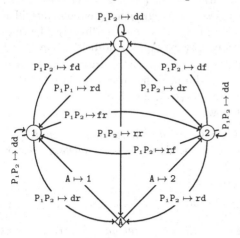

Fig. 1. Scheduler Arena $\mathcal{A}_S$

The whole scheduler system can reside in the following four states: I, 1, 2, and A. The idle state I indicates that both processes do not own the resource, while i, with $i \in \{1, 2\}$, denotes that process P_i is using it. Finally, the arbitrage state A represents the situation in which an action from the arbiter is required in order to solve a conflict between contending requests. For readability reasons, a decision is graphically represented by an arrow $\mapsto$ with a sequence of agents on left hand side and the sequence of corresponding actions on right hand side. Finally, the arena is extended to a CGS by using I as initial state and atomic propositions c, a_1, and a_2 such that $\mathsf{ap}(A) = \{c\}$, $\mathsf{ap}(1) = \{a_1\}$ and $\mathsf{ap}(2) = \{a_2\}$.

2.2 Syntax

Strategy Logic extends LTL by introducing two *strategy quantifiers* $\langle\!\langle x \rangle\!\rangle$ and $[\![x]\!]$, and an *agent binding* (a, x). Informally, these operators can be respectively read as *"there exists a strategy x"*, *"for all strategies x"*, and *"bind agent a to the strategy associated with x"*. More formally, for each agent a we consider a countable set of dedicated variables Vr_a and with Vr we denote the union of all such variables. Then, SL well formed formulas are defined as follows.

Definition 3. *Syntax. -* SL formulas *are defined by the following grammar:*

$$\varphi ::= p \mid \neg\varphi \mid \varphi \wedge \varphi \mid \varphi \vee \varphi \mid \mathrm{X}\varphi \mid \varphi\,\mathrm{U}\varphi \mid \varphi\,\mathrm{R}\varphi \mid \langle\!\langle x \rangle\!\rangle\varphi \mid [\![x]\!]\varphi \mid (a, x)\varphi,$$

where in (a, x) *we assume that* $x \in \mathrm{Vr}_a$.

The *free agents/variables* of a formula φ, free(φ), are the subset of Ag $\cup$ Vr containing *(i)* all agents a for which there is no binding (a, x) before the occurrence of a temporal operator and *(ii)* all variables x for which there is a binding (a, x) but no quantification $\langle\!\langle x \rangle\!\rangle$ or $[\![x]\!]$. A formula φ without free agents (resp., variables), i.e., with free$(\varphi) \cap$ Ag $= \emptyset$ (resp., free$(\varphi) \cap$ Vr $= \emptyset$), is named *agent-closed* (resp., *variable-closed*). If φ is both agent- and variable-closed, it is named *sentence*. By snt(φ) we denote the set of all sentences that are sub formulas of φ.

2.3   Semantics

Similarly as in FOL, the interpretation of a formula makes use of an assignment function which associates placeholders to some elements of the domain. In particular, an *assignment* is a (possibly partial) function $\chi \in \mathrm{Asg} \triangleq (\mathrm{Vr} \cup \mathrm{Ag}) \rightharpoonup \mathrm{Str}$ mapping variables and agents to strategies. An assignment χ is *complete* iff it is defined on all agents, *i.e.*, $\mathrm{Ag} \subseteq \mathrm{dom}(\chi)$. In this case, it directly identifies the profile $\chi_{\restriction \mathrm{Ag}}$ given by the restriction of χ to Ag. In addition, $\chi[e \mapsto \sigma]$, with $e \in \mathrm{Vr} \cup \mathrm{Ag}$ and $\sigma \in \mathrm{Str}$, is the assignment defined on $\mathrm{dom}(\chi[e \mapsto \sigma]) \triangleq \mathrm{dom}(\chi) \cup \{e\}$ which differs from χ only in the fact that e is associated with σ. Formally, $\chi[e \mapsto \sigma](e) = \sigma$ and $\chi[e \mapsto \sigma](e') = \chi(e')$, for all $e' \in \mathrm{dom}(\chi) \setminus \{e\}$.

The semantics of SL is defined as follows.

Definition 4. *Semantics. - Given a CGS $\mathcal{G}$, for all SL formulas φ, states $s \in$ St, and an assignment $\chi \in \mathrm{Asg}$ with $\mathrm{free}(\varphi) \subseteq \mathrm{dom}(\chi)$, the modeling relation $\mathcal{G}, \chi, s \models \varphi$ is inductively defined as follows.*

1. $\mathcal{G}, \chi, s \models p$ *if* $p \in \mathrm{ap}(s)$*, with* $p \in \mathrm{AP}$.
2. *Boolean operators are interpreted as usual.*
3. *For a variable* $x \in \mathrm{Vr}_a$*, it holds that:*
    (a) $\mathcal{G}, \chi, s \models \langle\!\langle x \rangle\!\rangle \varphi$ *if there exists an a-coherent strategy* $\sigma \in \mathrm{Str}$ *such that* $\mathcal{G}, \chi[x \mapsto \sigma], s \models \varphi$;
    (b) $\mathcal{G}, \chi, s \models [\![x]\!] \varphi$ *if for all a-coherent strategies* $\sigma \in \mathrm{Str}$ *it holds that* $\mathcal{G}, \chi[x \mapsto \sigma], s \models \varphi$.
4. $\mathcal{G}, \chi, s \models (a, x)\varphi$ *if* $\chi(x)$ *is coherent w.r.t. a and* $\mathcal{G}, \chi[a \mapsto \chi(x)], s \models \varphi$.
5. *Finally, if the assignment χ is also complete, for all formulas* φ, φ_1*, and* φ_2*, it holds that:*
    (a) $\mathcal{G}, \chi, s \models \mathrm{X}\varphi$ *if* $\mathrm{play}(\chi_{\restriction \mathrm{Ag}}, s) \models_{\mathrm{LTL}} \mathrm{X}\varphi$;
    (b) $\mathcal{G}, \chi, s \models \varphi_1 \mathrm{U} \varphi_2$ *if* $\mathrm{play}(\chi_{\restriction \mathrm{Ag}}, s) \models_{\mathrm{LTL}} \varphi_1 \mathrm{U} \varphi_2$;
    (c) $\mathcal{G}, \chi, s \models \varphi_1 \mathrm{R} \varphi_2$ *if,* $\mathrm{play}(\chi_{\restriction \mathrm{Ag}}, s) \models_{\mathrm{LTL}} \varphi_1 \mathrm{R} \varphi_2$.
    where $\models_{\mathrm{LTL}}$ *denotes the usual LTL semantics over paths.*

As the verification of a sentence φ does not depend on assignments, we omit them and write $\mathcal{G}, s \models \varphi$, for a generic s, and $\mathcal{G} \models \varphi$ when s is the initial state.

In the scheduler example, let $\varphi = \langle\!\langle x \rangle\!\rangle \langle\!\langle y_1 \rangle\!\rangle \langle\!\langle y_2 \rangle\!\rangle [\![z]\!] (\phi_1 \wedge \phi_2 \wedge \phi_3)$ where:

$$\phi_1 = (\mathrm{A}, x)(\mathrm{P}_1, y_1)(\mathrm{P}_2, z)\mathrm{G}(c \Rightarrow \mathrm{F}a_1),$$
$$\phi_2 = (\mathrm{A}, x)(\mathrm{P}_1, z)(\mathrm{P}_2, y_2)\mathrm{G}(c \Rightarrow \mathrm{F}a_2),$$
$$\phi_3 = [(\mathrm{A}, x)(\mathrm{P}_1, y_1)(\mathrm{P}_2, z)\mathrm{F}(c \Rightarrow \mathrm{X}a_1) \vee (\mathrm{A}, x)(\mathrm{P}_1, z)(\mathrm{P}_2, y_2)\mathrm{F}(c \Rightarrow \mathrm{X}a_2)].$$

Informally, the formula φ expresses that, whenever a conflict arises, A has a strategy x to avoid that one of the processes jeopardizes the other one by preventing the latter to access the resource. Moreover, it requires that a processes will suddenly get the resource (*i.e.*, a step after the conflict arises).

It is easy to see that φ is satisfied in I. Indeed, the arbiter strategy consists in alternating the access to the resource between the two processes, while they have to request it at most twice. Then, depending on an initial precedence, when the first conflict arises one of the two processes obtains the resource in the next state. Note that φ requires a unique strategy for the arbiter in order to coordinate with both processes independently. Therefore, it cannot be expressed in ATL⋆.

2.4   Fragments

Strategy Logic allows to freely compose LTL operators, bindings and strategy quantifiers. Such an expressiveness comes at a price of a NONELEMENTARYTIME complexity for the model checking problem. Therefore, it has been natural to investigate some syntactical fragments that can exhibit a better complexity.

A *quantification prefix* over a set $V \subseteq Vr$ is a finite word $\wp \in \{\langle\!\langle x \rangle\!\rangle, [\![x]\!] : x \in V\}^{|V|}$ of length $|V|$ such that each variable $x \in V$ occurs just once in $\wp$. By $Qn(V)$ we indicate the set of quantification prefixes over V, whereas $\langle\!\langle \wp \rangle\!\rangle$ (resp. $[\![\wp]\!]$) denote the set of variables occurring *existentially* (resp. *universally*) quantified in $\wp$. Similarly, a *binding prefix* over V is a word $\flat \in \{(a, x) : a \in Ag \wedge x \in V \cap Vr_a\}^{|Ag|}$ such that each agent in Ag occurs exactly once in $\flat$. By Bn we indicate the set of all binding prefixes.

Definition 5. *Fragments.* - Boolean Goal SL   *(SL[BG] for short) is defined by the following grammar:*

$$\varphi ::= LTL(\varphi) \mid \wp\psi,$$

$$\psi ::= \flat\varphi \mid \neg\psi \mid \psi \wedge \psi \mid \psi \vee \psi,$$

where $LTL(\varphi)$ stands for the usual LTL grammar and $\wp$ quantifies over all free variables of ψ. The One Goal SL   (SL[1G]), Conjunctive Goal SL   (SL[CG]) and Disjunctive Goal SL   (SL[DG]) are obtained from SL[BG] by restricting ψ to a single goal $\flat\varphi$, a conjunction of goals and a disjunction of goals, respectively.

The relevance of the Boolean Goal fragment derives from the fact that the majority of strategic notions (e.g. Nash and Dominant equilibria) resides in this fragment. However, the precise complexity of the model checking problem is still an open issue, whereas SL[1G], SL[CG] and SL[DG] have been proved to be 2EXPTIME-COMPLETE *w.r.t.* the length of the formula and PTIME-COMPLETE *w.r.t.* the size of the model.

3   Behavioral Semantics

In this section we formalize the behavioral semantics. First of all, we provide an intuition of the concept of behavioralness with an example.

Consider the 2-agent turn-based CGS in Figure 2, where square states are ruled by agent α, while circle states by the opponent β. Note that each possible play consists in a sequence alternating circle and square states. Moreover, α and β are free to decide the truth value of p and q, respectively, in the next state.

Consider now the formula $\varphi' = \langle\!\langle x \rangle\!\rangle [\![y]\!] \langle\!\langle z \rangle\!\rangle ((\alpha, x)(\beta, y)Fq \longleftrightarrow (\alpha, z)(\beta, y)Xp)$. Clearly, this formula can be satisfied as follows: if the binding $(\alpha, x)(\beta, y)$ determines a path that eventually makes q true, then in the first step the strategy z has to choose the action 0, 1 otherwise. However, since β is free to decide whether and when q will be true, the agent α cannot respond step by step but has, at the beginning of the game, to guess about the future moves of β. In particular, we say that φ', even if satisfiable, is not behavioral.

Roughly, a formula is behavioral if it can be satisfied by assigning strategies that in all possible histories depend only on what the other strategies do on the same history. Therefore, behavioralness establishes a locality principle in the inter-dependence among strategies.

Formally speaking, we need to introduce the concept of *dependence map* which is analogous to the Skolemization procedure in first order logic. Then, we provide the notion of *elementariness*, a general functional correspondent of what behavioral means for strategies. Let $\wp \in \mathrm{Qn}(V)$ be a quantification prefix over a set $V \subseteq \mathrm{Vr}$ of variables. For each variable $y \in \langle\!\langle \wp \rangle\!\rangle$, we use $\Delta(\wp, y)$ to denote the set of universally quantified variables $x \in [\![\wp]\!]$ that precede y in $\wp$, that are the variable on which y depends. A *valuation* of variables over a set D is a partial function $\mathsf{v} : \mathrm{Vr} \rightharpoonup \mathrm{D}$. By $\mathsf{Val}_\mathrm{D}(V) \triangleq V \to \mathrm{D}$ we denote the set of all valuation functions over D whose domain is V.

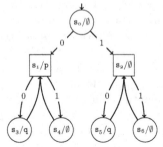

Fig. 2. A Critical Structure

A *dependence map* for $\wp$ over D is a function $\theta : \mathsf{Val}_\mathrm{D}([\![\wp]\!]) \to \mathsf{Val}_\mathrm{D}(V)$ satisfying the following properties: *(i)* $\theta(\mathsf{v})(x) = \mathsf{v}(x)$, for all $x \in [\![\wp]\!]$ and *(ii)*, for all $\mathsf{v}_1, \mathsf{v}_2 \in \mathsf{Val}_\mathrm{D}([\![\wp]\!])$ and $y \in \langle\!\langle \wp \rangle\!\rangle$, if $\mathsf{v}_1{\restriction}_{\Delta(\wp,y)} = \mathsf{v}_2{\restriction}_{\Delta(\wp,y)}$ then $\theta(\mathsf{v}_1)(y) = \theta(\mathsf{v}_2)(y)$, where $\mathsf{v}{\restriction}_{\Delta(\wp,y)}$ is the restriction of v to $\Delta(\wp, y)$. By $\mathsf{DM}_\mathrm{D}(\wp)$ we denote the set of all dependence maps of $\wp$ over D. Intuitively, Item (i) says that θ takes the same values of its argument w.r.t. the universal variables in $\wp$ and Item (ii) ensures that the value of θ w.r.t. an existential variable y in $\wp$ only depends on variables in $\Delta(\wp, y)$.

Due to the fundamental Skolem theorem reported in [19], for each SL formula $\varphi = \wp\psi$ and CGS $\mathcal{G}$, we have that $\mathcal{G} \models \varphi$ iff there exists a dependence map $\theta \in \mathsf{DM}_{\mathrm{Str}}(\wp)$ such that $\mathcal{G}, \theta(\chi), s_0 \models \psi$, for all $\chi \in \mathrm{Asg}$ such that $[\![\wp]\!] \subseteq \mathrm{dom}(\chi)$. This substantially characterizes SL semantics by means of the concept of dependence map. Then, the behavioral semantics essentially constraints the set of dependence maps that can be used to satisfy a formula by requiring them to be *elementary*.

Elementariness is a purely functional notion defined through the concept of *adjoint function*. Let D, T, U, and V be four sets, and $\mathsf{m} : (\mathrm{T} \to \mathrm{D})^\mathrm{U} \to (\mathrm{T} \to \mathrm{D})^\mathrm{V}$ and $\tilde{\mathsf{m}} : \mathrm{T} \to (\mathrm{D}^\mathrm{U} \to \mathrm{D}^\mathrm{V})$ two functions. Then, $\tilde{\mathsf{m}}$ is the adjoint of m if $\tilde{\mathsf{m}}(t)(\tilde{\mathsf{g}}(t))(x) = \mathsf{m}(\mathsf{g})(x)(t)$, for all $\mathsf{g} \in (\mathrm{T} \to \mathrm{D})^\mathrm{U}$, $x \in \mathrm{V}$, and $t \in \mathrm{T}$. Thus, a function m transforming a map of kind $(\mathrm{T} \to \mathrm{D})^\mathrm{U}$ into a new map of kind $(\mathrm{T} \to \mathrm{D})^\mathrm{V}$ has an adjoint $\tilde{\mathsf{m}}$ if such a transformation can be done point wisely w.r.t. the set T. Similarly, from an adjoint function it is possible to determine the original function unambiguously. Hence, there is a one to one correspondence between functions admitting an adjoint and the adjoint itself.

The formal meaning of the elementariness of a dependence map over generic functions follows.

Definition 6. *Elementary Dependence Maps.* - *Let $\wp \in \mathrm{Qn}(V)$ be a quantification prefix over a set $V \subseteq \mathrm{Vr}$ of variables, D and T two sets, and $\theta \in \mathsf{DM}_{\mathrm{T} \to \mathrm{D}}(\wp)$*

a dependence map for $\wp$ over T → D. *Then, θ is* elementary *if it admits an adjoint function.* $\mathsf{EDM}_{\text{T}\to\text{D}}(\wp)$ *denotes the set of all elementary dependence maps for $\wp$ over* T → D.

At this point, as mentioned above, we introduce a notion of *behavioral satisfiability*, in symbols $\models_\text{B}$, which requires the elementariness of dependence maps over strategies.

Definition 7. *Behavioral Semantics. - Let $\mathcal{G}$ be a CGS and $\varphi = \wp\psi$ an SL sentence where ψ is agent-closed and $\wp \in \text{Qn}(\text{free}(\psi))$. Then, $\mathcal{G}, s \models_\text{B} \varphi$ iff there exists a dependence map $\theta \in \mathsf{EDM}_{\text{Str}}(\wp)$ such that $\mathcal{G}, \theta(\chi), s \models \psi$, for all $\chi \in \text{Asg}$ such that $[\![\wp]\!] \subseteq \text{dom}(\chi)$.*

Observe that, differently from the classic semantics, the quantifications in a prefix are not treated individually but as an atomic block. This is due to the necessity of having a strict correlation between the point-wise structure of the quantified strategies.

4 Alternating-Goal Strategy Logic

We now introduce *Alternating-Goal Strategy Logic* (SL[AG], for short), which we prove to have a behavioral semantics and an elementary model-checking problem.

4.1 Syntax

We start introducing the syntax of SL[AG], which extend both SL[CG] and SL[DG] by allowing to nest the Boolean connectives through a right-linear grammar.

Definition 8 (SL[AG] **Syntax**). *The syntax of SL[AG] is defined as follows:*

$$\varphi ::= \text{LTL}(\varphi) \mid \wp\phi,$$
$$\phi ::= \flat\varphi \mid \flat\varphi \wedge \phi \mid \flat\varphi \vee \phi,$$

where $\wp \in \text{Qn}(\text{free}(\phi))$.

A sentence is *principal* if it is of the form $\wp\phi$, whereas it is *basic* in case the matrix ϕ generated by the second rule does not contain any further quantification. Also, with $\text{bnd}(\phi)$, we mean the set of all bindings occurring in ϕ.

The introduced logic SL[AG] allows to identify two dual chains of fragments, called *conjunctive-chain* and *disjunctive-chain*, of which SL[CG] and SL[DG] are the base case. To give an intuition, by using an analogy to the definition of classic dual hierarchies, each level i in a chain is built recursively by making use of formulas at level $i-1$ of the other one. To make this concept formal, we first need to introduce some notions that will be also useful in the following.

In the following, by *alternating combination* over a given set of elements E, we simply mean a syntactic expression obtained by the grammar $\eta := e \mid e \wedge \eta \mid e \vee \eta$, where $e \in$ E. The set of all these combinations is denoted by $\text{AC}(\text{E})$. In addition, $\text{AC}(\text{E}, k) \subseteq \text{AC}(\text{E})$ indicates the subset of those combinations having the number of alternation between the connectives $\wedge$ and $\vee$ bounded by $k \in \mathbb{N}$. Finally,

$\mathsf{sup} : \mathrm{BC(E)} \to 2^{\mathrm{E}}$ is the function assigning to each combination $\eta \in \mathrm{BC(E)}$ its support $\mathsf{sup}(\eta) \subseteq \mathrm{E}$, *i.e.*, the set of elements on which it is built. Furthermore, by means of its overloading $\mathsf{sup} : \mathrm{BC(E)} \times \mathbb{N} \to 2^{\mathrm{E}}$, we also denote the set $\mathsf{sup}(\eta, k) \subseteq \mathsf{sup}(\eta)$ of elements occurring in η at level $k \in \mathbb{N}$. As an example, consider the combination $\eta = \mathsf{e}_1 \wedge (\mathsf{e}_2 \vee \mathsf{e}_3 \vee (\mathsf{e}_4 \wedge \mathsf{e}_5)) \in \mathrm{AC(E, 3)}$ over $\mathrm{E} = \{\mathsf{e}_i : i \in \mathbb{N}\}$. It is immediate to see that $\mathsf{sup}(\eta) = \{\mathsf{e}_1, \mathsf{e}_2, \mathsf{e}_3, \mathsf{e}_4, \mathsf{e}_5\}$ and $\mathsf{sup}(\eta, 2) = \{\mathsf{e}_2, \mathsf{e}_3\}$.

Observe that every matrix ϕ of an $\mathrm{SL[AG]}$ principal sentence $\wp\phi$ is an alternating combination over the set of goals $\{\flat\varphi : \flat \in \mathrm{Bn} \wedge \varphi \in \mathrm{SL[AG]}\}$. From this fact, we can easily derive the existence of a whole hierarchy of logics of which $\mathrm{SL[CG]}$ and $\mathrm{SL[DG]}$ are just the base case. Indeed, for each $k \in \mathbb{N}$, we can define the logics $\mathrm{SL}[k\text{-}\mathrm{CG}]$ and $\mathrm{SL}[k\text{-}\mathrm{DG}]$ as the fragments of $\mathrm{SL[AG]}$ obtained by only admitting matrices ϕ starting with a conjunction and a disjunction, respectively, and having alternation level bounded by k. Note that the sentence used as an example in Subsection 2.3 is a basic sentence of $\mathrm{SL}[2\text{-}\mathrm{CG}]$.

4.2   Solution

We finally describe a polynomial reduction of the model-checking problem for $\mathrm{SL[AG]}$ to the same problem for $\mathrm{SL[1G]}$. This reduction provides us with both a proof of the behavioral semantics and a decision procedure whose complexity is not higher than the one for $\mathrm{ATL}^\star$, *i.e.*, 2ExpTime in the length of the specification and PTime in the size of the structure under analysis.

The reduction first consists of a conversion of the original CGS $\mathcal{G}$, on which we want to behaviorally verify the $\mathrm{SL[AG]}$ sentence $\varphi = \wp\phi$, in a new one $\mathcal{G}^\star$, in which we can keep track at the same time of a group of plays induced by φ, due to the different strategy bindings inside ϕ, that share a common history up to the current moment. Then, we check on the obtained structure a suitable $\mathrm{SL[1G]}$ sentence $\varphi^\star$ that, within its unique induced play, simulates those ones of the original sentence φ. In particular, every Boolean connective occurring in ϕ is replaced by a corresponding fresh agent in the new structure and their alternation is simply simulated by the one of the strategy quantifiers associated with these agents by means of the unique binding inside $\varphi^\star$.

To better describe the whole reduction, the transformation from $\mathcal{G}$ to $\mathcal{G}^\star$ is itself split in a conversion of the underlying arenas (see Construction 1) followed by a conversion of the associated labelings and initial states (see Construction 2).

The high-level idea behind the first construction is to build a composed arena $\mathcal{A}^\star$ in which each original state is paired with an alternating combination of bindings representing the part of the matrix ϕ of the original sentence $\varphi = \wp\phi$ to be still verified. The set of new agents is split into two components. First, we have the free variables of ϕ, called variable agents, that simulate the behavior of the original agents by choosing their actions between those of the original structure. Then, we have a fresh set of agents, one for each alternation level of the matrix, called numeric agents, that simulates the Boolean connective occurring in ϕ. Every one of the latter can either choose to verify a binding belonging to its own level or to pass the control to the successive agent. Finally, the new transition function just combines what the original one does for the binding chosen by the last active numeric agent with the update of the current combination. In particular, the latter is obtained by restricting the combination to the set of all bindings that go together in the same determined direction.

Construction 1 (Arena Conversion). *From an arena $\mathcal{A} = \langle \mathrm{Ag}, \mathrm{Ac}, \mathrm{St}, \mathrm{tr} \rangle$ and a k-bounded alternating combination $\eta_I \in \mathrm{AC}(\mathrm{B}, k)$ over a set of bindings $\mathrm{B} \subseteq \mathrm{Bn}(\mathrm{Ag})$ with $k \in \mathbb{N}$, we build the composed arena $\mathcal{A}^\star \triangleq \langle \mathrm{Ag}^\star, \mathrm{Ac}^\star, \mathrm{St}^\star, \mathrm{tr}^\star \rangle$ as follows:*

- *the new agents in $\mathrm{Ag}^\star \triangleq \{x \in \mathrm{Vr} : \exists \flat \in \mathrm{B} . x \in \mathrm{rng}(\flat)\} \cup [1, k]$ are represented by all variables bound by some binding and a range of numbers indicating all possible levels of alternation in η_I;*
- *the new actions in $\mathrm{Ac}^\star \triangleq \mathrm{Ac} \cup \mathrm{B} \cup \{\oplus\}$ are split into the original actions used by the variable agents and the bindings together with a fresh symbol used by the numeric agents;*
- *the new states in $\mathrm{St}^\star \triangleq \mathrm{St} \times \mathrm{AC}(\mathrm{B}, k)$ are pairs of original states and k-bounded alternating combinations over B indicating which parts of the initial combination η_I have to be verified from those states on.*

For each new state $s^\star = (s, \eta) \in \mathrm{St}^\star$, we can describe its set of active new decisions: for all $\delta^\star \in \mathrm{Dc}^\star$, it holds that $\delta^\star \in \mathrm{dc}^\star(s^\star)$ iff there exists a number $i \in [1, k]$ such that

- *the numeric agents from 0 to i are the only ones active on $\delta^\star$, i.e., $[1, i] \subseteq \mathrm{dom}(\delta^\star)$ and $]i, k] \cap \mathrm{dom}(\delta^\star) = \emptyset$;*
- *all numeric agents up to $i-1$ decide to give the control on the bindings to the successive agent, i.e., $\delta^\star(j) = \oplus$, for all $j \in [1, i[$;*
- *the numeric agent i chooses a binding occurring in the alternating combination η at level i, i.e., $\delta^\star(i) \in \mathrm{sup}(\eta, i)$;*
- *the original decision $\delta^\star \circ \delta^\star(i)$ obtained by the composition of the actions chosen by the variable agents with the binding chosen by the numeric agent i is active on the original state s, i.e., $\delta^\star \circ \delta^\star(i) \in \mathrm{dc}(s)$.*

To define the new transition function $\mathrm{tr}^\star$, we first need to introduce the projection function $\downarrow : \mathrm{AC}(\mathrm{B}, k) \times 2^\mathrm{B} \to \mathrm{AC}(\mathrm{B}, k)$ that, given a combination $\eta \in \mathrm{AC}(\mathrm{B}, k)$ and a set of bindings $\mathrm{B}' \subseteq \mathrm{B}$, returns a new combination $\eta \downarrow \mathrm{B}'$ obtained by deleting from η all bindings not in B'. At this point, for each state $s^\star = (s, \eta) \in \mathrm{St}^\star$ and decision $\delta^\star \in \mathrm{dc}^\star(s^\star)$ with $i \triangleq \mathrm{max}(\mathrm{dom}(\delta^\star) \cap [1, k])$, we define the transition function $\mathrm{tr}^\star(\delta^\star)(s^\star) \triangleq (s', \eta')$ as follows:

- *the original state s' is obtained as the successor of s following the original decision $\delta^\star \circ \delta^\star(i)$ obtained by functionally composing the new decision $\delta^\star$ with the function from Ag to Vr derived from the binding $\delta^\star(i)$, i.e., $s' \triangleq \mathrm{tr}(\delta^\star \circ \delta^\star(i))(s)$;*
- *the combination η' is obtained from η by removing all bindings whose plays do not pass through the original state s', i.e., $\eta' \triangleq \eta \downarrow \{\flat \in \mathrm{sup}(\eta) : s' = \mathrm{tr}(\delta^\star \circ \flat)(s)\}$, where $\delta^\star \circ \flat$ is the original decision obtained by composing the new decision $\delta^\star$ with the function $\flat : \mathrm{Ag} \to \mathrm{Vr}$ derived from the binding.*

To complete the conversion of $\mathcal{G}$ into the composed $\mathcal{G}^\star$, we need to define both the initial state and the labeling of the latter structure. Obviously, the new initial state just ensures that all bindings are pointing to the original initial state, since the corresponding plays have to start synchronously. This is done by associating it with the original alternating combination. As the labeling concerns, to distinguish the bindings that are active on a given new state from those that are not, we further label it with the support of the associated combination.

Construction 2 (Structure Conversion). *From a* CGS $\mathcal{G} = \langle \mathcal{A}, \mathrm{AP}, \mathsf{ap}, s_I \rangle$ *and a k-bounded alternating combination $\eta_I \in \mathrm{AC}(\mathrm{B}, k)$ over a set of bindings* $\mathrm{B} \subseteq \mathrm{Bn}(\mathrm{Ag})$ *with $k \in \mathbb{N}$, we build the composed* CGS $\mathcal{G}^\star \triangleq \langle \mathcal{A}^\star, \mathrm{AP}^\star, \mathsf{ap}^\star, s_I^\star \rangle$ *as follows:*

- *the arena $\mathcal{A}^\star$ is built as in Construction 1;*
- *the new atomic propositions in $\mathrm{AP}^\star \triangleq \mathrm{AP} \cup \mathrm{B}$ are represented by the original atomic propositions augmented with the bindings;*
- *the new labeling function $\mathsf{ap}^\star$ assigns to each new state $s^\star = (s, \eta) \in \mathrm{St}^\star$ the set $\mathsf{ap}^\star(s^\star) \triangleq \mathsf{ap}(s) \cup \mathrm{sup}(\eta)$ of original atomic propositions holding in s together with the bindings in the support of the current combination η;*
- *the new initial state $s_I^\star \triangleq (s_I, \eta_I)$ is constituted by the original initial state extended with the combination η_I.*

Finally, we need to introduce the SL[1G] sentence $\varphi^\star = \wp^\star \flat^\star \psi^\star$ to verify on the composed structure $\mathcal{G}^\star$. Since this has to simulate the original SL[AG] sentence $\varphi = \wp \phi$, they have to share the same quantification prefix $\wp$. Moreover, we need to suitably quantify the strategies to associate with the numeric agents, in order to act in place of the Boolean connective inside ϕ. In the end, the LTL temporal goal $\psi^\star$ is directly obtained from ϕ by replacing all bindings occurring in it with an apposite check of its presence in the current play.

Construction 3 (Sentence Conversion). *From an* SL[k-CG] *(resp.,* SL[k-DG]*) basic sentence $\varphi = \wp \phi$, with $k \in \mathbb{N}$, we obtain the* SL[1G] *basic sentence $\varphi^\star \triangleq \wp^\star \flat^\star \psi^\star$ as follows:*

- *the new quantification prefix $\wp^\star \triangleq \wp \wp'$ is the extension of the original one $\wp$ with the strategy quantifications of the numeric agents whose type depends on the alternation level, i.e., $\wp' \triangleq \prod_{i=1}^{k} \mathrm{Qn}_i$, with $\mathrm{Qn}_i \triangleq \langle\!\langle i \rangle\!\rangle$, if $i \equiv 0 \pmod{2}$ (resp., $i \not\equiv 0 \pmod{2}$), and $\mathrm{Qn}_i \triangleq [\![i]\!]$, otherwise;*
- *the new injective binding $\flat^\star \triangleq \prod_{x \in \mathrm{free}(\phi)} (x, x) \cdot \prod_{i=1}^{k} (i, i)$ simply associates each variable quantified in $\wp^\star$ with the new agent having the same name;*
- *the LTL formula $\psi^\star$ is derived from ϕ by substituting each goal $\flat \psi$ with either $\mathrm{G}\flat \wedge \psi$ or $\mathrm{G}\flat \to \psi$ in dependence of the level in which it resides, i.e., $\psi^\star \triangleq \overline{\phi, 0}$, where the translation function $\overline{\cdot}: \mathrm{X} \times \mathbb{N} \to \mathrm{LTL}$ is defined as follows:*
  - $\overline{\flat \psi, i} \triangleq \mathrm{G}\flat \wedge \psi$, *if $i \equiv 0 \pmod{2}$ (resp., $i \not\equiv 0 \pmod{2}$), and $\overline{\flat \psi, i} \triangleq \mathrm{G}\flat \to \psi$, otherwise, where $\flat \in \mathrm{B}$, $\psi \in \mathrm{LTL}$, and $i \in \mathbb{N}$;*
  - $\overline{\mathrm{Cn}_h \phi_h, i} \triangleq \mathrm{Cn}_h \overline{\phi_h, i+1}$, *where $\mathrm{Cn} \in \{\wedge, \vee\}$, $\phi_h \in \mathrm{X}$, and $i \in \mathbb{N}$;*
  where X is the set of all matrices of SL[AG].

We are now able to state the fundamental result about the reduction of the verification problem for SL[AG]. In the following, we shall then show how to use this reduction as a crucial building block on which to base the model-checking procedure for this fragment of SL.

Theorem 1 (SL[AG] Reduction). *Let $\mathcal{G}$ be a CGS and $\varphi = \wp\phi$ an SL[AG] basic sentence. Also, let $\mathcal{G}^\star$ be the composed CGS built in Construction 2, where $\eta_I \in \mathsf{AC}(\mathsf{bnd}(\phi))$ is the alternating combination over the set of bindings occurring in the matrix ϕ obtained by removing in the latter the LTL temporal part, and $\varphi^\star$ the SL[1G] basic sentence obtained in Construction 3. Then, $\mathcal{G} \models_B \varphi$ iff $\mathcal{G}^\star \models \varphi^\star$.*

Proof. First observe that, once the *if* direction is proved, the *only if* direction immediately follows. Indeed, suppose by contradiction that $\mathcal{G} \models_B \varphi$ but $\mathcal{G}^\star \not\models \varphi^\star$. Then, we have that $\mathcal{G}^\star \models \neg\varphi^\star$, so, $\mathcal{G}^\star \models (\neg\varphi)^\star$.[1] At this point, by the *if* direction, we have $\mathcal{G} \models_B \neg\varphi$, but this is impossible.

To prove that $\mathcal{G}^\star \models \varphi^\star$ implies $\mathcal{G} \models_B \varphi$, we simply show how to construct an elementary dependence map θ for the latter modeling relation starting from the one $\theta^\star$ of the former. Obviously, to do this we make use of the fact that SL[1G] is behavioral, *i.e.*, $\mathcal{G}^\star \models_B \varphi^\star$.

As first thing, we need a partial function $\mathsf{ext} : \mathsf{Hst} \rightharpoonup \mathsf{Hst}^\star$, which maps each history in the original structure $\mathcal{G}$ used to verify the sentence φ to the corresponding one in the composed structure $\mathcal{G}^\star$, where the extension of the original states with the alternating combinations is done coherently with the decision chosen by the agents. Formally, we have that:

1. the original initial state s_I is mapped to the new initial state (s_I, η_I), *i.e.*, $s_I \in \mathsf{dom}(\mathsf{ext})$ and $\mathsf{ext}(s_I) \triangleq (s_I, \eta_I)$;
2. for each original history $\rho \in \mathsf{dom}(\mathsf{ext})$ already mapped to the new history $\rho^\star \triangleq \mathsf{ext}(\rho)$ having $s^\star = (s, \eta) \triangleq \mathsf{lst}(\rho^\star)$ as last state and for all new decisions $\delta^\star \in \mathsf{dc}^\star(s^\star)$ having $i \triangleq \max(\mathsf{dom}(\delta^\star) \cap \mathbb{N})$ as active numeric agent, it holds that $\rho \cdot s' \in \mathsf{dom}(\mathsf{ext})$ and $\mathsf{ext}(\rho \cdot s') \triangleq \rho^\star \cdot (s', \eta')$, where:
   - the original state s' is obtained as the successor of s following the original decision $\delta^\star \circ \delta^\star(i)$, *i.e.*, $s' \triangleq \mathsf{tr}(\delta^\star \circ \delta^\star(i))(s)$;
   - the combination η' is obtained from η by removing all bindings whose plays do not pass through the the original state s', *i.e.*, $\eta' \triangleq \eta{\downarrow}\{\flat \in \mathsf{sup}(\eta) : s' = \mathsf{tr}(\delta^\star \circ \flat)(s)\}$.

Now, we can easily define the elementary dependence map θ by means of the adjoint functions as follows: $\widehat{\theta}(\rho) \triangleq \widehat{\theta^\star}(\mathsf{ext}(\rho))$, for all $\rho \in \mathsf{dom}(\mathsf{ext})$. Observe that, we do not need to prescribe any constraint on the value $\widehat{\theta}(\rho)$, for $\rho \in \mathsf{Hst} \setminus \mathsf{dom}(\mathsf{ext})$, since these histories are not used in the verification of the sentence.

At this point, it just remains to prove that $\mathcal{G}, \theta(\chi), s_I \models \phi$, for all $\chi \in \mathsf{Asg}$ such that $\mathsf{dom}(\chi) = [\![\wp]\!]$. We leave this as an exercise. □

By exploiting the above result, we can derive that classic and behavioral semantics for SL[AG] are equivalent, as stated in the following corollary.

---

[1] By $\neg\phi$, we actually mean the sentence in positive normal form equivalent to it.

Corollary 1 (SL[AG] **Behavioral Semantics**)**.** *Let* $\mathcal{G}$ *be a CGS and* φ *an* SL[AG] *sentence. Then,* $\mathcal{G} \models \varphi$ *iff* $\mathcal{G} \models_B \varphi$.

Proof. The proof simply proceeds by structural induction on the nesting of principal sentences. Here, we just show the base case, where $\varphi = \wp\phi$ is a basic sentence, and leave the easier inductive case to the reader. The *if* direction follows by definition of behavioral semantics. For the *only if* direction, we make use of a reasoning similar to the one done we have done in the previous theorem. Suppose by contradiction that $\mathcal{G} \models \varphi$ but $\mathcal{G} \not\models_B \varphi$. Then, by Theorem 1, we have that $\mathcal{G}^\star \not\models \varphi^\star$, so, $\mathcal{G}^\star \models \neg\varphi^\star$, which in turn implies $\mathcal{G}^\star \models (\neg\varphi)^\star$. By using again the previous theorem, we have $\mathcal{G} \models_B \neg\varphi$. Thus, by the *if* direction, we derive that $\mathcal{G} \models \neg\varphi$, which is impossible.

By inductively applying the reduction previously described on every principal subsentence of a given sentence of interest, we can reduce the model-checking problem of SL[AG] to a linear number of calls to the already known SL[1G] model-checking procedure [19, 22, 23]. Observe that, at each call, the arena conversion always applies to the original one. Instead, the structure conversion applies to a CGS augmented with a fresh proposition for each subsentence already analyzed. As for the CTL* model-checking procedure, the extra propositions only cost a linear factor in the computational complexity of the analyzed problem. From this, the following result directly derives.

Theorem 2 (Alternating Goal Complexity). *The model-checking problem of* SL[AG] *is 2*EXPTIME*-COMPLETE in the length of the specification and* PTIME*-COMPLETE in the size of the structure.*

Proof. As the lower bounds concern, the related results derive directly from the ATL* ones. Indeed, SL[AG] subsumes SL[1G], which in turn subsumes ATL*.

For the upper bound, consider a CGS $\mathcal{G}$ and an SL[AG] principal sentence $\varphi = \wp\phi$. If φ is basic, by exploiting the result of Theorem 1, we have that $\mathcal{G} \models \varphi$ iff $\mathcal{G}^\star \models \varphi^\star$. Therefore, the time complexity of the model-checking problem for φ against $\mathcal{G}$ is the sum of the time required by the reduction plus that of the same problem for $\varphi^\star$ against $\mathcal{G}^\star$. Both the time for building $\mathcal{G}^\star$ and its size are linear in the size of $\mathcal{G}$ and exponential in the number of bindings occurring in φ. The building of $\varphi^\star$, instead, is simply linear in the length of φ. The time complexity of the model checking for SL[1G], is known to be 2EXPTIME-COMPLETE in the length of $\varphi^\star$ and PTIME-COMPLETE in the size of $\mathcal{G}^\star$ [19]. Thus, the thesis for this case immediately follows.

If φ is not basic, we inductively solve the problem for all the immediate principal subsentences. Then, we enrich the labeling of $\mathcal{G}$ with fresh atomic propositions indicating whether a given subsentence holds in a certain state. Finally, we apply the procedure for the previous case on the new basic sentence φ' obtained from φ by substituting each immediate principal subsentence with the related atomic proposition. Hence, the thesis follows in this case too.

5   Discussion

In a recent paper titled *"What Makes ATL* Decidable? A Decidable Fragment of Strategy Logic"* [19], it has been argued for the first time that ATL* enjoys several positive properties thanks to its intrinsic *behavioral semantics*. In effect, several attempts of extending ATL* suffer from the fact that a choice of a strategy may depend on future strategies as well as on those over counterfactual plays. This is the case for both versions of *Strategy Logic* introduced in [6, 7] and [23].

As extensions of ATL* like SL are indispensable to represent key game-theoretic properties such as *Nash equilibria* and *sub-game perfect equilibria*[2], while the non-behavioral semantics is problematic to be implemented in practice, great effort has been devoted to find powerful fragments of SL for which the behavioral semantics suffices to evaluate the truth value of a formula.

Chronologically, the *Boolean-Goal* (SL[BG]) and the *One-Goal* (SL[1G]) fragments [19, 20], are the first two ones that have been investigated in this respect. It has been shown that, while SL[1G] enjoys all the main theoretic-properties of ATL*, including the behavioralness, the subsuming fragment SL[BG] does not. Notably, the model-checking problem for SL[1G] is 2ExpTime-complete (as for ATL*), while for SL[BG] the best existing algorithm requires non-elementary time. This has borne out the conjecture that dealing with a fragment holding a behavioral semantics is a sufficient condition to ensure an elementary procedure for such a decision problem. To enforce this, in [21], the *Conjunctive-Goal* (SL[CG]) and the *Disjunctive-Goal* (SL[DG]) fragments of SL[BG] have been introduced. Indeed, it has been shown that these logics strictly subsume SL[1G], are behavioral, and still retain a 2ExpTime-complete model-checking problem.

In this paper, we show that SL[CG] and SL[DG] are just at the bottom place of a hierarchy of behavioral fragments strictly contained in SL[BG] and that the conjecture still holds for all of them. Formally, we introduce Alternating-Goal Strategy Logic (SL[AG]) that imposes a precise alternation over the nesting of the Boolean connectives in SL[BG]. Precisely, in SL[AG], whenever there is a conjunction (disjunction), *at most one* of its conjunct (resp., disjunct) can be a disjunction (resp, conjunction). Note that allowing *two* instead of *one* conjunct/disjunct in the above definition would fall in a non-behavioral semantics [19].

As a future work, there are two lines of research we would like to follow. One is to prove the truth of the mentioned conjecture and possibly investigate whether it is also a *necessary* condition. The other one (also related to the necessary part of the conjecture) is to study the exact complexity of the model checking question of SL[BG], left open for some years now.

Acknowledgments. We thank an anonymous referee of the workshop LAMAS 2014 for having inspired us to introduce SL[AG].

---

[2] Note that sub-game perfect equilibria cannot be represented in the restricted turn-based two-player Strategy Logic version of Chatterjee, Henzinger and Piterman [10].

References

1. Ågotnes, T., Goranko, V., Jamroga, W.: Alternating-Time Temporal Logics with Irrevocable Strategies. In: TARK 2007, pp. 15–24 (2007)
2. Ågotnes, T., Walther, D.: A Logic of Strategic Ability Under Bounded Memory. JLLI 18(1), 55–77 (2009)
3. Alur, R., Henzinger, T.A., Kupferman, O.: Alternating-Time Temporal Logic. JACM 49(5), 672–713 (2002)
4. Brihaye, T., Da Costa, A., Laroussinie, F., Markey, N.: ATL with Strategy Contexts and Bounded Memory. In: Artemov, S., Nerode, A. (eds.) LFCS 2009. LNCS, vol. 5407, pp. 92–106. Springer, Heidelberg (2009)
5. Čermák, P., Lomuscio, A., Mogavero, F., Murano, A.: MCMAS-SLK: A Model Checker for the Verification of Strategy Logic Specifications. In: Biere, A., Bloem, R. (eds.) CAV 2014. LNCS, vol. 8559, pp. 525–532. Springer, Heidelberg (2014)
6. Chatterjee, K., Henzinger, T.A., Piterman, N.: Strategy Logic. In: Caires, L., Vasconcelos, V.T. (eds.) CONCUR 2007. LNCS, vol. 4703, pp. 59–73. Springer, Heidelberg (2007)
7. Chatterjee, K., Henzinger, T.A., Piterman, N.: Strategy Logic. IC 208(6), 677–693 (2010)
8. Emerson, E.A., Halpern, J.Y.: "Sometimes" and "Not Never" Revisited: On Branching Versus Linear Time. JACM 33(1), 151–178 (1986)
9. Finkbeiner, B., Schewe, S.: Coordination Logic. In: Dawar, A., Veith, H. (eds.) CSL 2010. LNCS, vol. 6247, pp. 305–319. Springer, Heidelberg (2010)
10. Fisman, D., Kupferman, O., Lustig, Y.: Rational Synthesis. In: Esparza, J., Majumdar, R. (eds.) TACAS 2010. LNCS, vol. 6015, pp. 190–204. Springer, Heidelberg (2010)
11. Jamroga, W., Murano, A.: On Module Checking and Strategies. In: AAMAS 2014, pp. 701–708. International Foundation for Autonomous Agents and Multiagent Systems (2014)
12. Jamroga, W., Penczek, W.: Specification and Verification of Multi-Agent Systems. In: Bezhanishvili, N., Goranko, V. (eds.) ESSLLI 2010/2011. LNCS, vol. 7388, pp. 210–263. Springer, Heidelberg (2012)
13. Jamroga, W., van der Hoek, W.: Agents that Know How to Play. FI 63(2-3), 185–219 (2004)
14. Kupferman, O., Vardi, M.Y., Wolper, P.: Module Checking. IC 164(2), 322–344 (2001)
15. Lomuscio, A., Qu, H., Raimondi, F.: MCMAS: A Model Checker for the Verification of Multi-Agent Systems. In: Bouajjani, A., Maler, O. (eds.) CAV 2009. LNCS, vol. 5643, pp. 682–688. Springer, Heidelberg (2009)
16. Lomuscio, A., Raimondi, F.: MCMAS: A Model Checker for Multi-agent Systems. In: Hermanns, H., Palsberg, J. (eds.) TACAS 2006. LNCS, vol. 3920, pp. 450–454. Springer, Heidelberg (2006)
17. Lomuscio, A., Raimondi, F.: Model Checking Knowledge, Strategies, and Games in Multi-Agent Systems. In: AAMAS 2006, pp. 161–168. International Foundation for Autonomous Agents and Multiagent Systems (2006)
18. Lopes, A.D.C., Laroussinie, F., Markey, N.: ATL with Strategy Contexts: Expressiveness and Model Checking. In: FSTTCS 2010. LIPIcs, vol. 8, pp. 120–132. Leibniz-Zentrum fuer Informatik (2010)
19. Mogavero, F., Murano, A., Perelli, G., Vardi, M.Y.: Reasoning About Strategies: On the Model-Checking Problem. Technical report, arXiv (2011)

20. Mogavero, F., Murano, A., Perelli, G., Vardi, M.Y.: What Makes ATL* Decidable? A Decidable Fragment of Strategy Logic. In: Koutny, M., Ulidowski, I. (eds.) CONCUR 2012. LNCS, vol. 7454, pp. 193–208. Springer, Heidelberg (2012)
21. Mogavero, F., Murano, A., Sauro, L.: On the Boundary of Behavioral Strategies. In: LICS 2013, pp. 263–272. IEEE Computer Society (2013)
22. Mogavero, F., Murano, A., Sauro, L.: Strategy Games: A Renewed Framework. In: AAMAS 2014, pp. 869–876. International Foundation for Autonomous Agents and Multiagent Systems (2014)
23. Mogavero, F., Murano, A., Vardi, M.Y.: Reasoning About Strategies. In: FSTTCS 2010. LIPIcs, vol. 8, pp. 133–144. Leibniz-Zentrum fuer Informatik (2010)
24. Mogavero, F., Murano, A., Vardi, M.Y.: Relentful Strategic Reasoning in Alternating-Time Temporal Logic. In: Clarke, E.M., Voronkov, A. (eds.) LPAR-16. LNCS (LNAI), vol. 6355, pp. 371–386. Springer, Heidelberg (2010)
25. Pinchinat, S.: A Generic Constructive Solution for Concurrent Games with Expressive Constraints on Strategies. In: Namjoshi, K.S., Yoneda, T., Higashino, T., Okamura, Y. (eds.) ATVA 2007. LNCS, vol. 4762, pp. 253–267. Springer, Heidelberg (2007)
26. Pnueli, A.: The Temporal Logic of Programs. In: FOCS 1977, pp. 46–57. IEEE Computer Society (1977)
27. Sauro, L., Villata, S.: Dependency in Cooperative Boolean Games. JLC 23(2), 425–444 (2013)
28. Schewe, S.: ATL* Satisfiability is 2EXPTIME-Complete. In: Aceto, L., Damgård, I., Goldberg, L.A., Halldórsson, M.M., Ingólfsdóttir, A., Walukiewicz, I. (eds.) ICALP 2008, Part II. LNCS, vol. 5126, pp. 373–385. Springer, Heidelberg (2008)
29. Schobbens, P.Y.: Alternating-Time Logic with Imperfect Recall 85(2), 82–93 (2004)
30. van der Hoek, W., Jamroga, W., Wooldridge, M.: A Logic for Strategic Reasoning. In: AAMAS 2005, pp. 157–164. Association for Computing Machinery (2005)
31. van der Hoek, W., Wooldridge, M.: Cooperation, Knowledge, and Time: Alternating-Time Temporal Epistemic Logic and its Applications. SL 75(1), 125–157 (2003)
32. Walther, D., van der Hoek, W., Wooldridge, M.: Alternating-Time Temporal Logic with Explicit Strategies. In: TARK 2007, pp. 269–278 (2007)

Synthesis and Verification of Uniform Strategies for Multi-agent Systems

Jerzy Pilecki[1], Marek A. Bednarczyk[2,3], and Wojciech Jamroga[4,5]

[1] Systems Research Institute, Polish Academy of Sciences, Poland
[2] Polish-Japahese Institute of Information Technology, Poland
[3] Institute of Computer Science, Polish Academy of Sciences, Poland
[4] CSC & SnT, University of Luxembourg, Luxembourg
[5] Department of Informatics, Clausthal University of Technology, Germany

Abstract. We present a model checking algorithm for alternating-time temporal logic (ATL) with imperfect information and imperfect recall. This variant of ATL is arguably most appropriate when it comes to modeling and specification of multi-agent systems. The related variant of model checking is known to be theoretically hard (Δ_2^P- to **PSPACE**-complete, depending on the assumptions), but virtually no *practical* attempts at it have been proposed so far. Our algorithm searches through the set of possible uniform strategies, utilizing a simple reduction technique. In consequence, it not only verifies existence of a suitable strategy but also produces one (if it exists). We validate the algorithm experimentally on a simple scalable class of models, with promising results.

Keywords: model checking, alternating-time logic, imperfect information, strategy synthesis.

1 Introduction

There is a growing number of works that study syntactic and semantic variants of *strategic logics*, in particular the alternating-time temporal logic ATL. Conceptually, the most interesting strand builds upon reasoning about temporal patterns and outcomes strategic play, limited by information available to the agents. The contributions are mainly theoretical, and include results concerning the conceptual soundness of a given semantics of ability [20,1,12], meta-logical properties [7], and the complexity of model checking [20,11,10]. However, there is very little research on actual *use* of the logics, in particular on practical algorithms for reasoning and/or verification.

This is somewhat easy to understand, since model checking of ATL variants with imperfect information has been proved Δ_2^P- to **PSPACE**-complete for agents playing positional (a.k.a. memoryless) strategies [20,11] and undecidable for agents with perfect recall of the past [9]. Moreover, the imperfect information semantics of ATL does not admit fixpoint equivalences [7], which makes incremental synthesis of strategies impossible, or at least cumbersome. Still, some other results [10,21] suggest that practical model checking of strategies with imperfect information might not be actually *that* harder than the standard perfect

N. Bulling et al. (Eds.): CLIMA XV, LNAI 8624, pp. 166–182, 2014.

information case, for which successful algorithms and model checkers already
exist [6,3,13,17,16]. Either way, we believe that the scientific approach requires
an extensive study of the practical hardness of the problem. This paper is our
first step in that direction.

We propose a novel model checking algorithm for a fragment of alternating-time
temporal logic with imperfect information and memoryless strategies (ATL$_{ir}$).
When model checking a formula of type $\langle\!\langle a \rangle\!\rangle \gamma$, the algorithm tries to synthesize
an executable (i.e., uniform) strategy for agent a that would enforce property γ.
The task requires to search through exponentially many strategies in the worst
case; however, we build on some observations that lead to a reduction of the search
space for certain instances of the problem. In consequence, a significant decrease in
complexity is possible for many practical instances.

Our algorithm comes in two variants: one based on exhaustive search through
the space of all uniform strategies, and another one based on a simple constructive heuristic. The latter variant tries to construct the strategy by "blindly"
following a single path in the model. We evaluate both variants experimentally
on a simple scalable class of models. In terms of comparison to existing results
we have faced a difficult problem, since there are virtually no results to compare
with. The only existing tool for MAS that verifies existence of executable strategies under imperfect information is an experimental version of MCMAS [19]. We
compare the performance of our algorithm to that version, with very promising
results. Moreover, some model checkers admit imperfect information *models* but
use perfect information (i.e., possibly non-executable) *strategies* in the semantics [3,17,16]. We compare the performance of our algorithm to one of those tools
(the standard version of MCMAS [16]) in order to get a grip on how imperfect
information changes the practical verification complexity. The only other model
checking algorithm for ATL$_{ir}$ that we know of [8] has been studied in [18], with
results that suggested bad performance.

2   Preliminaries

We begin by presenting the syntax and semantics of alternating-time temporal
logic, as well as defining the model checking problem formally.

2.1   ATL: What Agents Can Achieve

Alternating-time temporal logic (ATL) was proposed in [4,5] for reasoning about
abilities of agents in multi-agent systems. Intuitively, formula $\langle\!\langle A \rangle\!\rangle \varphi$ expresses
that the group of agents A has a collective strategy to enforce φ. The formal
syntax of ATL is given by the following grammar:

$$\varphi ::= p \mid \neg\varphi \mid \varphi \wedge \varphi \mid \langle\!\langle A \rangle\!\rangle X \, \varphi \mid \langle\!\langle A \rangle\!\rangle G \, \varphi \mid \langle\!\langle A \rangle\!\rangle \varphi \, \mathcal{U} \, \varphi.$$

where p is an atomic proposition, A is a subset of agents, and the operators X,
G, and $\mathcal{U}$ stand for "in the next state", "always from now on", and "strong until",
respectively. Additional operator F ("eventually") can be defined as $F \, \varphi \equiv \top \, \mathcal{U} \, \varphi$.

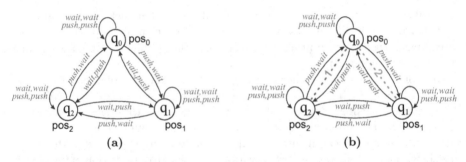

Fig. 1. Robots and carriage: (a) concurrent game structure M_1; (b) iCGS M_2

ATL is interpreted in a variant of transition systems where transitions are labeled with combinations of actions, one per agent. Formally, a *concurrent game structure* is a tuple $M = \langle \Sigma, Q, \Pi, \pi, d, \delta \rangle$, where: $\Sigma = \{1, \ldots, k\}$ is a finite nonempty set of *players* (also called *agents*), Q is a finite nonempty set of *states*, $\pi : Q \to 2^{\Pi}$ is the *labeling function*. Moreover, for each player $a \in \{1, \ldots, k\}$ and state $q \in Q$, $d_a(q) \geq 1$ gives the number of moves available to a at q; we identify the moves of a at q with the numbers $1, \ldots, d_a(q)$. For each state $q \in Q$, a *move vector* at q is a tuple $\langle j_1, \ldots, j_k \rangle$ such that $1 \leq j_a \leq d_a(q)$ for each player a. Furthermore, $D(q)$ denotes the set $\{1, \ldots, d_1(q)\} \times \ldots \times \{1, \ldots, d_k(q)\}$ of move vectors. Finally, δ is the deterministic *transition function* that returns a state $q' = \delta(q, j_1, \ldots, j_k)$ for each $q \in Q$ and $\langle j_1, \ldots, j_k \rangle \in D(q)$.

The meaning of ATL formulae is based on the notion of a strategy. A *memoryless strategy* for player $a \in \Sigma$ is a function $s_a : Q \to \mathbb{N}$ that maps every state q in the model to an action label $s_a(q) \leq d_a(q)$.[1] A *collective strategy* for agents $A \subseteq \Sigma$ is simply a tuple of strategies, one per agent in A. Each collective strategy S_A induces a set of computations (paths, runs). Formally, by $out(q, S_A)$ we will denote the set of infinite sequences of states that can occur from state q on when the players in A follow strategy S_A and the other players are free to do any actions. The semantic relation for ATL is defined inductively as follows:

- $M, q \models p$, for proposition $p \in \Pi$, iff $p \in \pi(q)$
- $M, q \models \neg\varphi$ iff $M, q \not\models \varphi$
- $M, q \models \varphi_1 \vee \varphi_2$ iff $M, q \models \varphi_1$ or $M, q \models \varphi_2$
- $M, q \models \langle\!\langle A \rangle\!\rangle X\varphi$ iff there exists a collective strategy S_A such that for all computations $\lambda \in out(q, S_A)$, we have $M, \lambda[1] \models \varphi$
- $M, q \models \langle\!\langle A \rangle\!\rangle G\varphi$ iff there exists a collective strategy S_A such that for all computations $\lambda \in out(q, S_A)$, and all positions $i \geq 0$, we have $M, \lambda[i] \models \varphi$.
- $M, q \models \langle\!\langle A \rangle\!\rangle \varphi_1 U \varphi_2$ iff there exists S_A such that for all $\lambda \in out(q, S_A)$ there is $i \geq 0$ with $M, \lambda[i] \models \varphi_2$ and for all $0 \leq j < i$ we have $M, \lambda[j] \models \varphi_1$.

---

[1] We depart from the assumption in [4,5] that agents have perfect recall of past situations. Note that both types of strategies (memoryless and perfect recall) yield equivalent semantics in case of standard ATL [5,20].

Example 1. An example concurrent game structure is depicted in Figure 1a. Some ATL formulae that hold in state q_0 of the model are: $\langle\!\langle 1,2\rangle\!\rangle F\,\mathsf{pos}_1$ (robots 1 and 2 have a collective strategy to make the carriage eventually reach position 1), $\neg\langle\!\langle 1\rangle\!\rangle F\,\mathsf{pos}_1$ (robot 1 cannot bring about it on its own), $\langle\!\langle 1\rangle\!\rangle G\,\neg\mathsf{pos}_1$ (on the other hand, robot 1 can singlehandedly avoid position 1 forever).

2.2 Abilities under Imperfect Information

The assumption that agents know the entire state of the system at each step of its execution is usually unrealistic; similarly, assuming perfect recall is not always practical [20,1,12]. The tension between *perfect* and *imperfect information*, as well as between *perfect* and *imperfect recall*, gives rise to the four "classical" semantic variants of ATL from [20]. On the level of models, we extend concurrent game structures to *imperfect information concurrent game structures (iCGS)* by adding indistinguishability relations $\sim_a\,\subseteq\,Q\times Q$, one per $a\in\Sigma$. Intuitively $q\sim_a q'$ iff a cannot distinguish q from q'. Then, *local states* of agent a can be defined as equivalence classes of the indistinguishability relation, denoted $[q]_{\sim_a}$.

In this paper, we are interested in the imperfect information + imperfect recall variant (ATL$_{ir}$), with the following semantics. First, we require strategies to be *uniform*, i.e., to specify the same choices in indistinguishable states; formally: if $q\sim_a q'$ then $s_a(q)=s_a(q')$. This ensures that the choice of an action does not depend on information that is inaccessible to the agent. Secondly, a collective strategy is uniform iff it consists only of uniform individual strategies. Thirdly, we update the semantic clauses from Section 2.1 by requiring all strategies to be uniform. Note that this semantics differs slightly from the one in [20] in that it looks only at the outcome paths starting from the current *objective* state of the system. We refer the interested reader to [7,2] for the philosophical discussion, and point out that it does not affect our performance results in Section 5, as the models in the experiments have a relatively small number of global states indistinguishable from the objective initial state. Moreover, model checking in the "subjective" semantics from [20] can be easily simulated in our "objective" semantics by having the environment agent inject nondeterminism on the first transition. We omit further details for lack of space.

Example 2. An example iCGS is depicted in Figure 1b. Now, formula $\langle\!\langle 1\rangle\!\rangle G\,\neg\mathsf{pos}_1$ does not hold in q_0 anymore: in order to avoid state q_1, robot 1 should wait in q_0 and push in q_1, which is not allowed in a uniform strategy.

2.3 Model Checking Problem

The decision problem of *local model checking* is typically defined as follows. Given a model M, an initial state q in the model, and a formula φ, determine whether $M, q\models\varphi$. Model checking of ATL with perfect information is known to be linear wrt the length of the formula and the number of global transitions in the model [4,5]. Model checking of ATL$_{ir}$ is much harder, namely $\mathbf{\Delta}_2^{\mathbf{P}}$-complete [20,11]. Moreover, for formulae with a single non-negated coalitional

modality it becomes **NP**-complete [20]. This is mainly because fixpoint characterizations of strategic modalities do *not* hold under imperfect information [7],
and hence purely incremental synthesis of winning strategies is not possible for
ATL_{ir}.

3   Towards ATL_{ir} Model Checking

As the starting point of our approach, we take the simple nondeterministic algorithm from [20] that model-checks formula $\langle\!\langle A \rangle\!\rangle \varphi$ in M, q:

1. Guess nondeterministically a collective uniform strategy S_A;
2. Perform CTL model checking of $\mathsf{A}\varphi$ ("for all paths φ") in $M \dagger S_A, q$, where
   $M \dagger S_A$ denotes model M "trimmed" according to strategy S_A.

For nested strategic modalities, the algorithm proceeds recursively (bottom-up).

In order to construct a working version of the algorithm, we need to determine
the order in which the space of solutions (i.e., strategies) will be searched. The
key to such determinization is a heuristic. With a good heuristic, we can hope
to achieve acceptable computation time at least for instances where a solution
exists. This has been experimentally observed for several classes of computationally hard problems, most notably SAT. Our heuristic is based on three factors.
First, we reduce the search space by exploring some equivalences between strategies. Secondly, we define a representation of strategies that minimizes the cost
of storing and processing a strategy, but even more importantly makes the algorithm try simpler solutions first. Thirdly, we define a subclass of strategies
that are relatively simple to construct and verify – which yields an incomplete
but reasonably efficient variant of the model checking algorithm. We present the
ideas in detail in the remainder of this section.

3.1   Restricting the Search Space

In case of ATL_{ir} model checking, the solutions are strategies that a coalition can
use to enforce a property.[2] Since the space of solutions is computationally large,
it is crucial for the algorithm to limit the search space as much as possible. We
limit the search space by identifying some equivalences between solutions.

Definition 1. *For a model M and strategy S for coalition A, we define a trimmed
model M_S as a restriction of model M, where agents from coalition A have their
choices restricted by S. $Q_S \subseteq Q$ will denote the set of states reachable in M_S. We
will call Q_S the* proper domain *of strategy S in model M.*

We also consider strategies that are not completely specified.

Definition 2. *An* incomplete *strategy is a strategy represented by a partial
rather than total function, i.e., $s : Q \rightharpoonup \mathbb{N}$. As usual, the* domain of s ($dom(s)$)
*is the subset of Q where the value of s is defined. The definitions of trimmed
model and proper domain can be easily extended to incomplete strategies.*

---

[2] From now on, when referring to strategies, we mean *uniform memoryless strategies*.

In the naive approach, we can take the domain of a strategy to be the whole Q. Note, however, that the assignment of actions for states in $Q \setminus Q_S$ does not have any significance, because those states are never reached with strategy S. We observe that strategies S_1, S_2 that assign identical actions in the same *proper domain* $Q_{S_1} = Q_{S_2}$ can be considered *equivalent*, regardless of actions assigned in $Q \setminus Q_{S_1}$. The equivalence class can be represented by a partial function which is only defined for the relevant states in Q, i.e., for states in Q_S.

Definition 3. *An incomplete strategy s is* proper *iff $dom(s) = Q_s$.*

Since only proper strategies are worth considering, we can significantly limit the searched strategy space by treating all strategies equivalent to S as a single proper strategy. This single proper strategy can be viewed a representative of an equivalence class of strategies. The size of each such equivalence class can be described as

$$\prod_{a \in A} \prod_{[q]_{\sim_a} \in [Q \setminus Q_S]_{\sim_a}} Act([q]_{\sim_a})$$

where $Act([q]_{\sim_a})$ denotes the number of actions available for agent a in the equivalence class of states $[q]_{\sim_a}$.

3.2 Representation of Partial Strategies

Proper strategies are incomplete in the sense that they leave the actions at unreachable states undefined. Still, in their proper domain, they are completely deterministic. In many cases it is worth considering *partial* strategies that leave some choices open, even in the reachable zone. The intuition is: in some states, all choices work equally well, and thus it is not necessary to fix a deterministic choice in those states.

Definition 4. *A partial strategy for agent a in model M is a nondeterministic, possibly incomplete strategy $s_a : Q \rightharpoonup 2^{\mathbb{N}}$ such that, for each $q \in dom(s)$, we have either $s_a(q) = d_a(q)$ or s_a is a singleton.*
The explicit part *of a partial strategy s_a is the part of s_a where $s_a(q)$ is always a singleton. The* implicit part *of a partial strategy s_a is the part of s_a where $s_a(q) = d(q)$. We will refer to the explicit and implicit parts of s_a as $expl(s_a)$ and $impl(s_a)$, respectively. Also, we will sometimes call $dom(expl(s))$ the* explicit domain *of s, and $dom(impl(s))$ the* implicit domain *of s.*

Definition 5. *We define the* size *of a strategy s as the number of indistinguishability classes of states contained in $dom(s)$. A partial strategy s is* empty *iff $expl(s)$ has size 0. Conversely, s is* fully determined *iff $impl(s)$ has size 0.*

In a model M, the move function D determines the sets of actions available to an agent in any state. A partial strategy can be seen as a possible restriction on the function. An empty strategy is just a strategy that imposes no restriction. A fully determined strategy, on the other hand, assigns a concrete action to every relevant state. All other partial strategies have explicit assignments for some states, and implicit for the others (according to the move function D).

Example 3. Consider a model with 2 states $Q = \{color, noColor\}$, with a single agent with 2 actions $Act = \{push, wait\}$. The move function in the model permits the execution of both actions in both states.

An empty strategy ES is equivalent to the move function, i.e. it permits the execution of both actions in both states as well. An example fully determined strategy CS defined in the following way: $CS(x) = \{$push if x = color, wait if x = noColor$\}$ assigns a single action for all states in Q_S, leaving the implicit strategy empty (of size 0). An example partial strategy PS defined in the explicit part in the following way: $PS_{explicit}(x) = \{$push if x = color$\}$ must have the implicit domain cover the rest of states in Q_S, and therefore the implicit strategy is: $PS_{implicit}(x) = \{\{$push, wait$\}$ if x = noColor$\}$.

The above concepts are so far only specified for individual strategies. This can be easily extended to coalitional strategies. A partial strategy for $A \subseteq \Sigma$ is simply a tuple of partial strategies for $a \in A$. It is empty iff all its components are empty, fully determined iff all its components are determined, etc.

3.3   Looking for Strategies on a Path

As we will see in Section 5, restricting the search to proper strategies and starting the synthesis from the empty partial strategy brings considerable computational benefits. In many cases, however, the space of potential solutions is still huge. In this section, we propose to consider a strict subclass of strategies that fix deterministic choices on a single path only, and leave choices off the path open. Our ultimate heuristic will be to look at such strategies only, which should work well for models with a limited degree of nondeterminism.

Definition 6. *We call a sequence of states $(q_1, \dots, q_n)$ a* line *iff there is a transition in M between every q_i and q_{i+1}.*

We call a line *$(q_1, \dots, q_n)$ a* lasso *in M iff there is a transition between q_n and some q_i, $1 \leq i \leq n$. Note that a lasso implicitly defines an infinite path that starts with $(q_1, \dots, q_n)$ and then cycles in the periodic part.*

Definition 7. *A partial strategy S is* path-based *iff $dom(expl(S))$ is a lasso in M_S. Moreover, S is* bounded path-based *iff $dom(expl(S))$ is a line in M_S.*

4   The SMC Model Checker

SMC (Strategic Model Checker)[3] is a software tool designed for model checking ATL_{ir} and synthesis of uniform strategies.

The current version of SMC can model-check ATL_{ir} formulae that contain at most a single coalitional modality. More precisely, the following formulae classes are supported:

---

[3] SMC is available online at `http://icr.uni.lu/wjamroga/smc.html`

- φ
- $\langle\!\langle A \rangle\!\rangle G \varphi$
- $\langle\!\langle A \rangle\!\rangle F \varphi$
- $\langle\!\langle A \rangle\!\rangle X \varphi$
- $\langle\!\langle A \rangle\!\rangle \varphi U \varphi'$

where φ, φ' are boolean formulae. Extension to the full logic of ATL_{ir} is planned as the next step. We note, however, that the importance of formulae with nested modalities is rather limited. For instance, formula $\langle\!\langle A \rangle\!\rangle F \langle\!\langle B \rangle\!\rangle G$ p refer to A'a ability to enable some ability of B – in this case, to maintain p forever. These kinds of properties are specified rather seldom; much more often, one wants to make sure that some agents A can bring about a *factual* state of affairs p (e.g., by specifying and verifying formula $\langle\!\langle A \rangle\!\rangle F$ p).

In this section, we present the algorithm behind SMC. We start with a general description, then provide a more detailed description of the most important step, and eventually an in-depth description of that step.

4.1   High-Level Description of the Algorithm

The general structure of the algorithm is as follows:

1. For formula of type $\langle\!\langle C \rangle\!\rangle \varphi$, synthesize a previously unverified strategy S_C to be verified;
2. Model-check the CTL formula $A\varphi$ in the trimmed model $M \dagger S_C$;
3. If step 2 returns *true* then terminate returning *true* together with the strategy S_C;
4. If all strategies have been verified, return *false* and terminate;
5. Else, return to start.

Step 1 (strategy synthesis step) is the most significant, as step 2 can be performed with the well-known fixpoint model checking algorithm for CTL, with a slightly modified pre-image function that operates on iCGS's. Points 3–5 are simple binary decision steps. Thus, our next move is to elaborate on step 1:

1. Start with an empty partial strategy and with the initial state;
2. In a loop, generate potential partial strategies by fixing actions for newly discovered states that do not have already fixed actions. These newly discovered states are required to be reachable with the employment of this strategy;
3. Continue the above step until a successful strategy is found or all strategies have been explored.

4.2   Low-Level Description of Strategy Synthesis

In order to implement the strategy synthesis step, we define the following structures. A *strategy task* $ST = \langle F, U, S \rangle$ consists of:

1. The set of *fixed* states F. For any state in F we have already assigned actions for all agents in the explicit domain of the partial strategy S;

2. The set of *unchecked* states U. States in U may have no explicit actions assigned in S yet for some or all of the agents;
3. The partial strategy S.

A *strategy tasks list* STL is a list of strategy tasks. We will implement STL as a sequential data structure (e.g. queue or stack) that stores the strategy tasks to be processed in the future.
The list is initialized with $STL_0 = \{\langle \emptyset, \{initialState\}, emptyPartialStrategy \rangle\}$.

The strategy synthesis algorithm proceeds as follows:

1. If $STL = \emptyset$, terminate with answer *no strategy found*. Otherwise remove a strategy task from STL in order to process it. This current strategy task will be referred to as $CST = \langle F, U, S \rangle$;
2. Fix a current state $CS \in U$ and do $F = F \cup \{CS\}$, $U = U \setminus \{CS\}$;
3. Generate all possible children strategies for S, reachable by fixing a previously unfixed action for the current state CS. (Note: This step generates strategies if at least one of the agents in the checked coalition has an unfixed action in the current state CS. We do not fix actions for agents that already have a fixed action in this state.)
4. If there were no new strategies generated in step 3, generate a new strategy task $\langle F, U, S \rangle$. (Note: the strategy is still S, but we have changed F and U in step 2.) Add this strategy task to STL if $U \neq \emptyset$. Assume S as current strategy;
5. If there were new strategies generated in step 3, process the first strategy as the current strategy. Postpone processing all *other* strategies except the first one by adding appropriate strategy tasks to STL. Do $U = \emptyset$ if path-centric synthesis is enabled. Add to U the successors (states reachable in a single step) of CS, that are not present in $F \cup U$.
6. If only unbounded (complete) strategies verification is enabled, ignore this step unless the current strategy is an unbounded (respectively, complete) strategy. Otherwise, pass the current strategy to the verification step (done by means of CTL fix-point model checking of the trimmed model $M \dagger S$). If the verification yields *true* result, terminate with answer *strategy found* and return the current strategy as witness;
7. Return to step 1.

In order to ensure that the algorithm is well-understood, some further explanations are needed. As stated in the high-level description, the crucial point is that we extend partial strategies by adding a single entry into the explicit domain of a partial strategy. For any agent in the checked coalition, we add a single entry that fixes the action in this state, unless such an action is already fixed. The possibility of this action being fixed in a previously unchecked global state stems from the presence of imperfect information. While this global state has certainly not been checked before, it might be indistinguishable for this particular agent with a state that has been checked before. In such a situation this agent has an action for the equivalence class containing both those states already fixed. Step 4 describes a very special case of such an event, where we have a previously unchecked global state that has already fixed actions for all agents in the coalition. Step 5 on the other hand describes a situation where at least one of the agents has no fixed action for this current global state, therefore has the possibility to extend his partial strategy by adding a new entry in the explicit domain of the strategy.

In step 5, if path-centric synthesis is enabled, the algorithm only considers as sources of strategy refinement states reachable from the current state (CS). This is achieved by doing $U = \emptyset$. Essentially, always only one successor of the current state CS is used to extend a strategy, then all other successors are forgotten. This leads to path-centric strategies.

4.3 Discussion

Our approach enables the capability of constructing strategies of limited explicit strategy size. To illustrate the idea that fully determined strategies with a large domain are not always required, we present an example where a partial strategy with the explicit domain size 1 is sufficient.

Example 4. Consider a model of a game of checkers with two players, a and b. The formula is $\langle\langle a\rangle\rangle F$playerAHasLessPiecesThanCurrently. The meaning of this formula is that agent a has a strategy to enforce himself having in the future at least one piece less than he currently has. The initial state of the model is an already started game where a move for a exists that forces b to capture a piece in the next transition of the system. Therefore there exists a successful partial strategy to satisfy the verified formula where the explicit domain of this strategy has size 1. In other words, a successful partial strategy that just assigns a single action in the initial state is possible to be constructed.

This example demonstrates that it is not necessary to build fully determined nor unbounded strategies sometimes. The output of this example can be a bounded path-based strategy of size 1, as the explicit part suffices as output. On the other hand, generating a fully determined strategy could easily require a domain size of 10^3 or more.

A proper partial strategy can be described by the explicit strategy part. This part can often be of small size, what the example above illustrates. Example benefits of smaller size of strategy domains are improved readability for humans and reduced memory/processing requirements for computers.

4.4 Variants of the Algorithm

In the experiments, we will use three different versions of the SMC algorithm. *SMC with branching strategy search* searches through all the proper strategies, which usually requires fixing choices for multiple successors of a given state (hence the "branching" moniker). *SMC with path-based strategy search* searches only through path-based strategies, and *SMC with bounded path-based strategy search* searches only through bounded path-based strategies.

We call a variant of SMC *sound* iff $SMC(M, q, \langle\!\langle A \rangle\!\rangle\varphi) = true$ implies $M, q, \langle\!\langle A \rangle\!\rangle \models \varphi$. Conversely, the variant of SMC is *complete* iff $M, q, \langle\!\langle A \rangle\!\rangle \models \varphi$ implies $SMC(M, q, \langle\!\langle A \rangle\!\rangle\varphi) = true$. The following claims are straightforward:

Theorem 1. *SMC with branching strategy search is sound and complete.*

Theorem 2. *SMC with (bounded or unbounded) path-based strategy search is sound but not necessarily complete.*

5   Experimental Results

In this section, we present experimental results obtained by running the SMC model checker on a parameterized class of models. All the tests have been conducted on a notebook with an Intel Core i7-3630QM CPU with dynamic clock speed of 2.4 GHz up to 3.4 GHz. The clock speed observed in the conducted tests was 3.2 GHz. The computer was equipped with 8 GB of RAM (two modules DDR3 PC3-12800, 800 MHz bus clock, effective data rate 1600 MT/s, in dual-channel configuration).

The experiments with SMC were conducted on Windows 7 OS, the experiments with MCMAS on Linux Ubuntu 12.04.2.

5.1   Working Example: Castles

For the experiments, we designed a simple scalable model called *Castles*. The model consists of one agent called *Environment* that keeps track of the health points of three castles, plus a number of agents called *Workers* each of whom works for the benefit of a castle. Health points (HP, ranging from 0 to 3) represent the current condition of the castle; 0 HP means that the castle is *defeated*.

Workers can execute the following actions:

1. attack a castle they do not work for,
2. defend the castle they do work for, or
3. do nothing.

Doing nothing is the only available action to a Worker of a defeated castle. No agent can defend its castle twice in a row, it must wait one step before being able to defend again. A castle gets damaged if the number of attackers is greater than the number of defenders, and the damage is equal to the difference. For example, if castle 3 is attacked by two agents, it loses 2 HP if not defended, or 1 HP if defended by a single agent. In the initial state, all the castles have 3 HP and every Worker can engage in defending its castle.

The indistinguishability relations for Workers are defined as follows. Every Worker knows if it can currently engage in defending its castle, and can observe for each castle if it is defeated or not. This defines 4 observable (boolean) variables for the agent. Now, $q \sim_a q'$ iff q, q' have the same values of the variables.

The model is parameterized by the number of agents and the allocation of Workers. For example, an instance with 1 worker assigned to the first castle, 3 workers assigned to the second and 4 to the third castle will be denoted by 9 (1, 3, 4).

5.2 Performance Results

We begin by presenting some performance results for the formula
$$\varphi_1 \equiv \langle\langle c12 \rangle\rangle F \text{ castle3Defeated}$$
saying that the agents working for castles 1 and 2 have a collective strategy
to defeat castle 3, no matter what the other agents do. Note that the formula
is true in all the models that we have tested. We used the SMC variant with
(unbounded) path-based strategy search. The timeout was set to 10 minutes.

N	Total time (ms)	1st step (ms)	2nd step (ms)	Peak memory (MB)
4 (1 1 1)	130	100	29	15
5 (1 1 2)	6 686	336	6 349	198
6 (2 1 2)	4 508	548	3 957	606
7 (2 2 2)	3 366	2 637	728	77
8 (3 2 2)	255 549	27 040	228 505	454

The table presents results for a sequence of models of various size. The columns
should be interpreted in the following way (from left to right):

1. The scalability factor N: the total number of agents (incl. Environment),
   followed by the number of agents working for Castles $1, 2, 3$ respectively;
2. Total "wall clock" time taken by the model checking algorithm in milliseconds
   (excluding the input parsing time);
3. "Wall clock" time taken by the first step of the algorithm (strategy synthesis);
4. "Wall clock" time taken by the second step (CTL verification);
5. Peak memory usage observed during the execution of the program in
   megabytes.[4]

5.3 Number of Generated Strategies

The table below presents the number of strategies processed by the algorithm,
which might be of an even greater interest than raw performance times. The SMC
variant, parameters of tests, and the formula are the same as in Section 5.2.

N	Agents	Potential strategies	Proper strategies	Tested strategies
4 (1 1 1)	2	$4.3 * 10^8$	283	1
5 (1 1 2)	2	$4.3 * 10^8$	229	4
6 (2 1 2)	3	$8.9 * 10^{12}$	3 507	3
7 (2 2 2)	4	$1.8 * 10^{17}$	$4, 4 * 10^5$	1
8 (3 2 2)	5	$3.8 * 10^{21}$	not calculated	3

The columns are interpreted as follows (left to right):

1. The scalability factor N;
2. The number of agents in the coalition for which a strategy is constructed;
3. The total number of *potential* strategies;
4. The total number of *proper unbounded path-based* strategies;
5. The number of strategies processed by the algorithm.

---

[4] Note that the default Java Virtual Machine makes it hard to determine the real
   maximum usage, as memory is freed nondeterministically.

5.4   Comparison to MCMAS

The only tool for ATL$_{ir}$ model checking that we are aware of is an experimental version of MCMAS [19], not yet released publicly at the time of writing this paper. Thanks to the authors of MCMAS who kindly provided us with the experimental version, we could compare the output of both model checkers. All the parameters of the experiments were like in Sections 5.2–5.3, except for the timeout (set to 120 minutes). Moreover, we used the following two formulae:

$$\varphi_1 \equiv \langle\!\langle c12 \rangle\!\rangle F \text{ castle3Defeated} \quad \text{(same as before; } true \text{ in the tested models)}$$
$$\varphi_2 \equiv \langle\!\langle w12 \rangle\!\rangle F \text{ allDefeated} \quad \text{(} false \text{ in the tested models)}$$

Formula φ_2 says that Workers 1 and 2 have a collective strategy to enforce that all the castles become defeated, no matter what the other agents do. The tables below compare the performance of both model checkers.

N	Formula	MCMAS execution time	SMC execution time
4 (1 1 1)	φ_1	72 s	0.1 s
5 (2 1 1)	φ_1	> 120 mins. (interrupted)	0.2 s
4 (1 1 1)	φ_2	78 s	5.4 s
5 (2 1 1)	φ_2	error	51 s

N	Formula	MCMAS tested strategies	SMC tested strategies
4 (1 1 1)	φ_1	$\approx 20\,000$	1
5 (2 1 1)	φ_1	$> 2 * 10^6$ (interrupted)	1
4 (1 1 1)	φ_2	$\approx 20\,000$	283
5 (2 1 1)	φ_2	error	106

It is important to note that MCMAS and SMC implement slightly different semantics of ATL$_{ir}$. While for SMC a strategy is successful if it succeeds on the paths starting from the actual initial state, MCMAS requires the strategy to succeed also on all the paths starting from indistinguishable states. For coalitional indistinguishability, MCMAS uses the "everybody knows" epistemic relation. A quick calculation shows that the initial epistemic class of a Worker contains $3^3 * 2^{W-1}$ states, where W is the number of Workers in the model. For a coalition of two Workers, there are $27 * 2^{W-1} + 27 * 2^{W-1} - 27 * 2^{W-2} = 81 * 2^{W-2}$ indistinguishable states. Thus, MCMAS needs to check 162 times more paths than SMC for $N = 4(1\ 1\ 1)$, and 324 times more paths for $N = 5(2\ 1\ 1)$.

5.5   Perfect vs. Imperfect Information Strategies

In this work, we also wanted to compare how model checking of abilities under imperfect information compares to the standard ATL case. To this end, we have compared the performance of SMC and the experimental version to the standard version of MCMAS [16]. The table reports model checking times (in milliseconds) for formula φ_1 in various instances of the *Castles* class.

N	perfect info (MCMAS)	imperfect info (SMC)	imperfect info (MCMAS)
4 (1 1 1)	43	130	72 000
5 (1 1 2)	70	6 686	timeout
6 (2 1 2)	250	4 508	timeout
7 (2 2 2)	954	3 366	timeout
8 (3 2 2)	1 996	255 549	timeout

5.6   Path-Based vs. Branching Strategy Search

So far, we have only presented experimental results for the (sound but incomplete) SMC variant using path-based strategy search. Here, we compare its performance to the complete variant, i.e., one that searches all the proper partial strategies. The table below gives the model checking times (in milliseconds) for formula φ_1 in different instances of the class of models.

N	Path-based strategy search	Branching strategy search
4 (1 1 1)	130	769
5 (1 1 2)	6 686	13 630
6 (2 1 2)	4 508	72 419
7 (2 2 2)	3 366	261 704
8 (3 2 2)	255 549	timeout

5.7   Example Output of Strategy Synthesis

One of the most interesting features of SMC is that it not only verifies existence of a suitable strategy, but also returns the strategy. Thus, SMC can be potentially used as a multi-agent planner. To conclude the section, we present some strategies produced by SMC for our working example. We use the model with $N = 5(1,1,2)$ and the formula $\varphi_3 \equiv \langle\!\langle c12 \rangle\!\rangle F$ castle3Damaged which says that Workers 1 and 2 have a collective strategy to decrease the HP of castle 3. For presentation purposes we have shortened the representation of agents' local states, e.g., we write "FFF" instead of "Environment.castle1Defeated = false, Environment.castle2Defeated = false, Environment.castle3Defeated = false".

While performing verification with (unbounded) path-based strategy search, the following solution was found after 2 attempts:

```
Agent Worker1 - Generated strategy:
(FFF, Worker1.canDefend = true): {defend}
(FFF, Worker1.canDefend = false): {attack3}
(TFT, Worker1.canDefend = true): {doNothing}

Agent Worker2 - Generated strategy:
(FFF, Worker2.canDefend = true): {attack3}
(TFF, Worker2.canDefend = true): {defend}
(TFT, Worker2.canDefend = true): {doNothing}
```

We also performed verification with bounded path-based strategy search. The following solution was found after 12 attempts:

```
Agent Worker1 - Generated strategy:
(FFF, Worker1.canDefend = true): {attack3}
Agent Worker2 - Generated strategy:
(FFF, Worker2.canDefend = true): {attack3}
```

6   Conclusions

Verification of strategic abilities under imperfect information has been extensively studied theoretically, but at the same time ignored as far as practical algorithms and tools are concerned. This paper reports our first step towards filling the gap. We propose and implement an algorithm for model checking ATL_{ir}, i.e., the variant of alternating-time logic based on uniform positional strategies. The experimental results are encouraging. In particular, our algorithm significantly outperformed the only other existing tool (an experimental version of MCMAS), despite the fact that MCMAS uses symbolic model checking techniques based on OBDD's, and our SMC operates purely on explicit representations of states.

Our algorithm enables speedup coming from two potential sources. First, it considers only so called proper strategies which are in fact equivalence classes of concrete strategies. A variant of SMC restricts the search even further by considering only so called path-based strategies. Secondly, strategies are sought incrementally, starting from simplest ones. In many scenarios, whenever a successful strategy exists, it can be found among the relatively simple ones. In those cases, our algorithm finds a good strategy after a number of attempts vastly smaller than the number of all proper strategies in the model. In the experiments, the first kind of speedup yielded reductions of the search space by order of 10^6 times up to 10^{12} times. The second kind of speedup yielded solutions after no more than 10 attempts for problems where the number of proper strategies ranged from order of 10^2 to 10^5. As a result, the strategy verification sub-routine was called only around $10^0 = 1$ times, yielding a speedup of the verification stage of order of 10^2 up to 10^5.

Despite the promising experimental results, our tests showed also that the problem itself *is* computationally difficult. We observed an overwhelming gap in performance between verification of strategic abilities for perfect vs. imperfect information strategies. On the other hand, there is still much room for improvement. In particular, we plan to employ symbolic model checking techniques (based on OBDD's and/or translation to SAT solvers) as well as parallelization using e.g. the DACFrame, Akka, or GridGain platforms for parallel computation (cf. also [15]). Further future work includes extending the syntax accepted by SMC to all ATL_{ir} formulae in negation normal form, more experiments with various benchmark models and formulae, and an extensive case study on an example of practical interest, e.g., verification of privacy and noninterference in a voting protocol. For the last task, an appropriate abstraction will have to be developed, possibly along the lines of [14].

Acknowledgements. This contribution has been supported by the Foundation for Polish Science under International PhD Projects in Intelligent Computing; project financed from The European Union within the Innovative Economy Operational Programme 2007-2013 and European Regional Development Fund. Wojciech Jamroga acknowledges the support of the FNR (National Research Fund) Luxembourg under project GALOT – INTER/DFG/12/06. We gratefully acknowledge the help of Hongyang Qu and Alessio Lomuscio who kindly provided us with the latest experimental version of MCMAS, as well as MCMAS model generators.

References

1. Ågotnes, T.: A note on syntactic characterization of incomplete information in ATEL. In: Procedings of Workshop on Knowledge and Games, pp. 34–42 (2004)
2. Ågotnes, T., Goranko, V., Jamroga, W., Wooldridge, M.: Knowledge and ability. In: van der Hoek, W., van Ditmarsch, H.P., Halpern, J.Y., Kooi, B.P. (eds.) Handbook of Logics for Knowledge and Belief. Springer (to appear, 2014)
3. Alur, R., de Alfaro, L., Grossu, R., Henzinger, T.A., Kang, M., Kirsch, C.M., Majumdar, R., Mang, F.Y.C., Wang, B.-Y.: jMocha: A model-checking tool that exploits design structure. In: Proceedings of ICSE, pp. 835–836 (2001)
4. Alur, R., Henzinger, T.A., Kupferman, O.: Alternating-time Temporal Logic. In: Proceedings of the 38th Annual Symposium on Foundations of Computer Science (FOCS), pp. 100–109. IEEE Computer Society Press (1997)
5. Alur, R., Henzinger, T.A., Kupferman, O.: Alternating-time Temporal Logic. Journal of the ACM 49, 672–713 (2002)
6. Alur, R., Henzinger, T.A., Mang, F.Y.C., Qadeer, S., Rajamani, S.K., Tasiran, S.: MOCHA: Modularity in model checking. In: Hu, A.J., Vardi, M.Y. (eds.) CAV 1998. LNCS, vol. 1427, pp. 521–525. Springer, Heidelberg (1998)
7. Bulling, N., Jamroga, W.: Comparing variants of strategic ability. Journal of Autonomous Agents and Multi-Agent Systems 28(3), 474–518 (2014)
8. Calta, J., Shkatov, D., Schlingloff, H.: Finding uniform strategies for multi-agent systems. In: Dix, J., Leite, J., Governatori, G., Jamroga, W. (eds.) CLIMA XI. LNCS, vol. 6245, pp. 135–152. Springer, Heidelberg (2010)
9. Dima, C., Tiplea, F.L.: Model-checking atl under imperfect information and perfect recall semantics is undecidable. CoRR, abs/1102.4225 (2011)
10. Jamroga, W., Ågotnes, T.: Modular interpreted systems: A preliminary report. Technical Report IfI-06-15, Clausthal University of Technology (2006)
11. Jamroga, W., Dix, J.: Model checking ATL_{ir} is indeed Δ_2^P-complete. In: Proceedings of EUMAS 2006 (2006)
12. Jamroga, W., van der Hoek, W.: Agents that know how to play. Fundamenta Informaticae 63(2-3), 185–219 (2004)
13. Kacprzak, M., Penczek, W.: Unbounded model checking for Alternating-time Temporal Logic. In: Proceedings of AAMAS 2004 (2004)
14. Köster, M., Lohmann, P.: Abstraction for model checking modular interpreted systems over ATL. In: Proceedings of AAMAS, pp. 1129–1130 (2011)
15. Kwiatkowska, M., Lomuscio, A., Qu, H.: Parallel model checking for temporal epistemic logic. In: Proceedings of ECAI, pp. 543–548 (2010)

16. Lomuscio, A., Qu, H., Raimondi, F.: MCMAS: A model checker for the verification of multi-agent systems. In: Bouajjani, A., Maler, O. (eds.) CAV 2009. LNCS, vol. 5643, pp. 682–688. Springer, Heidelberg (2009)
17. Lomuscio, A., Raimondi, F.: MCMAS: A model checker for multi-agent systems. In: Hermanns, H., Palsberg, J. (eds.) TACAS 2006. LNCS, vol. 3920, pp. 450–454. Springer, Heidelberg (2006)
18. Papalamprou, P.: Logic-based verification of games with imperfect information. Master thesis, University of Luxembourg (2013)
19. Qu, H., Lomuscio, A., Raimondi, F.: MCMAS with uniform strategies. Personal communication (2014)
20. Schobbens, P.Y.: Alternating-time logic with imperfect recall. Electronic Notes in Theoretical Computer Science 85(2), 82–93 (2004)
21. van der Hoek, W., Lomuscio, A., Wooldridge, M.: On the complexity of practical ATL model checking. In: Stone, P., Weiss, G. (eds.) Proceedings of AAMAS 2006, pp. 201–208 (2006)

Partial Information and Uniform Strategies

Hans van Ditmarsch and Sophia Knight

LORIA, CNRS – Université de Lorraine, France

Abstract. We present an alternating-time temporal epistemic logic with uniform strategies, interpreted in a novel way on transition systems for modelling situations in which agents with partial information interact to determine the way the system updates. This logic uATEL allows us to model what properties agents can enforce when they act according to strategies based on their knowledge. Apart from the usual memoryless strategies, we distinguish state-based memory, where agents recall the history of previous states, from perfect recall, where agents also recall their actions. We show that this makes a difference. Our logic includes three strategic operators for groups, representing the case where all the agents in the group cooperate actively, but do not share their knowledge, the case where some agents in the group may be passive, and the case where all the agents in the group share their knowledge. We include a detailed comparison to the literature on the subject.

1 Introduction

Linear temporal logic [15], Computation tree logic [6], and CTL* [7] are temporal logics for reasoning about distributed systems. LTL is concerned with infinite histories of states representing possible computations, CTL can reason about the branching structure of potential computations, and CTL* combines the expressive capabilities of both LTL and CTL. While the distributed systems that these logics model are implicitly understood to be systems consisting of many agents acting individually, there is no explicit mention of these agents or their actions in any of the above-mentioned temporal logics.

Alternating-time temporal logic [3] is a branching-time temporal logic for distributed systems where the effects of agents' actions are made explicit. In ATL, a formula of the form $\langle\langle \Gamma \rangle\rangle \bigcirc \varphi$, where Γ is a set of agents, $\bigcirc$ is the 'next' temporal modality, and φ is a state formula, signifies that the agents in the group Γ can cooperate to ensure that the formula φ is true in next state of the system, no matter what the agents who are not in Γ do. Thus, ATL provides a natural and interesting way of analyzing the properties of multi-agent systems, with the advantage of being able to analyse the effects of the actions of both specific agents and groups of agents.

Epistemic logic [13], on the other hand, is a different kind of modal logic which also models multi-agent systems, but only statically, without considering changes in these systems over time. Instead, epistemic logic is concerned with the agents' knowledge — another crucial aspect of multi-agent systems.

N. Bulling et al. (Eds.): CLIMA XV, LNAI 8624, pp. 183–198, 2014.
© Springer International Publishing Switzerland 2014

Thus, ATL is concerned with agents' abilities to control the outcomes of executions of dynamic multi-agent systems, while epistemic logic is concerned with agents' knowledge in static multi-agent systems. It is clear that combining these two focuses could yield a compelling and relevant logic for describing the interaction between agents' ability to act and their knowledge. Alternating-time temporal epistemic logic was proposed by [10] to combine knowledge and agency. Epistemic modalities are added to ATL, but the traditional semantics are used for both modalities. This approach allows some interesting applications, but since the original semantics are used for both modalities, the full interaction between the agents' knowledge and their actions is not captured. In particular, it is possible that an agent has different strategies in (epistemically) indistinguishable states of the system. It is reasonable not to allow this, and to require strategies to be *uniform*. For this, a strategy must correspond to what an agent knows.

Indeed, since [10] various proposals combining epistemic logic and ATL in a way that captures the interplay between agents' actions and their knowledge have been made, such as [12,16,11,2,4]. We discuss the related work in detail at the end of the paper, but we will point out some basic differences in our work here. The most novel aspect of our logic is that we allow agents with different memory abilities to interact in the same system. Many versions of epistemic ATL, for example [12,16], consider both full memory and memoryless agents (and implicitly, finite memory agents represented as memoryless agents). But in these logics, every agent in the entire system is assumed to have the same type of memory. It is interesting to consider systems where different agents have different memory abilities. For example, a system could consist of some simple, finite memory agents, interacting with other more sophisticated perfect memory agents. Furthermore, in some settings there may be a group of "friendly" agents with known memory capabilities, and a different group of adversarial agents with unknown memory capabilities. By modelling the friendly agents as limited memory agents and the adversaries as perfect memory agents, we can consider the worst case scenario, and verify security properties of a system.

Besides allowing the combination of agents with different memory capabilities, another novel aspect of our logic is that we allow agents to have arbitrary equivalence relations on histories. Just as agents in epistemic Kripke models are traditionally allowed to have any equivalence relations on the states of a system, our systems allow agents to have any equivalence relation on the histories of the system. For example, we can model an agent who has perfect recall, except she always forgets when the system has been in a specific state. Or we could model an agent who only remembers every other past state. Or an agent could remember everything, until the system enters a certain state, at which point the agent's memory is wiped out. Combined with the fact that different agents are allowed to have different types of equivalence relations on histories, allowing them to have arbitrary equivalence relations as well makes our systems quite general. As far as we know, ours are the only ATL-type systems that allow arbitrary equivalence relations on histories.

The ATL tradition, wherein agents are modelled but not actions, views perfect recall as remembering histories of states, whereas the PDL tradition [9], wherein actions are modelled but not agents, views perfect recall as remembering histories of actions. In our framework, these are available as different memory capabilities. Our definition of perfect recall is therefore different from that in [12,16,2], as it does not just consider past states, but also considers the agent's own past actions. We can also model what is elsewhere called perfect recall memory, but we call it 'state-based memory' since it is not as strong as our concept of perfect recall memory. Our definition of perfect recall models agents who remember all the past states of the system, but also remember their own past actions, and can reason about the effects of their actions.

In Section 2, we present epistemic concurrent games structures and we define strategies. In Section 3 we present our alternating-time temporal epistemic logic with uniform strategies. Section 4 compares our work to the tradition in ATL with epistemic operators.

2   Epistemic Concurrent Game Structures

In this section, we present a variation on concurrent game structures. We introduce an indistinguishability relation on the set of states for each agent, which puts a new requirement on the transition relation. This model is appropriate in our setting, because our goal is modelling agents with partial information about the state of the system and the effects of their actions on the outcome. The agents' partial information about the current state is represented by their indistinguishability relations, while the actions they can choose reflect the agents' limited information about the way the system updates.

Definition 1. *An* epistemic concurrent game structure *(ECGS) is a tuple* $\langle Q, \Pi, \Sigma, \mathcal{B}, \sim, \pi, Av, \delta \rangle$ *where*

- Q *is a set of states,*
- Π *is a set of propositions,*
- $\Sigma = \{a_1, ..., a_n\}$ *is a finite set of agents.*
- $\mathcal{B}$ *is a finite set of actions.*
- $\sim: \Sigma \to \mathcal{P}(Q \times Q)$ *is an equivalence function associating to each agent* a_i *an equivalence relation* $\sim_i$.
- $\pi : Q \to \Pi$ *is the valuation function,*
- $Av : Q \times \Sigma \to \mathcal{P}(\mathcal{B})$ *is the availability function defining the available actions for an agent in a state, with the requirement that for all* $q_1, q_2 \in Q$ *and all* $a_i \in \Sigma$: $Av(q_1, a_i) \neq \emptyset$, *and if* $q_1 \sim_i q_2$ *then* $Av(q_1, a_i) = Av(q_2, a_i)$.
- $\delta : Q \times \Sigma \times \mathcal{B} \to \mathcal{P}(Q)$ *is the transition function, with the* determinacy *requirement that for any* $q \in Q$, *for any* $(b_1, ..., b_n) \in \mathcal{B}^n$ *such that* $b_i \in Av(q, a_i)$ *for* $i = 1, ..., n$, *it is required that* $\bigcap_{i=1}^{n} \delta(q, a_i, b_i)$ *be a singleton.*

The uniformity requirement $Av(q_1, a_i) = Av(q_2, a_i)$ reflects the fact that an agent is aware of what actions are available, so if two states are indistinguishable to the agent, the same actions must be available.

We now define strategies in this setting. The notion of a strategy is dependent on an agent's knowledge about the state of the system: if an agent cannot distinguish two histories, then the agent cannot behave differently in those two histories. Thus, the definition of a strategy for an agent is modular with respect to the agent's equivalence relation on histories. So we will begin by defining strategies, and then we will define three interesting equivalence relations on histories.

In order to define strategies, we must first define histories in ECGS's. We need a few subsidiary definitions first. The following assume an n-agent ECGS $\langle Q, \Pi, \Sigma, \mathcal{B}, \sim, \pi, Av, \delta \rangle$.

Definition 2. *We extend the notion of available actions to a vector of n actions. For $q \in Q$, let $Av(q) = \{\langle b_1, b_2, ..., b_n \rangle \in \mathcal{B}^n \mid \forall a_i \in \Sigma, b_i \in Av(q, a_i)\}$.*

Definition 3. *For $q \in Q$ and $b^* \in Av(q)$, define the b^*-successor of q as follows: $Succ(q, b^*) = q'$ iff $\bigcap_{i=1}^{n} \delta(q, a_i, b_i) = \{q'\}$.*

Definition 4. *In an ECGS L, suppose $h = q_0.b_1^*.q_1.b_2^*.q_2...q_{k-1}.b_k^*.q_k$, where $q_j \in Q$ for $j \in \{0, ..., k\}$ and $b_j^* \in \mathcal{B}^n$ for $j \in \{1, ..., k\}$. Then h is a history for L if $q_j = Succ(q_{j-1}, b_j^*)$ for $j \in \{1, ..., k\}$. We denote the set of all histories for L as $Hist(L)$.*

Note that all histories are finite, even though infinite executions are possible.

Finally we can define a strategy. For this definition, we extend the Av function from state-agent pairs to history-agent pairs in the obvious way, as the set of actions available at the last state in the history: $Av(q_0.b_1.q_1...q_k, a_i) = Av(q_k, a_i)$.

Definition 5. *Given an ECGS L, let $\approx_i$ be an arbitrary equivalence relation on $Hist(L)$, and $a_i \in \Sigma$. A $\approx_i$ uniform strategy for a_i is a function $f_i : Hist(L) \to \mathcal{B}$ satisfying the following requirements:*

1. *For all $h \in Hist(L)$, $f_i(h) \in Av(h, a_i)$.*
2. *If $h_1 \approx_i h_2$ then $f(h_1) = f(h_2)$.*

Now that we have given the definition of a strategy with respect to a general equivalence relation, we present several interesting equivalence relations giving rise to different classes of strategies.

Definition 6. *Histories $h_1 = q_0...q_k$ and $h_2 = r_0...r_j$ are memoryless equivalent for agent a_i iff $q_k \sim_i r_j$. This is denoted $h_1 \sim_i^m h_2$. If f_i is a $\sim_i^m$ uniform strategy for agent a_i, then it is called a memoryless strategy for a_i.*

This equivalence relation describes agents who are only aware of the present state but forget everything that has already happened. Next we define strategies for agents who remember the past states of the system.

Definition 7. *For $h_1, h_2 \in H$ and $a_i \in \Sigma$, h_1 and h_2 are state memory equivalent, written $h_1 \sim_i^s h_2$ iff $h_1 = q_0.q_1...q_k$ and $h_2 = r_0.r_1...r_k$ and for $j = 0, ..., k$, $q_j \sim_i r_j$. If f_i is a $\sim_i^s$ uniform strategy for agent a_i, then it is called a strategy with state memory for a_i.*

This equivalence relation and class of strategies describe agents who remember all the past states of the system, but either do not remember their own actions, or do not reason about the effects of their own actions. Next we give the equivalence relations for agents who remember every state of the system, remember all their own actions, and understand all the effects of their actions.

Definition 8. *In an n-agent ECGS, histories h_1 and h_2 are* perfect-recall equivalent *for agent i, written $h_1 \sim_i^{pr} h_2$, iff either $h_1 = q_1$ and $h_2 = q_2$ (where $q_1, q_2 \in Q$) and $q_1 \sim_i q_2$, or $h_1 = q_0.b_1^*.q_1...q_{j-1}.b_j^*.q_j$ and $h_2 = r_0.c_1^*.r_1...r_{j-1}.c_j^*.r_j$ and all of the following conditions hold:*

1. $q_0.b_1^*.q_1...q_{j-1} \sim_i^{pr} r_0.c_1^*.r_1...r_{j-1}$, and
2. $q_j \sim_i r_j$, and
3. $b_i = c_i$ where $b_j^* = \langle b_1, ..., b_n \rangle$ and $c_j^* = \langle c_1, ..., c_n \rangle$.

The intuition behind this definition is an agent who remembers its own actions, and can reason about their effects, rather than an agent who just remembers the past states. The perfect recall agent does not observe or remember other agents' actions, however. State memory is often called perfect recall in ATL, whereas our perfect recall is more like PDL perfect recall. In our setting for epistemic ATL there is a real difference between the two. To motivate the definition of perfect recall equivalence, and the differences between the three types of memory we have discussed, consider the following single-agent example.

2.1   Example

A robot is in a simple maze made up of square spaces. The robot can only perceive whether there are walls immediately in front of, behind and to each side of it, and cannot perceive anything else about the state of the world. The robot has an orientation, either north, south, east or west, and a position in the maze, but the robot is not aware of its orientation and cannot perceive the position, but only the walls around it. We consider the following simple maze:

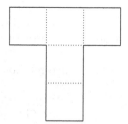

In the following pictures, the arrow represents the robot: both its orientation and its position in the maze. The state of the system consists of the position and orientation of the robot. So, for example, the following three states are indistinguishable:

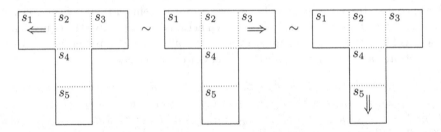

The following two states, however, are distinguishable, because in the first one, the robot perceives that there is only a wall in front, while in the second one it perceives that there are walls on either side:

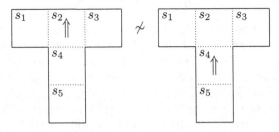

Also, the following two states are distinguishable for the robot, because it can distinguish between having an open space in front of it or behind it:

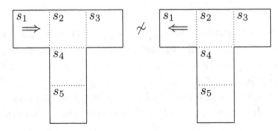

In the following, we denote the states of the system as pairs (s, o) where s is the robot's position in the system (s_1 through s_5), and o is its orientation ($n, s, e,$ or w).

So now we can state the full equivalence relation for the robot:

$$(s_1, n) \sim (s_3, s) \sim (s_5, w) \qquad (s_4, n) \sim (s_4, s) \qquad (s_2, n)$$
$$(s_1, e) \sim (s_3, w) \sim (s_5, n) \qquad (s_4, e) \sim (s_4, w) \qquad (s_2, e)$$
$$(s_1, s) \sim (s_3, n) \sim (s_5, e) \qquad\qquad\qquad\qquad (s_2, s)$$
$$(s_1, w) \sim (s_3, e) \sim (s_5, s) \qquad\qquad\qquad\qquad (s_2, w)$$

Those in the rightmost column are singleton equivalence classes, since the robot can distinguish the single wall being on its left, right, in front of or behind it.

The robot's actions are go left, go right, go forward or go back, denoted (l, r, f, b). All of these actions are available at every state. The forward action does not change the robot's orientation, but all of the other actions do. Furthermore, the actions change the robot's position if there is space available where the robot tries to go. However, if the robot for example goes left when there is a wall to its left, it changes its orientation but not its position. The following diagram shows the possible transitions between positions and orientations, the combination of which gives the state of the system. The left hand side shows the positions and the right hand side shows the orientations. The arrows in the left hand side are unlabelled because the identity of the transition action between positions depends on the robot's orientation in the starting position: for example, $(s_4, n) \xrightarrow{f} (s_2, n)$ whereas $(s_4, w) \xrightarrow{r} (s_2, n)$.

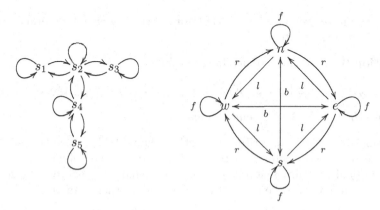

For clarity, here is part of the transition relation only for position s_1, for any orientation:

	f	r	b	l
(s_1, n)	(s_1, n)	(s_2, e)	(s_1, s)	(s_1, w)
(s_1, e)	(s_2, e)	(s_1, s)	(s_1, w)	(s_1, n)
(s_1, s)	(s_1, s)	(s_1, w)	(s_1, n)	(s_2, e)
(s_1, w)	(s_1, w)	(s_1, n)	(s_2, e)	(s_1, s)

Now, suppose that the robot knows the structure of the maze, but is dropped into a state without knowing its position or orientation. We want to investigate what the robot can achieve by taking actions to explore the system, depending on whether it is a memoryless, state memory, or perfect recall agent.

Suppose the robot starts out in state (s_4, n). Consider the following three sequences of actions.

1. $(s_4, n).b.(s_5, n)$
2. $(s_4, n).f.(s_2, n).l.(s_1, w)$
3. $(s_4, n).f.(s_2, n).r.(s_3, e)$

First of all, suppose the agent is memoryless. Then, the histories 1, 2, and 3 are all equivalent, since the last states are equivalent.

On the other hand, with state memory, the robot can distinguish 1 from 2. In fact, it is easy to see that the robot can distinguish any history that starts in position s_4 and ends in position s_5 from any history that starts in s_4 and ends in s_1. But the agent cannot distinguish 2 from 3. This is because the robot only looks at the past states, and $(s_1, w) \sim (s_3, e)$, as do the first two states in the histories. The robot does not consider its own past actions.

However, if the robot has perfect recall, it can also distinguish 2 and 3, since the two histories have different sequences of actions. Thus, with perfect recall, the agent is allowed to remember its own past actions and distinguish histories based on this information, as well as information about the states.

3   The Logic uATEL

In this section we present a logic uATEL for alternating-time temporal epistemic logic with uniform strategies.

Definition 9. *The syntax of* uATEL *is as follows.*

$$\varphi ::= p \mid \neg\varphi \mid \varphi \vee \varphi \mid K_i\varphi \mid \langle\!\langle A \rangle\!\rangle_\sharp \bigcirc \varphi \mid \langle\!\langle A \rangle\!\rangle_\sharp \Box\varphi \mid \langle\!\langle A \rangle\!\rangle_\sharp \varphi \mathcal{U}\varphi$$

where $p \in \Pi$, $i \in \Sigma$, $A \subseteq \Sigma$, *and* $\sharp$ *is one of* a, p *and* c.

For a single agent a_i, we write $\langle\!\langle a_i \rangle\!\rangle$ rather than $\langle\!\langle \{a_i\} \rangle\!\rangle$. We also use $\wedge$ and $\rightarrow$ in the usual way, defined in terms of $\vee$ and $\neg$. The subindices a, p, c for the coalitional modalities stand for different semantics. Before we give these semantics, we motivate the differences with some further examples.

Example 1. There are two agents, a_1 and a_2, and five states: s_0, s_1, s_2, w, and l. $s_0 \sim_1 s_1$ and $s_1 \sim_2 s_2$. There are three actions, b, c, and d, and two propositions, which we also call w (for win) and l (for lose), with $w \models w$ and $l \models l$. The transitions are as follows:

s_0	a_1			s_1	a_1			s_2	a_1		
	b	c	d		b	c	d		b	c	d
b	w	l	l	b	l	l	l	b	l	l	l
a_2 c	l	l	l	a_2 c	w	l	l	a_2 c	l	l	l
d	l	l	l	d	l	w	l	d	l	w	l

Here is a picture of the system, where all the transitions are available at s_0, s_1, and s_2, and the ones not displayed go to l.

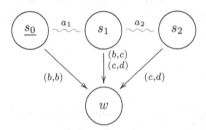

The question is, in state s_0, do the agents have a strategy to reach w? a_2 knows the state is s_0, so she will definitely do b. But a_1 does not know whether the state is s_0 or s_1. If the state were s_1, he would rationally want to do c, since a_2 would now know whether the state was s_1 or s_2, so a_2 would do d to be safe. So in s_0, a_1 wants to do b, but in s_1 a_1 wants to do c. The problem is that a_1 cannot distinguish s_0 and s_1, so he has no strategy to be sure to get the system to reach w. So our semantics must say that

$$s_0 \models \neg \langle\!\langle \{a_1, a_2\} \rangle\!\rangle \bigcirc w.$$

Now observe that this reasoning does not hold in the case of the general knowledge semantics, which only considers the union of equivalence relations for the agents in the group, so that in this case from state s_0 we only need to consider that state and s_1, but only with the common knowledge semantics, that it its transitive closure, in this case, all three states s_0, s_1, s_2. This is embodied in the semantics for $\langle\!\langle \{a_1, a_s\} \rangle\!\rangle_a$ (where a stands for 'active').

Given are an ECGS L and $q \in L$. For $\Gamma \subseteq \Sigma$, $\sim_\Gamma^*$ is the transitive reflexive closure of $\bigcup_{a_i \in \Gamma} \sim_i$. We use λ to denote an element of Q^+ (where Q is the set of states of L), and $\lambda[i]$ denotes the ith state in the string λ, starting from 0, e.g. if $\lambda = q_0.q_1.q_2$ then $\lambda[1] = q_1$. We also need to define a group strategy:

Definition 10. *For a group of agents $\Gamma \subseteq \Sigma$, we say $F = \{f_a \mid a \in \Gamma\}$ is a group strategy for Γ if for all $a_i \in \Gamma$, f_{a_i} is a uniform strategy for a_i.*

Now we can give a possible semantics for the "next" operator.

$(L, q) \models \langle\!\langle \Gamma \rangle\!\rangle_a \bigcirc \varphi$ iff there exists a group strategy F_Γ for Γ such that $\forall q' \sim_\Gamma^* q, \forall \lambda \in out(q', F_\Gamma), (L, \lambda[1]) \models \varphi$

This *active coalitional strategy* semantics matches with the intuitive notion of a group of agents having a strategy to reach a goal particularly in settings where all the agents in the group are active in trying to reach the goal, but also have other choices they could make which would prevent the goal from being reached. It is less intuitive in situations where there are agents in the group whose actions cannot affect the outcome of the system from a certain state, as we will see in the following example.

Example 2. Consider a system with two agents a_1 and a_2 and states $\{s_0, ..., s_4\}$, where $s_0 \sim_{a_1} s_1$ but not for a_2, and all the other states can be distinguished by both agents. There is one proposition p, only $s_2 \models p$, and the transitions are $\delta(s_0, a_1, e) = \{s_2, s_3\}$, $\delta(s_0, a_2, b) = \{s_2\}$, $\delta(s_0, a_2, c) = \{s_3\}$, $\delta(s_1, a_1, e) = \{s_4\}$, $\delta(s_1, a_2, d) = \{s_4\}$. So, a_1 has no effect on the execution of the system. At both starting states she can only choose e. Agent a_2, on the other hand, can distinguish s_0 and s_1, and at s_0, he can choose the b action to make p true, but at s_1, a_2 has only one choice and p cannot become true no matter what either agent does. So, we want that $s_0 \models \langle\!\langle a_2 \rangle\!\rangle \bigcirc p$ but, $s_0 \models \neg \langle\!\langle \{a_1, a_2\} \rangle\!\rangle \bigcirc p$.

Let us consider whether it is reasonable that the semantics tells us that $s_0 \models \neg \langle\!\langle \{a_1, a_2\} \rangle\!\rangle \bigcirc p$. On the one hand, it is strange to think that while the smaller group consisting only of a_2 can bring about $\bigcirc p$, the larger group $\{a_1, a_2\}$ cannot bring about $\bigcirc p$. In fact, this violates the property in traditional ATL that if $\Gamma_1 \subseteq \Gamma_2$ then $\langle\langle \Gamma_1 \rangle\rangle \bigcirc \varphi \to \langle\langle \Gamma_2 \rangle\rangle \bigcirc \varphi$ [8]. On the other hand, if we think of a group strategy as a strategy where all the agents in the group are active and aware that their actions will reach the outcome, this outcome is less surprising.

In the $\langle\langle \Gamma \rangle\rangle_a$ semantics above we indeed get that $s_0 \models \neg\langle\langle \{a_1, a_2\} \rangle\rangle_a \bigcirc p$. We now propose an alternative $\langle\langle \Gamma \rangle\rangle_p$ semantics (p for 'passive') that achieves $s_0 \models \langle\langle \{a_1, a_2\} \rangle\rangle_p \bigcirc p$.

$(L, q) \models \langle\langle \Gamma \rangle\rangle_p \bigcirc \varphi$ iff there exists a group strategy F_B for some $B \subseteq \Gamma$ such that $\forall q' \sim_B^* q, \forall \lambda \in out(q', F_B), (L, \lambda[1]) \models \varphi$.

This is the *passive coalitional strategy*. In the active strategy operator, the strategy works at all points that any agent considers possible, but in the passive operator, there is a subset of agents who control the strategy, and it works at all states they consider possible, but there are also passive agents in the group whose actions and knowledge make no difference.

We propose a third strategic operator as well. In the active and passive coalition operators the agents can coordinate their actions into a group strategy, but they cannot coordinate or combine their knowledge prior to acting. We would like to also analyze what a group of agents can achieve when they share all the knowledge they possess, as well as acting strategically together. We can model this situation simply by quantifying over the states that are equivalent to the current state for *all* agents in the group (i.e., the accessibility relation for *distributed knowledge* among that group), rather than quantifying over the states that are equivalent for *at least one* agent in the group, and recursively so (i.e., the accessibility relation for *common knowledge* among that group), as in the above semantics. We call this the communication strategy operator and annotate it with a c.

$(L, q) \models \langle\langle \Gamma \rangle\rangle_c \bigcirc \varphi$ iff there exists a group strategy F_Γ for Γ such that $\forall q' \in \{r \in Q \mid r \sim_i q \; \forall i \in \Gamma\}, \forall \lambda \in out(q', F_\Gamma), (L, \lambda[1]) \models \varphi$.

When the agents share their knowledge, the issue of active and passive strategies no longer arises, because they now coincide.

After these preparations, we now give the complete semantics of uATEL, wherein we have only spelled out the $\square$ and $\mathcal{U}$ versions for one of the three coalitional modalities (the other two are similar).

Definition 11 (Semantics of uATEL). *Let an ECGS L and a state q in L be given.*

- *for $p \in \Pi$, $L, q \models p$ iff $p \in \pi(q)$,*
- *$L, q \models \neg\varphi$ iff $L, q \not\models \varphi$,*
- *$L, q \models \varphi_1 \vee \varphi_2$ iff $L, q \models \varphi_1$ or $L, q \models \varphi_2$,*
- *$L, q \models K_i\varphi$ iff for all $q' \sim_i q$, $L, q' \models \varphi$.*
- *$L, q \models \langle\langle \Gamma \rangle\rangle_a \bigcirc \varphi$ iff there exists a group strategy F_Γ for Γ such that $\forall q' \sim_\Gamma^* q$, $\forall \lambda \in out(q', F_\Gamma)$, $L, \lambda[1] \models \varphi$,*

- $L, q \models \langle\!\langle \Gamma \rangle\!\rangle_a \Box\varphi$ iff there exists a group strategy F_Γ for Γ such that $\forall q' \sim_\Gamma^* q$, $\forall \lambda \in out(q', F_\Gamma)$, $L, \lambda[n] \models \varphi$ for all $n \geq 0$,
- $L, q \models \langle\!\langle \Gamma \rangle\!\rangle_a \varphi_1 \mathcal{U} \varphi_2$ iff there exists a group strategy F_Γ for Γ such that $\forall q' \sim_\Gamma^* q$, $\forall \lambda \in out(q', F_\Gamma)$, there exists $m \in \mathbb{N}$ such that $L, \lambda[m] \models \varphi_2$ and for all $0 \leq n \leq m$, $L, \lambda[n] \models \varphi_1$,
- $L, q \models \langle\!\langle \Gamma \rangle\!\rangle_p \bigcirc \varphi$ iff there exists a group strategy F_B for some $B \subseteq \Gamma$ such that $\forall q' \sim_B^* q$, $\forall \lambda \in out(q', F_B)$, $L, \lambda[1] \models \varphi$,
- $L, q \models \langle\!\langle \Gamma \rangle\!\rangle_c \bigcirc \varphi$ iff there exists a group strategy F_Γ for Γ such that $\forall q' \in \{r \in Q \mid r \sim_i q \text{ for all } i \in \Gamma\}$, $\forall \lambda \in out(q', F_\Gamma)$, $L, \lambda[1] \models \varphi$,

If φ holds at all states in all EGCS's, then we write $\models \varphi$ (for 'φ is valid').

Some elementary results for this semantics are as follows.

Proposition 1. *For all sets of agents Γ and for all formulas φ: $\models \langle\!\langle \Gamma \rangle\!\rangle_a \varphi \to \langle\!\langle \Gamma \rangle\!\rangle_p \varphi$ and $\models \langle\!\langle \Gamma \rangle\!\rangle_p \varphi \to \langle\!\langle \Gamma \rangle\!\rangle_c \varphi$.*

Proposition 2. *If $\Gamma_1 \subseteq \Gamma_2$, $\models \langle\!\langle \Gamma_1 \rangle\!\rangle_p \varphi \to \langle\!\langle \Gamma_2 \rangle\!\rangle_p \varphi$ and $\models \langle\!\langle \Gamma_1 \rangle\!\rangle_c \varphi \to \langle\!\langle \Gamma_2 \rangle\!\rangle_c \varphi$.*

Whereas this is *false*: "$\models \langle\!\langle \Gamma_1 \rangle\!\rangle_a \varphi \to \langle\!\langle \Gamma_2 \rangle\!\rangle_a \varphi$ implies $\models \langle\!\langle \Gamma_1 \rangle\!\rangle_c \varphi \to \langle\!\langle \Gamma_2 \rangle\!\rangle_c \varphi$." An obvious embedding is the following. We use $\models_{ATL}$ for the ATL semantics, and $\langle\!\langle \Gamma \rangle\!\rangle$ as the ATL coalitional operator. A *perfect information system M* is an ECGS such that for all agents i, for all states q and q', $q \sim_i q'$ iff $q = q'$.

Proposition 3. *$M, q \models_{ATL} \langle\!\langle \Gamma \rangle\!\rangle \varphi$ if and only if $M, q \models \langle\!\langle \Gamma \rangle\!\rangle_a \varphi$.*

3.1 Example

In this section, we present an extended example based on the following scenario. Consider a game played by two agents using a deck of cards with all the face cards (J,Q,K,A) removed. The deck is shuffled and each agent is given one card. Each agent sees their own card without revealing it to the other agent. Then each agent has the choice of trading their card for a different one from the deck, once, or keeping their card. The agents' goal is for the sum of their cards to be at least seven.

First we model this game as an ECGS. We model it as a three agent system, where a_1 and a_2 represent the two agents playing the game and the third agent, *env* represents the environment, resolving choices that would otherwise be nondeterministic. We define the set of states as

$$Q = \{(x, y, z) \mid x \in \{i, f\} \text{ and } y, z \in \{2, 3, ..., 10\}\},$$

where (i, y, z) represents an initial state where a_1 has card y and a_2 has card z, and (f, y, z) represents a final state, after the agents have decided whether to swap their cards, where a_1 has card y and a_2 has card z. The equivalence relations are as follows:

$$(x_1, y_1, z_1) \sim_1 (x_2, y_2, z_2) \text{ iff } x_1 = x_2 \text{ and } y_1 = y_2$$
$$(x_1, y_1, z_1) \sim_2 (x_2, y_2, z_2) \text{ iff } x_1 = x_2 \text{ and } z_1 = z_2$$
$$(x_1, y_1, z_1) \sim_{env} (x_2, y_2, z_2) \text{ iff } x_1 = x_2 \text{ and } y_1 = y_2 \text{ and } z_1 = z_2$$

The set of actions is $\mathcal{B} = \{swap, stay\} \cup \{(x, y) \mid x, y \in \{2, ..., 10\}\}$. The transition relation is as follows:

$$\delta((i, y, z), a_1, stay) = \{(f, y, z') \mid z' \in \{2, ..., 10\}\}$$
$$\delta((i, y, z), a_1, swap) = \{(f, y', z') \mid y', z' \in \{2, ..., 10\}\}$$
$$\delta((i, y, z), a_2, stay) = \{(f, y', z) \mid y' \in \{2, ..., 10\}\}$$
$$\delta((i, y, z), a_2, swap) = \{(f, y', z') \mid y', z' \in \{2, ..., 10\}\}$$
$$\delta((i, y, z), env, (y', z')) = \{(f, y, z), (f, y, z'), (f, y', z), (f, y', z')\}$$
$$\delta((f, y, z), a, stay) = \{(f, y, z)\} \text{ for all } a \in \Sigma$$

Thus, in an initial state, each agent chooses whether to keep their card or change it. If they change their card, the environment picks a new card for them. Then, in a final state, all three agents only have one action available, *stay*, which does not change the state (we only include this because our semantics require infinite runs).

Finally, our only proposition will be w, representing that the agents win, and $\pi((x, y, z)) = \{w\}$ iff $x = f$ and $y + z \geq 7$. Otherwise $\pi((x, y, z)) = \emptyset$.

Now we will investigate which formulas are true at certain states in this system. First, consider the state $(i, 8, 1)$: the first agent has an 8 and the second agent has 1. Intuitively, would we say that the group consisting of both agents has a winning strategy from this state? Of course,

$$(i, 8, 1) \models \neg \langle\!\langle a_2 \rangle\!\rangle_a \bigcirc w,$$

because acting alone a_2 has no strategy to ensure that they reach a winning state, but

$$(i, 8, 1) \models \langle\!\langle a_1 \rangle\!\rangle_a \bigcirc w,$$

because a_1 can use the strategy of keeping his card and be sure to win. But notice that

$$(i, 8, 1) \models \neg \langle\!\langle \{a_1, a_2\} \rangle\!\rangle_a \bigcirc w,$$

since, for example $(i, 1, 1) \sim_2 (i, 8, 1)$ and there is no strategy from $(i, 1, 1)$ for $\{a_1, a_2\}$ to achieve w in the next state. However, it is true that

$$(i, 8, 1) \models \langle\!\langle \{a_1, a_2\} \rangle\!\rangle_p \bigcirc w,$$

because $\{a_1\} \subseteq \{a_1, a_2\}$, and no matter what a_2 does, a_1 has a winning strategy. So there is a *passive* strategy for a_1 and a_2 to reach w at the next state, because a_2 has an active strategy for this goal, and nothing a_1 does can interfere with this accomplishment, so a_1 passively brings about w at the next state. And of course,

$$(i, 8, 1) \models \langle\!\langle \{a_1, a_2\} \rangle\!\rangle_c \bigcirc w.$$

Intuitively, this is because the agents share their knowledge and then decide on a strategy, so they both know that keeping their cards is a good strategy.

To highlight the differences between $\langle\!\langle \Gamma \rangle\!\rangle_c$ and the other two strategic operators, consider the state $(i, 4, 5)$. Here, we have both

$(i, 4, 5) \models \neg \langle\!\langle \{a_1, a_2\} \rangle\!\rangle_a \bigcirc w$, and $(i, 4, 5) \models \neg \langle\!\langle \{a_1, a_2\} \rangle\!\rangle_p \bigcirc w$.

Intuitively, this means that the agents do not have enough information about their current state to have either an active or a passive group strategy to reach a winning state. However, if the agents share all their information, they realize that both of them keeping their cards is a good group strategy. Thus,

$$(i, 4, 5) \models \langle\!\langle \{a_1, a_2\} \rangle\!\rangle_c \bigcirc w.$$

In terms of the semantics, this is because there are no other states that are equivalent to $(i, 4, 5)$ for both a_1 and a_2, so the group strategy only needs to guarantee the desired outcome at this single state.

4   Related Work

Uniform strategies In this paper we have only considered uniform strategies, since we are considering what agents are able to accomplish, and an agent must choose their actions based on their own knowledge. Non-uniform strategies, however, may be useful sometimes, for example for analyzing worst-case scenarios where agents could perhaps secretly communicate or otherwise gain unexpected knowledge. Only [10], the first paper about ATEL, does not consider uniform strategies. Interestingly, in the original paper on ATL there is a discussion of ATL with incomplete information, and uniform strategies are defined [3, p.706–710]. However, in their approach the agents' equivalence relations are defined in terms of propositions (i.e., valuations) rather than in terms of states, leading to many restrictions on the expressible formulas and making the logic quite complicated. It is well-known that in multi-agent Kripke models such an identification of states with valuations is very restrictive for the expressivity of a logic.

De re or de dicto A second major aspect of ATEL-type logics is whether they allow *de dicto* or *de re* strategies. A *de re* strategy to achieve something is a uniform strategy that will succeed starting from any state the agent considers possible. A *de dicto* strategy to achieve something, on the other hand, is a uniform strategy that will succeed from the present state, but not from every state the agent considers possible. So if an agent has a *de re* strategy to achieve something, the agent knows that he has the strategy and knows what the strategy is. But if the agent has a *de dicto* strategy, he does not know what the strategy is. Note that a *de dicto* strategy is in general uniform- even though it does not succeed from all the states the agent considers possible, it requires the agent to take the same action in all states that are equivalent for him.

In the current paper, we only consider *de re* strategies, as we are concerned with what agents can be sure to achieve based on their knowledge. While *de dicto* strategies are interesting from an outside perspective, they are not useful to the agents inside the system, trying to achieve certain goals. Like our logic, ATOL [12] and ATL with perfect and imperfect information and recall [16] can only express *de re* abilities, whereas other logics can only express *de dicto* abilities, for example Epistemic Coalition Logic in [2]. Some logics can express both *de dicto* and *de re* abilities. For example, in Constructive Strategic Logic [11], the basic group operator expresses *de dicto* ability, but combining this operator with a special epistemic operator expresses *de re* ability. In [4], six variants of epistemic ATL are considered, with both *de dicto* and *de re* abilities. It is shown that the expressiveness of ATL with *de re* abilities ("subjective abilities") and ATL with *de dicto* abilities ("objective abilities") are incomparable, both in the perfect recall and imperfect recall cases. Similar results are shown for ATL* with *de re* and *de dicto* abilities.

Coalitional operators In logics with uniform strategies the semantics for the coalitional operator (followed by next) has the following generic form

$$L, q \models \langle\langle \Gamma \rangle\rangle \bigcirc \varphi \text{ iff there exists a group strategy } F_\Gamma \text{ such that } \forall q' \sim^? q,$$
$$\forall \lambda \in out(q', F_\Gamma), \ L, \lambda[1] \models \varphi,$$

where the definition of $\sim^?$ is variable. Most often, the relation is either $\bigcup_{a \in H} \sim_a$ (general knowledge for group of agents H), as in [16], or it is $(\bigcup_{a \in H} \sim_a)^*$, the transitive closure of $\bigcup_{a \in H} \sim_a$ (common knowledge for H). We have seen in Example 1 that the former is not felicitous. Similarly, in [4], six varieties of ATL and six varieties of ATL* are compared, and the semantics of the ability operators in all the varieties of the logics are defined using the union of the equivalence relations of the agents (i.e., general knowledge). It would be interesting to know if defining the semantics in terms of the common knowledge relation would change the results presented in that paper.

In ATOL [12] the semantics of the ability operator is much more subtle. The operator is defined as follows, where A and Γ are groups of agents and $\mathcal{K}$ is either C, E or D, for common knowledge, general knowledge and distributed knowledge, respectively.

$$L, q \models \langle\langle A \rangle\rangle_{\mathcal{K}(\Gamma)} \bigcirc \varphi \text{ iff there is a group strategy } F_A \text{ such that } \forall q' \sim^{\mathcal{K}}_\Gamma$$
$$q, \forall \lambda \in out(q', S_A), \ L, \lambda[1] \models \varphi.$$

The ability operator in this logic is very powerful: not only does it subsume both the union relation semantics (which can be expressed as $\langle\langle A \rangle\rangle_{E(A)}$) and the common knowledge semantics (which can be expressed as $\langle\langle A \rangle\rangle_{C(A)}$), it is even possible to define the ability of one group of agents with respect to the knowledge of another group of agents. We have the following correspondence with our logic.

Proposition 4. *Consider a ECGS L with memoryless agents, and $q \in L$.*

1. $L, q \models \langle\langle \Gamma \rangle\rangle_a \varphi$ *if and only if* $L, q \models_{ATOL} \langle\langle \Gamma \rangle\rangle_{C(\Gamma)} \varphi$.
2. $L, q \models \langle\langle \Gamma \rangle\rangle_p \varphi$ *if and only if* $\exists \Gamma' \subseteq \Gamma$ *such that* $L, q \models_{ATOL} \langle\langle \Gamma' \rangle\rangle_{C(\Gamma')} \varphi$.
3. $L, q \models \langle\langle \Gamma \rangle\rangle_c \varphi$ *if and only if* $L, q \models_{ATOL} \langle\langle \Gamma \rangle\rangle_{D(\Gamma)} \varphi$.

In item 2, since we consider a finite set of agents, it follows that $L, q \models \langle\langle \Gamma \rangle\rangle_p \varphi$ if and only if $L, q \models_{ATOL} \bigvee_{\Gamma' \subseteq \Gamma} \langle\langle \Gamma' \rangle\rangle_{C(\Gamma')} \varphi$. So, for memoryless systems, our logic can be translated into ATOL. However, our system can deal with non-memoryless systems as well. Even for memoryless systems ATOL can express properties that our logic cannot express, such as $\langle\langle \Gamma_1 \rangle\rangle_{E(\Gamma_2)} \bigcirc \varphi$, where $\Gamma_2 \not\subseteq \Gamma_1$.

Memory Abilities Another difference among the various logics is whether they allow perfect recall or not. Traditional ATL [3] allows agents to have perfect recall, although it was shown in [4] that in the perfect information setting, for ATL it does not matter whether agents have perfect recall or not — this only matters in the case of ATL*. In [10] only perfect recall agents are considered. In [16], four different classes of operators are considered: IR for perfect information and recall, iR for imperfect information and perfect recall, Ir for perfect information and imperfect recall, and ir for imperfect information and recall. These different levels of abilities determine which strategies are considered admissible. Interestingly, in the logic of [16] it is possible to combine different ability operators within the same formula, for example $\langle\!\langle A \rangle\!\rangle_{iR} \bigcirc \langle\!\langle B \rangle\!\rangle_{Ir} \Box \varphi$ means that group A has an imperfect information perfect recall strategy so that at the next state group B will have a perfect information imperfect recall strategy to make φ always true. While being able to express such formulas is interesting, it is not clear what the meaning of them is—for example, if some of the agents are in both groups A and B in the above formula, it means that sometimes they are being considered as memoryless agents and sometimes as perfect recall agents. The logic ATOL [12] is mostly concerned with memoryless agents.

Combining memory abilities One of the new aspects of our work is the ability to represent models with agents of different ability in the same system and in the same logic. We do this by treating an agent's memory abilities as part of the underlying system rather than as an aspect of the semantics of the logic. This is similar to the way that each agent's knowledge is traditionally encoded in the system as an arbitrary equivalence relation on states, but now we encode an agent's knowledge as an equivalence relation on histories rather than on states. So, rather than being an aspect of the logic, the agent's memory ability becomes an aspect of the system. This makes it possible to discuss agents with different memory abilities in the same formula, which is impossible in the other varieties of epistemic ATL. For example, we can have a formula such as $\langle\!\langle ab \rangle\!\rangle \Box \varphi$ where a is an agent with perfect recall and b is a memoryless agent. This formula is not expressible in other logics.

5   Conclusion and Future Work

We have presented a logic for reasoning about the abilities of agents to cooperate to achieve a goal when they are uncertain about the state of the world. Our systems allow different agents to have different memory abilities. We presented a new definition of perfect recall, which takes the history of states and the history of actions into account.

We intend further to study the properties of this logic, such as decidability and complexity. For example, in [5], it is proven that model checking is undecidable for a variant of epistemic ATL with strategies based on common knowledge. We also wish to be able to describe memory abilities in the logical language. We are further contemplating dynamic operators for change of memory ability, and other levels of cooperation than the three considered in this paper.

Yet another future direction is that the logic uATEL may help to pave the way to a coalitional event logic. Pauly's game logic [14] corresponds to the next temporal fragment of ATEL, and this game logic is subsumed by the coalitional announcement logic (CAL) of [1]. Coalitional announcements are *public* events enacted by coalitions.

Acknowledgements. We thank the reviewers for their comments. Hans van Ditmarsch is also affiliated to the IMSc, Chennai, as associated researcher. This research is supported by European Research Council grant EPS 313360.

References

1. Ågotnes, T., van Ditmarsch, H.: Coalitions and announcements. In: Proc. of 7th AAMAS, pp. 673–680. IFAAMAS (2008)
2. Ågotnes, T., Alechina, N.: Epistemic coalition logic: completeness and complexity. In: AAMAS, pp. 1099–1106 (2012)
3. Alur, R., Henzinger, T.A., Kupferman, O.: Alternating-time temporal logic. J. ACM 49(5), 672–713 (2002)
4. Bulling, N., Jamroga, W.: Comparing variants of strategic ability: how uncertainty and memory influence general properties of games. Autonomous Agents and Multi-Agent Systems 28(3), 474–518 (2014)
5. Diaconu, R., Dima, C.: Model-checking alternating-time temporal logic with strategies based on common knowledge is undecidable. Applied Artificial Intelligence 26(4), 331–348 (2012)
6. Emerson, E.A., Clarke, E.M.: Using branching-time temporal logic to synthesize synchronization skeletons. Sci. Comput. Programm. 2, 241–266 (1982)
7. Emerson, E.A., Halpern, J.Y.: "sometimes" and "not never" revisited: on branching versus linear time temporal logic. J. ACM 33(1), 151–178 (1986)
8. Goranko, V., van Drimmelen, G.: Complete axiomatization and decidability of alternating-time temporal logic. Theor. Comp. Science 353(1-3), 93–117 (2006)
9. Harel, D., Kozen, D., Tiuryn, J.: Dynamic Logic. Foundations of Computing Series. MIT Press, Cambridge (2000)
10. van der Hoek, W., Wooldridge, M.: Cooperation, knowledge, and time: Alternating-time temporal epistemic logic and its applications. Stud. Log. 75(1), 125–157 (2003)
11. Jamroga, W., Ågotnes, T.: Constructive knowledge: what agents can achieve under imperfect information. Journal of Appl. Non-Classical Logics 17(4), 423–475 (2007)
12. Jamroga, W., van der Hoek, W.: Agents that know how to play. Fundam. Inform. 63(2-3), 185–219 (2004)
13. Kripke, S.: Semantical analysis of modal logic. Zeitschrift fur Mathematische Logik und Grundlagen der Mathematik (1963)
14. Pauly, M.: A modal logic for coalitional power in games. Journal of Logic and Computation 12(1), 149–166 (2002)
15. Pnueli, A.: The temporal logic of programs. In: The Eighteenth Annual IEEE Symposium on Foundations of Computer Science, pp. 46–57 (1977)
16. Schobbens, P.Y.: Alternating-time logic with imperfect recall. Electr. Notes Theor. Comput. Sci. 85(2), 82–93 (2004)

Author Index